THE
SPANISH
TABLE

The Food and Wines
of Spain

THE
FLAVOUR
OF
SPAIN

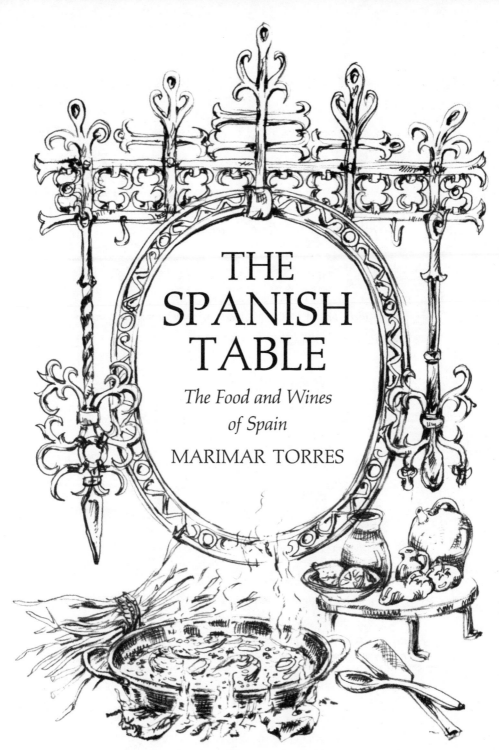

THE
SPANISH
TABLE

*The Food and Wines
of Spain*

MARIMAR TORRES

EBURY PRESS LONDON

To Rosalía,
my parents' cook,
who allowed me to follow her around as a child,

AND

To Ann Walker,
with whom I have shared many hours
of fun and experimentation in the kitchen

Published by Ebury Press
Division of The National Magazine Company Ltd
Colquhoun House, 27-37 Broadwick Street, London W1V 1FR

This edition published 1987

The Spanish Table was first published in America by Doubleday & Company, Inc in 1986

ISBN 0 85223 643 3

Illustrations by Jofre Vila

Filmset by Advanced Filmsetters (Glasgow) Ltd

Printed and bound in Great Britain at The Bath Press, Avon

nonconformist and my working in the family business represented a break with established traditions. The Torres family has owned vineyards in Spain since the seventeenth century, and has been actively involved in the wine business since 1870. My father, Miguel, is the fourth-generation proprietor, my two brothers and I are the fifth. When my brother Miguel, Jr, and I were in school, my father was already grooming him for the business. Something inside me said, I would like to do that, too.

Instead, my mother always arranged for me to study languages during the summer; that was more lady-like. By the time I was sixteen I was fluent in German, French and English, which is an enormous help today, of course. But I wanted to work with wine. When I was about ten, after really insisting, I was able to get a summer job at the winery, handing dirty bottles to the men who washed them for re-use.

I made my first trip to America with my father in 1967, when he came to visit American distributors and wine merchants. As his assistant/secretary, I learned a great deal and tried to persuade him to make me the family representative for our wines here in America. He simply wouldn't hear of it. Later on, however, he allowed me to travel by myself to promote Torres wines in Canada, where our distribution was just getting started. The liquor boards were very conservative and having a woman visit them was unheard of – it earned me a lot of publicity, and our sales began to soar. When I later married an American wine and food critic and came to live in California, I started Torres Wines North America in a corner of our living room. At that time, in 1975, our sales volume in the United States was 15,000 cases a year. Today it is well over 150,000 – and the office is no longer in my home.

Food and wine go so naturally together that, for me, each reinforces the other. Cooking has become my joy; I love working in the kitchen, I love the feel of the ingredients. I even like to clean squid for paella, one of the dishes I most enjoy preparing because you get to work with so many things. Basically it's like a painting – you have all these different components and assembling them all is a kind of thrill; you feel you are really creating something and it never comes out quite the same.

These experiences eventually led quite naturally to the idea of doing this book. As I delved more deeply into the history and lore of Spanish cooking, I realized how much it could appeal to the American palate. Americans have such a wonderful curiosity about food. The inventiveness of American cooks has led them to explore many different cuisines and many styles of cooking. I also have sensed recently a growing awareness of Spain through travel and the media, which has come about at the same time as the increasing interest in Spanish food. Certainly it is a cuisine that easily adapts to the bounty of American and British ingredients and those countries' appetites for interesting flavours.

CONTENTS

A WORD OF ACKNOWLEDGMENT

This book has been the culmination of a long-time dream to bring today's Spanish cuisine to North America. And perhaps more important, it has given me the opportunity to learn, during the years I devoted to it, a lot about my home country and its people. In my travels through Spain I found the most incredible cooperation from restaurant and winery owners, chefs and winemakers, all of whom are mentioned in the book.

In the United States, there are a great number of people who made the book possible. First of all, Ann Walker, with whom I made my first gastronomic-culinary journey around Spain, surveying the key restaurants; she has collaborated with me from the beginning in developing and double-testing all the recipes. Together we endeavoured to keep intact the idea of the chef who inspired the recipe while making it work with our ingredients – even to improve it, whenever possible. And for all this, I will never be able to thank Ann enough.

Throughout the testing of the recipes, two women were by my side, providing invaluable help: Bonnie Whyte, a great cook and patient friend; and Patricia Riquelme, who since 1980 has helped me with many of the dishes. And of course, I have to thank all my friends who acted as 'guinea pigs' and gave me their opinions about the numerous dishes they had to try at one dinner – often compensating by dieting the entire next week. In particular I want to thank Robert Finigan, for the great influence he has had on my appreciation of food since I came to live in America.

Another person in the United States who faithfully contributed her skills is Joann Shirley. She not only typed the book but helped immeasurably to improve my English – a much needed assistance, considering that I came to live here just ten years ago. And indeed, I have to thank my editor at Ebury Press, Veronica Sperling, for her kind advice and assistance.

One person without whom I might never have written this book is Dr Pierre Mornell, a writer himself who inspired and supported me in the project from the day I conceived the idea, and stood behind me convincing me that I could do it.

The book would have been an impossible task without Montse Painous, my assistant at my family's winery in Spain, who has been with me ever since I started to work there twenty years ago. Montse's devotion to this project ranged from helping me research the best restaurants and wineries to scheduling my trips, coordinating my visits and contacts – and patiently answering, by telex or telephone, my myriad of questions from here. Besides her, everybody at the winery and our representatives throughout Spain helped me with their contacts and experience.

There are many acknowledgments due to people in Spain. First, all the members of my family searched for the best recipes in their repertoire and also undertook endless – though wonderful – meals at Catalan restaurants, often paying for it with strict diets afterwards (my father paid by picking up the bill, too). My mother, especially, provided me with recipes galore from her voluminous files. My brother Miguel shared not only his many contacts in the wine and food world but also his wealth of knowledge, patiently answering the endless questions of a younger sister and allowing me to use the information contained in the wine books he has written.

Rosalía, the family cook, deserves special thanks. At eighty-six her memory is still vivid; she has often recounted for me the wonderful meals she cooked for my family since she started working for my grandmother at the age of nineteen.

Then there is a long list of Spanish wine and food authorities who gladly shared their knowledge and time with me. My good Catalan friend Mauricio Wiesenthal, a living encyclopedia on gastronomy and wine, helped me throughout the book but especially in the part about Catalan wines, for which he willingly wrote the Spanish draft. In Madrid, Dr Manuel Martínez Llopis, another gastronomic encyclopedia, opened for me his incredible recipe files and gave me much advice and information. Juan José Lapitz, a Basque who knows and loves food, helped me to understand his region's cuisine by taking me to the 'food sanctuaries' there and meeting the top chefs. José Carlos Capel, a *madrileño* who has lived in Andalucía and written about its cuisine, introduced me to the importance of the Andalusian cooking heritage. Lorenzo Millo helped me with the chapter about Valencia. Enric Canut, the young president of the Association for the Promotion of Farmhouse Cheeses, provided information about the incredible array of Spanish cheeses.

In the wine chapter, my mentors and guides were Antonio Larrea in Rioja, Xosé and Carmen Posada in Galicia, Isabel Mijares in Valdepeñas, José Antonio Mijares in La Mancha, and all the wineries that are mentioned in the section on sherry. Wine writer José Peñín also provided useful information about the Spanish wine regions.

In Spain's gastronomic world, Madrid publisher Miguel Rodríguez helped me with his advice and introduced me to the books' authors from his series about the cooking of each Spanish region. Catalan publisher Jaume Beltrán also provided me with numerous contacts and information. Clara María González de Amezúa, director of Spain's most renowned cooking school, Alambique, in Madrid, shared her knowledge and her mastery of Spanish regional cooking. Many great writers, among them Lluís Bettonica, Manuel Vázquez Montalbán, Jorge Victor Sueiro, Carmen Casas, Ana Lorente, Carlos Delgado, Nines Arenillas, Antonio Vergara, Esperanza Gallego, Ana María Calera, Mann Sierra and José María Busca Isusi, have provided me with excellent information, points of view and inspiration. And I should also mention Spain's best restaurant guide, *Gourmetour*, which steered me through the country with its sound, unbiased advice.

Last but not least, I owe this book to *a place* – Rancho La Puerta, a fitness resort in the Mexican desert, near San Diego, away from the world and from telephones,

INTRODUCTION

When I was growing up in Catalonia, the kitchen was always a place of fascination. I remember how I would sneak in and ask Rosalía, the family cook, if there was any job she could give me. Sometimes she would say, 'Well, you can scrub the floor,' but if I had been especially good she would let me get my hands into the flour – and that I loved.

This was rare, however, because in our home, as in many Spanish homes, the kitchen traditionally was the cook's domain. I was never allowed there without Rosalía's permission. My mother, Margarita, had little interest in cooking, although she did like making desserts. How she raised her eyebrows when I announced at the age of five or six that when I grew up, I wanted to be either a cook or a dancer.

My aunt Oriola is the real cook of the family. Some of the recipes in this book are ones I've taken from her and adapted. Aunt Oriola and Rosalía were really my mentors, although my love of cooking took a while to flower. For most of the twenty-nine years that I lived in Barcelona, I attached very little importance to cooking. Until I came to the United States, in fact, I rarely ventured into the kitchen at all; at that time it was felt that young women should spend their time at more 'elevated' pursuits. Cooking in Spain, until very recently, was laborious and unfashionable; it was the cook's chore.

America was a revelation to me. Here I found cooking upgraded to an art which most of my friends, both male and female, took pride in mastering. It wasn't considered a waste of time to spend two days preparing a lavish dinner. It was looked on as a labour of love, and one fully appreciated by guests who knew all the effort and creativity that had gone into the production. The first time I made paella, I remember the astonishment expressed by my friends – they loved it and raved about it. For me, it was just a simple paella, the same dish I had watched my grandmother's cook, Adriana, prepare numerous times. Whenever I entertained, I prepared traditional Spanish dishes and the response was always the same. People were delighted and fascinated by *real* Spanish cooking.

The enthusiastic reactions soon led friends who owned cooking schools to invite me as a guest instructor. That, too, was a revelation for me. What a surprise to learn that Americans thought of Spanish food as something spicy hot to be washed down with beer and tequila! It was gratifying to see their delight in discovering the flavours and food combinations in Spanish cooking, so different from those of Latin America, which were more familiar to them.

My life in America has been liberating for me in more ways than one. I have always, in terms of my country's social conventions, been something of a which provided me with peace and quiet, good exercise, excellent instructors who became supportive friends, and healthful food, all of which allowed me to concentrate and get the book written.

In order to understand the cuisine of Spain, it is important to realize that it is a country of 200,000 square miles and 37 million people with a tremendous variation in climates, people, history, cuisines, wines and culture. Spain has four *real* languages, as well as various dialects: Basque, spoken in north-central Spain and in southwest France; Galician, the language of the Peninsula's northwest region; Catalan – from Catalonia, my home region – also spoken in Valencia and the Balearics; and Castilian, the official Spanish language.

It always amuses me that people refer to my way of pronouncing my home town, Barcelona (Barth-elona), as my 'Castilian accent', when there is no such thing in Spain. *Castellano* or Castilian is a language, and from it emanate numerous dialects and different accents, throughout Spain and in Latin America, such as Andalusian, Mexican, and Argentinian. They all stem from the same language – *castellano*.

More and more Americans and Britons visit Spain every year, and I must confess that my proud Spanish heart fills with joy as I hear reports of 'the highlight of our trip'. Hospitality is one quality I believe inherent in the Spanish nature; we truly love to receive visitors. And indeed, if people make the effort to travel across an entire ocean from America, then we can't do enough to give them a good time.

The main meal in Spain is the midday *comida* or *almuerzo*, which is eaten rather late by American standards. At home we never had *comida* until three o'clock in the afternoon. Restaurants in Madrid and Barcelona are rarely filled before 3 pm, or before 10.30 pm. The evening meal, *cena*, at home was more of a light supper: a soup, some grilled fish with boiled vegetables, a piece of fruit for dessert. If we were entertaining or it was a special occasion, the meal would be more elaborate. If going out for dinner, we would often begin with drinks and *tapas*, the special Spanish version of hors d'oeuvres. In Spain the *tapas* bars are loaded with little dishes that include everything from salted almonds to kidneys in sherry sauce. It is great fun to go *de tapas*, the Spanish equivalent of bar-hopping, often making a meal of these appetizers in the evening.

We use lots of olive oil in cooking, which gives Spanish food much of its unique flavour. But since we are all health- and weight-conscious these days, I have found ways to use less fat in my recipes and make them lighter, retaining the flavour with fresh ingredients and herbs and seasonings. For instance, I usually drain off the oil or fat as much as possible, and often deglaze with wine or brandy, which add an extra flavour of their own. Wine is something I don't measure; it has flowed freely in our family since the seventeenth century.

A GASTRONOMIC TOUR THROUGH THE REGIONS OF SPAIN

There is not one Spanish cuisine; there are many. And they reflect the Spaniards' pride of regional identity and heritage, a legacy we are seeking to express and preserve with new enthusiasm in the Spain of today.

To know and understand the variation in the different cuisines of Spain, we will travel through the fifteen regions of the Peninsula. We will visit the cities and small towns, from the beaches to the mountains, exploring the meals and produce from the villagers as well as sophisticated restaurateurs. And best of all, their tastiest recipes will then follow!

CATALUNYA (CATALONIA)

While the many and varied cuisines of Spain are a delight to explore, I am naturally happiest cooking the dishes of Catalonia, or Catalunya, my home region. Catalan cuisine is one of the oldest, and most individual, of Spain – typical of the Catalonians themselves. We have always had a strong sense of our own identity that expresses itself in many ways – in our art, in our language, in our politics, in our lifestyle.

Catalonia is a region of 12,000 square miles sweeping down from the green and rugged Pyrenees to the beaches of the beautiful Costa Brava, north of Barcelona, and, to the south, the golden sands of the Costa Dorada. The land is a mixture of mountains and plains, which makes the climate and agriculture very varied.

Basically, there are two well-defined cuisines in Catalonia: the fisherman-style dishes of the coast, based on the bounty of seafood found only in the Mediterranean; and the more solid, sturdy preparations of the inland areas. In the Pyrenees the cooking is warm and comforting; I have some great memories of earthy, delicious meals by the fire after a day of skiing in the mountains, with the wind blowing outside over the snow-covered slopes.

The Pyrenees also provide the right environment for some of Catalonia's best cheeses, such as Serrat, dry or semi-dry with a classic, intense taste of the sheep's milk from which it is made; and de Arán, a slightly smoked, ball-shaped cow's milk cheese, its rind rubbed with rum. Another excellent cow's milk cheese is La Selva, made near Gerona; it can be fresh (white) or tender (pale yellow), both soft, creamy and delicate. A favourite Catalan dessert is the white fresh Mató, soft and moist, made from goat's or cow's milk, eaten with honey and walnuts. A true delicacy!

The wealth of Catalan cuisine relies on the wide range of produce available, from the alpine-type mushrooms – especially the unique, delicious *rovellons* – and herbs grown in the Pyrenees to the rice, fruits and vegetables grown south in the fertile Ebro River valley. The classic Mediterranean trilogy of olives, vineyards and wheat dominates in Catalonia. We also have a lot of game, from small wild birds like partridges and quail to rabbit and hare, dove, duck, goose (a Catalan speciality) and even deer. Basic staples also are fowl, veal, baby goat and, above all, pork, whose fat has been used as a cooking element throughout the centuries.

The History of Catalonia
The Greeks founded the city of Ampurias, on the Mediterranean, north of Barcelona. Today that district, L'Empordà (or Ampurdán in Castilian), with its dramatic Costa Brava, is one of Catalonia's main gastronomic centres and

according to my friend, gastronomic historian Manuel Martínez Llopis, it has the finest and most elaborate of all Spanish cuisines. The Romans later established in Tarragona – south of Barcelona – the capital of their Spanish empire, Hispania. Both Greeks and Romans had great influence in the cuisine of Catalonia, and in all of Spain. Remnants of many ancient cuisines, such as the Arab and Jewish custom of using lemon, honey and cinnamon in certain dishes, can be found in modern Catalonia. And spice traders from the Far East introduced a variety of other spices.

Catalan cuisine is Spain's oldest on record. The first Spanish cookbook (and one of the most ancient surviving in all of Europe) is the *Llibre de Sent Soví*, written in the Catalan language in the first half of the fourteenth century.

Barcelona is the commercial capital of all Spain. This as much as anything has given Catalonia its sophisticated, cosmopolitan character; it is much more European than the rest of the country. During the Renaissance, Barcelona ranked with Venice and Genoa as a great centre of trade and banking. Today it is still one of the most important ports on the Mediterranean. It was through Barcelona that pasta arrived in Spain, as Naples, Milan and Sicily belonged to the Spanish Crown during the fourteenth and fifteenth centuries. And Roussillon and Provence, today in southern France, were also part of Catalonia from 1160 to 1659 – hence the similarities among these cuisines.

The nineteenth century saw the development of Barcelona as a city of great restaurants. Today, it has over 10,000 eating establishments! The oldest of them, Can Culleretes, dates back to 1786. It was originally a *chocolatería* or chocolate house, which is similar to a coffee shop. Patrons would go there in the afternoon and drink hot chocolate with rolls or sweets. It was Spain that introduced chocolate to Europe from the New World, and in fact monopolized it until the seventeenth century. Chocolate is used a lot in Catalonia, but rather than as a basic ingredient for rich desserts, Catalans have traditionally used it to flavour and thicken savoury dishes.

Catalan Cuisine Today

There are six primary ingredients in Catalan cooking: olive oil, garlic, onions, tomatoes, nuts (almonds, hazelnuts and pine nuts) and dried fruits, particularly raisins and prunes. In addition, the four traditional herbs are oregano, rosemary, thyme and bay leaves.

The five essentials in Catalan cuisine are:

1. *Sofrito*, meaning long sautéing, consists of onion and tomato slowly sautéed in olive oil, sometimes with garlic, peppers or other ingredients. It is used as a basis for many dishes and sauces.

2. *Picada*, which literally means pounded, is usually a mixture of garlic, parsley, nuts, some toasted or fried bread and sometimes saffron or other spices. The ingredients are traditionally ground or pounded with a mortar and pestle, then added raw to the preparation while the cooking is in progress. *Picada* is used as a thickening and flavouring agent, and in a way is a complement to *sofrito*.

3. *Allioli*, an emulsion of pounded garlic and olive oil traditionally mixed

together in a mortar, is one of the most widely used sauces in Catalan cooking. It enhances grilled meats or fish, and can also enliven the flavour of a dish by stirring in just a spoonful at the end.

4. *Romesco* today is a sauce that evolved from a fish dish, Fish Stew, Tarragona Style (Romesco de Pescados), typical of the Tarragona area where there are lots of almond groves. A favourite accompaniment to grilled fish and vegetables, it is usually a paste of toasted almonds, garlic, sweet red peppers or *nyoras* (a type of dried mild red pepper), bread and tomatoes.

5. *Samfaina* is a mixture of onion, tomato, sweet pepper, aubergine and courgette, cut into small pieces and sautéed in olive oil. It is served to accompany meats, fowl, fish, even fried eggs or as an omelette filling.

A very basic utensil in the Catalan kitchen is the mortar and pestle. Despite the availability of modern conveniences like the blender and food processor (which I use for the most part), it is still frequently used to grind nuts and spices – as in the case of *picada* – and to prepare sauces such as *allioli* and *romesco*.

Catalans also like to cook with fruit, as in chicken with prunes, goose with pears, Duck with Figs (Pato con Higos), Squab with Peaches (Pintada al Melocotón) or Spinach with Pine Nuts and Raisins, Catalan Style (Espinacas a la Catalana). In fact, any dish prepared *a la catalana* is likely to contain pine nuts and raisins or prunes.

Finally, Catalans love grilled dishes, especially cooked outdoors on an open fire. *Parrillada*, a combination of grilled shellfish, seafood or meat, is a great favourite. We even barbecue vegetables, as in Assorted Grilled Vegetables, Catalan Style (Escalivada) or Baked Young Onions or Leeks (Ceballots).

PAÍS VALENCIANO

South of Catalonia, bordering the Mediterranean, is the País Valenciano – the home of paella, undoubtedly the most famous dish of Spanish origin known in America and Britain.

This region is the number one rice producer in Spain, and the grain has been cultivated there since Arab times. The Romans introduced the hydraulic system, and the Arabs expanded and perfected the irrigation in the low, swampy lands around Lake Albufera, south of the city of Valencia.

The cuisine of the coast is very different from that of the inland areas. The terrain is quite varied, since the region originated for political reasons rather than geographical unity. While the coastline has many small, fertile *huertas* or vegetable gardens and is heavily populated, the inland is mountainous and almost uninhabited, with rivers flowing through narrow canyons. Its cuisine is therefore earthy, substantial and high in calories – hardy food for a rigorous climate. It uses mountain products including aromatic herbs such as rosemary, thyme and savory, game such as partridge, hare or mountain rabbits. The flavourful snails are a traditional ingredient in many dishes, including the original Paella Valenciana (Classic Paella with Shellfish, Chicken and Pork). *Ollas* or stews, where everything – beans, potatoes, pork and sausages – is cooked together, are very popular.

The coastline of País Valenciano starts on the north with the town of Vinaroz, renowned for its delicious shrimp. Some say they are the finest in Spain (though on the southwest coast, Sanlúcar assuredly claims that honour). Just south of Vinaroz are the seaside resorts of Benicarló and Peñíscola, also well known for their shellfish.

The area around Castellón de la Plana is an ocean of orange trees and great agricultural wealth. The cooking here is quite similar to Catalonia's in its fisherman-style dishes, such as Fish Stew with Potatoes, Costa Brava Style ('Suquet' de Pescado), a stew of many varieties of fish, with a *sofrito* and *picada*.

One great dish from La Plana is *arròs a banda* (rice on the side), so called because the rice is cooked in a stock made from the local fish and shellfish, and is then served 'on the side'. As with all seafood rices *a la marinera*, or 'fisherman's style', this is accompanied by a Garlic Mayonnaise (Allioli) sauce. I personally find that the powerful taste of garlic rather overwhelms the delicate flavours of the dish; but the tradition comes from the old days, when *arròs a banda* was a two-course meal and the fish was served after the rice. Of course, it had very little flavour left after cooking for a long time to make the stock – hence it needed a strong sauce.

The area around the city of Valencia is called La Huerta, or the vegetable garden. It is the birthplace of paella and has the most representative gastronomy of the region. Despite its worldwide fame the dish is not very old, probably no more than 200 years. In the early days it was a Lenten dish made with vegetables, cod and snails. Some inventive farmer must have come up with the idea of adding a little meat from his barnyard to make it more festive. As it became adopted by restaurants, other more sophisticated ingredients were added, such as shellfish and even lobster, thus reaching the peak of refinement (and price!). Originally it was prepared over a wood fire, often made with vine cuttings. Even today, a *true* paella party is cooked out of doors – always by men – and served straight from the paella pan.

The name paella originates from the utensil in which the dish is cooked – the Catalan word for frying pan. Made of iron, it is round and shallow with two handles, and usually quite large, since paella is a dish for large numbers. At home, it should always be cooked on top of the stove, though restaurants often bake it because this method is faster.

The secret to a successful paella is the rice. Some cooks seem to attribute more importance to the other ingredients, but it is these that must contribute their flavour to the rice. It is essential to use short-grain rice, which is tastier than long-grain; the Italian-style rice, particularly the *arborio*, works very well. Valencia's cuisine abounds with rice dishes other than paella, and recipes for some of these are included in this book.

Lake Albufera, just south of Valencia, is a source of excellent fish, especially its unique eels, which are the basis for some delicious preparations. One of my favourites is *all-i-pebre d'anguilas* (garlic-and-pepper of eels), where the eels are simply poached with garlic, hot pepper and paprika *(pebre roig)*, accompanied by potatoes. The area is also well known for the quality of its ducks, and another classic dish is *arròs al forn amb ànec de l'Albufera* (baked rice with Albufera duck).

Alicante is the home of *turrones*, those amazing sweets which become an obligatory treat at Christmas. The cities of Jijona and Alicante – capital of the province – gave the name to *turrón de Jijona* and *de Alicante*, the two most typical. The basis for *turrón* is almonds, honey and egg white, but there are many different variations. *Alicante*, my favourite, is similar to French nougat but harder.

Farther south is the historic city of Elche, the date capital of Spain. Indeed, it has more than a million date palms, the highest concentration in all of Europe.

MURCIA

A small region nestling between Valencia and Andalucía, Murcia is best known for the cooking of its coastal area – especially the Mar Menor in the north – and of its Huerta Murciana, the fertile vegetable gardens along the banks of the Segura River. A third cuisine, of the Serranía or mountain range inland, is less important; it is shepherd style, with close ties to La Mancha. The best part is its sausages and meat, which combine to make *pastel murciano* – a pie dating back to the sixteenth century, filled with chopped meat, onion and spices, and covered with puff pastry – quite reminiscent of the Moroccan *bastilla*.

The Mar Menor (smaller sea), at the mouth of the Segura River, provides the area with its famous salt flats. A speciality here is *pescado a la sal*, or fish baked in salt, derived from a very ancient method of cooking. A whole fish is packed in a thick coating of coarse salt and baked; the salt forms an insulating cover and keeps the fish moist inside. The system is very simple but requires absolutely fresh fish. I particularly enjoy it with the tasty Mediterranean *dorada* and *lubina* (sea bass). The dish is found all over Spain, so if you have an opportunity, you must try it!

Also worth tasting is *arroz en caldero*, named after the deep cauldron, *caldero*, used by the fishermen to cook it. It is a fish rice dish similar to the Valencian *arròs a banda* but with the dried red peppers *nyoras*.

While the cooking of Mar Menor consists of simple preparations of the excellent local produce, that of the Huerta Murciana is more elaborate. It is based mostly on vegetables, for this is probably the wealthiest vegetable garden of Spain. Its red peppers, *pimientos morrones*, are the ones usually canned and exported. Great salads abound; I have fond memories of boat trips along the Murcian coast and of the salads we made, which the rocking of the boat seemed to mix in a special way – they were unparalleled!

Gazpacho murciano is a variation of the classic cold Andalusian soup. The ingredients are not puréed but cut into small dice, mixed with water, vinegar and olive oil, and sprinkled with dried oregano.

Finally, one of my favourite Murcian dishes is *cordero en ajo cabañil*: lamb and thinly sliced potatoes fried in olive oil are combined with a *majado* (mashed mixture) of raw chopped garlic, hot paprika and vinegar. Disarmingly simple, earthy and delicious.

A landmark of Murcian cuisine is Rincón de Pepe, a restaurant in the city of Murcia where you can try an array of the local produce and specialities.

Raimundo González-Frutos has done a fantastic job of gathering and developing the classic recipes from the region's cuisine.

ANDALUCÍA

This southernmost region is the only one in Spain with a coast on both the Mediterranean Sea and the Atlantic Ocean. Separated from the central plateau of Castile by the mountain range of Sierra Morena, it is full of light and sunshine.

Andalusian cuisine is, together with Catalan, the oldest in Spain, documented since the thirteenth century; yet its cuisine has been neglected until recently.

The Arabic Influence
Probably the most important fact in Andalucía's gastronomic history is that it developed from the Arabic culture (with Roman roots). The tenth to twelfth centuries saw the greatest splendour in the history of the Islamic world, and of Europe, in Córdoba – headquarters of the Califato or seat of the Arabic empire in Spain until the mid-thirteenth century – and later in Granada. Moreover, almost simultaneously, Jewish culture reached its peak in Spain.

At one point, all of Spain except the northern belt was under Islamic domination and influence. The part of the country occupied by the Arabs was known as Al-Andalus, hence the name Andalucía. This was the region where they stayed the longest (800 years) and which they loved the most. The great poets of Al-Andalus have left us a beautiful legacy of poems in praise of wine, women and ephebes (young boys), three of life's pleasures they thoroughly enjoyed – the last two in the open, the first discreetly, as it was forbidden to them.

The Desserts
The Arabic influence is perhaps most notable in the desserts. It is because of the Arab tradition that Spanish pastry making today is based 90 per cent on almonds. *Mazapán*, or marzipan, originally an Arab product, is made with almonds and sugar. Another of their legacies is *almíbar*, or sugar syrup, which made their desserts especially sweet.

The use of egg yolks in Spanish desserts seems to have originated in Jerez, because the egg whites were used to clarify sherry wines. The yolks were traditionally given as charity to convents, where nuns made their little custards, *natillas*, Egg Caramel Tarts (Tocinillos de Cielo), and so on, with them.

Oranges, perhaps the most Spanish of all fruits, were brought to Spain by the Arabs. Not only meant for desserts, they were also used in savoury dishes such as Chicken in Orange and Mint Sauce (Pollo con Salsa de Naranja y Menta).

Sevilla, Port of Entry from the New World
Sevilla welcomes the traveller with the charm of its baroque buildings, a reminder that in the sixteenth and seventeenth centuries it was one of the most opulent cities in Europe. After the discovery of America, its harbour on the Guadalquivir River was the gateway to Europe. It was through Sevilla that products such as

potatoes, sweetcorn, peppers, tomatoes, most dried beans, pineapple, avocado, peanuts and chocolate, arrived in Europe.

One famous old dish that evolved after America's discovery is gazpacho. It was originally the white Ajo Blanco de Málaga (Cold White Gazpacho from Málaga with Garlic and Almonds), made with bread, garlic, olive oil, vinegar and almonds; then tomatoes were substituted for almonds in Salmorejo de Córdoba (Thick Gazpacho from Córdoba), and later peppers and cucumbers were added for the classic Gazpacho Rojo de Sevilla (Cold Soup from Seville with Tomatoes and Vegetables) recipe.

Sherry wine vinegar is an ingredient I find irreplaceable in gazpacho as well as in some salads and marinades for the distinct flavour and fragrance it imparts. It has been used in Spain, especially in Andalucía, for many years. Fortunately, it has recently caught on in international cuisine, so today it is widely available in specialist shops and good supermarkets.

Andalucía and its Tapas

Sevilla is also the place to go for *tapas*, which may be the most fun part of Andalusian cuisine. Before lunch and dinnertime, you will see bars and taverns fill up with friendly groups who carry on animated conversations while nibbling on small portions of anything edible, from almonds and olives to tiny fried fish or boiled shellfish, *serrano* ham or sausages, fried fish roe, potato omelette, small casseroles of stews such as kidneys and tripe and any combination imaginable. They are having *tapas* – tasting the establishment's specialities while chatting with friends over a glass of wine, often a chilled fino sherry.

The origin of the word *tapa*, which literally means cover, seems to go back to the middle of the last century, from the name given to the slice of ham, cheese or bread used to cover the wineglass served to the horsemen as they arrived tired and thirsty at the roadside inn. The *tapa* protected the wineglass from dust or rain. In fact, the *tapa* was free – the patron paid only for the wine, which of course would be the famous *jerez* or sherry, the perfect accompaniment.

Of course you can enjoy *tapas* all over Spain, from Andalucía to Basque Country, but perhaps Sevilla is the only city where the best restaurants are *tapas* bars, offering an amazing assortment. I've never seen faster waiters; they need to be, because of the small portions and the variety one customer alone will consume. To keep track, trust prevails; the waiter will just ask what you had and charge for whatever you say. Some bars have a selection of small *tapas* (*pinchitos* or *banderillas*, combinations of three or four titbits skewered with a cocktail stick) all priced the same, and the waiter will count the sticks at the end to add up your bill. Sometimes he will draw a line on a slate for every portion you order, adding up the lines at the end.

The art of frying reaches the peak of perfection in the *tapas* bars of the cities of Cádiz and Málaga. Nowhere else will you find the tiny fish deepfried to a dry, crunchy outside and moist inside without any trace of oil. Indeed, not even the best tempura I have had in Japan can match the extraordinary taste of the Andalusian *pescadito frito*.

SUGGESTED RECIPES FOR SERVING AS TAPAS

The variety of *tapas* is almost as extensive as the entire Spanish gastronomy. A whole dinner may be turned into a *tapas* menu, simply by making smaller portions; I usually call *all* of my Spanish buffet meals *tapas* dinners!

Many recipes in this book can be prepared as *tapas* – try some of the dishes listed below. Any of the other recipes included in Fish and Shellfish (p. 79), Poultry and Game (p. 106) or Meat (p. 121) could in fact also be prepared as *tapas*, although they would not be found as such in Spain. To make them into a *tapa*, simply cut smaller pieces and serve them on a platter, chafing dish or in individual portions. And don't choose recipes that are delicate and refined; remember, *tapas* is more a style of eating, informal and unpretentious, than recipes per se.

Dips
(Best served with toasted French bread, cheese biscuits or raw vegetables.)
Garum (*Roman Dip*) 44
Mousse de 'Escalivada' (*Aubergine, Pepper and Tomato Dip*) 45
Pâté de Salmón Ahumado (*Smoked Salmon Pâté with Capers*) 48

ROMESCO SAUCES:
Salsa Roja (*Romesco-style Sauce for Grilled Fish*) 195
'Xató' (*Romesco-Style Sauce for 'Xatonada'*) 196
'Salbitxada' (*Romesco-Style Sauce for Grilled Vegetables*) 196
Romesco de L'Olivé (*Romesco Sauce with Ancho Chillis, Onion and Paprika*) 197
Romesco de Cal Isidre (*Romesco Sauce with Ancho Chillis and Baked Garlic/Tomato*) 198

ALLIOLI SAUCES:
Allioli (*Garlic Mayonnaise*) 199
Allioli de Miel (*Honey Garlic Mayonnaise*) 199
Allioli de Manzana (*Apple Garlic Mayonnaise*) 200
The *romescos* and *alliolis* are also great served with little skewers of chicken, prawns, fish, lamb, vegetables, meatballs, etc.

Pâtés and Terrines
(Baked in a mould. Can be served on toasted French bread or in slices.)
Mousse de Endibias con Salsa de Cabrales (*Endive Mousse with Blue Cheese Sauce*) 46
Corona de Gazpacho (*Gazpacho Mousse*) 47
Mousse de Salmón y Aguacate (*Salmon and Avocado Mousse*) 47
Pâté de Anchoa con Caviar (*Anchovy Pâté with Caviare Mayonnaise*) 49
Pâté de Cabrales a la Manzana (*Blue Cheese Pâté with Apples*) 50
Terrina de Conejo con Ciruelas (*Rabbit and Prune Terrine*) 51
Pastel de Jamón (*Ham Terrine*) 52
Pastel de Pescado Mediterráneo (*Mediterranean Fish Cake*) 83
Pastel de Krabarroka (*Basque Fish Mousse*) 84

Finger Foods

Huevos Rellenos de Anchoa (*Eggs Filled with Anchovies*)   35

Champiñones Rellenos al Jerez (*Stuffed Mushrooms with Sherry*)   37

Tartaletas de Caracoles a las Hierbas Aromáticas (*Snail Tartlets with Mushrooms and Aromatic Herbs*)   39

Caracoles sin Trabajo con Salsa de Berros (*Effortless Snails in a Watercress Sauce*)   40

Tartaletas de Riñones (*Kidney Tartlets*)   41

Tartitas de Berenjena (*Aubergine Tartlets*)   154

Pelotas (*Meatballs*)   132

Mejillones en Escabeche (*Mussels Marinated in a Wine, Vinegar and Herb Sauce*)   79

Pan con Tomate (*Bread with Tomato, Catalan Style*)   185

Tosta de Gambas (*Prawn Toast*)   83

Pollo Escabechado (*Chicken Marinated in Vinegar and Wine, Spices and Herbs*), served at room temperature, using wings or drumsticks   106

Vegetable Tapas

Zanahorias Aliñadas (*Carrots Seasoned with Herbs*)   36

Zanahoria Rallada con Naranja y Piñones (*Shredded Carrot Salad with Orange and Pine Nuts*)   65

Ensalada de Zanahoria al Jerez (*Carrot Salad with Sherry*)   66

Ensalada de Naranja y Aguacate (*Orange and Avocado Salad*)   66

Ensalada de Aguacate con Tomate (*Avocado and Tomato Salad*)   67

Ensalada de Aguacate y Pimientos Rojos (*Avocado and Red Pepper Salad*)   67

Ensalada de Endibias y Aguacates a la Salsa de Cabrales (*Endive and Avocado Salad with a Blue Cheese Sauce*)   68

Barquitos de Ensalada (*Colourful Salad Boats*)   69

Ensalada de Col Lombarda con Boquerones (*Red Cabbage Salad with Anchovies*)   70

Ensalada de Habas a la Hierbabuena (*Broad Bean Salad with Mint*)   70

Calabacines en Escabeche (*Courgettes Marinated in Vinegar and Mint*)   149

'Escalivada' (*Assorted Grilled Vegetables, Catalan Style*)   150

'Ceballots' (*Baked Young Onions or Leeks*)   151

Cebollitas a la Crema y al Perfume de Tomillo (*Button Onions in a Cream and Thyme Sauce*)   151

Confit de Cebollas (*Onion Relish*)   152

Espinacas a la Catalana (*Spinach with Pine Nuts and Raisins, Catalan Style*)   153

Pastelitos de Espinaca (*Spinach Custards*)   153

Flanes de Verduras (*Green Pea and Red Pepper Flans*)   156

Flanes de Setas (*Mushroom Flans*)   157

Alcachofas con Piñones (*Artichoke Stew with Pine Nuts*)   159

Pimientos Rellenos de Bacalao (*Red Peppers Stuffed with Cod*)   88

Fish and Meat Salads
'Xatonada' (*Catalan Tuna Salad with a Romesco-Style Sauce*)   72
Ensalada Templada de Bonito (*Warm Bonito Salad with Vegetables*)   73
Ensaladilla de Bonito (*Bonito Salad with Peppers, Onions and Tomatoes*)   74
'Esqueixada' (*Catalan Shredded Cod Salad*)   74
'Trinxat' de Rape (*Catalan Shredded Monkfish Salad*)   75
Ensalada de Verduras con Dos Gustos de Salmón (*Vegetable Salad with Fresh and Smoked Salmon*)   76
Ensalada Templada de Lentejas y Conejo al Curry (*Warm Curried Lentil and Rabbit Salad*)   77
Patatas Aliñadas con Gambas (*Potato Salad with Prawns*)   168

Tarts and Pies
(Cut into wedges or squares. Best served warm, but can also be served at room temperature.)
Tarta de Cebolla (*Onion Tart*)   42
Tarta de Puerros (*Leek Tart*)   43
Tortilla Española (*Spanish Potato Omelette*)   170
Tortilla de Berenjenas (*Aubergine Omelette*)   155
Pastel de Tortillas (*Three-Layer Omelette Torte*)   53
Pastel de Col (*Cabbage Torte*)   159
Coca de Tomate y Pimiento (*Flat Bread with Tomato and Pepper Topping*)   185
Empanada de Anchoas (*Anchovy and Onion Pie*)   189

Fish and Meat Stews
(Best served in a casserole, preferably earthenware, with fresh crusty bread to dip.)
Caracoles Picantes (*Snails in a Piquant Sauce*)   38
Guisantes Estofados a la Menta Fresca con Almejas (*Pea Stew with Fresh Mint and Clams*)   80
Bacalao al Ajoarriero (*Cod in a Tomato and Red Pepper Sauce*)   89
Bacalao a la Catalana con Pasas y Piñones (*Catalan-style Cod with Pine Nuts and Raisins*)   90
Riñones al Jerez (*Kidneys in a Sherry Sauce*)   125
Fabada Asturiana (*Bean Stew with Sausages, Asturian Style*)   127
Habas a la Catalana (*Broad Bean Stew, Catalan Style*)   128
Callos a la Gallega (*Tripe with Chick-peas, Ham and Sausage, Galician Style*)   129
Lengua Empiñonada (*Braised Tongue with Pine Nuts*)   126

The King of Hams: Jabugo

Pork has been a staple of Spanish gastronomy since Roman times, and curing its meat to make ham and sausages is an art that enjoyed a high social status in Spain for generations. In fact, for centuries pork was the only source of protein in many areas of Spain; the survival of a whole family often depended on preserving its meat to make it last throughout the year.

Jabugo is a little village seventy-five miles north of Huelva, nestling in the high peaks of the western end of the Sierra Morena mountain range. The name *jamón serrano* is given to the excellent Spanish cured mountain hams, for which Jabugo has the best reputation. Around the village there are plenty of leafy oak forests which provide the acorns the black Iberian pig, *cerdo ibérico*, loves to eat, and a cool mountain climate indispensable for curing the hams. The placid Iberian pig, originally related to the wild boar, at one time was found all over the Peninsula and the Balearic Islands; but today this breed abounds only in some areas of Andalucía and Extremadura. It produces the best hams because it has more veins of fine fat intermingled in its meat than any other kind of pig.

January and February are the best months to visit Jabugo: it's the peak season for the *matanza*, the pig butchering, an occasion for great festivities in the whole area. As a child, I never quite understood why a big party centred around the killing of a pig – until I read about its historic and religious connotation: it was a way for the Christians to differentiate themselves from the Jews and Arabs.

The *matanza* is an important gastronomic event which usually lasts three days. The *mataor* or butcher and the *matancera*, his female partner, are the orchestrators of the task, which calls for the help of everybody in the family and more. Everyone gets a job, from washing the tripe and intestines (a delicate chore assigned to the *matancera*) to chopping onions and garlic, baking bread for the sausages, building a fire or even making coffee. And intertwined with the work is the partying at night, feasts with classic, earthy, rather indigestible menus, all of it washed down with generous amounts of wine and spirits, notably the rough *aguardientes* obtained from pure unmatured distillation.

The process of curing the hams takes at least fifteen months and up to three years. First they are stored in salt for fifteen to twenty days, then washed and hung in drying rooms to exude the fat, and finally transferred to dark, humid cellars for maturing. *Chorizos, caña de lomo* and all sausages except the salami-style ones are smoked for about two months in dark rooms with terracotta-tile floors, watered down to maintain an 80–85 per cent humidity, and an oak fire in the middle. The smell of those thousands of appetizing sausages hanging from the ceiling is irresistible!

Bullfights

Another animal unique to Spain and native to Andalucía is the Iberian bull or *toro ibérico*. The origin of *corridas* or bullfights is obscure; some historians attribute it to the Cretan bullfighting, but that had a different purpose. While in old Crete it was purely an acrobatic game, in Spain the goal has always been to confront man and beast in a deadly struggle. The *corridas* started in the sixteenth or seventeenth century as a horseman's game, a legacy of medieval jousts, for the *matador* or bullfighter was on horseback. The eighteenth century saw the great development of cattle ranches in Andalucía, and with it the peak of bullfighting. *Rejoneadores*, or bullfighters on horseback, were until the late eighteenth century much more popular than *toreros*, the bullfighters on foot. Today it is the other way around.

The bull's meat is highly appreciated in Spain and quite in demand after a *corrida*. *Estofado de rabo de toro* is a bull-tail stew which I have enjoyed especially at El Caballo Rojo restaurant in Córdoba. One popular delicacy is *criadillas*, euphemistically called here Rocky Mountain oysters and in France *rognons blancs* – they are in fact the bull's testicles.

EXTREMADURA

Situated to the far west of the country, north of Andalucía, this region is one of the least inhabited of Spain. Many of the Spanish *conquistadores* – Pizarro, Hernán Cortés, Orellana, Cabeza de Vaca – came from Extremadura. It is a land of mountains and oak forests, dry climate in the summer and little rain in the winter.

The cuisine of Extremadura was chronicled as early as the sixteenth century by the monasteries. A very important cookbook of the time, that of the Benedictine monks of the Alcántara Monastery in Cáceres, was stolen and taken to France during the Napoleonic invasion of 1808. In fact, one of Auguste Escoffier's classic recipes, partridge *à la mode d'Alcántara*, has its origin in that cookbook. Another French classic, consommé, is also said to have developed from a recipe in the book, *consumido*.

Sheep are plentiful in the mountains around Badajoz; they are the basis for the shepherd-style lamb stew *caldereta de pastor*. Another shepherd's dish, *migas* (literally, breadcrumbs), found all through La Mancha to Murcia, is also very popular here, especially for breakfast. It is made in an iron pot, where some chopped garlic and green peppers have previously been sautéed. Day-old bread soaked in water is drained and crumbled, added to the pot and sautéed until golden. The dish is served with olives, grapes, uncured bacon, chorizo or other pork sausages. In Murcia I've indulged in it for breakfast with hot chocolate. Delicious!

The little town of Villanueva de la Serena, east of Badajoz, held the famous archives of La Mesta, which governed the routes of the nomadic shepherds from the thirteenth to the seventeenth or eighteenth century. In 1248, King Alphonse X the Wise established the 'Honourable Mesta Council of Castile's Shepherds' to protect the shepherds and their flocks from thieves during their periodic migrations to the north and south of Spain in summer and winter. A shepherd-style cuisine developed along these routes, and its influence in the area's gastronomy has remained to this day.

My favourite Extremaduran cheese is *queso de los Ibores*, a buttery, rich and mellow fresh goat cheese made in the area of Los Ibores in northeast Cáceres. It is also called *pimientonado* because the rind is usually brushed with oil and coated with paprika.

CASTILLA-LA-MANCHA

The Shepherd's Cuisine: Lamb and Game

The shepherd's legacy is most notable in this extensive region. La Mancha has an old, sturdy, dry-land farming cuisine, with pastoral recipes dating from the thirteenth century.

Gazpachos de pastor or *gazpachos manchegos*, found all over La Mancha, Extremadura and west Valencia, have nothing to do with the Andalusian cold vegetable soup gazpacho. They are made from whatever game the shepherds have to hand – hare, rabbit, partridge – together with ham, some mountain herbs, mushrooms, tomatoes and peppers. They are eaten with the *torta*, a heavy flour-and-water dough cooked on a stone hot from the fire; half the *torta* is broken into the pot and mixed with the gazpachos, and the other half is used as a spoon, in pieces. It is not a light meal – but certainly tasty.

The cuisine of La Mancha is limited, yet you can eat magnificently; it has the most abundant small game of all Spain. It is said that one good reason why King Philip II established Madrid as Spain's capital in the sixteenth century was because it was a convenient meeting point for his hunting parties.

Pisto manchego, a La Mancha classic, is found in many areas of Spain. It is the equivalent of the Catalan *samfaina* and the French ratatouille, only the vegetables are cut smaller and cooked longer. *Pisto* can be a delicious accompaniment to scrambled eggs or white rice, or to salt cod in *bacalao a la manchega*.

Don Quijote, the 'Man of La Mancha'

La Mancha is the land of Cervantes' Don Quijote, and the influence of this character in the area's history is extraordinary. Cervantes was, in fact, a satiric genius; he ridiculed his society and the establishment in a most subtle and effective way. The *hidalguía* or nobility was such that the hidalgos (noblemen) were not supposed to work, for they regarded work as improper; so they were mostly poor, but had to pretend to wealth. They were thin, like Don Quijote, because they starved. Paradoxically, while Spain dominated the world in the sixteenth and seventeenth centuries, there was tremendous hunger among its people. To conceal it, some hidalgos would sprinkle breadcrumbs over their beards before leaving home, as if they had just finished a banquet, and they would walk around with a toothpick.

Marzipan

Mazapán de Toledo is quite famous all over Spain. Legend has it that marzipan originated in the thirteenth century in the San Clemente nuns' convent of Toledo, during a siege of the city. Since bread was scarce, the nuns made a dough as a substitute for it, using the staples they had to hand – almonds and sugar. They called it *mazapán* or club bread, because it was hard as a club!

Little nuns' stories aside (Italians wouldn't agree with it anyway), the origin of marzipan is definitely Arab; their *maysaban* was a confection made with dried fruits and sugar, a very Islamic combination. But the craftsmanship of Toledo confectioners gave *mazapán* its fame and prestige. It is a treat to visit a marzipan shop there – my favourite is La Positiva, in Bargas – and watch the little figurines being shaped. They are baked briefly in a hot wood-fired oven, dipped in a sugar syrup (*almíbar*) and dried.

Manchego Cheese

Manchego is La Mancha's – and maybe Spain's – most famous cheese. It is made from sheep's milk and can range from *tierno* or tender – fresh, mellow and snow-white – to *seco* (dry), dark yellow and hard, with intense sheep taste and a little piquant. The one mostly found in this country is the *semi-seco*, mild and very tasty.

Saffron, 'the Gold of La Mancha'

This is also the land of saffron, the costliest spice in the world. Travelling through the plains of La Mancha in late October, you will see the fields covered with a colourful purple hue. It is from the hundreds of thousands of saffron flowers growing in small plots, alternating with the bare, just-harvested vineyards.

The world's finest-quality saffron is produced in Spain – mainly in the provinces of Albacete, Ciudad Real, Cuenca and Toledo – and the best is Mancha Superior. The harvest of 'the rose', as the saffron flower is called, lasts approximately twenty days starting around 15 October, the feast day of St Theresa – and it is the occasion for great celebrations. The little towns organize competitions, and the old men judge the youngsters' skill in peeling 'the rose'.

Native to the Orient, saffron arrived in Spain via the Arabs (*azafrán*, Spanish for saffron, derives from the Arabic word *za'faran* or yellow) although the Romans were already using it as a dye and spreading it on the floor to perfume their orgy rooms. Today, the red pistils of the purple saffron flower are highly appreciated in fine cuisine. And maybe the price won't seem as high when you consider the enormous amount of labour necessary to produce saffron.

Each flower has three pistils, and they have to be harvested daily, early in the morning, or the sun will spoil them. The men harvest the flowers, their backs bent over for hours, and the women peel them the same day – an exhausting task they perform while singing around a table. An experienced peeler will do a maximum of 2–3 oz a day, or about 10,000 flowers. Then the pistils must be dried in the evening without delay, a process which will reduce the crop to one quarter of its size.

If kept in airtight containers, away from heat and cold, light, and above all humidity, saffron will keep for several years. The La Mancha farmers treat it just like gold; they store it and sell it in time of need.

I always prefer to use saffron in threads – I buy it in Spain at about £1.60 per gram – rather than powdered, as the latter is more likely to be adulterated. Besides, the visual effect of the threads is much better. It is a good idea to mash it a bit in a mortar with a pestle, and always cook it in a warm liquid for at least 5 minutes, to release the flavour further. Never use it in excess, or it will impart a medicinal flavour; a small amount will go a long way. And when you do use it, you will appreciate it even more if you think of the La Mancha farmers who went to so much effort to produce it.

MADRID

The capital of Spain, itself a small autonomous region as of 1982, is the centre of all the regional cuisines of the country; all, that is, except Catalan. Catalonia has traditionally kept its cooking within its boundaries, and its representation in Madrid restaurants is quite minimal.

Madrileños love to wine and dine and have a good time. They make friends easily; it is said that in Barcelona it takes you much longer to make a friend, but when you do it's a friend for ever – in Madrid you make a friend in a minute, but the friendship may only last for the day. The city has excellent restaurants and hotels as well as great entertainment, from cabarets and flamenco dancing to theatre and museums. *Chateo* (meaning *chato*-hopping, from *chato* or small glass) is a favourite pastime. I've always had a terrific time in Madrid, and can happily use any excuse to spend a few days there.

A classic dish of Madrid cuisine is *cocido madrileño*, a delicious stew pot from the nineteenth century which blends meat, marrow and sausages (*chorizo* and *morcilla*) with cabbage, carrots, chick-peas and potatoes for a three-course meal of soup, vegetables and meats. *Besugo al horno* (baked sea bream) is a simple preparation with lemon and oil, designed to enhance the fresh taste of this excellent fish. *Callos a la madrileña*, a favourite *tapa* as well as a main course, is tripe stewed with ham and sausages, onion, garlic, paprika and spices.

Madrid has as much tradition in *tapas* as Andalucía; a *tapas* tour of Madrid can be an unforgettable experience. There are still, in the down-town quarter near the Plaza Mayor, old inns (*mesones*) and hostelries (*posadas*) from the sixteenth and seventeenth centuries, with an entrance for the horse-drawn carriages, since the guests came in stagecoaches. The typical streets Cava Baja, Cuchilleros and Arco de Cuchilleros are full of earthy *tapas* bars, among them the popular Cuevas de Luis Candelas (Caves of Luis Candelas, a legendary bandit of the time); the delightful Posada de la Villa, an old three-storey inn, beautifully restored and a fine restaurant, too; and Casa Botín, home of Madrid's most celebrated roasted suckling pig and a haunt of Hemingway, who made it famous in *Death in the Afternoon*.

Other Madrid landmarks in that area are Lhardy, which has been serving *cocido madrileño* since 1920, along with an array of wonderful *tapas*; and the old Valentín, started in 1899 by Valentín Fernández and run today by his son Félix, where you will eat the best *cocido* in the entire city. No matter how many wonderful new restaurants Madrid has, I always treasure the experience of a *tapas* dinner in the picturesque old section of the city.

CASTILLA-LEÓN

This region embraces the ancient kingdoms of Old Castile and León, a vast land rich in history and tradition which extends through the northern part of the

Castilian Plateau. To the northwest, it is flanked by the Montes de León, a mountain range where good cheese abounds.

The *hornos de asar* (literally, baking ovens), establishments specializing in serving *asados*, the roasted local meats, are probably the most important gastronomic heritage of the region. They are particularly typical of three provinces: Segovia, Valladolid and Burgos. Originally, *hornos de asar* were bread bakeries which used the Arabic *hornos de bóveda*, conically shaped adobe ovens where the fire is banked on one side and the heat circulates around. It was the custom, and still is, to take a young lamb to the bakery for roasting; bakeries use dried vine shoots to heat the fire and do a much better job of roasting than can be done in most homes, where ovens are often either too small or non-existent.

Roasted young animals such as lamb or suckling pigs are a true delicacy here. Nowhere can they bake a *lechazo*, the tender baby lamb fed only with its mother's milk, the way they do in Old Castile. And *tostón* or *cochinillo*, a suckling pig of about 3.6 kg (8 lb), is a speciality of the region, enjoyed by the Castilian kings of the fifteenth century. The quality test was – and still is – to carve it with the edge of a plate to prove its tenderness.

Segovia is well known for its Roman aqueduct, the finest example of Roman construction in Spain, as well as for its almost-as-famous restaurant alongside it, Mesón de Cándido. Cándido López, the 'Great Innkeeper of Castile', has served delicious roasted suckling pig and other specialities at his restaurant since 1931. Duque, the oldest *mesón* or country restaurant in Segovia, started by Dionisio Duque in 1895, is another favourite.

Sepúlveda, just northeast of Segovia and 70 miles from Madrid, is a particularly lovely town. I have enjoyed many a dish of roast lamb in its casual *hornos de asar*; my favourites are Cristóbal and Tinín. Also worthy of a visit is the charming village Pedraza de la Sierra, just a two-hour ride from Madrid. Walking through the beautifully kept cobblestone streets and peeping through the windows of the old farmhouses is a journey to days long past. Pedraza is the second residence of many wealthy *madrileños*, who have fortunately guarded it from being spoiled.

Castile is also the land of bread. The round loaves, crusty and golden on the outside and pure white inside, are made from the high-quality wheat grown all over the region. It is a compact bread, very tasty and quite different from any other I've had.

A legacy from the Arabs is *escabeche*, a way of sautéing and marinating fish or fowl with lemon or vinegar to preserve it. Originally *escabeches* were made along the Mediterranean coast, using the local fish; gradually they moved inland and today they are a speciality of northern Castile. The word comes from the Arab *sikbaj*, a word of Persian origin meaning acid food, as mentioned in the book *Thousand and One Nights*. I've had the best *escabeches* ever at Mesón de la Villa in Aranda de Duero, where Eugenio and Seri Herrero serve their famous *escabechados* – chicken, partridge, quail, rabbit, or whatever is in season. Mussels and trout also make excellent *escabeches*, and so do vegetables such as courgettes.

The area around Palencia, Valladolid and Zamora, north of the Duero River, is the fertile Tierra de Campos. The wide variety of vegetables provides the raw material for the delicious *menestra de verduras*, which I have enjoyed here as much as further east, in Navarra and Rioja. This same area is a paradise for small game such as doves and pigeons; they are stewed like larger game, in their own blood, and cooked with vegetables.

An important speciality of Tierra de Campos is its fresh white or dry cheese de Villalón or Pata de Mulo (donkey's leg, named after its shape), made from raw sheep's milk and native to the town of Villalón, near Valladolid. Other Castilian cheeses worth mentioning are the fresh white Burgos, made from sheep's milk, soft and moist; León, a cured cheese from sheep's milk found all over Old Castile, with a characteristic almondy flavour; and Zamora, a Manchego-style cheese which is more available and less expensive than the original Manchego.

In sum, the pantry of Old Castile is humble and sparse, yet tasty and hearty, preserving the natural flavours in a simple but nutritious way.

GALICIA

Galicia may be the most striking region of all Spain. To start with, the Galicians are Celts, therefore different from the rest of the Peninsula, which is of mostly Iberian ancestry. Their character is also unique: they are individualistic, epicurean, tradition-bound, cynical and great conversationalists. They are more Irish than Spanish! They are also good drinkers; while Spain's wine consumption is 15 gallons per capita, Galicia's is 35. The region even has its own language, *gallego* or Galician, similar to Portuguese.

Situated in the farthest northwest corner of the Iberian Peninsula, Galicia still maintains its ancestral purity, the small villages and country farms that add a colourful note to the green landscape. Driving around the region, one is startled by the lush, extraordinarily green and beautiful countryside. It has a very high rainfall and mild climate, tempered by the ocean currents. Everything grows there – from kiwis and avocados to *grelos*, the delicious greens that are a speciality of their cuisine.

The Camino de Santiago

Santiago de Compostela is the political, spiritual, religious and educational centre of the region – a city full of history, named after Santiago or St James the Greater, the patron saint of Spain. The city's origin goes back to the early days of the Reconquista, the Christians' 'reconquest' of Spain from the Moors, who had invaded the country in the year 711. The Reconquista started soon after in Asturias, the region next to Galicia, and lasted nearly eight centuries, until 1492. The Arabs never established themselves in northern Spain; hence they left no influence on that area's gastronomy.

In the beginning, the Reconquista did not progress very well. The Moors had a strong motivation, their religion: the Christians didn't – until, in the year 813, some fishermen claimed to have found the remains of the Apostle Santiago. The impact was great, and it gave the Christians a symbol, a spiritual reason to fight the Moors.

Around the eleventh century the Church issued a bull granting dispensation for all sins to those who would travel to Santiago and revere the Apostle's remains. This created the Camino de Santiago, or route followed by the pilgrims through northern Spain and France, and even from Germany. The Camino was a very important means of cultural and gastronomic communication; it brought foods and customs back and forth from other parts of Spain – and most important, from Europe.

The Gastronomy: A Wealth of Shellfish

With its 800 miles of winding coastline, Galicia has the longest exposure to the ocean of any Spanish region; thus its cuisine is based on seafood. Galician shellfish, in fact, is the most appreciated all over Spain.

The Galician coast also provides some spectacular landscapes, with its *rías* or deep bays similar to the Norwegian fiords. The tiny island of La Toja, inside the Arosa *ría*, is a paradisaical spot. A little farther south lies the village of Bayona and its famous Parador Nacional, with a breathtaking view over the Vigo *ría* and the ocean. It is a real treat to let an afternoon go by while sitting enjoying the scenery together with a sampling of the marvellous local shellfish – especially the *vieiras* (scallops), which in Galicia are a true delicacy. They are always eaten with the coral (roe), and served in their own shell; the most traditional way to prepare them is *a la gallega*, or Galician style, baked with oil, wine, onions and breadcrumbs, a simple recipe based on the freshness of the scallop itself.

Shellfish in Galicia is prepared very simply, so as to enhance its high quality. The most wonderful crab, lobsters, mussels, squid, *percebes* (goose barnacles), *cigalas*, which are similar to a Mediterranean lobster but the size of a large prawn, *zamburiñas* (small scallops) and many others are simply grilled, steamed or boiled. There is also an array of clams and oysters of many types, which are for the most part eaten raw, sprinkled with some lemon juice.

An experience I'll never forget was going to gather oysters from their own beds in the *bateas*, in the Arosa *ría* near Villagarcía. *Bateas* are like large stationary barges, made from cement and wood, with ropes hanging from them where mussels or oysters grow. We took a small boat early in the morning and, armed with a knife and some lemons, cut the oysters out and ate them with lemon juice right on the boat. A bottle of fresh *alvarinho* wine proved an exceptional accompaniment.

Another very popular mollusc in Galicia is *pulpo* or octopus. The thought of eating an animal with many slippery legs may be unappetizing, but in fact Spanish octopus is much tastier than any I've tried here. The preparation requires quite a bit of work, for you have to pound octopus vigorously for a long time to tenderize it. I remember when, in my childhood, my brothers would catch octopus in the summertime – it was much to the family cook's distress, as she knew hard work was in store for her!

One of the most common ways to cook octopus is *a feira*, or festive style – so called because it is eaten traditionally at village fairs – simply dressed with some olive oil and paprika.

Inland, the peasant cooking uses the basic farm produce in the nourishing *caldo gallego* (Galician broth), a homely meal-in-a-pot that combines pork and other local meat with potatoes, dried beans and vegetables. In the Galician speciality *lacón con grelos*, the greens are cooked with the famous *lacón*, or foreleg of the tasty local pork.

Empanada gallega (Galician pie) is another classic preparation, perhaps their best-known dish. It can be filled with meat such as chicken, veal, rabbit or pork; with fish such as sardines, eel or tuna; or with any shellfish. One of my favourites, and a little more unusual, is Anchovy and Onion Pie (Empanada de Anchoas).

Some of the best Spanish cheeses come from Galicia, all made from cow's milk. My favourites are Tetilla (little breast, after its shape), pale yellow, semi-soft, mild and flavourful; and San Simón, pear-shaped, semi-firm and creamy, delicately smoked, white and with reddish orange rind.

Two of my favourite Galician desserts are the almond tart (*tarta de almendras*) and Santiago Almond Torte (Tarta de Santiago); both have an almond base, but the first is different in that it has no flour, just a rich filling of ground almonds mixed with egg, sugar and grated lemon rind. And an excellent end to any meal is Witch's Brew (Queimada), with or instead of coffee.

ASTURIAS

East of Galicia is the Principality of Asturias, from which the heir to the Spanish crown gets his name. The current Prince of Asturias is King Juan Carlos's son, Felipe. The title dates back to 1388, when King Juan I of Castile granted it to his son as a wedding gift, and it has been handed down ever since to the heirs of the Kingdom of Castile. Asturias is also famous as the place where the Reconquista started: in Covadonga, a mountain refuge 50 miles east of Oviedo.

This is dried beans country, and the best-known dish is Bean Stew with Sausages, Asturian Style (Fabada Asturiana), a hearty stew which combines dried beans (*fabes*) with the *compango* – pork, chorizo and blood sausages. There is a definite resemblance between *fabada* and the French cassoulet of Carcassonne – one more influence from the Camino de Santiago pilgrims.

Asturias is rich in apples and cider, used to delicately garnish and flavour their excellent fish in the classic preparation *merluza a la sidra* (hake in a cider sauce).

The greatest variety of cheeses in the country is found all along the northern belt of Spain, in Galicia, Asturias, León, Cantabria and País Vasco; but Asturias is probably the country's single top producer. Its most famous cheese is named Picón after the Picos de Europa, and it is made in several little villages in that part of the Cantabrian mountain range. It is an outstanding blue-veined cheese made from a mixture of cow's, sheep's and goat's milk, wrapped in chestnut leaves and kept in humid caves where air circulates naturally. It is creamy and soft, with intense aroma and sharp taste, ranking with Gorgonzola and Roquefort in quality. The best known is Cabrales-Picón, made in the village of Cabrales.

Asturian cows also provide the best milk in Spain, a basic ingredient in *arroz con leche* (rice pudding). This is a very popular dessert throughout Spain, but particularly famous in this area.

CANTABRIA

Santander, the capital of Cantabria – the region east of Asturias – is an important port and fishing centre. Sardines, tuna, bonito and anchovies are among the best in Spain. The charming seaside village of Laredo, just east of Santander, is the main fishing centre as well as the tourist capital of the beautiful Costa Verde (Green Coast), now also known as the Cornisa Cantábrica. It is home as well of the excellent Risco restaurant, high on a hill overlooking the entire village, where I enjoyed an old dish from the Laredo fishermen: *pollo marino* (sea-style chicken), a euphemism for a tuna or bonito preparation from a time when chicken used to be more expensive than fish – certainly the other way around today!

Laredo is particularly well known for its *besugo* (sea bream), which, in the old days, was shipped to Madrid in carts, packed with lemon for preservation. From this derives the custom practised all over Spain of baking that fish with half slices of lemon stuck on top of it.

If you are in the area during the hunting season, don't miss trying venison from deer of the local reserve, which is marinated and cooked in red wine with a rich, dark sauce.

PAÍS VASCO (BASQUE COUNTRY)

Spanish Basque Country and its language are today known throughout Spain by their original Basque names – Euskadi and *euskera*. This is one of the most significant regions in the country, with a long history and great gastronomic tradition.

Basque and Catalan are undoubtedly the main cuisines in Spain today. But one big difference between them is that, while Basques have always exported theirs, we Catalans never took ours outside the region. There are Basque restaurants all over Spain, and in the United States too, but few Catalan ones.

Fish has traditionally been very important in Basque cuisine. For centuries the people have lived off the ocean's produce, not only from the nearby waters but farther away too. First fishing for whales and then for cod, they arrived in Newfoundland – even before Columbus discovered America. The old dish *marmitako* originated from the way Basque fishermen cooked tuna, bonito and other fish on board. In the beginning it was made with bread. After the discovery of America, potatoes were substituted for bread and later peppers and tomato were added. A great restaurant in which to eat *marmitako* is the long-established Nicolasa in San Sebastián.

Tiny squid (*calamares* or *chipirones*) are made into the only truly black dish in the world, squid in its own ink (*calamares en su tinta*). In the United States and Britain it is difficult to make the dish *really* black, for the squid are not caught on a hook, as they are in Spain, but with drag nets, and while they are in the net, the squid exude most of their ink.

Bilbao, capital of the Basque province of Vizcaya, is well known for its *bacalao* (salt cod). I've had the best *bacalao* dishes ever at Genaro Pildaín's historic Guría restaurant. His *bacalao a la vizcaína*, an old recipe for salt cod cooked in onions and dried red peppers, is famous. There are about 200 recipes to prepare *bacalao*, and you will find at least some in every Bilbao restaurant.

A wonderful Basque dish is *angulas* (baby eels), often prepared *al ajillo* – with garlic and hot peppers, served in boiling hot oil. The best known throughout Spain are those from Aguinaga, a small town 6 miles west of San Sebastián. *Angulas* are found only along the coast of the Bay of Biscay, in Spain and France. The reason is that eels lay their eggs in the Sargasso Sea, and the brood is transported by the Gulf Stream to Europe; they grow up to become adult eels (*anguilas*) in the rivers that flow into the Bay of Biscay, from where they swim back to the Sargasso Sea, and the process starts again. This is why there are no *angulas* in the United States, unfortunately; they are available only frozen or canned – and it just isn't the same thing.

San Sebastián, capital of the Guipúzcoa province, is the tourist as well as gastronomic capital of the Basque Country, where the most renowned restaurants are located. It was here in the seventies that a group of young, innovative chefs started the 'New Basque Cuisine', promoting their novel ideas with great success. Juan Mari Arzak took charge of the Arzak restaurant in the late sixties, and in a few years he made his cuisine famous throughout Spain and abroad. Pedro Subijana opened the Akelaŕe restaurant in 1972, and has today become one of Spain's top chefs. Both of these restaurants have a double star in the French Michelin Guide – the only two in the Basque Country to have been accorded such an honour.

It was also in San Sebastián that, on 1 January 1900, the first *sociedad gastronómica* (gastronomic society) was born. These are enormously popular in the matriarchal Basque society because they are reserved exclusively for men, who have there a place to gather, a kitchen to cook their own meals and a cellar in which to keep their best wines. The idea has prospered, especially in the last twenty-five years; in 1950 there were about 200 gastronomic societies in the region, and today there are over 1,000!

The atmosphere in these societies is one of equality and harmony. All members have the same status: the mayor may cook for the janitor, and the manager for the labourer. No political ideas are discussed; fine cooking is enjoyed and friendship promoted.

The area near the French border – notably the village of Zugarramurdi, some 30 miles from San Sebastián – was famous in the old days for its *akelarres*. Witches and sorcerers gathered around a male goat, invoking the devil, during their Saturday evening rituals – which always ended in an orgy. While the *akelarre* was being celebrated, the attendants roasted veal using a cooking method that had its origin in America. It is called *lindo*, a derivation of the name 'Indians' given to the region's emigrants who came back from the New World bringing not only silver but American customs as well. Several legs of veal are stuck in the ground around a large fire and turned by hand to cook evenly.

The variety of cheeses in the area is wide and excellent. They are mostly made with sheep's milk and range from fresh, white and tender curd cheeses, to those cured from raw milk. An array of smoked cheeses is also made there; the most famous – and my favourite – is Idiazábal, yellowish white, firm, with golden rind and an intense smoky flavour with a hint of mountain herbs.

NAVARRA

Travelling south from San Sebastián, you will drive along a winding road through green lush landscapes to Pamplona, the capital of Navarra, immortalized by Hemingway in his book *The Sun Also Rises*. I have enjoyed his wonderfully vivid description of the Sanfermines and the excitement of the running of the bulls in the week of 7 July to celebrate the day of San Fermín, the city's patron saint. It is a marathon week of eating and drinking and staying out in the streets all night.

The area around Lodosa, in the south of Navarra, is famous for its red peppers, notably the *pimientos del pico* (peppers of the beak, named after their beak-shaped ends). In September and October, a delicious smell perfumes the air of the little towns as the women roast peppers in front of their houses over wood fires; then they peel and bottle them, selling the jars for additional income.

Other types of fine red peppers grown in Spain are *choriceros* and *del cuerno*, found mostly in the Basque Country, and *morrones* in Aragón and Murcia; but reputedly the finest in all of Spain are *pimientos del pico*.

The northern mountain areas, in the Pyrenees, are a paradise for mushrooms and game such as dove and quail. Quail are combined with some very special beans, the tender *pochas* – available only at the beginning of the hunting season – in the wonderful autumn dish *codornices con pochas*.

One memorable cheese in Navarra is Roncal, named after the Pyrenees valley where it is made, from raw sheep's milk. It is firm, of ivory colour, slightly piquant, with a characteristic aroma and flavour.

Pamplona is renowned for its chorizos and other sausages, notably the slender flavourful *chistorra*. Ever since my first visit there I have been fascinated by the strings of sausages which hang outside the balconies of the homes, together with the red peppers, to dry. A truly colourful sight!

South of Pamplona, the banks of the Ebro River form the fertile area of La Ribera. Here vegetables and fruits grow abundantly, and the easy access to irrigation has made this area very fruitful. The cuisine is primarily based on vegetables; artichokes and asparagus, simply boiled and accompanied by a *vinagreta* sauce, are unique because of the natural flavour of the fresh ingredients.

La Ribera has a famous dish, *caldereta ribereña*, a country-style stew named after the cauldron in which it is made: deep, with three legs so a fire can be built underneath. Obviously an outdoor dish, it is cooked by the peasants and shepherds, and includes anything the land provides: meat and potatoes, maybe a few birds hunted in the morning, eels or trout caught in nearby rivers, some snails, and seasonal vegetables.

The city of Tudela – centre of La Ribera – had Hebrew, Islamic and Catholic communities living together from the tenth century. The Arab and Mediterranean influence is still visible in the way they stuff their morcillas (blood sausages) with pine nuts and raisins, flavouring them with cinnamon.

LA RIOJA

Logroño, the region's capital, is only 3 miles from Basque Country and the same from Navarra – hence La Rioja's cuisine is intimately joined to that of its two neighbours.

The name Rioja evokes wine; its reds are known all over the world. Curiously, though, *a la riojana* (Rioja-style) dishes do not use any wine, but always some kind of peppers – either red sweet peppers, fresh or dry, whole or ground (paprika), or the chillis called *guindillas* – and often chorizo.

Patatas a la riojana are a staple of the region. The potatoes are served with enough broth to almost make a soup; generous amounts of paprika and the delicious local chorizo provide a lot of flavour. Other classic *a la riojana* dishes are snails, tripe, pork loin, and salt cod cooked with tomatoes, onions and potatoes besides the peppers and the tasty chorizo.

The Rioja gardens are well known for their vegetables, and peppers are as important here as they are in Navarra. They are often chargrilled and served as an accompaniment to grilled meats or to the favourite Riojan dish, lamb chops roasted over a fire made with vine cuttings. A wonderful combination are quails stuffed in red peppers (*pimientos rellenos de codornices*).

Pork is excellent, often cooked quite simply, grilled or chargrilled. The cuisine here is earthy and country style, not too varied but very tasty.

The combination of the Riojan Ribera's fruits and the region's great wines makes for the delicious *melocotones al vino*, whole peaches cooked in red wine. And speaking of wine, the local Spiced Red Wine (Zurracapote) is worth a try.

ARAGÓN

This is a large region, bordering Catalonia and Valencia as well as the Pyrenees and France, Navarra and Castile; therefore its cuisine reflects the influence of these areas. Northern Aragón, around Huesca, is cold and mountainous. I've had many a warming meal there which tasted like heaven after a long day of skiing – peasant-style cooking at its best.

South in the Teruel province, the mountains of Serranía de Albarracín provide ideal conditions to make excellent *serrano* hams, which dry well in the cold mountain winds.

The region's central province, Zaragoza, in the Ebro River Valley, is flat and fertile. Vegetables and fruit trees are plentiful, and the candied fruits made here are very famous. Vineyards and olive trees grow very well, too; Cariñena makes sturdy, full-bodied wines, and Alcañiz produces excellent olive oil. Almond trees provide the basis for *guirlache*, the delicious candy made with caramelized sugar and almonds.

One of the most distinctive preparations is *salmorrejo* – which has nothing to do with the *salmorejo* or gazpacho-style thick soup of Andalucía. Here the name is given to a number of dishes with eggs such as *tortilla al salmorrejo*, an omelette with potatoes and rice covered with a garlic sauce, and *huevos al salmorrejo*, eggs poached with white wine and fillet of pork, sausages, chorizo, ham and asparagus.

The roasted meat can be excellent, and lamb is plentiful. A traditional way to roast meat, still used today with small animals like rabbits or hare, is *al entierro* or burial style. The animal is not skinned but cleaned, and stuffed with chopped garlic, onion, pork fat, ham and chorizo. Then it is placed in a hole in the ground, covered with earth, and a fire is built over it. When this turns into red-hot coals, an onion is placed on top; as soon as the onion is tender, the animal is cooked. It is then skinned and ready to eat.

BITS
AND
PIECES

Olive Oil

Olive oil is indispensable in preparing many of the recipes in this book. It will impart a more authentic 'Spanish' flavour to the food than a vegetable oil.

It is the fat most used along the Mediterranean for cooking, a heritage from the Greeks and Romans; the first records of its cultivation date back 6,000 years to the Middle East. It came to Spain through Tarragona from eastern Mediterranean traders, especially the Greeks, in the first millennium BC. But in northern Spain it was not used until the eighteenth century; before that, Galicia used mostly lard and the Basque Country used butter.

Together with Italy, Spain heads the list of olive oil producers in the world; over 5 million acres are dedicated to its cultivation, with an average annual production of 500,000 tons. Most of it is produced in the Andalusian provinces of Jaén, Córdoba and Sevilla, although some of the best olive oil is obtained in Catalonia. The area around the village of Borjas Blancas, east of Lérida, is particularly famous for the quality of its oil and is one of only four olive-producing areas in the country covered and controlled by an Appellation of Origin. So is the area of Siurana, west of Tarragona. Both oils are made from the *arbequina* olive, a small, round, greenish variety which stands out for its low acidity and fine, fruity flavour. The other two Appellations of Origin are in Andalucía: Sierra de Segura and Baena, north and west of Jaén respectively. The first uses the *picual* olives, dark and small; the second grows mostly the *picudo* variety, lighter in colour and pointed at the end.

Olive oil is extracted from its fruit by pressing; an olive contains between 18 and 30 per cent oil, depending on its ripeness, and an average of 20–22 per cent oil is obtained in the process. Olive oil can be consumed virgin, which means it has been obtained by cold pressing and not refined; virgin oil has the lowest acidity, from under 1 per cent in the extra virgin to under 1.5 per cent in the superfine virgin. It has a darker, greener colour and much fruitier taste; it is excellent for seasoning salads, but I find it too strong for cooking. Extra virgin olive oil is a special treat and well worth seeking out, even if expensive; buy it from a retailer you trust, so he can guide you to one that will suit your taste.

Refined olive oil has a higher acidity and limpid yellow colour. So-called pure olive oil is a mixture of refined and about 5–10 per cent of virgin. It is much less expensive, and I find it best for cooking.

When storing olive oil, it is important to keep it away from direct sunlight and at a temperature of 10–15°c (50–60°F).

Orange and Lemon Zest

Zest is the rind of an orange or lemon, without any of the white pith. Whenever a recipe calls for grated orange/lemon zest, I recommend you use a zester rather than grating the rind, as this releases the oils. If you don't have one, use a vegetable peeler to make very thin strips, and then chop them.

Breadcrumbs

Using soft white breadcrumbs as a binder in a stuffing is very common in Spanish cuisine. A filling made with all meat tends to be too heavy; adding breadcrumbs lightens the filling, and I find that the final product is much tastier.

Breadcrumbs can be made from white or wholemeal bread, but my recipes call for white bread because that is what we mostly use in Spain. I have indicated when commercial dry breadcrumbs should be used. These are grated much finer and are good for coating food, but not for a stuffing.

To make breadcrumbs it is better to use day-old bread, if possible. Remove the crusts and reduce the bread to crumbs, in the food processor. A 900 g (1 lb) loaf of bread will give you about 225 g (8 oz) breadcrumbs, after removing crusts. When using a cook's measure, don't pack it; the directions in my recipes are intended for loose measurements.

Roasting and Peeling Peppers

Red and green peppers are used a lot in Spanish cuisine, and many recipes in this book include them. Very often they are roasted and peeled – which may seem like a difficult task. But here are a few tips on how to do it easily.

Preheat the oven to 200°c (400°f) mark 6.

Place the peppers on an ungreased baking sheet in the oven for 30 minutes, turning them around occasionally, until they scorch and the skin blisters and puffs up, starting to blacken. Immediately put them in a paper bag and twist it shut; leave the peppers in it for 15–30 minutes. While they are still warm it will be fairly easy to skin them, scraping them with a small, sharp knife. Do not do this under running water, or the peppers will lose some of their flavour; and don't worry about getting every last bit of skin off.

This procedure will just precook the peppers; if they are to be baked later, they will not be overcooked. In fact I prefer peppers on the well-done side, not only because they are easier to digest but also because their flavours come through more fully. Roasted peppers are simply delicious as an accompaniment to grilled meats; in this case I like to sprinkle on some olive oil and salt after peeling and seeding them, maybe a touch of minced garlic, and put them back in the oven for another 15 minutes.

If you only have to peel 2 or 3 peppers, you may find it faster to skewer each pepper on a fork and hold it over a flame until the skin starts to blacken, turning it around so it scorches evenly all over. After each pepper has blistered, place it in a paper bag as directed above.

In Spain, peppers are often roasted over a wood fire, which naturally provides wonderful flavours. A barbecue is a great substitute, especially if you are going to serve the peppers roasted.

Flambéing

Spanish chefs – and Catalans in particular – are very fond of flambéing foods when cooking. This is done not as a decorative presentation but as part of the actual preparation, to add flavour and a bit of colour to the dish. The harsh alcohol flavours burn off quickly, and what is left is the essence of the brandy or other spirit used.

It is important to use a liquor with high alcohol content; you cannot flambé with wine. Both the liquor and the ingredients should be hot, and you should use a shallow pan. Pour in the liquid, shake the pan and, as soon as the liquor is hot, ignite with a match – but be very careful and do not stand too close to the pan, as it will burst into flames right away. This method will not only improve your dish but it is also dramatic and fun to do.

Caramelizing

My recipes often call for caramelizing, whether to line a dessert mould or to add colour and flavour to a savoury dish. The method simply consists of combining sugar with a little water in a heavy-based saucepan over a brisk heat. (You can actually caramelize sugar by itself, without water, but I find it easier to do when the sugar is dissolved in about 1 tbsp water to 50 g (2 oz) sugar.) Don't stir the mixture, just shake the pan gently; in about 4 minutes, the water will evaporate and the sugar will first melt, then turn to a thick golden liquid. At this point you must decide how dark a caramel you want – and quickly, since the colour turns from light golden to burnt brown very fast.

When used to line a mould, caramel will not only add a nice colour and flavour to your dessert but will also make it easier to unmould. In savoury dishes, the caramel is added to a hot liquid; it will hiss and smoke, but don't let that deter you – the caramel will soon dissolve, contributing a nice colour and extra flavour.

Equivalents

1 small onion	= 100 g (4 oz)
1 large onion	= 225 g (8 oz)
1 medium carrot	= 100 g (4 oz)
1 large carrot	= 175 g (6 oz)
1 large tomato	= 225 g (8 oz)
1 large pepper	= 175–225 g (6–8 oz)
1 small pepper	= 100–175 g (4–6 oz)
150 g (5 oz) chopped onion	= 1 medium
150 g (5 oz) chopped carrot	= 2 medium
225 g (8 oz) chopped tomato (unpeeled)	= 1 large
225 g (8 oz) chopped tomato (peeled and seeded)	= 2 large
225 g (8 oz) chopped pepper	= 1 large
150 g (5 oz) chopped leek	= 1 small (white part with $\frac{1}{3}$ of the green part)
15 ml (1 tbsp) minced garlic	= 3 large cloves
15 ml (1 tbsp) minced shallots	= 1 medium
50 g (2 oz) minced shallots	= 2 large
60 ml (4 tbsp) lemon juice	= 1 large lemon
125 ml (4 fl oz) orange juice	= 1 or 1½ large oranges
15 ml (1 tbsp) grated orange zest	= 1 large orange
15 ml (1 tbsp) grated lemon zest	= 2 medium lemons
10 ml (2 tsp) grated lemon zest	= 1 large lemon
1 large (1 cm/½ inch) slice white bread	= 25 g (1 oz)

FOOD AND WINE MENU PLANNING

Perhaps the most important thing to realize about matching food and wine is this: almost any wine tastes better with food and almost any food tastes better with wine. It's that simple. Don't be misled by self-appointed experts who tell you at great and boring length that you *must* drink a particular wine with a particular food.

In Spain, for example, wine is usually served with meals and, most often, you drink the wine of the particular area you are in, be it red or white; if it is red, you drink it straight through the meal and no nonsense about white wine with fish and red wine with meat.

However, the pairing of food and wine is fun and often rewarding, since different foods *do* change one's appreciation of the wine, and vice versa. As wine writer Larry Walker maintains, 'The integrity of neither should be violated. That is, the food should not be moulded to the wine, nor the wine be so homogenized that it becomes a kind of bland and universal "food wine". My only other quibble is that wine *is* food and should be part of the menu planning process from the beginning, designed to harmonize (not necessarily blend) with the rest of the menu.'

The only rule to follow is that you should try to find a balance and a harmony between the food and wine you are serving, almost as if you were composing a painting or planning a garden. You might begin with a specific dish, a main dish, something that is in season or maybe just on sale at the local market. Plan the rest of the menu around that dish, be it lamb or fish or aubergine. Then try to remember the taste of some of your favourite wines – will they harmonize? Will they be too acidic? Too sweet? Too heavy? As you can see, the more experience you have in tasting different wine and food combinations, the better you will be able to pair them. Some people enjoy keeping a kind of kitchen diary to help jog palate memory; I keep a record of all my dinners, guests, menus and wines, and make notes of what worked.

There are very few golden rules in serving wines; one I always follow is never to serve a wine of lower quality than the one which has gone before. The second is to suit the wines to the guests; if they are connoisseurs they should be offered fine wines, for even if the differences are small they will be able to appreciate the subtler overtones. With guests who are not experts, serve wines whose differences they can appreciate at once. The third rule is not to attach too much importance to old vintages; a wine that is too old is nothing but a memory, a museum piece.

I hope that through these pages you will learn to enjoy and use the exciting foods (and wines) of Spain; I believe they will add a strong, vivid note to your culinary repertoire.

APPETIZERS AND FIRST COURSES

Huevos Rellenos de Anchoa

· EGGS FILLED WITH ANCHOVIES ·

Stuffed eggs are as popular in Spain as they are in America and Britain; but these are out of the ordinary because of the interesting mixture of flavours. They make a delightful appetizer and are also very good in a salad, or with cold sausages and tomatoes, etc. *Serves 6.*

6 small eggs, or 12 quail's eggs
FOR THE FILLING
1 × 50 g (2 oz) can flat anchovy fillets,
  drained
2 medium cloves garlic
pinch of crushed hot red pepper flakes

50 ml (2 fl oz) olive oil
75 g (3 oz) grated Parmesan cheese
30 ml (2 tbsp) lemon juice
AS A GARNISH
6 black olives, unstoned (if using quail's
  eggs, use 12 olives)

To cook the eggs Place the eggs in a saucepan, cover with cold water and bring to the boil. Immediately reduce heat to very low and simmer, covered, for 10–15 minutes. (If you use quail's eggs, they will cook faster.) Place the eggs under cold water to prevent further cooking. Peel the eggs, cut them in half and carefully remove the yolks.

To prepare the filling   In a food processor, purée the anchovies with the garlic and pepper flakes; add the olive oil and Parmesan, and process until a thick paste is formed. Add the egg yolks and lemon juice, and mix thoroughly. Taste for seasoning.

To assemble the eggs   Using a piping bag, pipe the filling into the whites of the eggs. Cut the olives in half and remove the stones; place half an olive on top of each egg. Refrigerate for at least 1 hour before serving.

Zanahorias Aliñadas

· CARROTS SEASONED WITH HERBS ·

This is a classic dish served in Andalucía at *tapas* bars, and each cook takes pride in having the best recipe. One of the tastiest preparations I've had comes from Las Golondrinas, a wonderful place in the quintessential *tapas* city, Sevilla. Owner Luis Ribera *never* gives out his recipe, so I was very lucky to get it.

I serve these carrots usually as an appetizer, with toasted French bread; but they also make a delightful, light first course.   *Serves 6.*

900 g (2 lb) long slender carrots
4 large cloves garlic
7.5 ml (1½ tsp) dried oregano
3.75 ml (¾ tsp) cumin seeds
5 ml (1 tsp) dried coriander
1.25 ml (¼ tsp) crushed hot red pepper
   flakes
1.25 ml (¼ tsp) freshly ground black
   pepper
5 ml (1 tsp) salt
22.5 ml (1½ tbsp) sherry wine vinegar
125 ml (4 fl oz) olive oil
10 ml (2 tsp) chopped parsley

Peel the carrots and slice them into 2.5 cm (1 inch) thick rounds (if they are large, cut in half lengthways). Bring a large pan of salted water to the boil; add the carrots and cook over a medium heat for 8–10 minutes, or until the carrots are tender but still firm. Drain and place in a serving bowl.

In a food processor, grind together the garlic, oregano, cumin, coriander, pepper flakes, pepper and salt. Add the vinegar to form a paste. Add the oil in a thin stream and blend it all together. Transfer to the bowl with the carrots, add the parsley and mix well to coat the carrots with the dressing. Leave the carrots to marinate for 2 hours or longer. Serve at room temperature.

Champiñones Rellenos al Jerez

· STUFFED MUSHROOMS WITH SHERRY ·

Mushrooms are very often eaten as a *tapa* in Spain, and we frequently combine them with sherry in a sauce. But in this recipe sherry adds zest to the filling, an interesting variation on more traditional preparations. *Serves 6.*

18 *large mushrooms, 450–700 g*
  (1–1½ lb)
65 *g (2¼ oz) whole almonds*
15 *g (½ oz) soft white breadcrumbs*
  (pp. 31–2)
225 *g (8 oz) minced pork*
5 *ml (1 tsp) orange zest (p. 31)*

90 *ml (3 fl oz) flavourful dry or semi-dry*
  Spanish sherry, such as amontillado or
  oloroso
2.5 *ml (½ tsp) salt, or to taste*
1.25 *ml (¼ tsp) freshly ground black*
  pepper, or to taste
15–30 *ml (1–2 tbsp) olive oil*

Preheat the oven to 180°C (350°F) mark 4.

Wipe the mushrooms; remove the stems and chop finely. Set aside the mushroom caps. Toast the almonds in the oven for 12 minutes, and chop them coarsely in a food processor.

In a mixer or by hand, combine the mushroom stems, chopped almonds, breadcrumbs, pork, orange zest, sherry, salt and pepper. Pack the mushroom caps with the stuffing. Increase the oven temperature to 200°C (400°F) mark 6.

In a large frying pan, heat enough olive oil just to coat the bottom of the pan. Add the mushroom caps, filling side down, and sauté over a medium to low heat until the filling is golden brown – 2–3 minutes. Remove the mushrooms with a spatula and place on an oiled baking sheet, filling side up. Bake for about 20 minutes. Serve immediately.

A WORD ABOUT SNAILS

Snails are eaten in Spain quite often, but traditionally they have been cooked as a peasant dish – not as an elegant preparation, as is the case in France, for example. It is only recently that Spaniards have elevated snails to the status of a delicacy! The following recipes reflect both attitudes: the first one is an earthy, peasant-style dish; the other two are refined and delicate – one Catalan, and one Basque.

Snails have been popular along Spain's Mediterranean coast for a long time. Later on, the custom of eating snails expanded inland, and not long ago to the Basque Country. Custom has it that snails were eaten in the old times on vigil days, especially Holy Thursday, Good Friday and Christmas Eve, when Catholics were not allowed to eat meat – and snails were not considered to be meat. According to popular belief, the tastiest snails are those that grow up in the vineyards, but where there are no vineyards, those found in cemeteries are just as good. This was earnestly told to me by Pedro Subijana, owner of the Akelaŕe restaurant in San Sebastián, who is one of the most progressive chefs in Spain. His Effortless Snails in a Watercress Sauce (Caracoles sin Trabajo con Salsa de Berros) has become a classic of the New Basque Cuisine. A more traditional way to prepare snails is with tomato sauce or red peppers, combined with meat such as chorizo or ham.

Caracoles Picantes

· CATALAN – CARGOLS PICANTS ·

· SNAILS IN A PIQUANT SAUCE ·

This recipe comes from El Celler del Penedès, a country restaurant near Vilafranca del Penedès where chef/owner Pere Valls serves wonderful earthy dishes typical of Catalonia. A special feature of this dining spot is a huge *porrón* which they keep outside, full of wine, to welcome thirsty visitors. Used in the Catalan countryside, the *porrón* is a wine-drinking container with two spouts: a larger one through which you fill it, and a smaller one through which you pour the wine into your mouth, raising the *porrón* high with your hand. If you can raise it with one hand only, you are allowed to drink as much as you want free!

This gives you an idea of the kind of restaurant this is – friendly, hospitable and very Catalan. And so is this peasant-style snails recipe, with its classic Catalan *sofrito* and *picada*, flavourful and spicy. It can be served as an appetizer or first course, and would be wonderful as a *tapa* at a buffet dinner, served in a clay casserole as we do in Spain. In any case, make sure to accompany it with good crusty bread.   *Serves 6.*

FOR POACHING THE SNAILS
225 ml (8 fl oz) dry white wine
225 ml (8 fl oz) Brown Veal Stock
  (p. 192)
2.5 ml (½ tsp) fennel seeds
2 sprigs fresh thyme or 1.25 ml (¼ tsp)
  dried
36 large snails, frozen or canned about
  225 g (8 oz), drained weight
FOR THE SOFRITO
45 ml (3 tbsp) olive oil
3 large cloves garlic, finely chopped
1 small onion, chopped
450 g (1 lb) tomatoes, skinned, seeded
  and chopped
2.5 ml (½ tsp) crushed hot red pepper
  flakes

225 g (8 oz) ham knuckle bone, cut into 3
  or 4 pieces
225 ml (8 fl oz) Enriched Veal Stock
  (p. 193) or 475 ml (16 fl oz) Brown
  Veal Stock (p. 192)
225 ml (8 fl oz) full-bodied dry red wine
FOR THE PICADA
15 ml (1 tbsp) olive oil
1 medium slice white bread, about 15 g
  (¼ oz)
10 almonds, ground
½ sweet red pepper, cored, seeded and
  chopped
15 ml (1 tbsp) chopped parsley

To poach the snails   In a saucepan, combine the wine, stock, fennel and thyme; cook for 20 minutes over a medium to low heat, to reduce by about half. Drain the snails and rinse them under running water. Add them to the poaching liquid and cook for 5 minutes. Drain the snails and remove any fennel seeds that cling to them. Discard the liquid and reserve the snails.

To prepare the *sofrito*   In a heavy frying pan, heat the oil and add the garlic and onion; cook until soft, stirring. Add the tomatoes, pepper flakes and ham bone pieces; cook over a low heat for 30 minutes, to obtain a concentrated thick sauce.

Add the stock and wine, increase the heat to medium and cook until reduced to 225 ml (8 fl oz) – about 30 minutes. Remove and discard the ham bone pieces.

To prepare the *picada*   Heat the oil in a frying pan. Add the bread slice and fry over a medium heat until golden on both sides. In a food processor, finely grind the bread slice with the almonds, red pepper and parsley.

To assemble the dish   Add the *picada* to the *sofrito* in the pan and cook, stirring, for a few minutes until warm. Add the snails and cook just to heat them through. Taste for seasoning, and serve warm.

Tartaletas de Caracoles a las Hierbas Aromáticas

· CATALAN – TARTALETES DE CARGOLS A LAS HERBES AROMÀTIQUES ·

· SNAIL TARTLETS WITH MUSHROOMS AND AROMATIC HERBS ·

This delicate and sophisticated Catalan recipe will be enjoyed even by those who don't like snails – unless you tell them what's in it (I speak from experience!).

A creation of chef/owner Toya Roqué, of the Azulete restaurant in Barcelona, it is a good example of her inventive, new approach to turning a peasant food into an elegant dish.

For this recipe you need 6 individual shallow flan tins about 11 cm (4½ inches) in diameter. It is best if they are loose-based, as it will be easier to take them out after they are cooked. The Press-in Pastry, however, is not difficult to detach from the tin, because of its high butter content and absence of water.   *Serves 6.*

FOR THE TARTLETS
1 quantity Press-in Pastry (p. 177)
FOR THE FILLING
400 g (14 oz) canned snails, drained
   weight
25 g (1 oz) butter
4 shallots, finely chopped
175 g (6 oz) mushrooms, finely chopped
5 ml (1 tsp) finely chopped chervil or
   1.25 ml (¼ tsp) dried

3.75 ml (¾ tsp) finely chopped tarragon or
   1.25 ml (¼ tsp) dried
450 g (1 lb) tomatoes, skinned, seeded
   and finely chopped
225 ml (8 fl oz) double cream
3.75 ml (¾ tsp) salt
2.5 ml (½ tsp) freshly ground black pepper
AS A GARNISH
30 ml (2 tbsp) snipped chives

Preheat the oven to 220°c (425°F) mark 7.

To prepare the tartlets   Divide the pastry into 6 equal pieces 50 g (2 oz) each and, with your hands, press a piece into each tin. Refrigerate for at least 15 minutes.

Immediately bake in the oven for 10–15 minutes, or until golden. Allow to cool slightly, then remove the pastry cases from the tins and set aside.

Reduce the oven temperature to 190°c (375°F) mark 5.

To prepare the filling   Rinse the snails under cold running water and chop them. Heat the butter in a heavy frying pan; add the shallots and fry over a medium to low heat until translucent. Add the mushrooms and continue cooking until liquid evaporates. Add the chervil and tarragon, stir and cook for about 1 minute; add the tomatoes and cook over a medium heat until the liquid evaporates. Add the cream, salt and pepper; continue cooking for a few minutes until the mixture thickens slightly. Add the snails and cook for 5 minutes. Taste for seasoning.

To assemble the tartlets   Fill the tartlets with the mixture, distributing it evenly. Place the tartlets on a baking sheet in the oven and bake for about 10 minutes, or until they are golden brown.

Serve warm, with some chives sprinkled over the centre of each tartlet.

Caracoles sin Trabajo con Salsa de Berros

· EFFORTLESS SNAILS IN A WATERCRESS SAUCE ·

Pedro Subijana is one of the most representative chefs of modern Basque cuisine; he deserves much credit for the simplicity and delicacy of his recipes, such as this one.

Dining at his beautiful Akelaŕe restaurant in San Sebastián, high on a hill overlooking the Bay of Biscay, is an experience not to be forgotten. I particularly enjoyed these 'effortless snails'; he gave them this name because they are served without shells and are easy to eat. The dish may be effortless for the eater – but not so much for the cook. Yet I assure you, it is worth all the work you put into it, and will delight even those guests who wrinkle their noses at the thought of eating snails. *Serves 6.*

FOR THE PASTRY CASES
½ quantity *Puff Pastry (p. 178), chilled*
1 egg, beaten
FOR POACHING THE SNAILS
225 ml (8 fl oz) dry white wine
225 ml (8 fl oz) Brown Veal Stock
(p. 192)
2.5 ml (½ tsp) fennel seeds
2 sprigs fresh thyme or 1.25 ml (¼ tsp)
dried
115 g (4½ oz) snails, frozen or canned,
drained weight
FOR THE SAUCE
25 g (1 oz) butter

6 large cloves garlic, finely chopped
225 g (8 oz) unpeeled tomatoes, chopped
225 ml (8 fl oz) Enriched Veal Stock
(p. 193) or 475 ml (16 fl oz) Brown
Veal Stock (p. 192)
50 ml (2 fl oz) double cream
25 g (1 oz) watercress leaves, roughly
chopped
1.25 ml (¼ tsp) salt, or to taste
pinch of freshly ground white pepper, or
to taste
AS A GARNISH
a few sprigs watercress

Preheat the oven to 220°c (425°F) mark 7.

To prepare the pastry cases Roll out the pastry to about 3 mm (⅛ inch) thickness. Using a biscuit cutter of about 7.5 cm (3 inch) diameter, cut 12 rounds out of the pastry. Place 6 of the rounds on an ungreased baking sheet. Dip your finger in water and moisten a 1 cm (½ inch) ring around the edge of each round. Using a sharp-pointed knife or a 5 cm (2 inch) diameter biscuit cutter, make a line 1 cm (½ inch) in from the edge of the other 6 rounds. (Don't cut all the way through the dough, however, or it will not rise.) Place these 6 rounds on top of the others on the baking sheet. Brush the tops with the beaten egg. Bake in the oven for 8 minutes, then reduce the temperature to 190°c (375°F) mark 5 and bake for a further 10–15 minutes, or until the pastry is golden and the bottom starts to brown.

Remove the pastry cases from the oven and immediately cut through the round line you made earlier, lifting out the 'lid' carefully with a knife. If there is any soft puff pastry inside, scoop it out with a spoon and discard it. You now have 6 round little boxes with lids for your snails.

These pastry cases can be made up to 3 days ahead, stored in an airtight tin and warmed up at the last moment in a preheated oven, 150°c (300°F) mark 2, for 5 minutes.

To poach the snails Proceed as directed in the recipe for Snails in a Piquant Sauce (Caracoles Picantes) (p. 38).

To prepare the sauce Heat the butter in a large heavy frying pan; add the garlic and fry over a low heat for 2 minutes, or until soft. Add the tomatoes and cook over a low heat for 15 minutes. Add the stock and purée in a food processor or blender. Strain through a fine sieve, pressing the contents with the back of a spoon. Return the sauce to the pan and reduce to about 225 ml (8 fl oz). Add the cream and cook over a medium heat for 5–10 minutes, to thicken slightly. Add the snails, watercress, salt and pepper, and taste for seasoning.

To assemble the dish Gently heat snails in the sauce for just a couple of minutes, so they don't toughen. Place 1 pastry shell on each individual plate. Distribute the snail mixture evenly among the shells, letting the sauce overflow the top. Put the lids on at an angle – like cocked hats. Garnish with watercress sprigs.

Tartaletas de Riñones

· KIDNEY TARTLETS ·

It is very common in Spain for *tapas* bars to serve little tartlets filled with anything from chopped mushrooms to meat. The idea for these comes from Bar Oquendo, a popular *tapas* bar in San Sebastián which is famous for them and has been serving them since 1963, as owner José Mari Iriondo told me. *Makes 12 tartlets.*

FOR THE TARTLETS
½ quantity Press-in Pastry (p. 177)
FOR THE FILLING
300–350 g (10–12 oz) calf's or lamb's
   kidneys, fresh if possible
50 g (2 oz) butter
4 shallots, finely chopped

225 g (8 oz) tomatoes, skinned, seeded
   and chopped
125 ml (4 fl oz) dry Spanish sherry,
   preferably fino
1.25 ml (¼ tsp) salt, or to taste
2.5 ml (½ tsp) freshly ground black
   pepper, or to taste

To prepare the tartlets   Press the pastry into 12 tartlet tins of about 3.5 cm (1½ inch) diameter. Refrigerate for at least 15 minutes.

Preheat the oven to 220°c (425°F) mark 7.

Bake the pastry cases in the oven for 15 minutes, or until golden. Lower the oven temperature to 180°c (350°F) mark 4.

To prepare the filling   Trim the excess fat from the kidneys and finely chop them. Heat half the butter in a heavy frying pan and sauté the kidneys over a medium heat for 3–4 minutes. Set them aside.

In the same pan, heat the remaining butter and fry the shallots over a low heat, until very soft and golden. Stir in the tomatoes, and cook until all the liquid has evaporated. Add the sherry and cook until reduced by half. Return the kidneys and their juices to the pan. Add salt and pepper, and taste for seasoning. Set aside.

To assemble the dish   At the last minute, warm up the pastry cases for 5 minutes in the oven preheated to 180°c (350°F) mark 4. Divide the kidney mixture equally among them. Serve immediately, while still warm.

Tarta de Cebolla

· ONION TART ·

This recipe was inspired by a dish I had at Panier Fleuri, in San Sebastián. Chef/owner Tatús Fombellida is a young woman with a great restaurant family tradition; she has inherited the skill and taste of her parents – still alive but letting her run the show – while adding new ideas which reflect her own personality.

This onion tart is not 'new' in style, but different in that it contains no cream – and it is one of the best I have ever had. The secret is in the long cooking of the onions and their combination with the light, airy puff pastry.   *Serves 6–8.*

FOR THE TART
1 quantity Puff Pastry (p. 178)
FOR THE FILLING
100 g (4 oz) bacon, thickly sliced
40 g (1½ oz) butter

6 large onions, very thinly sliced
2.5 ml (½ tsp) salt, or to taste
1.25 ml (¼ tsp) freshly ground white
   pepper, or to taste

To prepare the tart   Roll out the pastry to fit a 22.5 cm (9 inch) loose-based flan tin, adding 3.5 cm (1½ inches) to the diameter. Cut the pastry into a circle with a sharp knife; handle the pastry as little as possible. (With puff pastry you will get

more rise if you cut the pastry before fitting it into the tin.) Place the pastry inside the tin, allowing the edges to drape a little over the sides. Refrigerate until needed.
To prepare the filling   Cut the bacon into tiny strips. Melt the butter in a large heavy frying pan and fry the bacon over a low heat for 10 minutes.

Preheat the oven to 220°c (425°F) mark 7.

Add the onions to the bacon in the pan and sprinkle with salt and pepper. Cook over a low heat until the onions are soft and deep golden; this will take 45–60 minutes. The onions must cook this long to get that mellow consistency which brings out their sweetness. Stir frequently while they are cooking.
To assemble the dish   Remove the pastry case from the refrigerator and fill with the onions. Place in the oven and bake for 30 minutes.

Serve warm, cut into wedges.

Tarta de Puerros

· CATALAN – PASTÍS DE PORROS ·

· LEEK TART ·

High in the Catalan Pyrenees Mountains, just a few miles from the French border, is Can Borrell, a unique inn and restaurant that blends old traditions of great Catalan cuisine with the personal style of Lola Pijoán. In 1976 she and her husband, Jaume Guillén, opened Can Borrell in the picturesque old village of Meranges, in one of the most beautiful regions of Catalonia, La Cerdanya. Can Borrell overlooks an endless bucolic valley, near two crystal-clear mountain lakes. The narrow winding roads you have to take to get there are well worth it. Lola and Jaume have achieved the impossible dream: living in an ideal place while attracting lovers of food and nature to eat and stay there.

This leek tart is one of Lola's favourite creations – and one of mine, too.   *Serves 8–10.*

100 g (4 oz) butter
1.4 kg (3 lb) leeks, trimmed and thinly
   sliced
1.25 ml (¼ tsp) salt, or to taste
2.5 ml (½ tsp) freshly ground black
   pepper, or to taste
pinch of cayenne, or to taste
1.25 ml (¼ tsp) freshly grated nutmeg, or
   to taste

4 eggs
225 ml (8 fl oz) double cream
FOR THE TART
1 quantity Pie Pastry (p. 177)
100 g (4 oz) Gruyère or Emmenthal
   cheese, grated

To prepare the filling   In a large saucepan, melt the butter and, over a very low heat, sauté the leeks until all their liquid has evaporated and they are reduced almost to a paste; it will take 45–60 minutes. Season with salt, pepper, cayenne and nutmeg and allow to cool. In a bowl, beat the eggs lightly. Add the cream and leeks; mix well.

Preheat the oven to 220°c (425°F) mark 7.

To prepare the tart   Roll out the pastry thinly to fit a 22.5 cm (9 inch) loose-based flan tin about 3.5 cm (1½ inches) deep. Trim away the excess dough round the edge. Line the pastry with foil, fill with rice or beans and bake blind for 15 minutes. Remove the foil and beans and bake for a further 5–10 minutes, until lightly golden. Remove from the oven.

Reduce the oven temperature to 190°c (375°F) mark 5.

To assemble the dish   Pour the leek mixture into the pastry case. Sprinkle the cheese on top. Bake in the oven for 45–60 minutes, until the cheese is golden. Serve warm.

Garum

· ROMAN DIP ·

Garum was a famous sauce used by the Romans, as we have learned from recipes of such Roman authors as Apicius, who lived in the days of Christ. We know it was obtained by the pressing of fish, herbs and salt in bronze cauldrons, which were placed in the sun with a stone weight on top. As time passed, the fish fermented, with the salt acting as a preservative. A wicker basket was dipped into the cauldron, and the solids gathered in the basket were *garum*. The strained liquid left was *liquamen*, similar to the fermented fish sauces of Southeast Asia – known in Vietnam as *ñuoc-mam* – used as a flavouring in many dishes and also as a dipping sauce. The Romans used *garum* to season many of their recipes.

In my travels through southern Spain I learned that the remains of some of the most important Roman *garum* factories had been discovered near Cádiz, Granada, and Cartagena, but I was unable to find a present-day *garum* preparation anywhere. It was in the Ampurdán restaurant in Figueras, capital of L'Empordà (Ampurdán) district in northern Catalonia, that I found *garum* served as a dip. And indeed, it was delicious – even if not quite like what the Romans used to flavour their cooking. I serve it as a dip with crackers, toast or raw vegetables.

Ampurdán's owner, Jaume Subirós, is the son-in-law of the late Josep Mercadé, who has been called one of the fathers of Catalan cuisine. Jaume not only carries on the restaurant tradition but has contributed new ideas and great talent, following the family's guidelines: raw materials of impeccable quality, handled with care and skill, and a total dedication to the development of Catalan cooking.   *Makes about 450 ml (¾ pint).*

2 hard-boiled eggs
4 anchovy fillets
30 ml (2 tbsp) drained capers
225 g (8 oz) drained purple olives, Greek
  kalamata type, stoned
225 g (8 oz) drained black olives, stoned
1.25 ml (¼ tsp) chopped tarragon leaves
  or a pinch of dried

30 ml (2 tbsp) full-bodied Spanish
  brandy
150 ml (¼ pint) olive oil
2.5 ml (½ tsp) freshly ground black
  pepper, or to taste

Remove the egg yolks from the whites. In a food processor or blender, purée the egg yolks, anchovies, capers, olives, tarragon and brandy. With the motor running, add the olive oil in a thin stream. Season with pepper to taste. Chill until serving time.

At the moment of serving, stir to blend in the olive oil, which will have separated a little. Pour the mixture into a small bowl. Chop the egg whites finely and sprinkle on top.

Mousse de 'Escalivada'

· CATALAN – ESCUMA D'ESCALIVADA ·

· AUBERGINE, PEPPER AND TOMATO DIP ·

Escalivada is a typical way of preparing vegetables in Catalonia which enhances their fresh flavour; they are simply grilled or baked and served sprinkled with olive oil, salt and pepper. Making a mousse out of it is a new version, in the classic style of the great Ampurdán restaurant in Figueras which has created so many dishes based on traditional Catalan recipes.

This attractively coloured purée is delicious served with cold or grilled meats, or as a dip with thin toasted rounds of a French stick.   *Serves 6–8.*

about 15 ml (1 tbsp) olive oil	*1.25 ml ($\frac{1}{4}$ tsp) crushed hot red pepper*
450 g (1 lb) aubergines	*flakes*
2 large red peppers	*45 ml (3 tbsp) red wine vinegar, or to*
1 large ripe tomato	*taste*
1 large potato, 225 g (8 oz)	*5 ml (1 tsp) salt*
2 large heads garlic	*2.5 ml ($\frac{1}{2}$ tsp) freshly ground black pepper*
1 small onion	

Preheat the oven to 200°c (400°F) mark 6.

Rub the unpeeled aubergines, peppers, tomato and potato with oil. Place them on an ungreased baking sheet in the oven, with the garlic heads and whole onion. Remove the tomato after 15–20 minutes; the aubergines and the peppers after 45 minutes; the potato, garlic and onion after 1 hour. They have to be well done; bake for longer if necessary.

Cut the potato in half, scoop out the flesh and mash with a fork; discard the skin. Peel the aubergines and onion and cut them up. Squeeze the garlic cloves, discarding the skin. Stem, seed and peel the peppers. Skin the tomato and seed it. Reserve the pepper and tomato juices.

Purée the onion, potato and pepper flakes in a food processor or blender. Add the remaining vegetables with their juices and process until smooth. Add the remaining ingredients. Taste for seasoning.

Allow to stand at room temperature for at least 2 hours, to let the flavours mingle. Serve at room temperature or chilled.

Mousse de Endibias con Salsa de Cabrales

· CATALAN – ESCUMA D'ENDÍVIES AMB SALSA DE CABRALES ·

· CHICORY MOUSSE WITH BLUE CHEESE SAUCE ·

Big Rock is one of the most 'in' restaurants on the fashionable Costa Brava, the coastal area north of Barcelona which many call the Spanish Riviera. Carles and Mari Carmen Camós opened Big Rock in Palamós in 1973, and from a simple little restaurant serving good honest Catalan home-style cooking, it has evolved into a gastronomic haven specializing in traditional dishes of L'Empordà district.

Most of Carles' recipes are perfect reproductions of old classics; but some, like this delicate mousse, show his inventive, newer approach to great cooking. Carles is a big, friendly, affable man who loves to chat with anybody interested in his food or his wines. He also told me he loves anything American or British – hence the name of his restaurant.   *Serves 8–10.*

FOR THE MOUSSE
40 g (1½ oz) butter
1 large leek, trimmed and chopped, with
   ⅓ of the green part
1 medium onion, chopped
450 g (1 lb) chicory, stems trimmed,
   chopped
50 g (2 oz) creamy blue cheese such as
   Danish Blue
6 eggs

salt and freshly ground white pepper to
   taste (optional)
FOR THE SAUCE
50 g (2 oz) creamy blue cheese
75 ml (3 fl oz) single cream
45 ml (3 tbsp) Mayonnaise (p. 198)
AS A GARNISH
2 heads chicory, stems trimmed and
   leaves separated
toasted rounds of French bread

To prepare the mousse   Melt the butter in a large heavy frying pan. Fry the leek with the onion over a low heat, stirring occasionally, until very soft and beginning to colour – at least 20 minutes. Stir in the chicory; cover and cook for 10–15 minutes, until very soft. Purée in a food processor or blender, together with the cheese and eggs. Taste for seasoning, adding salt and pepper if necessary (depending on the saltiness of the cheese).

Preheat the oven to 180°c (350°F) mark 4.

Butter generously a 1.1 litre (2 pint) ring mould and fill with the mixture. Place the mould in a roasting pan and pour in boiling water to come halfway up the sides of the mould. Bake in the oven, uncovered, for 45 minutes or until firm. Leave to cool completely.

To prepare the sauce   While the mousse is cooking, purée the cheese with the cream and mayonnaise in a food processor or blender until smooth. Chill in the refrigerator for an hour or two, to let the flavours mingle.

To assemble the mousse   When the mould is cold, turn it out on to a round serving platter. (Don't worry if it doesn't come out perfectly, scoop up with a rubber spatula any mousse that may have been pulled off and patch the surface to even it out.) Spread the sauce over and around the mousse.

Serve garnished with chicory leaves, with the toast handed separately.

Corona de Gazpacho

· GAZPACHO MOUSSE ·

Prepare 8 hours ahead, or the day before

An interesting variation of the classic Spanish dish, gazpacho, this colourful mousse is a perfect summer recipe, best made at the peak of the tomato season and when the vegetables have the most flavour. It makes an attractive appetizer; I always serve it with toasted thin rounds of French bread.   *Serves 12 as an appetizer.*

1 small red or green sweet pepper, cored,
  seeded and chopped
5 ml (1 tsp) chopped garlic
3.75 ml (¾ tsp) chopped, seeded, canned
  chilli pepper
½ small red onion, chopped
700 g (1½ lb) unpeeled ripe tomatoes,
  chopped
225 g (8 oz) cucumber, peeled and
  chopped
45 ml (3 tbsp) olive oil

50 ml (2 tbsp) sherry wine vinegar or a
  good red wine vinegar
2.5 ml (½ tsp) salt, or to taste
2.5 ml (½ tsp) freshly ground black
  pepper, or to taste
225 ml (8 fl oz) tomato juice
20 g (¾ oz) powdered gelatine
AS A GARNISH
1 lemon, thinly sliced
a few parsley sprigs

In a food processor or blender, purée the pepper with the garlic and the chilli pepper. Add the onion, tomatoes and cucumber and process until very smooth. Blend in the olive oil, vinegar, salt and pepper.

In a small saucepan, heat the tomato juice and, over a low heat, whisk in the gelatine until it is completely dissolved. With the motor running, immediately add the gelatine-tomato mixture to the vegetable purée. Taste for seasoning.

Pour the gazpacho into a lightly oiled 1.1 litre (2 pint) ring mould and chill in the refrigerator for 6 hours or overnight, until set.

To unmould, dip the bottom of the mould for just 2 or 3 seconds into a basin of warm water, and immediately invert on to a serving plate. Garnish with the lemon slices and parsley.

Mousse de Salmón y Aguacate

· SALMON AND AVOCADO MOUSSE ·

Smoked salmon is served often in Spain at fine restaurants or at elegant dinners in homes. El Amparo, one of Madrid's most creative restaurants and a particular favourite of mine, has added a new twist by introducing avocado, which blends very well with the flavour of smoked salmon and adds an interesting texture. It also provides a dramatic visual effect, a classic example of chef Ramón Ramírez's inventive approach to cooking.   *Serves 8.*

15 g (½ oz) powdered gelatine	225 g (8 oz) smoked salmon trimmings
1 egg	225 ml (8 fl oz) double cream
30 ml (2 tbsp) finely chopped onion	4 small, ripe (Haas) avocados
5 ml (1 tsp) English mustard powder	45 ml (3 tbsp) snipped chives
225 ml (8 fl oz) vegetable oil	AS A GARNISH (OPTIONAL)
30 ml (2 tbsp) lemon juice	snipped chives

Sprinkle the gelatine over 175 ml (6 fl oz) water and leave for a few minutes until spongy. Gently heat it in a small saucepan, just until it is completely dissolved. Set aside to cool.

In a food processor or blender, combine the egg, onion and mustard and process until thoroughly blended. Mix the oil and lemon juice together in a jug. With the motor running, gradually add the oil mixture to the egg and onion mixture; process for a further 10 seconds. Add the smoked salmon and purée. With the motor running, add the dissolved gelatine.

Refrigerate the mixture until it begins to set on the surface – about 15–25 minutes (if you find that it has set too much, just whisk it).

Meanwhile, whip the cream until it stands in soft peaks. Peel the avocados; cut them in half lengthways and remove the stones. Cut a slice from both ends of each avocado, leaving just the centre part, which has the hole from the stone. (When you slice into the mousse, you will get a beautiful design from the avocado curve which you would not have if you used the whole fruit.)

Fold the cream and chives into the salmon mixture. Rinse a 1.1 litre (2 pint) terrine with water. Pour some of the salmon mixture into the mould, to a depth of about 2.5 cm (1 inch). Place 4 of the avocado halves, cut side up, in a line down the centre of the mousse. Press avocados down, to prevent air pockets from forming. Cover with some more mousse, to about 8 mm–1 cm (¼–½ inch) over the avocados. Place the remaining 4 avocado halves, cut side up, over the first row. Cover with the remaining mousse mixture. Cover and refrigerate until serving.

To serve   Dip the terrine into a basin of warm water for just a few seconds. Invert on to a cutting board; the mousse should come out easily. Cut into slices and serve on individual plates, to show the attractive design of the mousse. If liked, serve sprinkled with a few chives.

This mousse can be prepared a day ahead, as long as it is not cut in advance. The avocado slices will darken when they are in contact with the air, but not as long as they are completely encased in the mousse.

Pâté de Salmón Ahumado

· SMOKED SALMON PÂTÉ ·

This recipe was inspired by a salmon pâté I had at Sacha in Madrid, a great restaurant which combines good food with a wonderful feeling of dining in someone's living room – largely as a result of the earthy personality of the owner, Pitila Mosquera. She serves this pâté as a little appetizer while you wait for your meal. The capers were not in her recipe; I have added them as I find they contribute an interesting note of texture and flavour. I would suggest serving this pâté as Pitila does, with toasted French bread rounds. *Serves 10–12.*

½ *medium onion*
225 g (8 oz) smoked salmon trimmings
225 ml (8 fl oz) double cream

2.5 ml (½ tsp) freshly ground white pepper
15 ml (1 tbsp) drained small capers

Peel and finely chop the onion in a food processor or blender. Add the salmon and purée. With the motor running, pour in the cream. Blend in pepper. Transfer to a bowl, fold in the capers and taste for seasoning. Refrigerate until serving time.

Pâté de Anchoa con Caviar

· *ANCHOVY PÂTÉ WITH CAVIARE MAYONNAISE* ·

This dish makes an elegant first course, interesting and light. The touch of caviare in the mayonnaise provides a nice contrast with the pungency of the anchovies in the pâté.

The idea came from a dish I had at Risco, a charming country-style restaurant in a hotel high on a hill overlooking the beach town of Laredo, in the northern region of Cantabria. Owners Zacarías and Inés Puente are warm, hospitable hosts, as proud of their domain as they are of their cuisine. *Serves 6.*

FOR THE PÂTÉ
2 × 50 g (2 oz) cans flat anchovy fillets,
  drained
4 eggs
225 ml (8 fl oz) double cream
1.25 ml (¼ tsp) freshly ground white
  pepper
FOR THE CAVIARE MAYONNAISE
1 whole egg

1 egg yolk
5 ml (1 tsp) Dijon mustard
125 ml (4 fl oz) olive oil
125 ml (4 fl oz) vegetable oil
10 ml (2 tsp) lemon juice
50 g (2 oz) black lumpfish roe

Preheat the oven to 180°C (350°F) mark 4.
To prepare the pâté In a food processor or blender, finely purée the anchovies; add the eggs, cream and pepper and process until smooth. Taste for seasoning. Butter a shallow 750 ml (1¼ pint) rectangular or round ovenproof mould. Line the base with buttered greaseproof paper. Pour the anchovy mixture into the mould.

Cover the mould and place it in a roasting pan. Pour in boiling water to come halfway up the sides of the mould. Place in the oven for 50–60 minutes, until slightly firm to the touch and a skewer inserted into the centre comes out clean. When cool, run a knife around the edges and unmould onto a serving plate. Carefully remove the lining paper. Refrigerate.

To prepare the caviare mayonnaise   In a food processor or blender, combine the egg, egg yolk and mustard. Combine the oils and lemon juice in a jug. With the motor running, slowly add the oil mixture to the eggs and mustard; the mixture will thicken and become a mayonnaise. (If the mixture separates, see Mayonnaise [Salsa Mayonesa] recipe (p. 198) for how to correct it.) Fold the lumpfish roe into the mayonnaise. Refrigerate until serving time.

To assemble the dish   When you are ready to serve, whisk the caviare mayonnaise and pour some over and around the pâté, handing the rest separately.

Pâté de Cabrales a la Manzana

· BLUE CHEESE PÂTÉ WITH APPLES ·

Start preparation at least 1 day ahead, by marinating chicken livers

I had this pâté at La Máquina restaurant in Madrid, which specializes in Asturian cuisine. This northern Spanish region produces the finest blue cheese in Spain, Cabrales-Picón; unfortunately that is hard to find outside Spain, but a very good substitute is a flavourful Danish Blue or Roquefort.

The combination of the blue cheese with the other ingredients in this pâté is interesting and different; the apples provide a refreshing contrast in taste and texture. I serve it with peeled apple wedges or toasted bread rounds; I personally prefer to spread it on the apple wedges, as they combine very well with the subtle taste of the blue cheese.   *Serves 6–8.*

450 g (1 lb) chicken livers	*125 ml (4 fl oz) double cream*
90 ml (6 tbsp) dry flavourful Spanish	*2.5 ml (½ tsp) salt*
sherry, such as amontillado	*1.25 ml (¼ tsp) freshly ground white*
90 ml (6 tbsp) full-bodied Spanish	*pepper*
brandy	*1 large tart dessert apple such as Granny*
100 g (4 oz) flavourful blue cheese	*Smith, about 175–225 g (6–8 oz)*
2 eggs	

In a non-metallic bowl, marinate the livers in half the sherry and brandy. Cover and refrigerate for at least 24 hours.

Preheat the oven to 180°c (350°f) mark 4.

Transfer the livers with their marinade to a saucepan. Bring to the boil, cover and reduce heat to very low. Cook gently for 10 minutes. With a slotted spoon, remove the livers from the liquid and transfer to a food processor or blender. (Discard the liquid in the pan.) Purée the livers with the cheese. Add the eggs and cream, the remaining sherry and brandy, salt and pepper; blend until smooth. Pour through a fine sieve into a bowl. Peel, core and grate the apple; immediately fold it into the pâté mixture.

Butter the sides and bottom of a 1 litre (1¾ pint) terrine, and pour in the pâté mixture. Cover tightly with foil and a lid. Place in a roasting pan and pour in boiling water to come halfway up the sides of the terrine. Bake in the oven for 60 minutes, or until the pâté is firm and shrinks from the sides of the terrine.

Allow the pâté to cool before refrigerating. Serve at room temperature. (It is always a good idea to keep pâtés in the refrigerator for a day before serving, to allow the flavours to develop.)

Terrina de Conejo con Ciruelas

· CATALAN – TERRINA DE CONILL AMB PRUNES ·

· RABBIT AND PRUNE TERRINE ·

Start preparation 1 day or at least 10 hours ahead

This is another recipe inspired by the Ampurdán restaurant in Figueras. You can serve it as an appetizer, with toasted, thinly sliced French bread rounds, or as a first course, as Jaume Subirós does. It goes very well with Apple Garlic Mayonnaise (Allioli de Manzana, (p. 200)).

The combination of flavours in this dish is as successful as the presentation is attractive. The prunes and fresh herbs complement the rabbit and other meats, and the carrots add pretty spots of colour. *Serves 10–12.*

200 g (7 oz) carrots, peeled and cut into
  6 mm (¼ inch) dice
225 g (8 oz) boneless rabbit
225 g (8 oz) boneless lean pork
225 g (8 oz) pork fat, including whatever
  fat is trimmed from the pork cut
225 g (8 oz) lean cooked ham, cut into
  1 cm (½ inch) dice
1 large onion, finely chopped
3 large cloves garlic, finely chopped

175 g (6 oz) coarsely chopped, stoned
  prunes
125 ml (4 fl oz) full-bodied Spanish
  brandy
10 ml (2 tsp) chopped rosemary
10 ml (2 tsp) chopped thyme
5 ml (1 tsp) salt
5 ml (1 tsp) freshly ground black pepper
125 ml (4 fl oz) fino sherry or other dry
  Spanish sherry

In a saucepan, bring about 1.1 litres (2 pints) salted water to the boil. Blanch the carrots for 2 minutes; drain and set aside.

Cut the rabbit, pork and pork fat into pieces, and chop them coarsely. (If using a food processor, do this in small batches and be careful not to reduce to a paste.)

In a non-metallic bowl, mix the chopped meats with the ham, onion, garlic, prunes, reserved carrots and brandy. Allow the mixture to marinate at room temperature for 2 hours or longer.

Preheat the oven to 170°c (325°f) mark 3.

Add the rosemary, thyme, salt and pepper to the meat mixture; mix well. Oil a 1.7 litre (3 pint) terrine and pack the mixture into it. Pour the sherry over. Cover the terrine with foil and a lid. Place in a roasting pan and pour in the boiling water to come halfway up the sides of the terrine. Bake in the oven for 2 hours. Allow to cool, covered, at room temperature, then refrigerate overnight or for at least 4 hours. Serve at room temperature.

Pastel de Jamón

· HAM TERRINE ·

This is a favourite recipe from my mother's buffet parties; it is easy to whip up, and can be prepared the day before. She made this terrine with truffles, which in Spain are more affordable than in the United States or Britain. I tried it once and certainly enjoyed the delicacy – but it was hard to recuperate from paying the grocery bill. So I found that adding a fresh herb such as sage in place of the truffles is an excellent substitution. Some fine commercial duck liver pâtés with truffles and brandy are not too expensive and also work very well.

This dish has the consistency of a pâté, and I like it best served as a first course. The tomato sauce adds an interesting fresh flavour; it should be made shortly before serving.   *Serves 8.*

FOR THE TERRINE
25 g (1 oz) butter
25 g (1 oz) plain flour
225 ml (8 fl oz) milk
350 g (12 oz) lean cooked ham, finely
   chopped
100 g (4 oz) duck or pork liver pâté
10 ml (2 tsp) finely chopped sage or 5 ml
   (1 tsp) dried
4 eggs, beaten
30–45 ml (3 tbsp) amontillado or other
   flavourful Spanish sherry
2.5 ml (½ tsp) freshly ground black
   pepper, or to taste
FOR THE TOMATO SAUCE
15 g (½ oz) fresh parsley

700 g (1½ lb) ripe tomatoes, skinned and
   seeded
22.5 ml (1½ tbsp) tomato purée
30 ml (2 tbsp) sherry wine vinegar or red
   wine vinegar
45 ml (3 tbsp) fine olive oil, extra virgin
   if possible
2.5 ml (½ tsp) salt, or to taste
5 ml (1 tsp) freshly ground black pepper,
   or to taste
AS A GARNISH
24 French beans, trimmed and lightly
   steamed
16 cherry tomatoes

Preheat the oven to 180°c (350°F) mark 4.

To prepare the terrine   In a small saucepan, melt the butter; add the flour and cook for about 1 minute. Add the milk and continue cooking over a medium heat, whisking constantly until the sauce is thickened and smooth. Cook for 1 minute and remove from heat. Set aside.

In a bowl, mix the ham, pâté, sage, eggs, sherry and pepper. Add the white sauce and blend well. Taste for seasoning; salt will probably not be necessary.

Butter a 1.1 litre (2 pint) loaf tin and line the base with a piece of buttered greaseproof paper. Pour the mixture into the tin, cover and place in a roasting pan. Pour in boiling water to come halfway up the sides of the tin. Bake in the oven for 30 minutes; remove it from the water, uncover and bake for 25–30 minutes, until a skewer inserted into the centre comes out clean. Allow to cool.

To prepare the tomato sauce   Finely chop the parsley in a food processor or blender. Add the remaining ingredients and purée. Taste for seasoning; the sauce should have a sharp flavour.

To assemble the dish   Unmould the terrine on to a board and cut it into 16 slices. Spoon some tomato sauce on each dish, place 2 slices of terrine on top, arrange 3 green beans on one side of the terrine and 2 tomatoes on the other. Serve at room temperature.

Pastel de Tortillas

· THREE-LAYER OMELETTE TORTE ·

This triple-layered omelette, with its fresh tomato sauce, was a favourite at home; my mother often served it as a festive first course for lunch on Sundays. I find it can make a lunch in itself, accompanied by a salad. While not difficult to prepare, it is unusual and visually very attractive.   *Serves 6.*

FOR THE OMELETTES
1 large potato, 350 g (12 oz), peeled and
  sliced into wafer-thin pieces, about
  2 cm (¾ inch) in diameter (can be done
  in food processor)
3.75 ml (¾ tsp) salt
3.75 ml (¾ tsp) freshly ground black
  pepper
about 125 ml (4 fl oz) olive oil
1 large onion, peeled and thinly sliced
12 eggs
450 g (1 lb) red sweet peppers, cored,
  seeded and coarsely chopped

350 g (12 oz) French beans, topped,
  tailed and finely diced
FOR THE SAUCE
30 ml (2 tbsp) olive oil
1 small onion, chopped
900 g (2 lb) unpeeled ripe tomatoes,
  chopped
7.5 ml (1½ tsp) tomato purée
1.25 ml (¼ tsp) salt, or to taste
1.25 ml (¼ tsp) freshly ground black pepper
dash of cayenne (optional)
AS A GARNISH
about 50 g (2 oz) grated Parmesan cheese

To prepare the omelettes   Season the potato with 1.25 ml (¼ tsp) each salt and pepper. Heat the oil in a non-stick frying pan and, over a medium heat, fry the potato until golden-brown and crisp. Drain, leaving 15–30 ml (1–2 tbsp) oil in the pan (reserve the remainder) and add the onion; fry over a low heat until soft – about 10 minutes. Beat 4 of the eggs in a bowl; stir in the potatoes and onions.

 Wipe the pan clean and heat 15 ml (1 tbsp) of the reserved oil. Pour in the egg mixture and cook over a low heat just until the omelette is barely set – about 3 minutes. Place over the pan an inverted plate slightly larger than the pan, and turn out the omelette on to it; slide the omelette back into the pan. Cook until cooked through – about 2 more minutes. Slide the omelette on to a round heated serving plate and keep warm.

 Pour a further 30 ml (2 tbsp) oil into the pan and add the peppers; cook over a medium heat until dry – about 15 minutes. Beat 4 of the remaining eggs with 1.25 ml (¼ tsp) each salt and pepper; stir in the peppers. Wipe the pan clean and add a further 15 ml (1 tbsp) oil. Pour in the egg mixture and cook the omelette in the same way as the previous one. Slide it on to the potato omelette on the plate.

 Meanwhile, bring a large pan of salted water to the boil. Add the beans and cook until tender but still crisp – 5 minutes; drain. Beat the remaining 4 eggs with 1.25 ml (¼ tsp) each salt and pepper. Stir in the green beans. Wipe the pan clean and add a further 15 ml (1 tbsp) oil. Pour in the egg mixture and make the omelette in the same way as the previous ones. Slide it on to the pepper omelette.

To make the sauce   Heat the oil in a frying pan and fry the onion over a low heat until soft – about 5 minutes. Add the tomatoes and cook over a medium heat for 15 minutes. Stir in the tomato purée, salt, pepper and cayenne, if liked. Transfer to a food processor or blender and purée. Strain through a fine sieve.

To assemble the dish   Preheat the oven to 180°c (350°f) mark 4. Reheat the omelette torte in the oven and pour the sauce over, drizzling over the sides. Sprinkle some cheese on top and the rest separately in a bowl. Serve warm.

SOUPS

Gazpacho Rojo de Sevilla

· *COLD SOUP FROM SEVILLA WITH TOMATO AND VEGETABLES* ·

Gazpacho is undoubtedly the most popular cold soup in Spain, one you will find in many restaurants during the hot summer months – especially in the south, where it originated. An Andalusian grand lady, Eugenia de Montijo, took it to France in the nineteenth century when she married Napoleon III, and there it became very fashionable, along with many other cold Andalusian soups.

There are numerous variations of gazpacho: white and red, thick and thin, puréed and diced – even warm ones for the wintertime, although I don't find them as interesting as the cold soups. In the old days it was hard work to make gazpacho, for the ingredients had to be puréed by hand; I remember having it very seldom at home – until my mother brought back a blender from a trip to the United States!

The following recipe is my own adaptation of the classic red gazpacho, original to Sevilla and the most widespread of all. After making it many times over the years, I find this *the* perfect recipe for my taste.   *Serves 6.*

FOR THE SOUP
1.4 kg (3 lb) very ripe tomatoes, skinned,
   seeded and chopped
½ large red sweet pepper, cored, seeded
   and chopped
½ large cucumber, peeled and chopped
5 ml (1 tsp) finely chopped garlic
60 ml (4 tbsp) fine olive oil, preferably
   extra virgin
150 ml (¼ pint) sherry wine vinegar, or to
   taste
2.5 ml (½ tsp) salt, or to taste

2.5 ml (½ tsp) freshly ground black
   pepper, or to taste
FOR THE GARNISH
30 ml (2 tbsp) olive oil
2 × 1 cm (½ inch) thick slices of bread,
   without crusts, finely diced
1 large tomato, skinned, seeded and
   finely diced
½ large red sweet pepper, cored, seeded
   and finely diced
½ large cucumber, peeled and finely diced
½ red onion, finely chopped

To prepare the soup   Purée the vegetables in a food processor or blender with
the garlic, oil, vinegar, salt and pepper. Add 225 ml (8 fl oz) water, or more if you
prefer a thinner soup. Refrigerate for at least 5 hours.

To prepare the garnish   In a small frying pan, heat the oil and fry the bread over
a medium to high heat until golden; drain on kitchen paper. Place the vegetables
and croûtons in separate bowls and pass them as garnishes with the chilled soup.

Ajo Blanco de Málaga

· COLD WHITE GAZPACHO FROM MÁLAGA WITH GARLIC AND ALMONDS ·

This is an understated, light cold soup, original to Málaga but found all over
Andalucía, perfect for the hot summer days of this southern region. The recipe is of
Arab origin, going back to the tenth century. It is made from the produce of the
Andalusian soil: almonds, bread, garlic, sherry vinegar and grapes. When grapes are
not in season, you can substitute other fruits, such as apples, pears or melon.

One of the best *ajo blancos* I had in southern Spain was at El Fogón, the delightful
restaurant run by Lalo Grosso and her family in Puerto de Santa Maria, near Cádiz.
Her daughter, María José, manages El Fogón and also lives in the little villa where the
restaurant is. This naturally makes for the pleasant, comfortable feeling of dining in
someone's home.   *Serves 6.*

100 g (4 oz) blanched almonds
350 g (12 oz) white bread, crusts
   removed, 700 g (1½ lb) before trimming
   crusts
3 large cloves garlic
2 eggs
225 ml (8 fl oz) olive oil

150 ml (¼ pint) sherry wine vinegar
5 ml (1 tsp) salt, or to taste
AS A GARNISH
18 sweet seedless green grapes or about
   100 g (4 oz) diced peeled apple, pear
   or melon

Place the almonds in a bowl and cover with boiling water; leave to soak for 1 hour.
Soak the bread in 1.4 litres (2½ pints) cold water.

In a food processor or blender, purée the drained almonds until they are reduced to a fine paste. Add the garlic and eggs; process to blend well. In a jug, mix the oil and vinegar; with the motor running, add the mixture in a thin stream. Drain the bread, squeezing it with your hands; reserve the water. Add the bread to the other ingredients and purée. Add salt and taste for seasoning.

Transfer the mixture to a large non-metallic bowl and add the reserved water; you may dilute it with more water, to the consistency you desire. Cover the soup and chill for 3–4 hours or longer; it will keep in the refrigerator for at least 2–3 days.

To serve, place 3 grapes in each serving bowl and ladle the soup on top. If you used other diced fruits, hand them separately.

Salmorejo de Córdoba

· THICK GAZPACHO FROM CÓRDOBA ·

Salmorejo is a gazpacho soup without water, original to the city of Córdoba but now found all over Andalucía, with minor variations in the ingredients and garnish. This is the classic recipe, as served by Pepe García-Marín at El Caballo Rojo, an excellent restaurant in Córdoba where Pepe features the most authentic and interesting dishes of Andalusian cuisine. He has done a fantastic job researching old Arab recipes which were practically lost, and adapting them to today's cooking methods and ingredients. *Serves 4–6.*

100 g (4 oz) white bread, preferably 1 or 2 days old, crusts removed, about 225 g (8 oz) before trimming crusts
900 g (2 lb) ripe tomatoes, skinned and seeded
5 ml (1 tsp) finely chopped garlic
2 egg yolks
22.5 ml (1½ tbsp) sherry wine vinegar or a fine red wine vinegar

2.5 ml (½ tsp) salt
1.25 ml (¼ tsp) freshly ground white pepper
150 ml (¼ pint) fine olive oil, preferably extra virgin
AS A GARNISH
1 hard-boiled egg, chopped
50 g (2 oz) thinly sliced prosciutto, cut into 2.5 cm (1 inch) strips

In a bowl, soak the bread in about 175 ml (6 fl oz) cold water. With your hands, squeeze the excess water from bread; purée it with the tomatoes and garlic in a food processor or blender. Add the egg yolks, vinegar, salt and pepper. With the motor running, add the olive oil and blend well. Chill the soup for at least 4–6 hours before serving.

Hand the hard-boiled eggs and prosciutto in separate bowls, as a garnish.

Crema Fría de Melón a la Hierbabuena

· COLD MELON CREAM SOUP WITH MINT ·

El Cenador del Prado has been a success since it opened in Madrid in 1984. It is a delightful, bright and cheerful restaurant, new in style and in its approach to cooking, owned by the young Herranz brothers: Tomás, the chef, and Ramón, the manager.

Tomás is never afraid to experiment with new ideas; yet many of his recipes have a very traditional, even old-fashioned background. This cold melon soup has a perfect balance of ingredients; he serves it garnished with tiny prawns and julienned fresh mint, but I usually garnish it with just a whole mint leaf and 3 melon balls in each bowl.   *Serves 6.*

2 large, ripe Ogen or Charentais melons, total weight 2.3–2.7 kg (5–6 lb)
15 ml (1 tbsp) cornflour
225 ml (8 fl oz) port, plus 90 ml (6 tbsp)
1.25 ml (¼ tsp) salt

225 ml (8 fl oz) double cream
AS A GARNISH
18 melon balls, cut from the 2 melons
6 fresh mint leaves
12 peeled prawns (optional)

Cut the melons in half and remove the seeds. Using a small melon-baller, scoop out 18 balls; set aside for the garnish.

Peel the melons and cut them up. Place them in a saucepan with 225 ml (8 fl oz) water, and bring slowly to the boil. Dissolve the cornflour in 225 ml (8 fl oz) of the port and add to the melon as soon as the water boils. Cook over a low heat, stirring, until thickened – about 15 minutes. Season with the salt. Purée and strain through a medium nylon sieve. Chill. When the soup is very cold, add the cream and the remaining port.

Serve cold, each bowl garnished with 3 melon balls, a fresh mint leaf and the prawns, if liked.

Sopa de Tomate y Hierbabuena con Almendras

· CATALAN – SOPA DE TOMÀQUET I MENTA AMB AMETLLES ·

· COLD TOMATO MINT SOUP WITH ALMONDS ·

On a warm summer evening in Barcelona, this was the perfect starter for a family feast at El Racó d'en Binu, an outstanding restaurant in Argentona, near Barcelona. It is refreshing, light and interesting.

Chef/owner Francesc Fortí has risen to the top echelon of new Catalan cuisine in Spain, combining the finest local produce with his own highly creative ideas. Francesc represents the third generation since Albino Fortí, 'Grandpa Binu' – after whom the restaurant was named when it opened in 1970 – started the great Fortí family cooking tradition.   *Serves 4–6.*

50 g (2 oz) butter
350 g (12 oz) onions, finely chopped
450 g (1 lb) courgettes, coarsely chopped
450 g (1 lb) unpeeled ripe tomatoes,
   puréed

900 ml (1½ pints) Chicken Stock (p. 191)
5 ml (1 tsp) salt
2.5 ml (½ tsp) freshly ground white pepper
6 large fresh mint leaves, chopped
25 g (1 oz) flaked almonds

In a medium to large frying pan, melt the butter and fry the onions over a low heat until soft and golden – about 20 minutes. Add the courgettes and cook until tender – about 15 minutes. Purée in a food processor or blender. Transfer to a large saucepan. Add the puréed tomatoes and stock. Bring to the boil and immediately turn off the heat. Strain through a fine sieve. Add salt, pepper and mint; taste for seasoning. Chill.

Preheat the oven to 180°c (350°F) mark 4. Toast the almonds for 3–4 minutes, or until golden.

Serve the soup cold, with toasted almonds sprinkled on each bowl.

Crema de Hinojo

· CATALAN – SOPA DE FONOLL ·

· CREAM OF FENNEL SOUP ·

Martinet is a picturesque little town nestling in the Catalan Pyrenees. In 1975, on a paradisaical spot in the outskirts, Josep and Dolores Boix opened an inn with an exceptional restaurant, Can Boix. Their cuisine aims at enhancing the finest produce of the bountiful area, La Cerdanya, and the dishes are prepared with care and imagination – the work of a great chef.

I had this soup there on a warm summer day, and it was served cold; but at home I've made it warm and found it just as good. When making it cold, I have substituted yogurt for cream and found this added a fresh, tangy flavour (and decreased the calories a bit, too!). I also thinned it some more, adding another 225 ml (8 fl oz) stock at the end.   Serves 6.

50 g (2 oz) butter
5 ml (1 tsp) finely chopped garlic
2 medium onions, finely chopped
2 heads fennel, about 900 g (2 lb), stems
   and leaves trimmed, chopped
900 ml (1½ pints) Chicken Stock (p. 191),
   1.1 litres (2 pints) if served cold

15 ml (1 tbsp) orange zest (p. 31)
125 ml (4 fl oz) double cream or yogurt, if
   served cold
10 ml (2 tsp) salt, or to taste
2.5 ml (½ tsp) freshly ground white
   pepper, or to taste

In a large saucepan, melt the butter and fry the garlic and onion over a low heat for 10 minutes. Add the fennel and cook for a further 20–30 minutes, stirring occasionally. Add the chicken stock and orange zest. Bring to the boil, reduce the heat to very low and cook, covered, for 30 minutes or until the vegetables are very tender. Purée and strain through a medium sieve. Stir in the cream and season with salt and pepper. Reheat and serve warm. (If served cold, add yogurt when chilled.)

Crema de Remolacha

· BEETROOT CREAM SOUP ·

This flavourful soup is another creation of Lalo Grosso, one of many delicacies she serves at her charming restaurant in Puerto de Santa María, El Fogón. I like beetroot, but I've never had it taste as good as in this recipe!   *Serves 4–5.*

50 g (2 oz) butter
1 medium onion, chopped
1 large leek, about 225 g (8 oz), finely
   chopped, with ¼ of the green part
5 ml (1 tsp) finely chopped garlic
900 g (2 lb) beetroot, peeled and finely
   chopped
15 ml (1 tbsp) sherry wine vinegar

225 ml (8 fl oz) fino sherry or other
   flavourful dry Spanish sherry
900 ml (1½ pints) Chicken Stock (p. 191)
5 ml (1 tsp) sugar
125 ml (4 fl oz) double cream
2.5 ml (½ tsp) salt, or to taste
1.25 ml (¼ tsp) freshly ground white
   pepper, or to taste

Heat the butter in a large heavy saucepan or flameproof casserole. Over a low heat, fry the onion, leek and garlic until very soft and golden – 30–45 minutes. Add the beetroot, stir and sauté for about 4 minutes. Add the vinegar, sherry, stock and sugar. Bring to the boil, reduce heat to low and cook, partially covered, for 45 minutes. Uncover and cook for a further 15–20 minutes, until the beetroot is very tender.

Purée in a food processor or blender and strain through a medium sieve. Return the soup to the pan; add the cream, salt and pepper. Taste for seasoning. Serve warm or chilled.

Crema de Tomillo

· CATALAN – SOPA DE FARIGOLA ·

· THYME CREAM SOUP ·

I have enjoyed this soup at two restaurants: Lola Pijoán's Can Borrell in Meranges, in the Catalan Pyrenees, and Montse Guillén in Barcelona. That is no wonder, because Lola is Montse's mother!

This is a classic Catalan soup made with fresh thyme, earthy and heartwarming; it was Montse's idea, though, to add the quail's eggs as a garnish – her note of 'new' style, and one that goes very well here.   *Serves 4–6.*

FOR THE VEGETABLE STOCK
30 ml (2 tbsp) olive oil
1 large onion, chopped
1 medium celery stick, chopped
2 large carrots, scraped and chopped
1 large leek, trimmed and chopped, with
  ⅔ of the green part
1 small bunch thyme
2 bay leaves
10–12 black peppercorns
FOR THE SOUP
1 large bunch thyme

1 large head garlic or about 40 unpeeled
  cloves, finely chopped
125 ml (4 fl oz) double cream
5 ml (1 tsp) salt
pinch of freshly ground white pepper
AS A GARNISH, PER SERVING
2–3 thin French bread slices, rubbed with
  garlic, sprinkled with olive oil and
  toasted in the oven
2 quail's eggs, poached (optional)
1 sprig thyme

To prepare the stock   Heat the oil in a large heavy saucepan and fry the onions, celery, carrots, leek and the small bunch of thyme over a very low heat until soft and very brown – about 45 minutes. Stir occasionally to prevent the vegetables from burning, but allow them to become quite golden.

Add the bay leaves and peppercorns, and cover with 1.8 litres (3¼ pints) water. Bring to the boil, immediately reduce heat to very low and simmer, covered, for 1 hour. Strain the stock into another pan, pressing the contents of the colander gently with a spoon.

To prepare the soup   Add the large bunch of thyme and garlic cloves to the stock. Increase the heat and boil briskly for 20 minutes. Strain the soup. Add the cream and heat through. Season with salt and pepper. Taste for seasoning.

To assemble the dish   Place 2–3 toasted bread rounds at the bottom of each serving bowl; place poached quail's eggs, if liked, on top, and pour the soup over. Add a thyme sprig and tell each guest to swish it through the soup before eating; this will intensify the thyme flavour.

Sopa de Hierbabuena

· MINT SOUP ·

This recipe was given to me by a young woman from Extremadura, Cristina Tristancho. At nineteen, she not only is a superb cook but has been doing a terrific job of revitalizing old recipes from her native region which have been forgotten, and incorporating them in today's cuisine.

A perfect example is this shepherd-style soup, which will surprise you with the simplicity and compatibility of its ingredients. It also has an attractive presentation, especially when served in a round earthenware casserole, 20–22.5 cm (8–9 inches) in diameter.   Serves 6–8.

1.8 litres (3¼ pints) Chicken Stock (p. 191)
6 large cloves garlic, finely chopped
25 g (1 oz) chopped mint leaves
5 ml (1 tsp) salt

450 g (1 lb) loaf of white bread, at least
  1 day old, crusts removed, and thinly
  sliced
75 g (3 oz) Gruyère cheese, grated

In a saucepan, combine the stock with the garlic, 5 ml (1 tsp) of the mint leaves and the salt. Bring to the boil, reduce the heat to low and simmer for 5–6 minutes. Preheat the grill.

In a shallow ovenproof casserole, preferably earthenware, place bread slices in a layer. Sprinkle some chopped mint over and continue alternating layers, ending with a layer of bread. Pour the hot stock over the bread. Sprinkle with the cheese and place under the grill until the cheese is bubbling and golden. Serve immediately.

Sopa de Pescadores

· CATALAN – SOPA DE PESCADORS ·

· FISHERMEN'S SOUP, MEDITERRANEAN STYLE ·

Practically every restaurant along the Mediterranean coast of Spain serves wonderful fish soups; they have the raw materials right at hand. To reproduce them here I have found it essential to make a double fish stock (that is, use a Fish Fumet (p. 194) instead of water as a basis to make the second fumet), and to use only fresh white fish.

One restaurant that comes to mind when I think of great fish soup is Mare Nostrum, in the seaside resort of Sitges, south of Barcelona, where my parents have had their summer home since 1950 – the same year Josep Martí opened Mare Nostrum. And it has been one of the top restaurants in town ever since, particularly noted for its fisherman-style cuisine.   Serves 8.

FOR THE SECOND FUMET
30 ml (2 tbsp) olive oil
1 large onion, chopped
3 large garlic cloves, chopped
1.1 kg (2½ lb) unpeeled ripe tomatoes, chopped
fish heads and bones reserved from filleting 900 g (2 lb) fish, or about 1.8 kg (4 lb) fish trimmings (see Note below)
225 ml (8 fl oz) dry white wine
2–3 leeks, trimmed and sliced, with about ⅔ of the green part
1 large onion, peeled and sliced
1 medium carrot, sliced or coarsely chopped
3–4 unpeeled cloves garlic, crushed

bundle of herbs made with parsley (with plenty of stems), 2 bay leaves and 2 sprigs each thyme, rosemary, savory or sage
15 ml (1 tbsp) orange zest (p. 31)
1 quantity Fish Fumet (p. 194)
FOR THE SOUP
900 g (2 lb) white fish fillets
8 large prawns, in the shell
125 ml (4 fl oz) dry white wine
16 mussels or small clams, shells scrubbed
215 g (7½ oz) short-grain rice
2.5 ml (½ tsp) saffron threads or 1.25 ml (¼ tsp) powdered saffron
3.75 ml (¾ tsp) salt, or to taste
2.5 ml (½ tsp) freshly ground black pepper

(Note: You may buy the whole fish and have the fishmonger fillet it for you, giving you the heads and bones for the second fumet. You will need about 2.7 kg (6 lb) whole fish to get 900 g (2 lb) fillets. Discard skins, fins and intestines. Clean and rinse well fish heads and bones to remove all blood and gills.)

To prepare the second fumet Heat the oil in a large flameproof casserole or stock pot; fry the chopped onion and chopped garlic over a low heat for about 10 minutes. Add the tomatoes and cook over a medium heat until the liquid has evaporated. Add the fish heads and bones and the wine. Bring to the boil, stir and cook over a high heat for 5 minutes to evaporate the alcohol. Add the leeks, sliced onion, carrot, crushed garlic, bundle of herbs, orange zest and fish fumet; bring to the boil, immediately reduce heat to very low and skim the scum from the surface. Simmer, partially covered, for 35 minutes. During this time, skim off the scum.

To prepare the soup Remove any bones from the fish fillets with tweezers or pliers, and cut the fillets into chunks. Rinse the prawns and pat dry. Set aside.

In a large saucepan, bring the wine to the boil. Add the mussels or clams, on a rack, and steam, covered, until they open – about 4–5 minutes for mussels, 5–10 minutes for clams. Set them aside and reserve steaming liquid. Discard any that have not opened.

Strain the second fumet through a colander, pressing down the bones and vegetables gently with a spoon. Add the mussel or clam steaming liquid to the fumet. Strain again through a fine sieve into a large saucepan. Bring to the boil and add the rice, saffron, salt and pepper. Gradually add the fish fillets and prawns. Bear in mind that the rice will take about 20 minutes to cook, the fish fillets 7–8 minutes, medium prawns 3–4 minutes – all depending on size. At the last minute, add the mussels or clams. Taste for seasoning. Serve immediately.

Fideos con Almejas

· NOODLES WITH CLAMS ·

I found the best version of this traditional Galician dish at Chocolate, the outstanding restaurant in the fishermen's village of Vilaxoán, near Pontevedra. Josefa Cores, the friendly chef and owner, feels that women play an important role in Galician cooking. Yet their work is understated and behind the scenes, while the man is up front and does the P.R. Josefa's husband, Manolo, is a great cook too – though often away running their restaurant in Caracas, Venezuela!

Meanwhile, the women in the family run the show. The restaurant, however, is named after Manolo's nickname, 'Chocolate'. *Serves 6.*

100 ml (3½ fl oz) olive oil
4 large cloves garlic, finely chopped
1 small onion, finely chopped
1 large red sweet pepper, cored, seeded
  and chopped
450 g (1 lb) ripe tomatoes, skinned and
  chopped
1.5 litres (2¾ pints) Fish Fumet (p. 194)
2.5 ml (½ tsp) saffron threads
30 ml (2 tbsp) chopped parsley

1 bay leaf
5 ml (1 tsp) salt, or to taste
3.75 ml (¾ tsp) freshly ground black
  pepper, or to taste
225 g (8 oz) fine egg noodles, broken into
  5 cm (2 inch) pieces
225 ml (8 fl oz) dry white wine
1.4 kg (3 lb) small live clams, shells
  scrubbed, about 8 per 450 g (1 lb)
300 g (10 oz) frozen peas

Heat 60 ml (4 tbsp) of the oil in a large flameproof casserole; fry the garlic and onion over a low heat for about 10 minutes, until soft. Add the pepper and tomatoes and fry gently for a further 20 minutes, stirring occasionally. Add the fumet and bring to the boil. Stir in the saffron, parsley, bay leaf, salt and pepper. Set aside.

Heat the oil in a large saucepan. Over a medium to high heat sauté the noodles, stirring, until golden. Add about 900 ml (1½ pints) of liquid from the casserole, a cup at a time, stirring, to allow the noodles to absorb the liquid gradually. Remove from heat.

In a large saucepan, bring the wine to the boil. Add the clams, on a rack, and steam them, covered, over medium to high heat for 5–10 minutes or until they open. Set the clams aside and keep warm. Discard any that do not open. Strain the liquid from the pan into the casserole.

Remove the bay leaf from the casserole and pour contents into the pan with the noodles; stir in peas and cook for 5 minutes. Add the clams and taste for seasoning. Serve immediately.

VEGETABLE SALADS

Zanahoria Rallada con Naranja y Piñones

· SHREDDED CARROT SALAD WITH ORANGE AND PINE NUTS ·

The famous Zalacaín restaurant in Madrid serves this refreshing salad as a little nibble before the meal. I also find it very nice as a light first course.   *Serves 6.*

700 g (1½ lb) young, slender, tender
  carrots
125 ml (4 fl oz) fresh orange juice

15 ml (1 tbsp) lemon juice
15 ml (1 tbsp) olive oil
25 g (1 oz) pine nuts

Peel and shred the carrots (you can do this in a food processor). Place them in a bowl with the orange and lemon juice. Stir and allow to marinate for 10–30 minutes.

Meanwhile, heat the oil in a small pan and sauté the pine nuts until golden. Drain on kitchen paper. Just before serving, toss the nuts with the carrots.

Ensalada de Zanahoria al Jerez

· CARROT SALAD WITH SHERRY ·

The idea for this flavourful salad came from Rincón de Pepe restaurant in Murcia, where chef/owner Raimundo González-Frutos has developed a number of recipes based on the local produce.   *Serves 4–6.*

FOR THE DRESSING
7.5 ml (1½ tsp) Dijon mustard
50 ml (2 fl oz) sherry wine vinegar
50 ml (2 fl oz) amontillado or other full-
  flavoured dry Spanish sherry

FOR THE SALAD
1 bunch watercress, rinsed and drained
450 g (1 lb) young, slender, tender
  carrots, peeled and grated

In a bowl, mix together the ingredients for the dressing, beating with a fork or whisk. Trim the watercress of all stems, keeping only the leaves. Place in a salad bowl with the carrots. Just before serving, toss watercress and carrots with the dressing.

Ensalada de Naranja y Aguacate

· ORANGE AND AVOCADO SALAD ·

This salad could be a Californian recipe – yet I had it as an appetizer at Els Capellans, a restaurant in the lovely hotel Huerto del Cura in the town of Elche, near Alicante, in the País Valenciano region.   *Serves 6.*

FOR THE SALAD
3 oranges
3 avocados (preferably Haas)
15 ml (1 tbsp) chopped tarragon or mint
FOR THE DRESSING
7.5 ml (1½ tsp) lemon juice

22.5 ml (1½ tbsp) sherry wine vinegar or
  red wine vinegar
75 ml (5 tbsp) olive oil
3.75 ml (¾ tsp) Dijon mustard
1.25 ml (¼ tsp) salt
2.5 ml (½ tsp) freshly ground black pepper

Peel the oranges and cut them into segments, discarding the pith and membrane. Peel the avocados and cut into slices approximately the same size as the oranges. (Don't peel avocados more than 30 minutes before serving time, or they will discolour, unless you pour the vinaigrette over them.) Arrange decoratively in circles on individual serving plates, alternating orange and avocado slices. Sprinkle tarragon or mint on top.

Whisk together all dressing ingredients and drizzle over each plate.

Ensalada de Aguacate con Tomate

· AVOCADO AND TOMATO SALAD ·

La Gabarra restaurant opened in Madrid in October 1982, and it has been a hit ever since. Owner Fernando Jover enjoyed cooking all his life, although he grew up in an upper-class environment in northern Spain where it was not considered appropriate for a man to cook. He started his first 'serious' restaurant in Bilbao. A boat lover, he named La Gabarra after the word for barges in Bilbao and northern Spain.

Fernando features a cuisine that mixes traditional Basque preparations with superb novelties such as this salad, which successfully combines textures and flavours. *Serves 6.*

3 small avocados (preferably Haas)
60 ml (4 tbsp) sherry wine vinegar
4 large tomatoes, skinned
8 large basil leaves, finely shredded
1 small round lettuce, finely shredded,
   you need only half a lettuce, so use just

the inner leaves, which are paler and
   more tender
90 ml (6 tbsp) olive oil
5 ml (1 tsp) salt
2.5 ml ($\frac{1}{2}$ tsp) freshly ground black pepper

Cut the avocados in half lengthways, remove the stones and peel the fruits. Brush about 15 ml (1 tbsp) of the vinegar over the avocados to prevent them from discolouring.

Seed and dice 3 of the tomatoes; in a bowl, toss with the basil leaves. Thinly slice the remaining tomato and cut each slice into quarters.

Just before serving, line 6 salad plates with the shredded lettuce. Using the small side of a melon-baller, scoop out 4 balls from the cut side of each half avocado; set these aside. In a bowl, mix the olive oil, remaining vinegar and salt and pepper; pour this dressing over the tomatoes and basil, and toss. Fill the avocado halves with the mixture, and arrange the avocado balls on top. Place 1 avocado half over the lettuce on each plate, and garnish with 3 or 4 quartered tomato slices around the avocado.

Ensalada de Aguacate y Pimientos Rojos

· AVOCADO AND RED PEPPER SALAD ·

It was at Wallis – a new, very creative restaurant in Madrid – that I had *ensalada de aguacate y pimientos del piquillo*, a delightful combination of very fine red peppers roasted over a wood fire, with thin slices of avocado. Also in Madrid, the outstanding restaurant Cabo Mayor serves anchovies with avocados in a very elegant dish – so both of these ideas inspired me to create this recipe. *Serves 8.*

4 large red sweet peppers
about 15 ml (1 tbsp) olive oil
2 ripe avocados (preferably Haas)
10 canned flat anchovy fillets, drained

37.5 ml (2½ tbsp) balsamic vinegar
2.5 ml (½ tsp) freshly ground white pepper
45 ml (3 tbsp) snipped chives

Preheat the oven to 200°C (400°F) mark 6. Rub the peppers with the oil. Roast and peel them according to directions for roasting and peeling peppers (p. 32).

Cut the peppers in half lengthways and remove the seeds. If some peppers break up a bit while peeling them, don't worry; just try to keep them as whole as possible. Place half peppers (or quarters, or even strips, if they have broken up) on an ungreased baking sheet and return them to the oven for 15 minutes.

Remove the pits from the avocados and scoop out the flesh into the food processor or blender. Purée with the anchovies and vinegar. Add white pepper and taste for seasoning; it will probably not need any salt, as the anchovies are quite salty themselves.

Place half a pepper on each plate. Arrange a spoonful of avocado purée at the base of the pepper. Sprinkle the chives over the peppers and serve immediately.

Ensalada de Endibias y Aguacates a la Salsa de Cabrales

· CATALAN – AMANIDA D'ENDÌVIES I ALVOCAT AMB SALSA DE CABRALES ·

· CHICORY AND AVOCADO SALAD WITH A BLUE CHEESE SAUCE ·

The Font brothers' Sa Punta restaurant, opened in 1976, is one of the prettiest in Spain. High up on a rock in the village of Pals, in the northern Catalan district of L'Empordà, near Gerona, it overlooks the Mediterranean through beautiful pine woods; a small white sandy beach is just 200 yards away. In the pleasant summer season of the Costa Brava, you can dine outside as well as in an elegant indoor dining room.

Jaume Font, the chef, is an artist. His cooking, basically Catalan, features some classic recipes from L'Empordà to which he adds his own personality and imagination. His wife, Mari Carmen, and his brother José run the dining room with charm and efficiency.

I loved this salad, one of their ideas, because of the flavour combinations as well as its attractive presentation.   Serves 8.

FOR THE DRESSING
50 g (2 oz) creamy blue cheese such as
   Danish Blue
150 ml (¼ pint) single cream
7.5 ml (1½ tsp) dry Spanish sherry,
   preferably fino
7.5 ml (1½ tsp) sherry wine vinegar

1.25 ml (¼ tsp) salt, or to taste
1.25 ml (¼ tsp) freshly ground black
   pepper, or to taste
FOR THE SALAD
3 medium heads chicory
3 medium carrots, peeled
2 large avocados (preferably Haas)

To prepare the dressing In a bowl, mash the cheese with a fork in 30 ml (2 tbsp) of the cream. Add the remaining dressing ingredients and mix well.

To prepare the salad Cut the chicory crossways into very thin strips. Cut the carrots into thin strips, or grate them coarsely, using a food processor. Toss the chicory and carrots with the dressing in the bowl.

Shortly before serving (to prevent them from discolouring), cut the avocados in half lengthways and remove the stones. Peel the avocados and cut them into quarters lengthways. Make a 'fan' of each quarter, by making 3 or 4 slices not quite all the way through at the base and fanning the slices out.

To serve, arrange an avocado fan on one side of each individual plate, and chicory/carrot mixture at the base of the avocado.

Barquitos de Ensalada

· COLOURFUL SALAD BOATS ·

This is a recipe from my mother which makes a very nice autumn or winter salad, as it uses fennel, apple and red cabbage. The orange adds a touch of colour as well as nice flavour contrast. I often served it in Spain at buffet parties, for it looks very pretty and is a perfect palate cleanser between courses. *Serves 6–8.*

FOR THE DRESSING
150 ml (¼ pint) olive oil
50 ml (2 tbsp) sherry wine vinegar or red
    wine vinegar
5 ml (1 tsp) Dijon mustard
10 ml (2 tsp) chopped tarragon or
    3.75 ml (¾ tsp) dried
2.5 ml (½ tsp) salt, or to taste
1.25 ml (¼ tsp) freshly ground black
    pepper, or to taste

FOR THE SALAD
150 g (5 oz) red cabbage, finely shredded
150 g (5 oz) fennel, finely chopped
2 celery sticks, finely chopped
1 small tart dessert apple, such as
    Granny Smith, finely chopped
2 small oranges, peeled, seeded and
    finely chopped
1 small red onion, very thinly sliced
6–8 large lettuce leaves

In a salad bowl, combine the dressing ingredients and whisk well. Toss the dressing with the cabbage, fennel, celery, apple, orange and onion. Place lettuce leaves on individual plates and spoon the salad mixture on to each. Serve chilled.

Ensalada de Col Lombarda con Boquerones

· *CATALAN – AMANIDA DE COL LLOMBARDA AMB SEITONS* ·

· *RED CABBAGE SALAD WITH ANCHOVIES* ·

Start preparation 1 day ahead

The idea for this salad came from a lovely little restaurant in Barcelona, L'Olivé. Owner Josep Olivé uses the small fish *boquerones*, which don't exist in the United States or Britain; they are white and less pungent than anchovies. But the recipe works really well with anchovies, too.   *Serves 8.*

900 g (2 lb) red cabbage, finely shredded
90 ml (6 tbsp) sherry wine vinegar or red
*   wine vinegar*
10 ml (2 tsp) salt

1 × 50 g (2 oz) can flat anchovy fillets,
*   drained*
125 ml (4 fl oz) olive oil
90 ml (6 tbsp) chopped parsley

In a large saucepan, combine the cabbage with the vinegar, salt and 450 ml ($\frac{3}{4}$ pint) water. Bring to the boil, reduce the heat to medium-low and cook, covered, for 15 minutes. Let it stand, covered and unrefrigerated, for about 24 hours.

Purée the anchovies in a food processor or blender with the olive oil. Drain and squeeze excess moisture from the cabbage; place it in a large bowl. Toss with the anchovy-olive oil mixture and the parsley. Serve cold or at room temperature.

Ensalada de Habas a la Hierbabuena

· *CATALAN – AMANIDA DE FAVES A LA MENTA* ·

· *BROAD BEAN SALAD WITH MINT* ·

This salad has become a classic of Catalan cuisine. It is an original recipe from the late master chef Josep Mercadé, featured by his son-in-law Jaume Subirós at the great restaurant Ampurdán in Figueras, near Gerona. He uses fava beans which go very well with prosciutto, and the mint provides a touch of freshness.

Fava beans are widely available in Spain, fresh and frozen; broad beans make an excellent alternative. You can buy them while they are available and store them shelled and blanched in your freezer; if the skins are too tough, peel them after blanching. *Serves 8.*

FOR THE SALAD
700 g (1$\frac{1}{2}$ lb) shelled young broad beans,
*   about 3.6 kg (4 lb) before shelling*
100 g (4 oz) lean, good-quality

prosciutto, sliced medium-thin, cut
*   into 6 mm ($\frac{1}{4}$ inch) strips*
1 small round lettuce, finely shredded
5 large mint leaves, cut into thin strips

FOR THE DRESSING
50–75 ml (2–3 tbsp) Dijon mustard
125 ml (4 fl oz) olive oil
45–60 ml (3–4 tbsp) red wine vinegar, to
   taste

5 ml (1 tsp) freshly ground black pepper,
   or to taste
2.5 ml (½ tsp) salt, or to taste

Bring a large amount of salted water to the boil in a saucepan. Add the beans and cook until tender – 5–7 minutes. Drain and allow to cool. Transfer the beans to a large salad bowl. Add the ham, lettuce and mint.

Combine all the dressing ingredients in a bowl and whisk until well blended. Taste for seasoning.

Just before serving, pour the dressing over the salad and toss gently until the lettuce is evenly coated. Serve at room temperature.

FISH AND MEAT SALADS

'Xatonada'

This is a classic recipe from the Catalan district of El Vendrell, in the Low Penedès. El Celler del Penedès, the excellent country-style restaurant near Vilafranca del Penedès, serves a delicious *xatonada*, and chef/owner Pere Valls was more than happy to share his recipe with me.

The name *xatonada* is derived from the word *xató*, the *romesco*-style sauce which is basic to the dish. It makes a delightful cold luncheon salad as well as a first course for dinner. In Catalonia it is traditional to serve it on Ash Wednesday.   *Serves 6.*

1 curly lettuce
1 × 200 g (7 oz) can tuna, in olive oil
2 small tomatoes, each cut into 6 wedges
2 hard-boiled eggs, each cut into 6
   wedges

1 × 50 g (2 oz) can flat anchovy fillets
100 g (4 oz) small black olives, unstoned
1 quantity Xató (p. 196)

Separate, wash and dry the lettuce leaves; arrange them as a bed on individual plates. In a bowl, flake the tuna very finely with your fingers; distribute it evenly on each plate, mounding it in the centre. Arrange 2 tomato wedges on the sides of each plate, and 2 egg wedges; put 1 anchovy fillet across each egg wedge. Sprinkle olives on top.

Place a small mound of *xató* on each plate, and hand the remaining sauce separately in a bowl. Serve at room temperature.

Ensalada Templada de Bonito

· WARM BONITO SALAD WITH VEGETABLES ·

This is one of the most imaginative and delicate fish salads I have had in Spain. It comes from one of my favourite restaurants in San Sebastián, Akelaŕe, inspired by chef/owner Pedro Subijana. I have made it with bonito, tuna and small scallops, and it has always been a success. Monkfish would also be good in this salad.   *Serves 6.*

FOR THE FISH MARINADE
450 g (1 lb) bonito or tuna fillets,
   or 350 g (12 oz) monkfish tails or fresh
   scallops
45 ml (3 tbsp) cider vinegar
5 ml (1 tsp) coriander seeds, lightly
   crushed
FOR THE DRESSING
30 ml (2 tbsp) cider vinegar
2.5 ml (½ tsp) Dijon mustard
2.5 ml (½ tsp) salt

pinch of freshly ground black pepper
90 ml (6 tbsp) finest-quality olive oil,
   extra virgin if possible
FOR THE SALAD
100 g (4 oz) red cabbage, finely shredded
100 g (4 oz) alfalfa sprouts
100 g (4 oz) carrots, cut into thin strips
50 g (2 oz) mâche (lamb's lettuce)
2 heads chicory, leaves separated and
   soaked in cold water

To marinate the fish   Toss the bonito, tuna, monkfish or scallops with the vinegar and coriander seeds and leave for 10 minutes. Drain.

To prepare the dressing   In a food processor or blender, thoroughly combine the vinegar, mustard, salt and pepper. Add the oil slowly in a thin stream.

Preheat the grill.

To prepare the salad   Toss the cabbage, sprouts, carrots and lettuce together with 30 ml (2 tbsp) of the dressing. Use half of this mixture to line 6 salad plates. Drain and pat dry the chicory leaves; arrange them in a circle on top of the cabbage mixture. Sprinkle the remaining cabbage mixture over the chicory.

Place the fish on the oiled grill pan and grill until cooked through. When the fish is cool enough to handle, remove any skin, shred the flesh with your fingers, and place a small heap in the middle of the vegetables on each plate.

Heat the remaining dressing in a small pan, stirring. Pour some of the hot dressing over each salad plate and serve immediately.

Ensaladilla de Bonito

· BONITO SALAD WITH PEPPERS, ONIONS AND TOMATOES ·

This refreshing salad was inspired by a dish I had at Los Remos restaurant, in the beach town of San Roque, near the southern city of Cádiz. As I sat down on their lovely patio waiting for a meal which promised to be memorable, owner Alejandro Fernández brought me this salad as an unpretentious little *tapa*. I thought it could make a delightful summer lunch dish. Again, monkfish or tuna could be substituted for bonito.   *Serves 4–6.*

FOR THE POACHING LIQUID
225 ml (8 fl oz) dry white wine
1 medium unpeeled carrot, sliced
1 large onion, sliced
1 bay leaf
3 sprigs parsley
1–2 sprigs thyme or 1.25 ml (¼ tsp) dried
1–2 sprigs tarragon or 1.25 ml (¼ tsp) dried
700 g (1½ lb) bonito fillets or monkfish tails

FOR THE VEGETABLES
1 large green pepper, cored, seeded and finely diced
1 medium onion, finely chopped
2 large firm ripe tomatoes, skinned, seeded and finely diced

FOR THE DRESSING
125 ml (4 fl oz) olive oil
60 ml (4 tbsp) red wine vinegar
5 ml (1 tsp) salt
3.75 ml (¾ tsp) freshly ground black pepper

Combine all the ingredients for the poaching liquid with 1.2 litres (2 pints) water in a saucepan large enough to hold the fish. Bring to the boil, reduce heat to low and simmer, partially covered, for 30 minutes. Add the fish, cover and poach for 8–10 minutes, depending on the size and type of fish – just enough to barely cook it.

Remove the fish from liquid, drain and let it cool. Remove any skin, and cut the flesh into 6 mm (¼ inch) cubes. Place the vegetables in a large serving bowl, and toss with the fish.

Combine all the dressing ingredients in a bowl, beating with a fork or whisk. Pour over the salad and leave to stand at room temperature for 1–2 hours. Serve lightly chilled.

'Esqueixada'

· CATALAN SHREDDED COD SALAD ·

Start preparation 2 days in advance, by soaking cod in water

Catalonia is the only region in Spain where you will find salt cod served cold and uncooked, in this very traditional salad. It makes a delicious first course; even those who are not used to salt cod have found this a favourite at my dinner parties.

Recently I had an excellent version of *esqueixada* at Tritón in Barcelona, a very home-style, traditional restaurant, which features country Catalan cooking. Owner Joaquín 'Quimet' Vidal, always friendly and attentive, has built a reputation for the quality and consistency of his food. *Serves 6–8.*

450 g (1 lb) boneless dried salt cod, see
  Salt Cod (p. 87)
1 small red or green pepper, cored, seeded
  and sliced into thin rings
½ large red onion, thinly sliced, separated
  into rings
1 large firm ripe unpeeled tomato, thinly
  sliced
150 ml (¼ pint) fruity olive oil

50 ml (2 fl oz) red wine vinegar
4 large cloves garlic, finely chopped
2.5 ml (½ tsp) freshly ground black
  pepper, or to taste
salt to taste, if necessary
AS A GARNISH
50 g (2 oz) black unstoned olives
2 hard-boiled eggs, quartered

Cover the salt cod with water and soak for 48 hours, changing the water several times – 5 or 6 if possible. Drain and press the cod with your hands to remove excess water. Discard any skin or bones. With your fingers, shred the cod into thin strips and place in a salad bowl.

Toss the pepper, onion and tomato with the cod. In a bowl combine the oil, vinegar, garlic and black pepper, beating to blend well. Pour over the cod and, with your hands, mix and toss to coat the cod and vegetables. Taste for seasoning.

Arrange on a platter or in a bowl, and garnish attractively with olives and hard-boiled eggs.

'Trinxat' de Rape

· CATALAN – TRINXAT DE RAP ·

· CATALAN SHREDDED MONKFISH SALAD ·

This recipe comes from one of the top restaurants in Catalonia and, for that matter, in Spain: Eldorado Petit, which Lluís Cruañas opened 12 years ago as a small restaurant in the seaside village of Sant Felíu de Guixols, in the heart of the famed Costa Brava. I remember Eldorado Petit as a tiny dining spot where everything on the limited menu was great. Today, Lluís is a brilliant representative of Catalan cooking, and in 1984 he opened another restaurant of the same name in Barcelona, which has very quickly established itself among the best in the city.

I had this dish for lunch on a hot summer day, and it couldn't have been more appropriate. It can make a delightful first course, too. *Serves 6.*

FOR THE FISH
900 g (2 lb) monkfish tails
15 ml (1 tbsp) sherry wine vinegar

1 bay leaf
6 black peppercorns

FOR THE DRESSING
450 g (1 lb) ripe tomatoes, skinned,
   seeded and diced very small, by hand
15 ml (1 tbsp) snipped chives
125 ml (4 fl oz)double cream
15 ml (1 tbsp) dry Spanish sherry, such as
   amontillado
45 ml (3 tbsp) sherry wine vinegar, or to
   taste
10 ml (2 tsp) salt, or to taste

5 ml (1 tsp) freshly ground white pepper,
   or to taste
FOR THE SALAD
2 large ripe tomatoes, skinned and thinly
   sliced
½ small red onion, peeled and very thinly
   sliced
½ large cucumber, peeled and thinly
   sliced

To cook the fish   Place the monkfish in a saucepan with the vinegar, bay leaf and peppercorns. Add water to cover, bring to the boil and immediately reduce the heat to low; simmer for 10–12 minutes, or until the fish is cooked. Drain.

To prepare the dressing   In a non-metallic bowl, combine all the dressing ingredients and let stand for at least 30 minutes.

To assemble the salad   Press the fish with your hands to squeeze out as much water as possible. Remove the loose greyish skin and membranes. With your fingers, shred the flesh very finely. Once more, squeeze water out of the fish with your hands. Toss the fish with the dressing in the bowl and refrigerate until serving time, between 1 and 3 hours.

To serve, arrange a bed of the thinly sliced tomatoes, onion and cucumber on a serving platter, and place a mound of fish salad on top.

Ensalada de Verduras con Dos Gustos de Salmón

· VEGETABLE SALAD WITH FRESH AND SMOKED SALMON ·

Cabo Mayor restaurant in Madrid is one of the most interesting exponents of new cuisine in Spain. Víctor Merino and his son-in-law, Pedro Larumbe, have created a number of fascinating recipes; I was particularly impressed with this one. The combination of fresh and smoked salmon is perfectly balanced with the other ingredients, and the presentation is most attractive as well.   *Serves 6.*

FOR THE SALAD
450 g (1 lb) salmon fillets, skinned
15 ml (1 tbsp) tarragon or sherry wine
   vinegar
2.5 ml (½ tsp) salt
175 g (6 oz) smoked salmon
24 French beans, topped and tailed
100 g (4 oz) young slender carrots, peeled
1 large turnip, peeled
50 g (2 oz) watercress leaves

30 ml (2 tbsp) snipped chives
FOR THE DRESSING
45 ml (3 tbsp) olive oil
30 ml (2 tbsp) tarragon or sherry wine
   vinegar
2.5 ml (½ tsp) salt
1.25 ml (¼ tsp) freshly ground white
   pepper
AS A GARNISH
a few sprigs watercress

To prepare the salad Cut the salmon fillets into very thin strips about 5 cm (2 inches) long. In a bowl, combine the vinegar with the salt and toss the salmon strips in it. Let stand for about 10 minutes (don't leave it much longer or the vinegar will cook the salmon). Drain and set the salmon aside.

Cut the smoked salmon into strips about the same size as the fresh salmon. Set aside.

Cut the beans, carrots and turnip into very thin strips about 5 cm (2 inches) long. In a saucepan, bring salted water to the boil and cook each vegetable separately until tender but still crisp (2 or 3 minutes after the water has returned to the boil). Drain each vegetable and refresh under cold running water. Pat dry and set vegetables aside in a bowl. Add the watercress and chives.

To prepare the dressing Whisk together the dressing ingredients.

To assemble the salad In a salad bowl, combine the fresh and smoked salmon with the vegetables. Toss with the dressing. This is a scantily dressed salad, but the sharpness of the dressing mingles nicely with the sweetness of the fish and the crunchiness of the vegetables.

Serve on individual plates, arranging the salad in little heaps with a watercress sprig on the side.

Ensalada Templada de Lentejas y Conejo al Curry

· CATALAN – AMANIDA DE LLENTÍES I CONILL AL CURRY ·

· WARM CURRIED LENTIL AND RABBIT SALAD ·

This recipe was inspired by a dish I had at Azulete, one of Barcelona's most innovative and exciting restaurants. Chef/owner Toya Roqué represents the current wave of women cooks who have made headlines in Spain. This is one of her creations – a dish as original as it is representative of Catalonia's new style of cooking. *Serves 8.*

FOR THE SALAD
2 bunches watercress or mâche (lamb's
   lettuce)
4 medium carrots, peeled
150 g (5 oz) red lentils
1.4 litres (2¼ pints) Chicken Stock
   (p. 191)
FOR THE RABBIT
25 g (1 oz) butter
1 celery stick, chopped
1 medium onion, chopped
15 ml (1 tbsp) curry powder
125 ml (4 fl oz) dry white wine
hind and forelegs of 1 rabbit (see Note
   overleaf)

5 ml (1 tsp) salt
2.5 ml (½ tsp) freshly ground black
   pepper
FOR THE DRESSING
10 ml (2 tsp) finely chopped garlic
50 ml (2 fl oz) cider vinegar
30 ml (2 tbsp) apple juice
5 ml (1 tsp) sugar
5 ml (1 tsp) mustard powder
5 ml (1 tsp) curry powder
2.5 ml (½ tsp) salt
2.5 ml (½ tsp) freshly ground black
   pepper
150 ml (¼ pint) vegetable oil

(Note: For this recipe you will need only a rabbit's hind legs and forelegs. You can use the body or saddle for Stuffed Rabbit Saddle with Vegetables (Silla de Conejo Rellena con Verduras) (p. 117).

To prepare the salad   Trim the stems from the watercress or mâche, saving only the leaves. Set aside in the refrigerator. Dice 3 of the carrots very finely. Chop the remaining carrot and set aside.

Wash and pick over the lentils. Bring the stock to the boil in a large saucepan. Add the lentils, return to the boil and reduce heat to simmer. Cook, uncovered, for 15 minutes. Add the diced carrots and cook for a further 15 minutes, or until the lentils are soft but not mushy. Strain the lentils and carrots and set aside. Reserve the stock.

To cook the rabbit   Melt the butter in a deep frying pan. Add the chopped carrot, celery and onion and fry until soft – about 5 minutes. Stir in the curry powder. Add the wine and cook over a medium heat for a further 5 minutes, or until the liquid has evaporated. Add 225 ml (8 fl oz) of the reserved stock (use the remainder in another recipe), and bring to the boil. Season the rabbit with salt and pepper. Reduce heat to very low and place the rabbit legs on top of the vegetables; cover and cook over a low heat for 45 minutes, turning the rabbit pieces several times. Remove the rabbit and dice the meat to about the size of the diced carrots. Set aside.

To prepare the dressing   In a food processor or blender, combine all the dressing ingredients except the oil. With the motor running, slowly add the oil, until the dressing thickens. Transfer to a saucepan and heat gently.

To assemble the dish   In a bowl, mix the rabbit with carrots and lentils. Toss the mixture with the dressing in the pan. Line 8 salad plates with the salad greens; pile the rabbit mixture in the middle, and serve immediately. The combination of warm and cold adds to the interest of this salad.

FISH AND SHELLFISH

Mejillones en Escabeche

· MUSSELS MARINATED IN A WINE, VINEGAR AND HERB SAUCE ·

This is a recipe from my mother, who made it at home, usually with sardines – a classic Spanish recipe of Arab origin. Since fresh sardines are not as common in the United States or Britain as they are in Spain, I found that mussels work very well too.

This dish can be served as a first course, as an appetizer or even as a main course for a light lunch. In either case, be sure to accompany it with lots of crusty bread to dip in the delicious sauce – Peasant Bread (Pan de Payés) (p. 179) is perfect with it. *Serves 6–8.*

225 ml (8 fl oz) dry white wine
1.4 kg (3 lb) mussels, well scrubbed
125 ml (4 fl oz) olive oil
6 large cloves garlic, finely chopped
30 ml (2 tbsp) finely chopped thyme
   or 10 ml (2 tsp) dried
30 ml (2 tbsp) finely chopped parsley
2 bay leaves, middle vein removed,
   crushed

150 ml ($\frac{1}{4}$ pint) balsamic vinegar
5 ml (1 tsp) paprika
5 ml (1 tsp) lemon zest (p. 31)
1.25 ml ($\frac{1}{4}$ tsp) salt, or to taste
2.5 ml ($\frac{1}{2}$ tsp) freshly ground black
   pepper, or to taste
pinch of cayenne

In a large saucepan, bring the wine to the boil. Add the mussels, on a rack, cover and steam over medium to high heat for 4–5 minutes. Transfer the mussels to a plate, discarding any that have not opened. Reduce the liquid in the pan to 175 ml (6 fl oz). Strain and reserve.

Heat the oil in a frying pan and fry the garlic over a low heat until golden. Add the thyme, parsley and bay leaves; cook for 2–3 minutes, stirring. Turn off the heat; add the reserved mussel steaming liquid, vinegar, paprika, lemon zest, salt, pepper and cayenne. Taste for seasoning.

Remove the mussels from their shells, reserving half of each shell. Place the mussels in a non-metallic bowl, add the sauce and let them marinate for at least 2 hours before serving. (If longer, cover and refrigerate; but bring to room temperature before serving.)

To serve, arrange the mussels on a serving plate in their half shells. Pour some sauce over, and hand the remaining sauce separately.

Guisantes Estofados a la Menta Fresca con Almejas

· CATALAN – PESOLS ESTOFATS A LA MENTA FRESCA AMB COPINYAS ·

· PEA STEW WITH FRESH MINT AND CLAMS ·

The idea for this dish came from Sa Punta restaurant in Pals (Costa Brava, near Gerona) where Jaume Font features classic and new dishes of Catalan cuisine. Mixing peas with mint is a traditional combination of L'Empordà, the district where Pals is. The freshness of the mint comes through perfectly with the peas, blending very well with the clams.

This is not a very soupy stew, but I serve it in soup bowls – and always accompanied with good crusty bread.   Serves 4–6.

40 g (1½ oz) butter
1 large onion, finely chopped
25 g (1 oz) finely chopped mint
450 g (1 lb) shelled peas, fresh or frozen
2.5 ml (½ tsp) salt

125 ml (4 fl oz) dry white wine
1.8 kg (4 lb) small clams, try to get
    10–12 per 450 g (1 lb), well scrubbed
AS A GARNISH
1 sprig mint per person

In a large flameproof casserole, melt the butter and fry the onion with the mint until very soft – about 20 minutes. Add the peas and salt, cover and cook until the peas are tender – about 15 minutes for fresh peas, 5 minutes for frozen.

Meanwhile, in a large saucepan, bring the wine to the boil. Add the clams, on a rack, and steam them until they open – 5–10 minutes. Add them to the pea stew, discarding any that have not opened. Strain the wine and juices from steaming the clams through a fine sieve into the stew. Taste for seasoning. Serve warm in soup bowls, garnished with a mint sprig.

Trucha Escabechada

· TROUT MARINATED IN VINEGAR WITH ONIONS AND CARROTS ·

Start preparation the day before

Fish *en escabeche* make delightful cold luncheon dishes, and trout is a favourite in Spain for this type of preparation. O'Pazo restaurant in Madrid, which owner Evaristo García has made famous for its fresh fish and shellfish, serves an excellent *trucha escabechada* in the style of this recipe.   *Serves 6.*

FOR THE TROUT
6 small trout, cleaned
about 125 ml (4 fl oz) olive oil
65 g (2½ oz) plain flour
5 ml (1 tsp) salt
1.25 ml (¼ tsp) freshly ground black
  pepper
FOR THE MARINADE
12 large cloves garlic, cut into slices
1 medium carrot, peeled and very thinly
  sliced

1 medium onion, thinly sliced
350 ml (12 fl oz) white wine vinegar
1 bay leaf
1–2 sprigs parsley
2.5 ml (½ tsp) crushed hot red pepper
  flakes
AS A GARNISH
parsley sprigs
lemon slices
30 ml (2 tbsp) chopped parsley

To cook the trout   Rinse the trout and pat dry. Heat the oil in a large frying pan with a lid. Combine the flour, salt and pepper in a polythene bag; add the trout, one at a time, shaking to coat thoroughly. Place the trout in the pan and cook over a high heat until golden – about 3 minutes on each side – turning only once. Remove the trout to an earthenware casserole.

To prepare the marinade   Add the garlic to the oil in the frying pan and fry until golden; remove with a slotted spoon and drain on kitchen paper. Add the carrot and onion to the pan and fry over a low heat for 10 minutes. Add the vinegar, bay leaf, parsley, hot pepper flakes and 225 ml (8 fl oz) water. Cover and simmer over a very low heat for 20 minutes.

Pour the marinade over the trout, and arrange garlic over them; reserve 30–45 ml (2–3 tbsp) garlic to use later as a garnish. Cover the casserole and refrigerate for 24 hours. During this time, turn the trout several times in the marinade.

Remove the trout from the refrigerator 2 hours before serving. Arrange them on a serving platter (or serve directly from the casserole). Pour the marinade, garlic, onion and carrot over. Garnish with the parsley sprigs and lemon slices; sprinkle the reserved garlic and the chopped parsley on top.

Tosta de Gambas

· PRAWN TOAST ·

Koldo Lasa, in his early thirties, is the youngest offspring of a great dynasty of cooks, which began when Francisco Lasa started a roadside inn in 1929. He had many children, who all devoted themselves to cooking – as did the grandchildren, too! Since the mid-1970s, Koldo has been running Hostal Lasa in Bergara, near San Sebastián, my favourite of all the various restaurants the family has scattered around northern Spain. Koldo has given his own creative touch to the Lasas' traditional Basque recipes.

Tosta de gambas makes a delightful first course or a light luncheon dish. It is perfect accompanied by a vegetable salad.   *Serves 4.*

700 g (1½ lb) small raw prawns, in the
shell
40 g (1½ oz) butter
225 ml (8 fl oz) full-bodied Spanish
brandy
450 ml (¾ pint) Fish Fumet (p. 194)
125 ml (4 fl oz) double cream

15 ml (1 tbsp) finely chopped parsley
2.5 ml (½ tsp) salt
2.5 ml (½ tsp) freshly ground white pepper
6–8 slices Loaf Bread (see Note below),
cut 1 cm (½ inch) thick
AS A GARNISH
15 ml (1 tbsp) snipped chives

(Note: Loaf Bread (Pan de Molde) (p. 180) is ideal for this recipe. You will need only a few slices for this dish, but you can serve the bread throughout the meal, or use it later – it makes wonderful toast! Or you can use any white bread, sliced and toasted.)

Peel the prawns, reserving the shells. Sauté the shells in 25 g (1 oz) of the butter in a frying pan for 1–2 minutes. Add half the brandy; when hot, flambé (pp. 32–3). When the flames subside, add the fumet; bring to the boil, reduce the heat to low and cook, uncovered, for 15 minutes, pressing down the shells with a spoon from time to time. Strain through a fine sieve, pressing down the shells with a spoon, and reserve the liquid.

Sauté the prawns over a medium to high heat in the remaining butter for 1 minute; add the remaining brandy, increase the heat and, when hot, flambé. After 1–2 minutes, douse with the reserved prawn liquid. Remove the prawns with a slotted spoon and reserve.

Over a high heat, cook the sauce until reduced to about 175 ml (6 fl oz). Add the cream, parsley, salt and pepper, and cook over a medium heat for about 5 minutes. Taste for seasoning.

Trim the crusts from the bread slices; cut them in half and toast them; place on individual plates. Return the prawns to the pan, just to heat through. Arrange the prawns on top of the toast and pour the sauce over, making sure it soaks the bread. Sprinkle chives on top. Serve warm.

Langostinos a la Crema de Perejil

· CATALAN – LLAGOSTINS A LA CREMA DE JULIVERT ·

· PRAWNS IN A PARSLEY CREAM ·

The secret of the great Cal Isidre restaurant is that every morning Isidre Gironés goes to the best market in Barcelona, La Bouquería, and personally selects the produce for the day's menu. His wife, Montserrat, is the charming hostess. This recipe was inspired by a delightful dish I had there. *Serves 6.*

700 g (1½ lb) medium or medium–small
  prawns in the shell
50 g (2 oz) butter
225 ml (8 fl oz) dry white wine
225 ml (8 fl oz) Fish Fumet (p. 194)
50 g (2 oz) chopped parsley

4–5 large cloves garlic, finely chopped
125 ml (4 fl oz) double cream
2.5 ml (½ tsp) salt
1.25 ml (¼ tsp) freshly ground black
  pepper

Shell the prawns and set them aside. In a medium frying pan, melt the butter and sauté the prawn shells over a low heat for 20–30 minutes. Stir occasionally and press the shells with the back of a spatula to extract as much of their flavour as possible. Add the wine, increase the heat to medium-high and cook, stirring, until the wine is reduced to about 125 ml (4 fl oz). Strain through a fine sieve into a medium saucepan, pressing the shells down with a spoon to get all the juices through. Add the fumet to the skillet, stirring and scraping with a wooden spatula to loosen any sediment left in the skillet. Pour the fumet through the sieve into the pan with the wine mixture. Discard the prawn shells.

Blanch the parsley: put it in a strainer and dip it for just a few seconds into a saucepan of boiling water. Drain and stir it into the sauce. Add the garlic and cook over a low heat for 2 minutes. Add the cream and cook over a medium heat until reduced by about one third or to desired consistency. Season with salt and pepper. Add the prawns and cook them, stirring, for 2–3 minutes or until done (depending on their size). Serve immediately.

Pastel de Pescado Mediterráneo

· CATALAN – PASTÍS DE PEIX MEDITERRANI ·

· MEDITERRANEAN FISH CAKE ·

This is a recipe from my sister-in-law, Mahle, one of the first I made in the United States – and a hit from day one. It is easy to make, and all you need is good fish.

Mahle serves it often at buffet dinners or as a first course. It also works very well as an appetizer on toast, because it is like a fish terrine. I guess it is a precursor of *nouvelle cuisine* fish mousses; not your usual mousse type but meatier, more country style. *Serves 8.*

60 ml (4 tbsp) olive oil
700 g (1½ lb) flavourful fresh fish, such as monkfish, halibut or sea bass
125 ml (4 fl oz) full-bodied Spanish brandy
1 large onion, finely chopped
3 cloves garlic, finely chopped
900 g (2 lb) tomatoes, skinned, seeded and chopped
15 ml (1 tbsp) chopped mixed fresh herbs, such as thyme, oregano or rosemary

50 ml (2 fl oz) dry white wine
5 ml (1 tsp) salt
2.5 ml (½ tsp) freshly ground black pepper
225 g (8 oz) peeled prawns, coarsely chopped
100 g (4 oz) crab meat, shredded
6 eggs, beaten
about 25 g (1 oz) dry breadcrumbs
AS A GARNISH
30 ml (2 tbsp) drained large capers
8 prawns, cooked and peeled, tails left intact

Heat half the oil in a frying pan, and, over a medium heat, fry the fish for 3 minutes. Add the brandy and, when hot, flambé. When the flames subside, remove the fish and allow to cool.

Add the remaining oil to the pan and, over a low heat, fry the onion and garlic until golden. Add the tomatoes, herbs, wine, salt and pepper; increase the heat to medium-high and cook until thick. Purée half the sauce and reserve. Transfer the remaining sauce to a bowl.

Preheat the oven to 180°c (350°F) mark 4.

Skin, bone and flake the fish. Add to the bowl, together with the raw prawns and crabmeat. Taste for seasoning. Stir in the beaten eggs and mix well.

Oil a 20 × 12.5 cm (8 × 5 inch) loaf tin. Add the breadcrumbs and shake to coat the bottom and sides; tap off any excess. Pour in the fish mixture. Place the tin in a roasting pan and pour in boiling water to come halfway up the sides of the tin. Bake in the oven for 30 minutes. Remove from the roasting pan and bake for a further 1 hour or until a skewer inserted into the centre comes out clean.

Unmould and serve either hot or cold, covered with the tomato sauce. Garnish with the capers around the edges, and arrange the whole prawns around the cake.

Pastel de Krabarroka

· *BASQUE FISH MOUSSE* ·

Juan Mari Arzak is today one of Spain's most renowned chefs. His excellent Arzak restaurant in San Sebastián – the gastronomic centre of the Basque Country – is enhanced by his charming personality. He has developed many interesting dishes found today in restaurants throughout Spain, among them this fish mousse, which has become a classic of New Basque Cuisine.

The fish used by Arzak for this dish is *krabarroka*, the Basque name for the fish known in the rest of Spain as *gallineta*, in France as *rascasse*, and in the United States as cabezone. It is a rockfish, ugly and with many bones, yet very tasty. But you can use any moist, flavourful white fish, such as monkfish or even cod. I must say I have changed the recipe somewhat – adding, for instance, a little saffron, which Arzak does not use but which contributes a lovely note of flavour. This delicate dish will make an elegant first course or a delicious main course for luncheon.   *Serves 8.*

450 g (1 lb) cabezone fillets or monkfish
  tails
FOR THE POACHING LIQUID
225 ml (8 fl oz) dry white wine
1 medium unpeeled carrot, sliced
1 small onion, sliced
1 small celery stick, sliced
1 bay leaf
1 sprig parsley
1 sprig thyme or 1.25 ml (¼ tsp) dried
FOR THE MOUSSE
about 30 ml (2 tbsp) fine dry breadcrumbs
15 g (½ oz) butter

30 ml (2 tbsp) finely chopped onion
450 g (1 lb) tomatoes, skinned but not
  seeded, chopped
2.5 ml (½ tsp) saffron threads
1 bay leaf
7.5 ml (1½ tsp) tomato purée
225 ml (8 fl oz) double cream
8 eggs
2.5 ml (½ tsp) salt, or to taste
2.5 ml (½ tsp) freshly ground white pepper
AS AN ACCOMPANIMENT
half quantity Mayonnaise (p. 198);
  make whole recipe and use half

To poach the fish   In a saucepan large enough to hold the fish, combine all the ingredients for the poaching liquid. Add 600 ml (1 pint) water, bring to the boil and simmer, partially covered, for 30 minutes. Add the fish to the liquid, cover and simmer just until cooked through – 8–10 minutes. Remove any skin and bones. (You can strain the liquid and save to use as a light fumet.) Set the fish aside.

Preheat the oven to 200°c (400°F) mark 6.

To prepare the mousse   Butter an ovenproof 1.4 litre (2½ pint) ring mould, add the breadcrumbs and turn to cover all the bottom and sides. Tap off any excess. Refrigerate the mould to set the crumbs – about 10 minutes – while you prepare the mousse.

Melt the butter in a medium frying pan and fry the onion until soft. Add the tomatoes, saffron and bay leaf; cook over a medium to low heat until the liquid has evaporated. Remove the bay leaf. Purée the tomato mixture in a food processor or blender. Blend in the tomato purée, cream, eggs, salt and pepper. Add the fish and blend again briefly, until it is chopped but not puréed. Taste for seasoning. Remove the mould from the refrigerator and pour the mixture into it.

Place the mould in a roasting pan and pour in boiling water to come halfway up the sides of the mould. Bake in the oven for about 45 minutes or, until a skewer inserted into the centre comes out clean.

Allow to cool, then run a knife around the edges and unmould onto a serving plate. Serve at room temperature, with the mayonnaise handed separately.

Crêpes de Txangurro

· PANCAKES STUFFED WITH CRAB ·

This is another dish that Juan Mari Arzak has made into a classic of 'New Basque Cuisine' by adding his personal touch to a traditional recipe. *Txangurro* is a Basque preparation of shredded crab with an 'American' sauce; but it is his idea to stuff it in a pancake and add a delicate sauce to it.

I have served this dish as a first course for dinner and as a main course for lunch, accompanied by a salad.   *Serves 6.*

FOR THE PANCAKES
3 eggs
100 g (4 oz) plain flour
225 ml (8 fl oz) milk
15 ml (1 tbsp) full-bodied Spanish brandy
about 25 g (1 oz) butter for frying
FOR THE FILLING
75 g (3 oz) butter
2 medium carrots, peeled and finely chopped
6 shallots, finely chopped

30 ml (2 tbsp) garlic, finely chopped
700 g (1½ lb) tomatoes, skinned, seeded and chopped
125 ml (4 fl oz) full-bodied Spanish brandy
350 ml (12 fl oz) Fish Fumet (p. 194)
225 ml (8 fl oz) double cream
salt and freshly ground black pepper to taste, if necessary
450 g (1 lb) crabmeat
FOR THE SAUCE
225 ml (8 fl oz) Fish Fumet (p. 194)

To prepare the pancakes   In a food processor or blender, combine all the pancake ingredients except the butter, and blend until very smooth. Leave the batter to stand for about 30 minutes.

In a crêpe pan or a 17.5 cm (7 inch) heavy frying pan, heat a tiny nut of butter until very hot. Add about 30 ml (2 tbsp) of the batter and, over a medium heat, very quickly swirl the batter around so that it coats the bottom of the pan. The pancake should be as thin as possible. Cook the pancake until the edges start to draw away from the sides of the pan; the bottom should be golden. Invert the pan over a firm surface – a wooden board, for example – and give it a sound whack to release the pancake. (Don't worry if the first pancake takes a little longer and doesn't come out perfectly; the rest of them will be faster and better.) Set the pancakes aside. You should have at least 12 pancakes.

To prepare the filling   In a heavy frying pan, melt the butter and add the carrots, shallots and garlic. Fry over a low heat until very soft and golden – about 15 minutes. Add the tomatoes, increase the heat and cook until the liquid has evaporated. Add the brandy and flambé (pp. 32–3). When the flames subside, add the fish fumet and reduce by half. Add the cream and cook over a medium heat until slightly thickened – 2 or 3 minutes. Taste for seasoning, adding salt and pepper if necessary. Reserve 225 ml (8 fl oz) of this sauce. Add the crab to the pan, stir and heat through.

To assemble the pancakes   Divide the crab mixture equally among the pancakes, and roll them up. Place them, seam side down, on an ovenproof serving platter or baking dish.

Preheat the grill.

To prepare the sauce Purée the reserved sauce with the fumet, and strain through a fine sieve into a saucepan. Heat through and pour over the crab pancakes. Place the platter under the grill just until the tops turn golden, and serve immediately.

SALT COD

Salt cod dishes, found all over Spain, are among the best offerings of the Mediterranean countries. In the following pages you will find several of my favourite recipes, as well as Catalan Shredded Cod Salad ('Esqueixada') in the Fish and Meat Salads chapter (p. 74).

Cod was originally a northern product, first found in Norway in the ninth century. Yet Spain and Portugal are the main creators of recipes for salt cod, which paradoxically we have always imported, at least since the fifteenth century. The best comes from Newfoundland, and also from Scotland and Norway. Basques were the first to eat it in Spain, as they caught it when fishing for whales in northern Europe; but Basque cuisine kept within its boundaries until well into the nineteenth century – while since the fifteenth, salt cod has been cooked in Catalonia. It probably came there from the South of France, which has old dishes such as *brandade de morue* (shredded salt cod with olive oil, garlic and milk), original to Nîmes and also found in Spain.

Salt cod, dry and hard as a wooden board, can be turned into a juicy, exquisite delicacy. Not all salt cod is the same quality, though; when buying it, be sure the fillets are thick and the flesh white. If they are thin and yellowish, they are old and will be stringy. If you are not going to use it right away, store it in your refrigerator and it will keep for at least 2 or 3 months.

Salt cod needs to be soaked in cold water for about two days before using it, changing the water 5 or 6 times during the process, as directed in my recipes. After this operation, the cod will no longer be salty. If you are short of time and the recipe calls for shredded cod, shred it before soaking; it will take less time to freshen.

Salt cod has a distinct flavour, very different from fresh cod, which I personally enjoy very much. Even though today we have other methods of preserving fish, the unique flavour of salt cod is important in the following recipes; you will not get the same results with fresh cod.

Pimientos Rellenos de Bacalao

· RED PEPPERS STUFFED WITH COD ·

Start preparation 2 days in advance, by soaking cod in water

Stuffed red peppers are a dish found very often all over Spain. Meat-stuffed peppers are more traditional and old-fashioned; to prepare them with seafood is a newer approach. My favourite stuffing is salt cod, as served at the Rekondo restaurant in San Sebastián. And yet this is not a 'New Basque Cuisine'-style restaurant; Chomín and Mari Carmen Rekondo serve sound, classic Basque cooking. Besides its excellent food, the restaurant is famous for Chomín's amazing cellar, which he built in 1975 and today has 80,000 bottles!

To prepare this dish, any small sweet red peppers will work; but the kind called pimientos are perfect for stuffing, because they are meatier and it is easier to prevent them from breaking. Whatever peppers you use, don't worry if they fall apart a bit; the stuffing will help to hold them together – and when you arrange them on the plate they will look fine.

When red peppers are not in season, you can also use green peppers – although I find that the red ones are sweeter and more colourful.   *Serves 8.*

FOR THE PEPPERS
450 g (1 lb) boneless dried salt cod
8 medium red sweet peppers
50 g (2 oz) soft white breadcrumbs
   (pp. 31–2)
65 ml (2½ fl oz) milk
30 ml (2 tbsp) olive oil
6 large cloves garlic, chopped
1 medium onion, chopped
3.75 ml (¾ tsp) freshly ground black
   pepper, or to taste
salt to taste, if necessary
2 eggs, beaten

15 ml (1 tbsp) chopped parsley
FOR THE SAUCE
30 ml (2 tbsp) olive oil
1 onion, sliced
225 g (8 oz) carrots, peeled and coarsely
   chopped
225 ml (8 fl oz) dry white wine
15 ml (1 tbsp) tomato purée
chopped fresh parsley
15 ml (1 tbsp) paprika, or to taste
pinch of cayenne
350 ml (12 fl oz) Chicken Stock (p. 191)

To prepare the cod   Soak the cod in water to cover for 48 hours, changing the water 5 or 6 times. Drain and press the cod with your hands to remove excess water. Discard any skin or bones left and, with your hands or a knife, flake the cod into small pieces. Set aside.

To stuff the peppers   Preheat the oven to 200°c (400°F) mark 6. Roast and peel the peppers as described on p. 32. Core each pepper and remove the seeds, trying to keep the peppers whole as far as possible. Turn the oven temperature down to 180°c (350°F) mark 4.

Soak the breadcrumbs in the milk. Heat the oil in a frying pan; add the garlic and onion, and fry over a low heat until soft – about 5 minutes. Add the cod and cook over a medium heat for 5 minutes. Squeeze the breadcrumbs dry and discard the milk. Add the crumbs to the pan; stir in the pepper, taste for seasoning and add salt if necessary. Off the heat, add the eggs and parsley.

Using a teaspoon or a piping bag filled with the cod mixture, divide the filling evenly among the peppers. Set them in an oiled baking dish.

To prepare the sauce In a saucepan, heat the oil and add the onion and carrots; fry over a medium to low heat for 10 minutes. Add the wine, increase the heat to high and cook for about 5 minutes, until the liquid has evaporated. Stir in the tomato purée, half the parsley, the paprika, cayenne and stock. Simmer over a low heat for 30 minutes, uncovered. Purée the mixture in a food processor or blender. Taste for seasoning.

To assemble the dish Pour the sauce over the peppers, covering them evenly. Bake in the oven for 20 minutes. Just before serving, sprinkle the peppers with the remaining parsley.

Bacalao al Ajoarriero

· COD IN A TOMATO AND RED PEPPER SAUCE ·

Start preparation 2 days in advance, by soaking cod in water

This is a very old dish, original to the northern region of Navarra. The name *ajoarriero* literally translates as 'garlic muleteer', because it was often prepared for muleteers as they arrived at the roadside inns, carrying their goods in mule-drawn carts. It was a handy preparation; the sauce was ready, and the shredded cod was added quickly.

A dish of such humble origin is today served at many smart restaurants, sometimes refined by the addition of expensive shellfish. Iñaqui Oyarbide, who is from Navarra, has made his *ajoarriero* with lobster famous at Madrid's superb Príncipe de Viana restaurant. I also enjoy it with prawns, as it is served in the Basque Country at Dos Hermanas restaurant in Vitoria.

But the only shellfish that could originally have been part of *ajoarriero* is crayfish, from the nearby rivers. One recipe I treasure is Hemingway's favourite, given to me by Manuel Martínez-Llopis, a gastronomic historian who has the greatest collection of recipes and their stories. It includes crayfish and prawns, besides other untraditional ingredients such as white wine, mushrooms and various herbs. Traditional or not, it is delicious!

The following is a classic recipe, the way I've had it at Pamplona's top restaurant, Josetxo. You will find it an instant success, whether served as a first course or as an appetizer, accompanied by toasted French bread.   *Serves 4–6.*

450 g (1 lb) boneless dried salt cod
30 ml (2 tbsp) olive oil
12 large cloves garlic, finely chopped
1 medium onion, chopped
2 medium red sweet peppers, cored,
  seeded and thinly sliced

450 g (1 lb) unpeeled tomatoes, chopped
pinch of crushed hot red pepper flakes
1.25 ml ($\frac{1}{4}$ tsp) freshly ground white
  pepper, or to taste
salt to taste, if necessary

Soak the cod in water to cover for 48 hours, changing the water 5 or 6 times. Drain and press cod with your hands to remove excess water. Discard any skin or bones, and flake it finely with your fingers.

Heat the oil in a flameproof casserole or saucepan. Add the garlic and onion and fry until soft, then add the red peppers and fry for 5 minutes over a medium heat, stirring. Add the tomatoes, red pepper flakes and white pepper. Cook over a medium heat until the mixture becomes very thick – about 15 minutes. Purée this sauce in a food processor or blender.

Return the sauce to the casserole or pan. Add the flaked cod and cook over a medium to low heat for about 10 minutes. It should have a thick consistency, with all the flavours mingled. Taste for seasoning; salt will probably not be necessary.

Bacalao a la Catalana con Pasas y Piñones

· CATALAN – BACALLÀ A LA CATALANA AMB PANSES I PINYONS ·

· CATALAN-STYLE COD WITH PINE NUTS AND RAISINS ·

Start preparation 2 days in advance, by soaking cod in water

This dish has the classic ingredients of Catalan cuisine: *sofrito*, *picada*, even pine nuts and raisins, which automatically qualify the dish to be named *a la catalana*. I have served it with equal success as a first course, a main course and an appetizer or *tapa*, cutting the cod into smaller pieces. Moreover, it can be made ahead and reheated at the last moment.

The following two cod recipes come from Jaume de Provença, one of my favourite restaurants in Barcelona not only for its high standards but because it is Catalan to the bone. Owner/chef Jaume Bargues has contributed a lot to bringing my region's cuisine to the top rank it enjoys today. He is imaginative and talented, always creating new dishes but also keeping some great old traditionals, such as this one.　*Serves 4–6.*

450 g (1 lb) boneless dried salt cod
FOR THE SOFRITO
45 ml (3 tbsp) olive oil
1 large onion, finely chopped
4 large cloves garlic, finely chopped
900 g (2 lb) ripe tomatoes, skinned and
　chopped
15 ml (1 tbsp) chopped parsley
25 g (1 oz) pine nuts
25 g (1 oz) raisins
FOR THE PICADA
15 ml (1 tbsp) olive oil (optional)

1 large slice white bread, cut 1 cm
　(½ inch) thick
12 blanched almonds
12 hazelnuts
3 large cloves garlic
15 ml (1 tbsp) chopped parsley
225 ml (8 fl oz) dry white wine
450 ml (¾ pint) Fish Fumet (p. 194)
2.5 ml (½ tsp) salt
1.25 ml (¼ tsp) freshly ground black
　pepper

Soak the cod in water to cover for 48 hours, changing the water 5 or 6 times. Drain and press the cod with your hands to eliminate excess water. Remove any skin and bones, and cut the flesh into 4 or 6 serving pieces.

To prepare the *sofrito* Heat 30 ml (2 tbsp) of the oil in a flameproof casserole. Add the onion and garlic and fry gently, for at least 20 minutes, until quite golden.

Add the tomatoes and parsley and fry until all the liquid has evaporated – about 30 minutes or longer.

Meanwhile, heat the remaining oil in a small frying pan and fry the pine nuts and raisins until the nuts are golden and the raisins plump. Remove them and set aside. Reserve the oil in the pan.

Preheat the oven to 180°c (350°F) mark 4.

To prepare the *picada* Add a further 15 ml (1 tbsp) oil to the pan if necessary, and fry the bread until golden. Toast the almonds in the oven for 15 minutes, and the hazelnuts for 12 minutes; rub the hazelnuts in a damp tea-towel to remove most of the skins. In a food processor, finely chop the fried bread with the garlic, almonds, hazelnuts and parsley.

Add the wine to the tomato mixture, increase the heat and cook until all the liquid has evaporated. Add the fumet, bring to the boil and stir in the *picada*. Season with salt and pepper. Add the cod and cook, uncovered, over a medium to low heat for 10 minutes. Taste for seasoning. Add the pine nuts and raisins. Serve warm.

Bacalao a la Mousse de Allioli

· CATALAN – BACALLÀ A L'ESCUMA D'ALLIOLI ·

· COD IN AN ALLIOLI MOUSSE ·

Start preparation 2 days in advance, by soaking cod in water

This recipe is based on an old Catalan combination, salt cod with *allioli*. Yet the idea of making an airy mousse out of a garlic mayonnaise is new and exciting – characteristic of Jaume Bargues's style. The dish has become a classic of new-style Catalan cuisine. It is easily prepared and can be served as a main or first course, depending on the portions.   *Serves 4–6.*

450 g (1 lb) boneless dried salt cod
FOR THE MOUSSE
2 large heads garlic
2 eggs, separated

225 ml (8 fl oz) olive oil
15 ml (1 tbsp) lemon juice
1.25 ml ($\frac{1}{4}$ tsp) salt
pinch of cayenne

Soak the fish in water to cover for 48 hours, changing the water 5 or 6 times. Drain and press the cod with your hands to eliminate excess water. Remove any skin or bones left. Set aside.

Preheat the oven to 200°c (400°F) mark 6.

Bake the whole garlic heads in the oven for 45 minutes. Allow to cool, then cut off about one third of the garlic head tops, up to where you can see the cloves, and squeeze them out with your fingers. You should have about 45 ml (3 tbsp).

In a food processor or blender, beat the garlic with the egg yolks until thick. In a jug, mix the oil, lemon juice, salt and cayenne, beating with a fork. With the motor running, add the oil mixture to the egg yolks and garlic very slowly, in a thin stream; the mixture will thicken and acquire the consistency of a thick mayonnaise. (If the mixture separates or curdles or does not thicken, see the Mayonnaise (Salsa Mayonesa) recipe on p. 198 for a way to correct it.)

Transfer the *allioli* to a bowl. Beat the egg whites until stiff, and fold them into the *allioli*.

Cut the cod into 4 or 6 serving pieces, making sure they are all the same thickness; if some of them are too thin, put 2 thin ones on top of each other to level out all the pieces. Lay the cod in an oiled ovenproof casserole and cover with the mousse. Just before serving, bake in the oven, uncovered, for 10–15 minutes, or until the mousse is golden on top.

Atún Mechado al Horno

· BRAISED TUNA STUDDED WITH ANCHOVIES ·

A few miles outside Granada is the little village of Dúrcal, with an old mill owned for generations by the Carrillo family. In 1978, young Manuel Carrillo decided to restore it and made it the home of the Gastronomic Academy of Granada. He has since devoted himself to researching old Arab recipes, developing them with chef Luis Rico.

Manuel made the old mill into a beautiful restaurant, appropriately called El Molino (The Mill), where he serves those old specialities. But he does not like it to be called a restaurant; in fact, it is more like a working museum, and a wonderful place to visit. The mill provides the flour for their crusty breads, which are made daily in the old oven. The kitchen is also from the old days, with wood and coal stoves – and a silver-haired, grandmotherly cook named Aurora who fits perfectly into the environment. *Serves 6.*

FOR THE FISH
9 canned flat anchovy fillets
900 g (2 lb) fresh tuna, cut into 6 fillets
15 ml (1 tbsp) lemon juice
1.25 ml ($\frac{1}{4}$ tsp) salt
1.25 ml ($\frac{1}{4}$ tsp) freshly ground black
　pepper
FOR THE VEGETABLES
30 ml (2 tbsp) olive oil
700 g (1$\frac{1}{2}$ lb) onions, thinly sliced
4 large cloves garlic, finely chopped

225 g (8 oz) carrots, peeled and thinly
　sliced into rounds
225 g (8 oz) ripe tomatoes, skinned,
　seeded and chopped
1 large green sweet pepper, cut into thin
　strips lengthways
15 ml (1 tbsp) finely chopped parsley
5 ml (1 tsp) salt
1.25 ml ($\frac{1}{4}$ tsp) freshly ground black
　pepper
2 bay leaves

To stud the tuna　Cut each anchovy into 3 pieces. With the point of a sharp knife, make a slit in the tuna flesh and stick 4–5 pieces of anchovy into each tuna fillet at different points; press into the opening with your finger. Sprinkle the fillets with lemon juice, salt and pepper. Set aside.

To prepare the vegetables　In a large frying pan, heat the oil and slowly fry the onions, garlic and carrots over a low heat until very soft – about 45 minutes. Add the tomatoes, pepper strips, parsley, salt and pepper; cook until the peppers are soft and all the liquid has evaporated – about 15 minutes.

To assemble the dish   Preheat the oven to 180°c (350°F) mark 4.

In a casserole that can accommodate the tuna fillets in a single layer, place half the vegetables in a layer; put the tuna fillets on top, tuck the bay leaves in beside the tuna and cover with the remaining vegetables. Cover and bake in the oven for about 30 minutes, or until the fish is cooked.

Chicharro con Juliana de Verduras

· MACKEREL WITH A JULIENNE OF LEEKS AND CARROTS ·

In the old part of San Sebastián there is a small restaurant, Kokotxa, which in recent years has become a star in the Basque Country. It is run by three young men: chef Iñaki Muguruza and brothers Guillermo and Gastón Nogués. Their cuisine is modern and rather Basque-French in style, as attested by this recipe.

I like to serve this dish in small portions as a first course; it provides a colourful, appetizing beginning for an elegant dinner.   *Serves 6.*

FOR THE SAUCE
75 g (3 oz) butter
4 shallots, finely chopped
700 g (1½ lb) leeks, trimmed and cut into
    thin strips (see Note below)
3 medium carrots, peeled and cut into
    thin strips
125 ml (4 fl oz) double cream
2.5 ml (½ tsp) salt, or to taste
pinch of freshly ground white pepper, or
    to taste

FOR THE FISH
3 mackerel, each weighing about 700 g
    (1½ lb), each cut into 2 fillets, with the
    skin on
30 ml (2 tbsp) olive oil
30 ml (2 tbsp) sherry wine vinegar or a
    good red wine vinegar
AS A GARNISH
15 ml (1 tbsp) finely chopped parsley

(Note: To slice the leeks thinly, cut them in half lengthways, separate the leaves and, one by one, roll them up lengthways and slice across horizontally.)

Preheat the oven to 180°c (350°F) mark 4.

To prepare the sauce   Melt the butter in a frying pan and fry the shallots over a low heat until golden. Add the leeks and carrots and fry until soft – 15–20 minutes. Add the cream, salt and pepper. Taste for seasoning. Reserve the sauce.

To cook the fish   Oil a casserole. Place the mackerel fillets in the casserole in a single layer, skin side down. Pour oil and vinegar over. Bake, uncovered, in the oven for 8 minutes.

To assemble the dish   Pour the sauce over the mackerel fillets and sprinkle with parsley. Serve immediately.

Pescado 'Koskera'

· FISH IN A PARSLEY AND PEA SAUCE, BASQUE STYLE ·

This recipe is a perfect example of the simple, tasty cooking in the Basque 'gastronomic societies'. It was prepared for me by the president of the Cofradía Vasca de Gastronomía (Basque Gastronomic Society) in San Sebastián. These societies are reserved exclusively for men, so I was very honoured to be invited!   Serves 6.

60 ml (4 tbsp) olive oil
1 large onion, sliced
3 large cloves garlic, finely chopped
125 ml (4 fl oz) dry white wine
450 ml (¾ pint) Fish Fumet (p. 194)
100 g (4 oz) shelled fresh or frozen petits pois

25 g (1 oz) finely chopped parsley
2.5 ml (½ tsp) salt, or to taste
2.5 ml (½ tsp) freshly ground black
   pepper, or to taste
900 g (2 lb) fish fillets, such as turbot
   or cod

Heat half the oil in a frying pan and fry the onion and garlic over a low heat for about 15 minutes, until very soft and starting to colour. Add the wine, increase the heat and cook rapidly until the wine evaporates. Add the fumet and cook over a medium heat for 5 minutes. Purée the mixture in a food processor or blender and return it to the pan. Stir in the peas, parsley, salt and pepper.

Heat the remaining oil in a flameproof casserole or a frying pan large enough to hold the fish fillets in 1 layer. Fry the fish over a medium heat, until golden. Pour the sauce over the fish and cook for about 3 minutes, or until the fish is done. Serve straight from the casserole, or on individual dishes.

Pescado Braseado en Hojas de Col con Salsa al Cava

· BRAISED FISH WRAPPED IN CABBAGE LEAVES WITH A CHAMPAGNE SAUCE ·

One of Madrid's most reputable, traditional and consistently good restaurants over the years is Jockey. Founded by Clodoaldo Cortés in 1945, it has flourished under his son, Luis Eduardo, and director Félix Rodríguez, who runs the elegant dining room with the efficiency of a great professional.

From the beginning, chef Clemencio Fuentes has shown his mastery of the art of cooking. This delicate dish with a 'new' touch is adapted from one of his creations. Serves 6.

900 g (2 lb) green cabbage, preferably Savoy
700 g (1½ lb) cod, cut into 12 thin fillets
3.75 ml (¾ tsp) salt
2.5 ml (½ tsp) freshly ground black pepper
50 g (2 oz) butter

3 shallots, finely chopped
225 g (8 oz) mushrooms, finely chopped
450 ml (¾ pint) champagne
450 ml (¾ pint) Fish Fumet (p. 194)
125 ml (4 fl oz) double cream

Core the cabbage and cook it, whole, in boiling salted water to cover for 15 minutes. Drain and separate the leaves. Lay 12 leaves flat (if necessary, 2 leaves can be patched together). Arrange 1 fish fillet on top of each leaf, and sprinkle them with 1.25 ml ($\frac{1}{4}$ tsp) each salt and pepper.

Melt the butter in a frying pan and fry the shallots for 5 minutes over a low heat. Add the mushrooms 2.5 ml ($\frac{1}{2}$ tsp) salt and 1.25 ml ($\frac{1}{4}$ tsp) pepper; cook for 15 minutes. Add half the champagne and cook over a high heat until evaporated.

Divide the mushroom mixture among the fish pieces. Fold the fillets over and wrap 1 cabbage leaf around each fillet. Place them seam side down in a frying pan large enough to hold all of them in a single layer.

In a pan, bring the fumet and remaining champagne to the boil, and reduce to 225 ml (8 fl oz). Add cream and cook over a medium heat for 5 minutes. Pour over the cabbage rolls. Bring to the boil, reduce the heat to low, cover and cook for 15 minutes. Transfer the cabbage rolls to a serving platter and reduce the sauce to desired consistency. Taste for seasoning. Pour over the fish and serve immediately.

Rodaballo Soufflé a la Albahaca

· CATALAN – TURBOT SOUFFLÉ AMB ALFÀBREGA ·

· TURBOT WITH BASIL SOUFFLÉ ·

Another creation of the outstanding Ampurdán restaurant in Figueras (near Gerona, in the northern Catalan district of L'Empordà) is this superb combination of a fine fresh fish – turbot from the Mediterranean is excellent – with aromatic basil in a light, airy sauce.

If you don't have turbot, I have found that the recipe works very well with any firm white fish, as long as it is fresh. The sauce will accent the flavour! *Serves 6.*

FOR THE POACHING LIQUID
225 ml (8 fl oz) dry white wine
6 black peppercorns
2 sprigs parsley
2 sprigs fresh basil
900 g (2 lb) turbot fillets or other fresh firm white fish, cut into 6 pieces
225 ml (8 fl oz) double cream

3 eggs, separated
25 g (1 oz) chopped basil
2.5 ml ($\frac{1}{2}$ tsp) salt
1.25 ml ($\frac{1}{4}$ tsp) freshly ground white pepper
15 g ($\frac{1}{2}$ oz) butter
450 g (1 lb) firm ripe tomatoes, skinned, seeded and finely diced

Combine the ingredients for the poaching liquid in a saucepan large enough to hold the fish; bring to the boil. Reduce the heat and simmer, covered, for 30 minutes. Add the fish fillets and poach for 6–7 minutes, just until cooked through. Remove any skin or bones. Discard the poaching liquid.

In a small saucepan, cook the cream over a medium heat until reduced by half. In a large bowl, beat egg yolks; add the hot cream slowly, stirring. Add the chopped basil, salt and pepper. Whisk the egg whites until stiff, and fold them into the mixture.

Preheat the grill.

In a frying pan, melt the butter and add the tomatoes; cook for 1 minute, just to heat them through. Transfer the tomatoes to an ovenproof plate, arranging them in a bed. Place the fish fillets on top, and pour the cream sauce over. Place under the grill until golden, and serve immediately.

Salmón al Vapor con Salsa de Vino Tinto

· CATALAN – SALMÓ AL VAPOR AMB SALSA DE VI NEGRE ·

· FRESH SALMON IN A RED WINE SAUCE ·

This recipe comes from a restaurant in Barcelona – one of the city's best, too – but I'm not sure how Catalan it is because Neichel is owned by a great Alsatian chef, Jean-Louis Neichel. He is in fact a disciple of French master Alain Chapel, and his recipes show a creative refinement worthy of the finest international cuisine. For me, more important than regional cuisines are personal styles, and good chefs and poor chefs; Jean-Louis is an extraordinary one, and I'm glad he decided to establish his restaurant in Barcelona.

I prefer this dish as a main course in which case the recipe should serve 4 rather than 6. Because of the red wine in the sauce, it goes very well with an elegant, medium-bodied red wine. Neichel serves it garnished with thinly sliced, lightly sautéed mushroom caps and a poached spinach leaf on top of each salmon piece, which I find adds a lovely note of colour and flavour; you can use the spinach leaves on which the salmon was poached.   *Serves 4–6.*

FOR THE SAUCE
30 ml (2 tbsp) olive oil
1 small onion, finely chopped
1 small celery stick, finely chopped
1 medium carrot, trimmed but unpeeled,
    finely chopped
½ small leek, finely chopped
300 ml (½ pint) plus 15 ml (1 tbsp)
    medium-bodied dry red wine
225 ml (8 fl oz) Enriched Veal Stock
    (p. 193) or 450 ml (¾ pint) Brown
    Veal Stock (p. 192)

225 ml (8 fl oz) Fish Fumet (p. 194)
15 ml (1 tbsp) lemon juice
75 g (3 oz) butter, cut into small pieces
salt to taste
FOR THE SALMON
several large spinach leaves, to line the
    steamer
900 g (2 lb) salmon fillets, skinned and
    cut into 4 or 6 pieces
salt for sprinkling the salmon

To prepare the sauce   Heat the oil in a large frying pan and fry the vegetables over a low heat until soft and golden – about 30 minutes. Add 125 ml (4 fl oz) of the wine and increase the heat until the wine has evaporated, scraping the pan with a wooden spatula to loosen any sediment stuck to the bottom. Add a further 225 ml (8 fl oz) wine, the stock and fumet. Increase the heat and cook briskly to reduce by about half. Purée and strain through a fine sieve. Return to the pan and cook further, until reduced to 225 ml (8 fl oz).

Turn the heat to low; stir in the lemon juice and remaining 15 ml (1 tbsp) wine. Whisk the butter pieces, one by one, into the sauce, being careful it does not come to the boil. Taste for seasoning, and add salt if necessary. This sauce may be prepared ahead and heated up in a double boiler at the last moment.

To prepare the salmon   Line a steamer with spinach leaves. Place the salmon fillets on top, and sprinkle lightly with salt. Place the steamer over a saucepan containing 2.5 cm (1 inch) boiling water. Cover and cook over a low heat for 5–10 minutes, depending on the thickness of the fillets, just until done.

To serve the dish   Arrange the fillets on a serving platter or individual plates, pour some of the sauce over and hand the remaining sauce separately in a sauceboat.

Escalopas de Salmón con Vieiras y Pimientos Verdes

· SALMON WITH SCALLOPS IN A GREEN PEPPER SAUCE ·

The brilliant idea for this combination of flavours is a good example of the style of Peñas Arriba, a new restaurant in Madrid that is the team effort of two men in their twenties: José Luis Seco – 'Chiqui' to everybody – and Javier Otaduy, the chef. Some of their recipes are inspired by the cuisine of Cantabria, the northern region where Chiqui lived and learned to cook before going to Madrid.

This dish can be served as a main course or, cutting the recipe in half, as an elegant appetizer.   *Serves 6.*

FOR THE SAUCE
30 ml (2 tbsp) olive oil
450 g (1 lb) green sweet peppers, cored,
   seeded and cut into strips lengthways
125 ml (4 fl oz) double cream
2.5 ml ($\frac{1}{2}$ tsp) salt
1.25 ml ($\frac{1}{4}$ tsp) freshly ground white
   pepper
FOR THE SEAFOOD
25 g (1 oz) butter

2 shallots, finely chopped
225 ml (8 fl oz) dry white wine
900 g (2 lb) salmon fillets, cut into 12
   pieces
12 large scallops
AS A GARNISH
30 ml (2 tbsp) snipped chives
25 g (1 oz) red lumpfish roe

To prepare the sauce   Heat the oil in a frying pan; over a low heat fry the green peppers for about 20 minutes, stirring occasionally, until very tender and golden. Stir in the cream, salt and pepper; bring to the boil and turn off heat. Set aside.

To prepare the seafood   Heat the butter in a frying pan wide enough to hold the salmon fillets in a single layer. Fry the shallots over a low heat for 5 minutes. Add the wine and bring to the boil. Add the salmon fillets, reduce the heat to low and cover. Cook for 7–10 minutes, or until the salmon is cooked through. Transfer the salmon to a serving platter and keep warm.

Pour the contents of the skillet into a food processor or blender and purée, together with the green peppers and their sauce. Return to the pan, heat through and add the scallops. Cook over a low heat, covered, for 3 minutes or until the scallops are just cooked through; they should feel barely firm to the touch.

To assemble the dish   Place 1 scallop on top of each salmon fillet and pour the sauce over. Sprinkle the scallops with chives and lumpfish roe.

Rape con Romero

· MONKFISH WITH ROSEMARY ·

Pedro Subijana shows again in this recipe his flair for simplicity, characteristic of many dishes he serves at his Akelaŕe restaurant in San Sebastián. It is based on the freshness of ingredients and on his skill in combining them in a way that works extraordinarily well.   *Serves 6.*

900 g (2 lb) monkfish tails	*2.5 ml (½ tsp) salt*
15 ml (1 tbsp) olive oil	*1.25 ml (¼ tsp) freshly ground black*
15 g (½ oz) butter	*pepper*
45 ml (3 tbsp) finely chopped shallot	*15 ml (1 tbsp) chopped rosemary*
30 ml (2 tbsp) finely chopped garlic	*450 g (1 lb) ripe firm tomatoes, skinned,*
225 ml (8 fl oz) dry white wine	*seeded and diced finely*

Preheat the oven to 180°c (350°F) mark 4.

Remove the skin and membranes from the monkfish. Place the fish in a buttered roasting pan and bake in the oven for 15 minutes. When cool, cut the large part of the fish into medallions, and the narrow tail section into fillets. Discard the juices in the pan.

In a wide frying pan, heat oil and butter. Add the shallots and garlic and fry over a low heat until soft. Pour in the wine and cook briskly for 2–3 minutes. Add the fish to the pan, turning it to coat with the sauce. Add salt and pepper, sprinkle with the rosemary and add the diced tomatoes. Cook, uncovered, just to heat the tomatoes through – about 1 minute – so the sauce retains a very fresh tomato taste. Taste for seasoning. Serve immediately.

Rape con Nueces

· MONKFISH IN A WALNUT CREAM SAUCE ·

Alejandro Fernández and his staff at Los Remos, a delightful restaurant on a tiny beach in the Bay of Algeciras – right across from the African coast – have created, over the twenty-five or more years it has been open, a well-deserved reputation for one of the top cuisines in the south. Alejandro has assembled a variety of recipes featuring local produce, such as this great combination of monkfish with the richness of walnuts in a cream sauce. Because of its complexity, I usually serve it as a main course; in that case, the recipe should be for 4 rather than 6.   *Serves 4–6.*

900 g (2 lb) monkfish tails	50 ml (2 fl oz) Pernod
30 ml (2 tbsp) olive oil	50 ml (2 fl oz) full-bodied Spanish
40 g (1½ oz) butter	brandy
3 large cloves garlic, finely chopped	450 ml (¾ pint) Fish Fumet (p. 194)
100 g (4 oz) finely chopped onion	125 ml (4 fl oz) double cream
150 g (5 oz) finely chopped leek	3.75 ml (¾ tsp) salt, or to taste
175 g (6 oz) walnuts, coarsely chopped	2.5 ml (½ tsp) freshly ground white pepper

Preheat the oven to 180°c (350°F) mark 4.

To cook the fish   Remove the skin and membranes from the monkfish. Place in a buttered roasting pan and bake in the oven for 15 minutes. Allow to cool for about 10 minutes. Cut the fish into medallions and reserve the juices in the pan.

To prepare the sauce   In a frying pan, heat the oil and 30 ml (2 tbsp) of the butter. Over a medium to low heat, fry the garlic, onion and leek until very golden, almost brown – about 20 minutes. Add 50 g (2 oz) of the walnuts and cook slowly for 10 minutes, stirring. Pour in the Pernod and brandy, increase heat and, when hot, flambé (pp. 32–3); cook until the flames subside, shaking pan. Transfer to a food processor or blender and purée with the reserved pan juices, fumet, cream, salt and pepper. Strain through a fine sieve into a frying pan large enough to hold the fish. Sauté the remaining walnuts slowly in the remaining butter for about 5 minutes; add to the pan. Taste for seasoning.

Add the fish medallions to the pan and heat through, coating with the sauce; transfer to a serving plate and serve immediately.

Pescado 'a l'All Cremat'

· CATALAN – PEIX A L'ALL CREMAT ·

· FISH IN A BURNED GARLIC SAUCE ·

Cremat in Catalan means burned – but don't let this put you off trying this country-style Catalan recipe. You won't find the sauce garlicky, just very flavourful. It is an old fisherman's dish, according to Xavier Mestres, chef/owner of L'Avi Pau restaurant in Cunit, south of Barcelona. And he should know, for his grandfather Pau was a fisherman – besides being a great cook and restaurateur. This is why Xavier named the restaurant after him, *avi* being Catalan for grandfather.

Peix a l'all cremat is a very popular dish in Catalonia, but L'Avi Pau's rendition is the inspiration for this recipe. It makes a nice first course, and is light enough to carry over to the main dish. I usually prefer to serve it accompanied by a medium-bodied red wine.   *Serves 6.*

60 ml (4 tbsp) olive oil
1 large head garlic, or about 20 large
    cloves, peeled and cut into slivers
225 g (8 oz) ripe tomatoes, seeded and
    finely chopped

700 g (1½ lb) sea bass fillets or other firm,
    white, fresh fish, cut into 6 pieces
2.5 ml (½ tsp) salt

In Spain, this dish traditionally would be cooked and served in a clay casserole; but if you don't have that, use any flameproof casserole or non-metallic pan with high sides, large enough to hold the fish fillets in a single layer.

Heat the oil and add the garlic; cook slowly over a low heat until the garlic is dark brown – 10–15 minutes. Keep stirring so it does not turn black and burn – but it should be really dark brown (this will give the colour and wonderful flavour to the sauce). Add the tomatoes and continue to cook, over medium to low heat, until all the liquid has evaporated. Add 450 ml (¾ pint) water, bring to the boil and reduce by about half. Add the fish fillets in a single layer and sprinkle with salt. Reduce the heat to medium and cook the fish, turning it once, for 3–4 minutes on each side, depending on the thickness of the fillets. Serve immediately, from the same casserole.

Zarzuela de Mariscos

· CATALAN – SARSUELA DE MARISC ·

· SHELLFISH STEW, BARCELONA STYLE ·

Catalans are known for their love of music, as are most Spaniards. There is a Catalan saying, 'Pinch a man on the streets of Barcelona – if he doesn't cry out in tune he's not Catalan.' Our love of music and food combine in this dish, a classic recipe from the area around Barcelona. *Zarzuela* is the Spanish term for light opera or operetta. As most seafood lovers would agree, the dish is a colourful production worthy of Gilbert and Sullivan.

Zarzuela is featured in a number of seafood restaurants in Barcelona. One of them, Casa Costa (a lively place in the popular seaport quarter), serves a special rendition with lobster, called '*Ópera*' to signify that it's even better – the ultimate.

One of my favourite places for *zarzuela* is Peixerot, a delightful old restaurant in the fishing village of Vilanova i la Geltrú, south of Barcelona, owned by brothers Jordi, Joan and Josep Mestres. I have spent many a lovely summer evening dining on the restaurant patio, enjoying their excellent fish preparations. *Serves 6.*

125 ml (4 fl oz) olive oil
2 large onions, finely chopped
2 large red or green sweet peppers, preferably red, cored, seeded and cut into thin strips lengthways
50 g (2 oz) lean prosciutto, cut into strips
1.4 kg (3 lb) tomatoes, skinned, seeded and chopped
4 large cloves garlic, finely chopped
50 g (2 oz) ground almonds
2.5 ml (½ tsp) saffron threads
3 bay leaves
5 ml (1 tsp) dried thyme
5 ml (1 tsp) rosemary leaves or 2.5 ml (½ tsp) dried
10 ml (2 tsp) salt, or to taste

2.5 ml (½ tsp) freshly ground black pepper, or to taste
2.5 ml (½ tsp) crushed hot red pepper flakes
225 ml (8 fl oz) dry white wine
750 ml (1¼ pints) Fish Fumet (p. 194)
15 ml (1 tbsp) lemon juice
12 small clams, shells scrubbed
12 small mussels, shells scrubbed
6 large prawns in the shell
450 g (1 lb) scallops
700 g (1½ lb) squid, cleaned and cut into rings (see Rice in a Casserole with Shellfish, p. 165)
AS A GARNISH
6 lemon wedges

In a large flameproof casserole, heat the oil and fry the onions and peppers for 5 minutes or until soft. Stir in the prosciutto and cook for 3–4 minutes. Add the tomatoes and cook rapidly until all the liquid has evaporated. Stir in the garlic, almonds, saffron, bay leaves, thyme, rosemary, salt, pepper, pepper flakes, wine, fumet and lemon juice. Bring to the boil. Add the clams and mussels; cover, reduce the heat to medium and cook for 10 minutes. Add the prawns, scallops and squid and cook for a further 5 minutes. Taste for seasoning and serve from the casserole, garnished with lemon wedges.

Romesco de Pescados

· CATALAN – ROMESCO DE PEIX ·

· FISH STEW, TARRAGONA STYLE ·

Tarragona and the nearby district of El Vendrell are the home of romesco, the sauce which originated from the fisherman-style preparation for the local fish. Practically all restaurants in the area serve romesco as a sauce, but only a few serve the dish romesco de pescados; one of my favourites is Casa Morros in Torredembarra, near Tarragona, where it is one of Juan Morros's specialities.

The dried nyoras peppers, found all along the Mediterranean coast from Catalonia to Murcia, are the key to this dish. They are round, small, dark red peppers, with just a trace of spiciness and extremely flavourful. Unfortunately they do not exist in the United States or Britain, but I have found that ancho or pasilla chillis (also called dried poblanos or pisados) work very well. If you cannot find these, any other kind of sweet-mild, flavourful dried chilli peppers will do.   Serves 6–8.

2 dried sweet red chilli peppers
65 g (2½ oz) whole almonds
45–75 ml (3–5 tbsp) olive oil
2 large slices of white bread, cut 1 cm
  (½ inch) thick
4 large cloves garlic, finely chopped
1 medium onion, finely chopped
225 ml (8 fl oz) dry white wine

450 ml (¾ pint) Fish Fumet (p. 194)
5 ml (1 tsp) salt, or to taste
1.25 ml (¼ tsp) freshly ground black
  pepper, or to taste
1.4 kg (3 lb) fish fillets, cut into 18
  chunks, you may use one or more types
  of fish: red mullet, cod, sea bass, etc.

Preheat the oven to 180°c (350°F) mark 4.

Place the chillis in a saucepan and cover them with water. Bring to the boil, reduce heat to low and simmer for 10 minutes. Turn off the heat, cover and leave to stand for 45 minutes. Reserve 225 ml (8 fl oz) of the soaking water. Core, seed and peel the chillis. Set aside.

Toast the almonds in the oven for 15 minutes. Grind them very finely. Set aside.

Heat 30–45 ml (2–3 tbsp) oil in a frying pan and fry the bread until golden. Set aside.

Fry the garlic and onion in 15–30 ml (1–2 tbsp) oil over a very low heat until soft and golden – at least 20 minutes. (You may add small amounts of water if they dry out.) Add the wine, increase the heat and cook briskly until reduced to 50 ml (2 fl oz). Purée in a food processor or blender with the chillis, almonds, bread, the reserved water from soaking the chillis and the fumet. Season with 2.5 ml (½ tsp) salt and the pepper.

Pour the sauce into a large frying pan and heat through. Season the fish with the remaining salt, add to the sauce and turn to coat. Reduce the heat to low and cook, covered, for about 10 minutes or until the fillets are done. Taste for seasoning. The sauce should not be further reduced; this is a rather soupy stew. Serve with lots of bread to dip in the sauce!

'Suquet' de Pescado

· CATALAN – SUQUET DE PEIX ·

· FISH STEW WITH POTATOES, COSTA BRAVA STYLE ·

This is an old classic dish from the fishermen of the Costa Brava, the dramatic coast north of Barcelona. Many restaurants serve it, and each recipe is very different; this comes from Big Rock, in the fishing village of Palamós, where Carles Camós serves some truly authentic local fisherman dishes.

As is traditional with fisherman-style preparations, this is served with Garlic Mayonnaise (Allioli) on the side, which indeed offers a nice contrast between the sweetness of the red peppers and onions in the dish and the sharpness of the garlic in the sauce. *Serves 6.*

FOR THE SOFRITO
125 ml (4 fl oz) olive oil
4 large onions, finely chopped
2 large red sweet peppers, cored, seeded
　and finely chopped
450 g (1 lb) ripe tomatoes, skinned,
　seeded and chopped
FOR THE FISH AND POTATOES
45 ml (3 tbsp) olive oil
900 g (2 lb) fresh firm white fish fillets,
　such as red mullet, cut into pieces
plain flour for coating the fish
3 large cloves garlic, finely chopped
30 ml (2 tbsp) chopped parsley
125 ml (4 fl oz) full-bodied Spanish
　brandy

900 ml (1½ pints) Fish Fumet (p. 194)
450 g (1 lb) potatoes, peeled and thinly
　sliced
5 ml (1 tsp) salt, or to taste
2.5 ml (½ tsp) freshly ground black
　pepper, or to taste
FOR THE PICADA
25 g (1 oz) whole almonds
15 ml (1 tbsp) olive oil
1 thin slice of white bread, about 15 g
　(½ oz)
2 large cloves garlic
AS AN ACCOMPANIMENT
1 quantity Garlic Mayonnaise (p. 199)

To prepare the *sofrito* In a large flameproof casserole, preferably earthenware, heat the oil and fry the onions and peppers over a medium to low heat. The secret to this dish is in frying the onions and peppers for a very long time – 45 minutes to 1 hour – until the onions are almost caramelized. Towards the end you may have to reduce the heat to low, perhaps even add a little water so the vegetables don't burn – but they must be very brown. Add the tomatoes and cook until all the liquid has evaporated.

To cook the fish and potatoes Heat the oil in a frying pan large enough to accommodate all of the fish. Coat the fish with the flour and fry over a medium heat very briefly on both sides. Set the fish aside, draining on kitchen paper. Add the garlic and parsley to the pan and fry until the garlic is soft. Add the brandy and cook over a high heat until almost evaporated. Transfer the contents of the pan to the casserole with the vegetable mixture; add the fumet and potatoes. Bring to the boil and cook over a medium to low heat for about 20 minutes or longer, until the potatoes are tender. Season with salt and pepper.

To prepare the *picada* Preheat the oven to 180°c (350°F) mark 4. Toast the almonds in the oven for 15 minutes. In a small frying pan, heat the olive oil and, when very hot, fry the bread until golden on both sides. In a food processor, very finely grind the almonds, fried bread and garlic.

When the potatoes are tender, stir in the *picada*. Add the fish fillets and cook for a further 7 minutes, until the fish is cooked.

Serve warm, handing the *allioli* separately so guests can have as much or as little as they want – depending on how much they like garlic.

Langosta con Pollo 'Mar y Montaña'

· CATALAN – LLAGOSTA AMB POLLASTRE 'MAR I MUNTANYA' ·

· LOBSTER AND CHICKEN WITH NUTS AND CHOCOLATE ·

This unusual combination, with its *picada* which includes not only the traditional hazelnuts, garlic and herbs, but also chocolate, is a speciality of Catalan cuisine and specifically of L'Empordà. It is a classic dish from the Costa Brava, north of Barcelona, where it originated at the beginning of this century.

One of my favourite versions is that of Eldorado Petit, the great restaurant in Sant Felíu de Guixols. Lluís Cruañas calls the dish *mar i muntanya*, or 'sea and mountain', because of the combination of produce from both areas in L'Empordà. Lluís feels it is one of the most elegant and interesting Catalan recipes – and I certainly agree with him.   *Serves 8.*

3–4 lobsters, total weight about 2.8 kg (6 lb)

FOR THE BROTH
30 ml (2 tbsp) olive oil
350 g (12 oz) unpeeled carrots, sliced or coarsely chopped
1 large onion, sliced
25 g (1 oz) celery leaves
2 bay leaves

FOR THE CHICKENS
2 chickens about 1.4 kg (3 lb) each, cut into 8 pieces, livers reserved
5 ml (1 tsp) salt
2.5 ml (½ tsp) freshly ground black pepper
30 ml (2 tbsp) olive oil

FOR THE SOFRITO
450 g (1 lb) onions, chopped

700 g (1½ lb) tomatoes, skinned, seeded and chopped
225 ml (8 fl oz) dry white wine

FOR THE PICADA
65 g (2½ oz) hazelnuts
100 g (4 oz) unsweetened baking chocolate
6 large cloves garlic
25 g (1 oz) chopped parsley
30 ml (2 tbsp) chopped thyme or 5 ml (1 tsp) dried
15 ml (1 tbsp) chopped oregano or 5 ml (1 tsp) dried
10 ml (2 tsp) orange zest (p. 31)
2.5 ml (½ tsp) saffron threads or 1.25 ml (¼ tsp) powdered saffron
2.5 ml (½ tsp) ground cinnamon

To prepare the lobsters   In a large saucepan, bring about 4.5 litres (8 pints) water to the boil. Drop in 1 lobster at a time – it will turn pink. As soon as it stops moving – a minute or two – remove the lobster from the pot and set aside. Bring the water back to a rapid boil before dropping in the next lobster. Let the lobsters cool, and reserve the water.

When the lobsters have cooled enough to handle, remove their tails: grasp the body in one hand and the tail in the other, twist the tail and pull; it will come free easily. Remove the claws in the same manner. Cut each tail (complete with shell) crossways into 2 or 3 pieces (depending on size). Set aside the tails and claws. (In order to make it easier to remove the tail meat from the shell at the table, you may cut off the inner membrane/shell with a pair of scissors.)

To prepare the broth   Heat the oil in a pan and fry the carrots and onion until soft – 6–8 minutes. Add to the saucepan with the reserved water, together with the lobster bodies, celery and bay leaves. Bring to the boil, reduce the heat to low and simmer, partially covered, for 30 minutes. Strain the broth and pour it back into the pan. Cook it over high heat until reduced to 1.4 litres (2½ pints). Set aside.

To prepare the chickens Poach the chicken livers in simmering water to cover for 10 minutes; drain and reserve the livers. Pat the chicken pieces dry, and season with salt and pepper. In a large frying pan, heat 30 ml (2 tbsp) oil and fry the chicken pieces, over a medium heat, until golden. Set them aside. Pour off the fat, leaving about 30 ml (2 tbsp) in the pan.

To cook lobsters and chickens in the *sofrito* Add the onions to the fat in the pan, and fry over a low heat until soft. Add the tomatoes and cook until all the liquid has evaporated. Add the wine and cook until it has evaporated. Transfer this mixture to the large pan with the reduced broth. Add the chicken pieces and cook for 20 minutes over a medium heat, covered. Add the lobster tails and claws; cook for 10 minutes.

Remove the chicken and lobster pieces from the sauce (reserve sauce) to a large, deep ovenproof platter; in Spain we traditionally use an earthenware casserole. Arrange the lobster and chicken pieces decoratively, except for the claws. Transfer these to a cutting board, and remove the meat from the claws by cracking the shells soundly with a hammer. Add the meat from the claws to the serving platter; keep warm.

To prepare the *picada* Preheat the oven to 180°c (350°f) mark 4. Toast the hazelnuts in the oven for 12 minutes and rub them in a damp tea-towel to remove most of the skins. In a food processor, blend the hazelnuts with the chicken livers and remaining *picada* ingredients.

To assemble the dish Stir the *picada* into the reserved sauce. Cook for 5 minutes, stirring; taste for seasoning. Pour the sauce over the chicken and lobster pieces on the platter, and serve immediately.

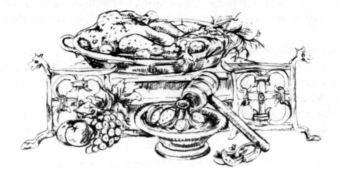

POULTRY AND GAME

Pollo Escabechado

· *CHICKEN MARINATED IN VINEGAR AND WINE, SPICES AND HERBS* ·

Start preparation 1 or 2 days in advance

Aranda de Duero is a small town between Burgos and Segovia, in the middle of the northern Castilian Plateau. One good reason for going there is to dine at Mesón de la Villa and visit its hospitable owners, Eugenio and Seri Herrero; he with his colourful moustache and she with her warm, motherly disposition are the friendliest hosts you can imagine.

Escabeche is an old way of cooking and preserving food, a legacy from the Arabs; although originally introduced along the Mediterranean, today it is most representative of northern Castile – and one of Seri's specialities. She prepares *escabechados* of fowl and small game, such as quail, partridge, rabbit and chicken; I chose this recipe because chicken is most widely available here.   *Serves 4–6.*

1 × 1.6 kg (3½ lb) ovenready chicken	*5 ml (1 tsp) salt*
125 ml (4 fl oz) olive oil	*15 ml (1 tbsp) dried thyme*
3 large onions, thinly sliced	*6 bay leaves*
1 head garlic, peeled, left in whole cloves	*8 whole cloves*
450 ml (¾ pint) red wine vinegar	*15 black peppercorns, lightly crushed*
450 ml (¾ pint) medium-bodied dry red	AS A GARNISH
wine	*12 sprigs watercress*

Prick the chicken all over with a skewer. Pat it dry.

Heat the oil in a large flameproof casserole. Over a medium to high heat, sauté the chicken on all sides until lightly golden. Remove from the casserole and set aside.

In the same oil, fry the onions over a medium heat until soft and golden. Return the chicken to the casserole, breast side down. Add all the remaining ingredients and bring to the boil. Reduce the heat to low, cover and cook for 45 minutes, turning the chicken once.

Cut up the chicken into serving pieces and place them in a bowl. Pour the contents of casserole over the chicken. Cover and refrigerate for at least 1 day and up to 4 days.

Remove the surface fat; bring to room temperature before serving. Arrange the chicken pieces, onions and herbs in a single layer in an earthenware casserole or on a serving platter. Garnish with watercress sprigs and serve immediately.

Pollo en Pepitoria de Rosalía

· ROSALÍA'S CHICKEN STEW WITH VEGETABLES ·

This is a homely, good chicken stew recipe dating from the sixteenth century, when the Provence region of southern France was a part of Catalonia. It was the favourite chicken recipe of Rosalía, my parents' cook – and I think her best.   *Serves 4.*

1×1.6 kg (3½ lb) ovenready chicken, cut
   into 8 serving pieces
8.75 ml (1¾ tsp) salt
3.75 ml (¾ tsp) freshly ground black
   pepper
30 ml (2 tbsp) olive oil
16 pickling onions, peeled
350 g (12 oz) carrots, peeled and sliced
   into 1 cm (½ inch) rounds
8 small new potatoes, unpeeled

1 bay leaf
225 ml (8 fl oz) dry white wine
450 ml (¾ pint) Chicken Stock (p. 191)
FOR THE PICADA
65 g (2½ oz) whole almonds
3 large cloves garlic, peeled
2.5 ml (½ tsp) saffron threads or 1.25 ml
   (¼ tsp) powdered saffron
3 hard-boiled eggs

Pat the chicken dry and season with 1.25 ml (¼ tsp) each salt and pepper. Heat the oil in a large frying pan and, over a medium to high heat, brown the chicken pieces. Transfer them to a large flameproof casserole. Add the onions and carrots to the frying pan and cook them, stirring, for 10 minutes or until they start to brown. Add them to the casserole, and arrange the potatoes around the chicken. Tuck the bay leaf in the middle, and sprinkle with the remaining salt and pepper.

Remove most of the fat in the pan and deglaze with the wine. Cook over a high heat, stirring and scraping, for 2–3 minutes; pour the liquid over the chicken in the casserole. Add the stock and bring to the boil. Reduce the heat to very low, cover and simmer for 45 minutes. Remove the chicken and vegetables and set aside. Discard the bay leaf.

To prepare the *picada*   In a food processor, finely grind the almonds with the garlic; add the saffron and egg yolks (reserve the whites). Add enough liquid from the casserole to form a paste.

Whisk the *picada* into the casserole and boil to reduce the liquid to about 450 ml (¾ pint). Taste for seasoning. Return the chicken and vegetables to the casserole and turn to coat in the sauce. Chop the egg whites and sprinkle over as a garnish.

Pollo con Salsa de Naranja y Menta

· CHICKEN IN ORANGE AND MINT SAUCE ·

The Arabs brought mint and oranges to Spain, and this dish combines both ingredients in an unusual recipe of definite Arab influence.   *Serves 4–6.*

3 boneless chicken breasts, cut in half,
  skinned
2.5 ml (½ tsp) freshly ground black pepper
2.5 ml (½ tsp) salt
30 ml (2 tbsp) olive oil
125 ml (4 fl oz) oloroso or other medium-
  dry, flavourful Spanish sherry

225 ml (8 fl oz) orange juice
150 ml (¼ pint) Chicken Stock (p. 191)
30 ml (2 tbsp) orange zest (p. 31)
30 ml (2 tbsp) chopped mint
AS A GARNISH
4–6 thin orange slices
a few sprigs fresh mint

Season the chicken breasts with salt and pepper. Heat the oil in a large frying pan and, over a high heat, sauté the chicken pieces very briefly, just until they start to brown, to seal. Transfer the chicken to a plate.

Deglaze the pan with the sherry. Add the orange juice, chicken stock and orange zest. Bring to the boil, then turn heat down to low and add the chicken breasts with their juices. Simmer, uncovered, for 10 minutes or until the chicken pieces are done. Turn them over once while cooking. Transfer the chicken to a serving platter and keep warm.

Bring the liquid to a rolling boil and add the mint. Reduce to about 175 ml (6 fl oz). Taste for seasoning.

Pour the sauce over the chicken. Serve garnished with orange slices and mint sprigs.

Pollito de Grano al Vino de Jerez

· CHICKEN FLAVOURED WITH SHERRY, IN A SHERRY SAUCE ·

Start preparation 9 hours ahead or the day before, by injecting the chicken with the sherries

Here is another outstanding creation from Madrid's El Amparo, the restaurant where Ramón Ramírez has developed some of the most imaginative recipes of today's

Spanish cuisine. Ramón is from Málaga, and this dish has a clear Andalusian inspiration.

To prepare it you will need a flavour injector – and if you've never used one, you are in for a treat. I find it so much fun to inject the sherry into the chicken that I always have trouble sticking to the maximum 125 ml (4 fl oz) indicated in the recipe! *Serves 4.*

FOR THE CHICKEN
1 × 1.6 kg (3½ lb) ovenready chicken
75–125 ml (3–4 fl oz) oloroso or other
   flavourful medium-dry Spanish sherry
75–125 ml (3–4 fl oz) fino or other
   flavourful dry Spanish sherry
salt and freshly ground black pepper
FOR THE SAUCE
125 ml (4 fl oz) sherry wine vinegar

350 ml (12 fl oz) Chicken Stock (p. 191)
225 ml (8 fl oz) double cream .
125 ml (4 fl oz) oloroso or other
   flavourful medium-dry Spanish sherry
2.5 ml (½ tsp) salt
1.25 ml (¼ tsp) freshly ground white
   pepper

To prepare the chicken At least 8 hours before cooking (or the day before), inject the chicken with the sherries, using a flavour injector fitted with a needle, making several punctures. Inject the oloroso sherry into the breast and wings, and the fino into the legs. Turn the chicken over, to inject the back of the thighs. Cover and refrigerate until 1 hour before cooking time.

Preheat the oven to 200°C (400°F) mark 6.

Rub the inside of the chicken with salt and pepper. (Reserve any sherry and juices drained from the chicken.) Place the chicken in a roasting pan, breast side up, and bake in the oven for 45 minutes; it should be slightly underdone. Transfer the chicken to a board and cut it into 4 serving pieces.

To prepare the sauce With a spoon, remove most of the fat from the pan. Add the vinegar and deglaze the pan over a high heat; transfer the mixture to a frying pan or casserole large enough to accommodate the chicken quarters. Cook the vinegar down to a glaze; add the stock and reserved chicken juices, and reduce to 125 ml (4 fl oz). Add the cream and oloroso; reduce by half, over a medium heat. Add salt and pepper.

To assemble the dish Add the chicken quarters and their juices, turning to coat with the sauce, and cook until the chicken is done. If the sauce is too thin, remove the chicken to a serving platter and reduce to desired consistency. Taste for seasoning. Pour the sauce over the chicken and serve.

Pintada al Melocotón

· SQUAB WITH PEACHES ·

This is one of those recipes from my mother's file for special occasions. *Pintada* is Spanish for the French *pintade* or *pintadeau*, a game bird similar to a guinea fowl. I have found that squab works beautifully in this recipe. *Serves 6.*

6 squabs, 350–450 g (¾–1 lb) each or
  ovenready poussins
salt and freshly ground black pepper
30 ml (2 tbsp) olive oil
40 g (1½ oz) butter
1 large carrot, sliced
1 large onion, sliced
6 large, firm but ripe peaches
900 ml (1½ pints) Brown Veal Stock
  (p. 192)
4 large unpeeled cloves garlic, crushed

1 × 7.5 cm (3 inch) cinnamon stick
50 ml (2 fl oz) full-bodied Spanish
  brandy
50 ml (2 fl oz) orange liqueur, such as
  Grand Marnier or Curaçao
1 bay leaf
3 sprigs parsley
1–2 sprigs fresh thyme
150 ml (¼ pint) balsamic vinegar or a fine
  red wine vinegar
50 g (2 oz) pine nuts

Clean the birds. Pat dry and season lightly with salt and pepper. In a flameproof casserole large enough to hold all the squabs, heat the oil and 30 ml (2 tbsp) of the butter; brown the squabs over a medium heat. Set the squabs aside. Add the carrot and onion and sauté until golden.

Meanwhile, peel the peaches; first dip them briefly – 4 or 5 seconds – in boiling water, then remove the skins. Halve the peaches and reserve them with their stones.

Preheat the oven to 170°c (325°F) mark 3.

Return the squabs to the casserole, over the carrot and onion; add the stock, garlic, cinnamon, brandy, liqueur, herbs and peach stones. Cover the squabs tightly with a double thickness of foil, and cover the casserole with a lid. Cook the squabs in the oven for 30 minutes. Turn the squabs and add the peaches; cover again with foil and the lid, and cook for a further 30 minutes.

Remove the squabs and peaches; cut off the trussing string. Strain the cooking liquid through a fine sieve into a saucepan. Return the squabs and peaches to the casserole; keep warm. Reduce the braising liquid to desired consistency (by about one third). Add the vinegar, and cook for 2–3 minutes. Taste for seasoning.

Meanwhile, heat the remaining butter in a small frying pan and sauté the pine nuts until golden. Add them to the finished sauce. Pour over the peaches and squabs, and serve immediately.

Capones al Agridulce

· CATALAN – CAPONS A L'AGREDOLÇ ·

· POUSSINS IN A SWEET AND SOUR SAUCE ·

Start preparation 9–10 hours ahead or the day before, by marinating poussins

The idea for this recipe came from one of Barcelona's oldest and most prestigious restaurants, Reno. For 30 years it has blended classic and new concepts in traditional cooking under the direction of Josep Juliá. Reno is a serious, elegant restaurant: attentive service, select ingredients and skillful preparation have combined to assure continuity of quality over the years.

The sweet and sour combination, found all over the Mediterranean, is a legacy from the Arabs. It enhances a mild bird, such as poussin, giving it a spicy, flavourful appeal.   *Serves 4.*

4 ovenready poussins, about 700 g (1½ lb)
  each
FOR THE MARINADE
450 ml (¾ pint) red wine vinegar
10 ml (2 tsp) ground cloves
25 g (1 oz) chopped mint
FOR THE POUSSINS
30 ml (2 tbsp) olive oil
25 g (1 oz) butter
2 medium onions, chopped

5 ml (1 tsp) salt
1.25 ml (¼ tsp) freshly ground black
  pepper
450 ml (¾ pint) Chicken Stock (p. 191)
90 g (3½ oz) sugar
125 ml (4 fl oz) red wine vinegar
125 ml (4 fl oz) full-bodied Spanish
  brandy
AS A GARNISH
a few sprigs fresh mint

Pat the poussins dry. Prick them all over with a skewer.

To prepare the marinade   Place the poussins in a non-metallic bowl and pour the vinegar over them. Add the cloves and mint; toss to coat. Cover and refrigerate for at least 8 hours, turning the poussins several times.

Remove the poussins from the refrigerator 2 hours before cooking. Discard the marinade, and wipe the poussins dry with kitchen paper. Set aside.

To prepare the hens   In a flameproof casserole, large enough to hold all the poussins, heat the oil and butter. Over a medium to low heat, fry the onions until soft. Add the poussins to the casserole and sprinkle with salt and pepper; pour over the stock. Bring to the boil and immediately reduce the heat to low; cover tightly with a double thickness of foil, place the lid over the casserole and simmer gently for 30 minutes.

Preheat the oven to 180°c (350°F) mark 4.

Remove the poussins from the casserole, reserving the stock; brush off the onion clinging to them and put the poussins in a roasting pan. Brush them with olive oil and bake in the oven, uncovered, for 30 minutes.

Meanwhile, strain the stock from the casserole and discard the onions. Skim the stock and return it to the casserole. In a small saucepan, caramelize the sugar (p. 33): dissolve the sugar in 15–30 ml (1–2 tbsp) water; over a medium to high heat, cook until it turns golden brown. Pour the caramelized sugar into the casserole with the stock; it will hiss and solidify, but don't worry – it will melt later. Add the vinegar and cook over a high heat until reduced to 350 ml (12 fl oz).

When the poussins are cooked, place them on a serving platter and keep warm. Pour off the fat from the roasting pan and deglaze with the brandy; add the mixture to the sauce.

To assemble the dish   Pour some of the sauce over the poussins and garnish with mint sprigs. Hand the remaining sauce separately in a sauce-boat.

MAKING AN ESSENCE OF MEAT FOR POULTRY AND GAME DISHES

In the following recipes I have incorporated a cooking technique from my friend and teacher Madeleine Kamman, who has mastered the concept of essences of meat. It involves making a double stock – that is, cooking the necks, wings, backs and other bones in a basic brown veal stock for a long time. If you do not feel up to the task, you can simply simmer these in water for 25 minutes to make a broth, skim it and reduce to about 225 ml (8 fl oz). But if you appreciate the little extra flavour in your sauces, the additional effort involved in making a veal stock to prepare the essence will be worthwhile.

Pato con Aceitunas

· CATALAN – ÀNEC AMB OLIVES ·

· DUCK WITH OLIVES ·

This recipe was given to me by Xavier Grifoll, chef of a little restaurant in Barcelona called Tiró Mimet. *Tiró* in old Catalan means duck, and that's Xavier's speciality. He once owned a restaurant in La Cerdanya, the northern region of Catalonia bordering on France at the Pyrenees Mountains, where one of the classic dishes is duck with turnips; a special kind of turnips, though, not at all like ours, as I found out after several tries. So following his suggestion, I made it with olives – and it was a hit. *Serves 4.*

1 × 1.8–2.3 kg (4–5 lb) duck, cut into 4
   serving pieces, fat, wings, back and
   neck reserved
FOR THE ESSENCE
reserved wings, back and neck of the duck
600 ml (1 pint) Brown Veal Stock
   (p. 192)
FOR THE DUCK
9 large cloves garlic, finely chopped
1 large onion, chopped
1 medium leek, chopped, with ⅓ of the
   green part

2 medium red sweet peppers, cored,
   seeded and cut into thin strips
   lengthways
700 g (1½ lb) unpeeled tomatoes, chopped
125 ml (4 fl oz) full-bodied Spanish
   brandy
125 ml (4 fl oz) dry white wine
175 g (6 oz) green flavourful olives,
   unstoned
25 g (1 oz) chopped parsley

To prepare the essence   Remove the fat from the duck, and most of the skin from reserved wings, back and neck; cut these into small pieces. Fry in a frying pan with 15–30 ml (1–2 tbsp) duck fat, stirring around until they are very brown. Transfer the duck pieces to a medium saucepan. Pour off the fat from the frying pan and deglaze with about 125 ml (4 fl oz) of the stock. Pour the mixture into the saucepan. Add some more stock and simmer, uncovered, over a very low heat. Keep turning the pieces over and adding more stock, little by little, as it evaporates. Cook for about 2 hours, or until reduced to 225 ml (8 fl oz). Strain the essence and reserve. Discard the bones.

To prepare the duck In a large flameproof casserole, fry the duck breasts and legs over a low heat until golden on all sides – about 30 minutes. The duck exudes its own fat, so you will not need to add any to the pan. Set the breasts and legs aside.

Pour off all but 30–45 ml (2–3 tbsp) of the fat. Add the garlic, onion and leek; fry slowly until soft – about 10 minutes. Add the peppers and tomatoes, and cook over a medium heat until all the liquid has evaporated. Add the brandy and, when hot, flambé (pp. 32–3). When the flames subside, add the wine and bring to the boil. Stir in the olives and parsley. Return the duck breasts and legs to the casserole, cover and simmer over a very low heat for about 1 hour.

To assemble the dish Add the reserved essence. If the sauce is too thin, remove the duck to a platter and cook the sauce over a high heat until reduced to desired consistency. Taste for seasoning, adding salt and pepper if necessary. Serve duck directly from the casserole, or arrange it on a serving platter, covering with the sauce.

Pato con Higos

· CATALAN – ÀNEC AMB FIGUES ·

· DUCK WITH FIGS ·

This is a delightful example of the traditional Catalan way to cook meats or poultry with fruits. Some of the finest ducks I've eaten come from L'Empordà, the bountiful region in northeast Catalonia, and are often cooked with pears, apples or other fruits.

Agut d'Avignon, the outstanding restaurant in the picturesque old part of Barcelona, near the Ramblas promenade, features duck with figs among other classic specialities of L'Empordà. The late owner Ramón Cabau told me he prefers to make the dish with dried figs, although I've made it with both fresh and dried and enjoyed them equally – but following his advice, my recipe calls for dried figs. *Serves 4.*

225 g (8 oz) dried figs
1 × 1.8–2.3 kg (4–5 lb) duck, cut into 4
    serving pieces, liver, fat, wings, back
    and neck reserved (see Note below)
FOR THE ESSENCE
reserved wings, back and neck of the
    duck
600 ml (1 pint) Brown Veal Stock
    (p. 192)

FOR THE DUCK
salt and freshly ground black pepper
225 ml (8 fl oz) dry Spanish sherry,
    preferably amontillado or a dry oloroso
FOR THE SAUCE
zest and juice of 1 large orange (p. 31)
30 ml (2 tbsp) finest-quality Spanish
    brandy
pinch of ground cinnamon

(Note: You will need the duck's liver for this recipe; if there isn't one, substitute 3 chicken livers.)

Cover the figs with 225 ml (8 fl oz) boiling water and soak for 2 hours. Stem the figs and reserve the figs and water.

To prepare the essence   Proceed as described in the previous recipe on pp. 112–13.

To cook the duck   Pat the duck pieces dry with kitchen paper and season with salt and pepper. In a frying pan with a lid, heat some of the duck fat and, over a medium to high heat, brown the duck quarters. Pour off the fat, add 125 ml (4 fl oz) of the sherry, cover tightly with a double thickness of foil and the lid. Braise for 45 minutes over a low heat.

To prepare the sauce   Simmer the liver in 50–125 ml (2–4 fl oz) reserved fig soaking water – just to cover – for 15 minutes. In a food processor or blender, purée the drained liver with 4 of the figs; add the orange zest and juice, brandy, cinnamon and liquid from simmering the livers. Reserve the sauce.

To assemble the dish   Set the duck quarters aside and skim the contents of the pan. Add the remaining sherry and cook until reduced by about half. Stir in the reserved sauce, duck essence and fig soaking water. Return the duck to the pan. Add the remaining figs, cover and cook for 20 minutes. Remove the duck and figs to a serving platter and keep warm.

Reduce the sauce further, if necessary, to desired consistency. Taste for seasoning. Pour some sauce over the duck and hand the remaining sauce separately in a sauce-boat.

Perdiz con 'Farcellets' de Col a la Ampurdanesa

· CATALAN – *PERDIU AMB FARCELLETS DE COL A L'EMPORDANESA* ·

· *PARTRIDGE WITH CABBAGE CROQUETTES, L'EMPORDÀ STYLE* ·

Partridge with cabbage is one of the oldest dishes of classic Catalan cooking, traced back to the fifteenth century. In a very Catalan way, the cabbage is cooked with the birds and made into croquettes (*farcellets*), which are absolutely delicious.

Partridge is prepared in many different ways all over Catalonia. In Barcelona, partridge with cabbage is served at several Catalan restaurants. I have particularly enjoyed it at Quo Vadis, an old, prestigious establishment which specializes in classic dishes of the area prepared with top-quality local produce; owner Martí Forcada, an enthusiast of Catalan cooking, willingly shared his recipe with me. The following is a combination of Martí's recipe and an old recipe from L'Empordà district in northern Catalonia, given to me by my friend, gastronomic historian Manuel Martínez-Llopis. *Serves 8.*

FOR THE PARTRIDGES
900 ml (1½ pints) Chicken Stock (p. 191)
1 large green cabbage, cored and
    quartered
8 ovenready partridges, necks and feet
    reserved
8 rashers bacon, rinded
salt and freshly ground black pepper
pinch of freshly grated nutmeg
30 ml (2 tbsp) olive oil
450 g (1 lb) carrots, chopped
1 large onion, chopped

4 large cloves garlic, finely chopped
15 ml (1 tbsp) chopped oregano or 5 ml
    (1 tsp) dried
15 ml (1 tbsp) chopped thyme or 5 ml
    (1 tsp) dried
4 cloves
350 ml (12 fl oz) medium-bodied dry red
    wine
FOR THE FARCELLETS
1 egg, beaten
plain flour for coating
olive oil for frying .

To prepare the partridges In a large saucepan, bring the stock to the boil and add the cabbage. Reduce the heat and cook for 20 minutes, covered. Drain the cabbage and separate the leaves; reserve the cabbage and stock.

Pat the partridges dry. Loosen the skin covering their breasts and slide ½ bacon rasher under the skin of each bird. Season with salt, pepper and nutmeg. Heat the oil in a large flameproof casserole. Cut the remaining bacon into small strips and fry over a low heat for 5 minutes. Add the partridges, increase the heat to medium-high and sauté until lightly golden. (Add the feet and necks too, if you have them.) Set the partridges aside.

Reduce the heat to medium-low and add the carrots, onion and garlic; fry for 15 minutes, or until soft and golden. Add the herbs, cloves, wine and reserved chicken stock. Bring to the boil, place the partridges on top and cover with the cabbage leaves. Cover the casserole with a lid and cook over a low heat for 1 hour.

Drain the cabbage leaves and set aside. Remove the partridges to a serving platter and keep warm. Strain the contents of casserole through a fine sieve and return the sauce to the casserole. Increase the heat to high and reduce to about 450 ml (¾ pint).

To prepare the *farcellets* Form the cabbage leaves into 5 cm (2 inch) dumplings; don't roll the leaves, just press with the palms of your hands to shape them into tight balls. Put the egg and flour in separate shallow bowls. Dip each cabbage ball first into the egg and then into the flour to coat. Have a frying pan ready with hot oil to a depth of 5 cm (1 inch) and, over a medium to high heat, sauté the cabbage dumplings until golden. Drain on kitchen paper.

To assemble the dish Arrange the *farcellets* around the partridges, pour some sauce over and hand the rest separately in a sauce-boat.

Conejo con Hierbas al Vino Tinto

· CATALAN – CONILL AMB HERBES AL VI NEGRE ·

· RABBIT COOKED IN RED WINE WITH HERBS ·

Start preparation at least 8 hours ahead or the day before, by marinating the rabbit

Here's a recipe from the great cook in my family, Aunt Oriola. You will love this dish; it is a classic Catalan combination, mixing chocolate and almonds with the traditional Catalan herbs: rosemary, thyme, oregano and bay leaves.   *Serves 8.*

FOR THE MARINADE
1 × 750 ml (1¼ pint) bottle full-bodied dry red wine
3 large cloves garlic, finely chopped
2 bay leaves
30 ml (2 tbsp) finely chopped herbs, such as oregano, rosemary and thyme, if dried, use 15 ml (1 tbsp)
3 large shallots, finely chopped
2 rabbits, total weight about 2.3 kg (5 lb), cut into quarters
FOR THE RABBITS
30 ml (2 tbsp) olive oil

150 ml (¼ pint) full-bodied Spanish brandy
1 × 7.5 cm (3 inch) stick cinnamon
50 g (2 oz) unsweetened cooking chocolate, grated or chopped
1.1 kg (2½ lb) tomatoes, skinned, seeded and chopped
2.5 ml (½ tsp) salt, or to taste
2.5 ml (½ tsp) freshly ground black pepper, or to taste
30 ml (2 tbsp) lemon juice
AS A GARNISH
100 g (4 oz) flaked almonds, toasted

To prepare the marinade   In a large non-metallic bowl, mix the wine, garlic, bay leaves, herbs and shallots. Add the rabbit and marinate for at least 6 hours, covered and refrigerated. Turn the pieces occasionally. Pat the rabbit dry and reserve the marinade.

To cook the rabbit   Heat the oil in a large flameproof casserole. Brown the rabbit pieces over a medium heat. Set them aside.

Deglaze the casserole with the brandy. Add the marinating liquid with the herbs and bring to the boil. Stir in the cinnamon stick, chocolate, tomatoes, salt and pepper. Reduce heat to very low and return the rabbit to casserole. Cover and simmer for 1 hour, turning the rabbit pieces occasionally.

To assemble the dish   Transfer the rabbit to a serving platter and keep warm. Discard the cinnamon stick and bay leaves. Increase the heat to high and cook the sauce until reduced by half. Stir in the lemon juice. Taste for seasoning. Pour the sauce over the rabbit and sprinkle the almonds on top just before serving.

Silla de Conejo Rellena con Verduras

· CATALAN – SELLA DE CONILL FARCIDA AMB VERDURES ·

· STUFFED RABBIT SADDLE WITH VEGETABLES ·

Rabbit is eaten a lot in Catalonia, usually grilled, braised or prepared in some country-style fashion. But this is different; here is a truly elegant way of preparing rabbit. It is another recipe inspired by Toya Roqué, chef/owner of the Azulete restaurant in Barcelona. She told me she came up with the idea from her days of cooking in southern France.   *Serves 4.*

1 rabbit, about 1.1 kg (2½ lb), see Note
  below
FOR THE ESSENCE
reserved bones of the rabbit
15 ml (1 tbsp) olive oil
about 450 ml (¾ pint) Brown Veal Stock
  (p. 192)
FOR THE STUFFING
15 ml (1 tbsp) olive oil
50 g (2 oz) finely chopped onion
100 g (4 oz) mushrooms, finely chopped
225 g (8 oz) calf's kidneys
3.75 ml (¾ tsp) salt, or to taste
1.25 ml (¼ tsp) freshly ground black
  pepper, or to taste
150 ml (¼ pint) full-bodied Spanish
  brandy

25 g (1 oz) white breadcrumbs
  (pp. 31–2)
FOR THE VEGETABLE GARNISH
20 pickling onions, peeled, about 900 g
  (2 lb)
3 medium slender carrots, peeled,
  quartered lengthways and cut into
  2.5 cm (1 inch) lengths
20 very small mushrooms, stems trimmed
225 g (8 oz) French beans, topped, tailed
  and cut into 2.5 cm (1 inch) lengths
2.5 ml (½ tsp) salt
50 ml (2 fl oz) Madeira wine or a
  flavourful dry Spanish sherry such as
  amontillado or a dry oloroso

(Note: You will, in fact, need only the body of the rabbit, but you may use the legs for another dish such as Warm Curried Rabbit and Lentil Salad (Ensalada Templada de Lentejas y Conejo al Curry) (p. 77). The rabbit must be boned, which you may do yourself as directed below, or prevail on your butcher to do. Reserve all fat and bones for later use in this recipe.)

Soak the top and bottom of an unglazed earthenware casserole in cold water for at least 15 minutes before use.

To bone the rabbit   Cut off the front and back legs at the joint nearest the body. Using a sharp boning knife, cut and scrape away the meat from the rib cage and backbone so that you will have a large, thin, boneless piece of meat, about 20–25 cm (8–10 inches) long by 12.5–17.5 cm (5–7 inches) wide. If you can't separate the skin from the backbone and you end up with 2 half pieces, don't worry – just patch them together. If there are any holes in the skin, don't worry either. Place the boned rabbit on top of a piece of greaseproof paper, giving it a rectangular shape as much as possible. Overlap any holes, covering them with meat; you should not see the paper through the meat, or the stuffing will ooze out of the holes while the rabbit is cooking. Place another piece of greaseproof paper on top and pound it gently to even out the surface.

To prepare the essence   Cut the rabbit bones into small pieces and sauté in the oil until very brown on all sides. Remove the bones, pour off the fat and deglaze the pan with 125 ml (4 fl oz) stock. Return the bones to the pan and simmer, uncovered, over a very low heat, turning the pieces occasionally. As the liquid evaporates, gradually add the remaining stock. Cook for about 2 hours, or until reduced to 225 ml (8 fl oz). Strain the essence and reserve. Discard the bones.

To prepare the stuffing   Heat the oil in a frying pan and fry the onion over a medium to low heat; after 2–3 minutes, add mushrooms. Meanwhile, cut the kidneys in half lengthways, trim off all the fat and membrane and chop the kidneys finely; add to the onions and mushrooms. Sprinkle with salt and pepper and cook over a low heat for about 5 minutes, stirring often. Add the brandy and, when hot, flambé (pp. 32–3). When the flames subside, add the breadcrumbs. Taste for seasoning. Transfer the mixture to a food processor and pulse just 4 or 5 times (or chop coarsely by hand).

To assemble the rabbit   Place the stuffing in a line down the middle of the boned rabbit. Fold up the ends and sides to cover the filling – like wrapping a parcel. Line the reserved fat along the seams. Tie the string tightly around the rabbit parcel at 2.5 cm (1 inch) intervals, and twice lengthways. Tie it around again between the intervals. It should look like a tiny little bundle, long and narrow.

To cook the rabbit with the vegetables   Drain the water from the casserole. Place the vegetables in the casserole, and put the rabbit over them; sprinkle with salt, and pour the reserved essence and Madeira over. Cover and place the casserole on the middle shelf of a cold oven. Set the temperature to 240°c (475°F) mark 9 and cook for 40 minutes.

To serve the dish   Slice the rabbit and place on a long serving platter, surrounded by the vegetables. Pour some sauce over the rabbit, and hand the remainder separately in a sauce-boat.

Pavo Relleno a la Catalana

· CATALAN – *GALL DINDI FARCIT A LA CATALANA* ·

· ROAST TURKEY STUFFED WITH DRIED FRUITS, NUTS AND SAUSAGE ·

Start preparation at least 7 hours in advance

Turkey is very seldom eaten in Spain, but it is traditional at Christmas. At home we always have it stuffed with prunes, apricots, apples, raisins, pine nuts and sausages: a delicious, very Catalan combination. Before turkey came from America, a rooster (*gall* in Catalan) was used; this tradition goes back to documents of the thirteenth century.

I always wished we'd have it more often than once a year – and by itself. At Christmas, you see, it comes *after* the Meat and Vegetable Stew with a Pasta Soup

(Cocido Catalán or Escudella i Carn d'Olla (p. 130)), by which time I am never able to appreciate it!

There is a consolation, though: just as traditional and wonderful is the *arroz de San Esteban* (rice of St Stephen, the patron saint on Boxing Day), which naturally is made with all the turkey leftovers. And that is a very vivid memory of my childhood Christmases: looking forward to the next day's turkey rice. *Serves 8, with leftovers.*

1 × 5 kg (11 lb) ovenready turkey, neck,
   liver and giblets reserved
FOR THE STOCK
1 large onion, chopped
2 medium unpeeled carrots, chopped
1 small celery stick, chopped
3 sprigs parsley
2 bay leaves
1 sprig thyme, or a pinch of dried
1.4 litres (2½ pints) Chicken Stock
   (p. 191) or water
FOR THE STUFFING
350 g (12 oz) stoned prunes
225 g (8 oz) dried apricots
50 g (2 oz) raisins

50 ml (2 fl oz) olive oil
700 g (1½ lb) mild Italian sausage, sliced
   into 1 cm (½ inch) pieces
150 g (5 oz) pine nuts
450 g (1 lb) tart dessert apples such as
   Granny Smith, peeled and cut into
   2 cm (¾ inch) dice
5 ml (1 tsp) salt
2.5 ml (½ tsp) freshly ground black pepper
FOR THE TURKEY AND ITS SAUCE
10 ml (2 tsp) salt
5 ml (1 tsp) freshly ground black pepper
125 ml (4 fl oz) full-bodied Spanish
   brandy

To prepare the stock Combine the turkey neck, liver and giblets in a large saucepan with all the stock ingredients. Bring to the boil, immediately reduce the heat to very low and cook, almost covered, for 2 hours. Strain the stock and reserve. Discard the neck and innards.

To prepare the stuffing While the stock is cooking, place the prunes, apricots and raisins in a bowl and cover with boiling water. Soak them for about 2 hours. Drain and reserve them. Discard the soaking water.

In a large frying pan, heat the oil and, over a low heat, sauté the sausage and pine nuts until the sausage is cooked and the pine nuts are golden. Add the prunes, apricots, raisins and apples; cook, stirring, for about 5 minutes. Stir in the salt and pepper. Transfer the stuffing to a bowl. Add 125 ml (4 fl oz) of the stock and deglaze the pan. Stir this mixture into the stuffing in the bowl.

Preheat the oven to 180°C (350°F) mark 4.

To cook the turkey Season the inside of the turkey with 5 ml (1 tsp) salt and 2.5 ml (½ tsp) pepper. Stuff it with the fruits, nuts and sausage filling. Truss.

Place the turkey, breast side up, in a roasting pan. Pour 225 ml (8 fl oz) of the stock over the turkey and roast in the oven for 2–2½ hours, or until cooked through. Baste with the stock from time to time, adding more as needed (you may end up using it all – especially if you have an electric oven).

To prepare the sauce Transfer the turkey to a cutting board and pour the juices into a saucepan. Add the brandy to the roasting pan and deglaze it, scraping the sides with a wooden spatula to loosen any sediment stuck to the pan. Pour this mixture into the saucepan with the turkey juices, and add also any remaining stock which was not used for basting. You may reduce it to desired sauce consistency; if you used all or most of the stock for basting, you probably won't need to. Season with the remaining salt and 2.5 ml ($\frac{1}{2}$ tsp) pepper, or to taste. Strain the sauce and hand in a sauce-boat.

MEAT

Mollejas de Ternera al Oporto

· VEAL SWEETBREADS IN A PORT SAUCE ·

Young and talented, Pedro Subijana is a master and a pioneer in the art of cooking. His Akelañe restaurant in San Sebastián is a great exponent of the New Basque Cuisine. This recipe, delicate and elegant, is among my favourites. I usually serve it accompanied by Home-Style White Rice (Arroz Blanco Hervido) (p. 160). *Serves 4–6.*

FOR THE SWEETBREADS
1.4 kg (2½ lb) fresh calf's sweetbreads
15 ml (1 tbsp) lemon juice
25 g (1 oz) butter
30 ml (2 tbsp) olive oil
3.75 ml (¾ tsp) salt, or to taste
2.5 ml (½ tsp) freshly ground black
   pepper, or to taste
FOR THE SAUCE
450 ml (¾ pint) port wine

30 ml (2 tbsp) olive oil
150 g (5 oz) leeks, trimmed and thinly
   sliced
2 celery sticks, chopped
150 g (5 oz) unpeeled carrots, chopped
450 g (1 lb) tomatoes, seeded and
   chopped
225 ml (8 fl oz) Enriched Veal Stock
   (p. 193) or 450 ml (¾ pint) Brown
   Veal Stock (p. 192)

To prepare the sweetbreads Soak the sweetbreads in cold water for 2 hours, changing the water 3 times. Drain the sweetbreads and place them in a saucepan. Cover with cold water and add the lemon juice. Bring to the boil, reduce the heat to low and simmer for 5 minutes. Drain the sweetbreads and immediately plunge them into a bowl of cold water; this will make them firmer. After a few minutes, drain the sweetbreads and separate the kernels, removing the tubes and connecting tissue. The pieces should be smaller than bite size. Pat dry with kitchen paper.

In a frying pan that will accommodate all the sweetbreads in a single layer, heat the butter and oil. When the butter is melted and the oil hot, add the sweetbreads. Sprinkle with salt and pepper. Cook over a medium to high heat, without stirring, for about 3 minutes. Turn the sweetbreads and sauté quickly until lightly browned – about 7 further minutes. With a slotted spoon, remove the sweetbreads from the pan and set aside.

To prepare the sauce   Deglaze the pan with about 125 ml (4 fl oz) of the port, cooking over high heat until reduced to a glaze. Add the oil; fry leek, celery and carrot until soft – 15–20 minutes. Add the tomatoes and cook quickly until all the liquid has evaporated. Transfer to a food processor or blender, and purée with the veal stock.

Add the remaining port to the pan and cook over a high heat until reduced by about half. Strain the puréed vegetable mixture through a fine sieve into the pan with the port and cook over a high heat until reduced to about 350 ml (12 fl oz). Taste for seasoning.

To assemble the dish   Return the sweetbreads to the sauce and heat through. Serve immediately.

Mollejitas a la Salsa de Miel y Vinagre de Jerez

· *CATALAN – PEDRERETS A LA SALSA DE MEL I VINAGRE DE XERÈS* ·

· *SWEETBREADS IN A HONEY AND SHERRY VINEGAR SAUCE* ·

The combination of vinegar and honey in a sauce is characteristic of southern Spain, where the Arab influence is most notable; but this recipe comes from a Catalan chef, Toya Roqué, owner of the Azulete restaurant in Barcelona. Her menu features a wide variety of dishes with different influences, to all of which she has added her ingenious touch.

This dish will combine very well with the flavour of Saffron Rice (Arroz con Azafrán) (p. 161).   *Serves 4–6.*

FOR THE SWEETBREADS
1.4 kg (2¼ lb) fresh calf's or lamb's
   sweetbreads, see Note below
15 ml (1 tbsp) lemon juice
25 g (1 oz) butter
30 ml (2 tbsp) olive oil
2.5 ml (½ tsp) salt
2.5 ml (½ tsp) freshly ground black pepper

FOR THE SAUCE
37.5 ml (2½ tbsp) sherry wine vinegar, or
   to taste
50 ml (2 fl oz) fino sherry, or other
   flavourful dry Spanish sherry
4 shallots, peeled and finely chopped
75 g (3 oz) finely chopped onion
225 ml (8 fl oz) Enriched Veal Stock
   (p. 193) or 450 ml (¾ pint) Brown Veal
   Stock (p. 192)
15 ml (1 tbsp) clear honey

(Note: Toya uses lamb's sweetbreads in her recipe, which are delicious if they can be found fresh. I have made this dish with both lamb's and calf's, and it comes out just as well with either; most important is that the sweetbreads be fresh. Lamb's sweetbreads are smaller and firmer than calf's.)

To prepare the sweetbreads Soak the sweetbreads in cold water for 2 hours and prepare them as described in the previous recipe on pp. 121–2.

In a frying pan that will accommodate all the sweetbreads in a single layer, heat the butter and oil. When the butter is melted and the oil hot, add the sweetbreads. Sprinkle with salt and pepper. Cook over a medium to high heat, without stirring, for about 3 minutes. Turn the sweetbreads and cook quickly until golden – about 7 further minutes. Set the sweetbreads aside.

To prepare the sauce Deglaze the pan with vinegar and sherry; cook over a high heat, stirring, until reduced to a glaze. Reduce the heat to low and add the shallots and onions; fry for about 5 minutes, until soft. Add the veal stock and cook over a high heat until reduced to about 350 ml (12 fl oz). Stir in the honey and taste for seasoning.

To assemble the dish Return the sweetbreads to the pan and turn to coat with the sauce. Serve immediately.

Hojaldre de Mollejas al Aroma de Alcaparras

· *SWEETBREADS IN PUFF PASTRY WITH A CAPER SAUCE* ·

Huelva, in the furthest western province of Andalucía, is probably not a city to which you would think of making a special gastronomic trip; yet La Muralla is a restaurant that could make you change your mind. Luis de la Osa and Bartolomé Albarracín opened it in 1982, and they have devoted themselves to reproducing local dishes which had been forgotten; a remarkable feat which has gained them a well-deserved reputation. Besides, both are tremendously friendly and hospitable – like true Andalusians – and they delight in receiving visitors who show an interest in their food and their accomplishments. This recipe is inspired by a memorable dish I had there. *Serves 6.*

FOR THE PASTRY CASES
1 quantity Puff Pastry (p. 178)
1 egg, beaten
FOR THE SWEETBREADS
700 g (1½ lb) calf's sweetbreads
15 ml (1 tbsp) lemon juice
50 g (2 oz) butter
4 shallots, finely chopped
125 ml (4 fl oz) full-bodied Spanish brandy

225 ml (8 fl oz) Enriched Veal Stock (p. 193) or 450 ml (¾ pint) Brown Veal Stock (p. 192)
125 ml (4 fl oz) double cream
30 ml (2 tbsp) olive oil
1.25 ml (¼ tsp) freshly ground black pepper, or to taste
1.25 ml (¼ tsp) salt, or to taste
45 ml (3 tbsp) capers

Preheat the oven to 220°c (425°F) mark 7.

To prepare the pastry cases Roll out the puff pastry into a rectangular shape about 3 mm ($\frac{1}{8}$ inch) thick. Using a sharp knife, cut into a rectangle exactly 30 × 40 cm (12 × 16 inches). Cut this rectangle into 12 × 10 cm (4 inch) squares. Place 6 of these squares on an ungreased baking sheet. Dip your finger in water and moisten a 1 cm ($\frac{1}{2}$ inch) border around the edge of each square. Using a sharp pointed knife, make a line 1 cm ($\frac{1}{2}$ inch) from the edge of the other 6 squares. (Don't cut all the way through the dough, however, or it will not rise.) Place these 6 squares on top of the other squares on the baking sheet. Try to handle with your fingers as little as possible, and don't pat the edges; the pastry will rise better. Brush the tops with the beaten egg. Bake in the oven for 8 minutes, then reduce the temperature to 190°c (375°F) mark 5 and bake for a further 10–15 minutes, or until the pastry is golden and the bases begin to brown.

Remove the pastry cases from the oven and immediately cut through the square line you made earlier, lifting out the 6 'lids' carefully with a knife. If there is any soft puff pastry inside, scoop it out with a teaspoon and discard it. You now have 6 neat square boxes with lids for your sweetbreads.

(These biscuits may be made up to 3 days ahead, and heated just before serving in a preheated 150°c (300°F) mark 2 oven for 5 minutes.)

To prepare the sweetbreads   Soak the sweetbreads in water for 2 hours and prepare them as directed in Veal Sweetbreads in a Port Sauce (Mollejas de Ternera al Oporto) (p. 121).

In a frying pan, heat half the butter and fry the shallots over a low heat until soft. Add the brandy and, when hot, flambé (pp. 32–3). When the flames subside, add the stock and reduce to about 175 ml (6 fl oz). Stir in the cream; bring to the boil and turn off the heat. Cover and set aside.

In a heavy frying pan large enough to accommodate all the sweetbreads in a single layer, heat the oil and remaining butter. When the butter is melted and the oil hot, add the sweetbreads; season with salt and pepper and sauté over a medium to high heat for about 3 minutes, without stirring. Turn the sweetbreads over and cook for a further 7 minutes.

Heat the sauce in its pan and add the sweetbreads. Add the capers and heat through, stirring. Taste for seasoning.

To assemble the dish   Divide the sweetbread mixture among the pastry cases and pour the sauce over the sweetbreads. Place the 'lids' on top and serve immediately.

Hígado Glaseado con Manzana y Naranja

· GLAZED LIVER WITH APPLE AND ORANGE ·

Casa Alcalde, right in the heart of the colourful old quarter in San Sebastián, is an institution. I remember going there many years ago, while walking around that picturesque part of the city, and indulging in their marvellous Jabugo hams and other terrific *tapas*. Since young Joseba Iraizoz took charge of the legendary establishment in

1981, there has been a resurgence in the kitchen. While you still can meander along the bar crowded with zillions of *tapas*, the small rustic restaurant in the back features superb traditional Basque cuisine as well as some novelties that have come out of Joseba's imagination.

Such is this delicate dish, which he actually makes with fresh goose *foie gras*. Since that is hard to find here, I followed his recommendation and tried it with calf's liver – it truly works! It is a brilliant combination, and also quick to prepare; but it has to be assembled at the last minute, so I usually make it for smaller parties. I have served it as an appetizer, and as a main dish preceded by a fish course.   *Serves 4.*

1 large navel orange, peeled and sliced
 into 4 × 1 cm (½ inch) rounds, ends
 discarded
25 g (1 oz) butter
30 ml (2 tbsp) clear honey
30 ml (2 tbsp) sherry wine vinegar or red
 wine vinegar
1 large tart dessert apple such as Granny

Smith, peeled, cored and sliced into
 4 × 1 cm (½ inch) rounds, ends
 discarded
450 g (1 lb) calf's liver, cut on the
 diagonal into 4 thin slices
150 ml (¼ pint) full-bodied Spanish
 brandy
4 gherkins, sliced into fans

Heat a heavy frying pan and, when very hot, add the orange slices. Fry them quickly over a high heat, on each side, until they turn brown. Add half the butter, honey and vinegar. Cook the oranges over a medium heat in this sauce just until the butter melts. Transfer the oranges to 4 individual heated plates.

Add the apple rounds to the pan and cook over a medium heat until tender – 5–7 minutes. Add about 2 tablespoons water to the pan during the cooking. Arrange the apple slices next to the orange slices.

Add the remaining butter to the pan and, when hot, fry the liver over medium to high heat for 30 seconds on each side. Add the brandy and flambé (pp. 32–3). Cook quickly until the liquid has evaporated. Add the remaining honey and vinegar. Cook until the liver is glazed – 1 minute on each side. Place the liver over the orange and apple slices. Arrange a gherkin fan on top of each liver piece and pour the juices from the pan over. Serve immediately.

Riñones al Jerez

· *KIDNEYS IN A SHERRY SAUCE* ·

Beasaín is a small town 30 miles south of San Sebastián, and probably its main claim to fame is its Castillo restaurant. The name is renowned in Basque gastronomy; José Castillo has been doing a fantastic job on behalf of the region's cuisine, researching and compiling old recipes in his books, and travelling widely to promote them. José Juan, his son, is the chef at Beasaín's Castillo, which he runs together with his wife, Ana Mari, José Juan's recipes are traditional and perfectly executed, such as this version of kidneys in a sherry sauce, a classic dish with his personal touch.

If served as a main course, Home-Style White Rice (Arroz Blanco Hervido) (p. 160) is an ideal accompaniment. In Spain it is often served as a *tapa*, with good crusty bread to dip in the sauce.   *Serves 4–6.*

1.4 kg (3 lb) fresh calf's kidneys
125 ml (4 fl oz) milk
50 ml (2 fl oz) olive oil
3.75 ml (¾ tsp) salt
2.5 ml (½ tsp) freshly ground black
  pepper, or to taste
225 ml (8 fl oz) dry Spanish sherry,
  preferably a fino or amontillado
9 large cloves garlic, finely chopped
1 large onion, finely chopped

125 ml (4 fl oz) Enriched Veal Stock
  (p. 193) or 225 ml (8 fl oz) Brown
  Veal Stock (p. 192)
1 bay leaf, middle vein removed,
  crumbled
30 ml (2 tbsp) finely chopped parsley
100 g (4 oz) prosciutto, sliced not too
  thin, cut with scissors into 2.5 cm
  (1 inch) strips

Put the kidneys into a bowl with the milk. Add water to cover and leave for 1 hour. Drain the kidneys and cut in half lengthways; trim off the fat and cut them into 1 cm (½ inch) pieces. Discard the milk.

In a large pan, heat 30 ml (2 tbsp) of the oil and sauté the kidneys for 2 minutes over a high heat. Stir in 1.25 ml (¼ tsp) each salt and pepper. Remove kidneys with a slotted spoon and set aside. Add the sherry to the juices in the pan and cook until the liquid is reduced to about 50 ml (2 fl oz). Set aside.

In a large frying pan, heat the remaining oil and fry the garlic with the onion over low heat until soft – about 10 minutes. Add the stock, the reduced sauce from the pan, a bay leaf, parsley, prosciutto, 2.5 ml (½ tsp) salt and 1.25 ml (¼ tsp) pepper. Cook over a medium heat for 5 minutes (10 minutes if you used Brown Veal Stock). Stir in the kidneys and their juices. Simmer over a low heat for a further 5 minutes. Serve warm.

Lengua Empiñonada

· BRAISED TONGUE WITH PINE NUTS ·

La Fragua is probably the most typical and best-known restaurant in Valladolid, northwest of Madrid, in the middle of Old Castile. Roasted suckling animals as well as great bread are among their specialities. The restaurant is beautifully decorated with Old Castilian motifs, and the kitchen reflects that approach; earthy stews, such as this one, are classics of the menu. Besides, José Antonio Garrote is a delightful host, always pleased to welcome anybody interested in Castilian cuisine. The food is excellent – and so is the cellar, José Antonio's pride, full of wonderful old vintages sure to warm your journey!   *Serves 4–6.*

FOR THE TONGUE
1 × 1.4–1.6 kg (2½–3 lb) ox tongue
2 medium leeks, trimmed and sliced
1 large onion, sliced

4 large cloves garlic, unpeeled and
  mashed
6 black peppercorns

FOR THE SAUCE
30 ml (2 tbsp) olive oil
1 large onion, finely chopped
4 large cloves garlic, finely chopped
pinch of crushed hot red pepper flakes
700 g (1½ lb) unpeeled tomatoes, chopped
225 ml (8 fl oz) Brown Veal Stock
   (p. 192)

450 g (1 lb) young, slender carrots,
   peeled and cut into 1 cm (½ inch)
   diagonal slices
5 ml (1 tsp) salt, or to taste
2.5 ml (½ tsp) freshly ground black
   pepper, or to taste
25 g (1 oz) pine nuts

To cook the tongue   Place the tongue in a large saucepan with the leeks, onion, garlic and peppercorns. Pour over enough boiling water to cover, bring to the boil again, reduce the heat to low and cook, uncovered, for 2 hours.

Drain the tongue, reserving the liquid. When the tongue is cool enough to handle, peel it and remove the bone and fatty glands on each side. Cut into 6 mm (¼ inch) slices. Set aside.

To prepare the sauce   Skim the fat from the reserved cooking liquid; there should not be much fat, just lift it with a spoon. Transfer to a saucepan and, over high heat, reduce it to 350 ml (12 fl oz).

In a frying pan, heat the oil and over a low heat, fry the onion and garlic with the pepper flakes for 10 minutes or until soft. Add the tomatoes and cook until all the liquid has evaporated. Transfer to a food processor or blender, add the reduced cooking liquid and purée. Strain through a medium sieve or a food mill. Transfer to a flameproof casserole (preferably earthenware) and add the stock, carrots and tongue slices. Bring to the boil, reduce the heat to low and cook at a simmer, partially covered, until the carrots and tongue are tender – about 30–45 minutes. Add salt and pepper to taste. The sauce should not be thick, and it will probably not need reducing; but if it is too thin, remove the tongue and carrots to a platter and reduce to desired consistency.

In a small frying pan, fry the pine nuts, stirring, until they turn golden; add to the casserole. Serve hot.

Fabada Asturiana

· BEAN STEW WITH SAUSAGES, ASTURIAN STYLE ·

Start preparation the day before, by soaking beans overnight

This is the greatest dish from Asturias: a hearty, nourishing stew very suitable for the cold winter days of that northern region. The meats used in Spain are not quite what we have here, but I have found that you can get excellent results with ham knuckle and good pork sausages; my favourites are chorizo-style and blood sausages. I must add that I've served this good country dish many times, and it's always been a success.

You are bound to find *fabada* served at any restaurant in Asturias, but it is a particular speciality of La Máquina, an old farmhouse turned restaurant in Oviedo. María García-Rodríguez cooks, while her husband, Ramón, goes in search of the best local beans, *fabes*, and the *compango*, the mixture of pork meats and sausages that accompanies the beans.

Like all bean stews, this will be even better the next day. I always keep it in an earthenware casserole, which brings out the best flavours.   *Serves 6–8.*

450 g (1 lb) large lima beans
30 ml (1 tbsp) olive oil
100 g (4 oz) bacon rashers, rinded and
  cut into thin strips
12 large cloves garlic, finely chopped
4 onions, sliced
450 g (1 lb) leeks, trimmed and sliced
1 large carrot, peeled and coarsely
  chopped
2 ham knuckles about 900 g (2 lb),
  chopped into small pieces

450 g (1 lb) flavourful, spicy pork
  sausages (preferably blood sausage,
  such as Italian blood pudding or black
  pudding, and chorizo), cut into 2 cm
  (¾ inch) pieces
2 bay leaves
15 ml (1 tbsp) paprika
salt and freshly ground black pepper to
  taste, if necessary

Place the beans in a bowl and soak them overnight to cover by 5 cm (2 inches). Next day, drain the beans and reserve the soaking water.

In a very large flameproof casserole or saucepan, heat the oil and cook the bacon over a low heat for 3–4 minutes. Add the garlic, onions, leek and carrot; cook for 30 minutes, stirring occasionally.

Add the ham knuckles, sausages, bay leaves, paprika and beans; add the reserved water to barely cover. Bring to the boil; skim off the scum and fat from the top, reduce the heat and simmer, partially covered, over a very low heat for about 2½ hours, or until the beans are tender. Remove the ham knuckles and skim the surface of the stew. Take off the meat from ham knuckles and return it to the pan. Discard the bay leaves. Taste for seasoning. Serve warm, preferably from an earthenware casserole.

Habas a la Catalana

· CATALAN – FAVES A LA CATALANA ·

· BROAD BEAN STEW, CATALAN STYLE ·

This is a classic Catalan dish – a wonderful earthy, peasant one, most comforting on a cold day. It is served at many country restaurants in my home region, usually as a small first course; but I have always made it here as a main dish, and a hearty one at that. If it's reheated and served the next day, the flavours will be even better. It is traditionally cooked in an earthenware casserole; this brings out especially good flavour.

I have enjoyed this dish many times at one of my favourite restaurants, Cal Joan, in Vilafranca del Penedès – one of the warmest, most authentic and finest restaurants in the whole area. Joan Samsó and his wife, María, ran the restaurant until he died recently; now his son, Quico, is the chef. He has added to his father's classic Catalan cooking the innovativeness of a young man who loves to cook.   *Serves 8.*

1.8–2.7 kg (4–6 lb) unshelled broad
  beans or 2 × 300 g (10 oz) packages
  frozen broad beans, defrosted
30 ml (2 tbsp) olive oil
225 g (8 oz) streaky bacon rashers,
  rinded and cut in strips
2 medium onions, chopped
4 large cloves garlic, finely chopped

450 g (1 lb) pork sausages
450 g (1 lb) blood pork sausage, such as
  Italian blood pudding or black
  pudding
75 ml (3 tbsp) chopped mint
1 large or 2 small bay leaves
225 ml (8 fl oz) dry white wine
750 ml (1¼ pints) Chicken Stock (p. 191)

Shell the beans. (If they are not young and their skins are tough, blanch them for 2 or 3 minutes and peel them. When you open the pod, you will know that they are old if the small husk attached to the pod is black.)

In a flameproof casserole, heat the oil and fry the bacon over low heat for about 10 minutes. Remove it and set aside. Add the onions and garlic to the casserole and fry until golden – about 20 minutes. Add the beans and toss for 4–5 minutes.

Put about 125 ml (4 fl oz) water in a frying pan and add the sausages. Pierce them with a fork and cook for 3–5 minutes, until lightly browned. Cut them into 2.5 cm (1 inch) slices and add to the beans. Add the bacon, 15 ml (1 tbsp) of the mint, the bay leaf and wine. Add the stock, bring to the boil, reduce the heat to low and cook, covered, for 1 hour or more, until the beans are quite soft. If you find the sauce too thin, cook, uncovered, for a further 15 minutes or until the sauce reaches desired consistency; it should be rather soupy. Taste for seasoning. At the last minute, add the remaining mint, stir and serve.

Callos a la Gallega

· *TRIPE WITH CHICK-PEAS, HAM AND SAUSAGE, GALICIAN STYLE* ·

Tripe is very bland by itself, so it provides an excellent vehicle for all the other good things in this recipe. It is another of those dishes you can make a day ahead and reheat, for even better flavour. I always serve it as a first course directly from the casserole, accompanied by Peasant Bread (Pan de Payés) (p. 179) or a good crusty bread to dip in the sauce.

In Galicia the classic preparation includes chick peas (garbanzo beans). This recipe is an adaptation of that of Moncho Vilas, whose Vilas restaurant in Santiago de Compostela is my favourite in the city. His cooking is down-to-earth home style, enhancing in a simple way the beautiful produce of Galicia.   *Serve 8–10.*

900 g (2 lb) tripe
30 ml (2 tbsp) olive oil
1 large onion, finely chopped
4 large cloves garlic, finely chopped
900 g (2 lb) unpeeled tomatoes, chopped
2 × 425 g (15 oz) cans chick-peas,
   drained
1 × 450 g (1 lb) ham knuckle, chopped
   into small pieces

225 g (8 oz) chorizo-style sausage, sliced
   into 1 cm (½ inch) rounds
5 ml (1 tsp) chopped thyme
1.25 ml (¼ tsp) crushed hot red pepper
   flakes, or to taste
10 ml (2 tsp) salt, or to taste
2.5 ml (½ tsp) freshly ground black
   pepper, or to taste
30 ml (2 tbsp) finely chopped parsley

Soak the tripe in cold water for 30 minutes. Drain and cut into very thin strips.

Heat the oil in a large flameproof casserole. Fry the onion and garlic until golden – about 20 minutes; add the tomatoes and cook until all the liquid has evaporated. Add the chick-peas, ham knuckle, chorizo, thyme, pepper flakes, salt and pepper. Cook for 5 minutes and stir in the tripe. Simmer very slowly, covered, for at least 2 hours. Remove the meat from the ham knuckle and put it back into the casserole. Taste for seasoning. Just before serving, sprinkle parsley on top.

Cocido Catalán

· CATALAN – ESCUDELLA I CARN D'OLLA ·

· MEAT AND VEGETABLE STEW WITH A PASTA SOUP ·

Start preparation the day before, by soaking beans overnight, or use canned beans

Escudella i carn d'olla is the most typical Catalan dish – a true meal-in-a-pot, in the family of boiled dinners like the French *pot-au-feu* and the Italian *bollito misto*. In the old days, it was the staple meal for those who lived in the country. I remember my grandmother saying that when she was young, they had it five or six days a week! A special *escudella* was reserved for Christmas Day, and today it still is a classic Catalan Christmas dish.

The idea is to simmer flavourful meats and sausages with vegetables. The broth is served as a first course with pasta – traditionally, large shell pasta or *galets*. The main course will be the meats and vegetables. And at Christmas, if you can believe it, we have the turkey after that!

Here is my version of *escudella* – subject to any changes according to your taste. For instance, in Spain we pass around some fine olive oil to drizzle over the vegetables; but I enjoy a dab of Garlic Mayonnaise (Allioli) (p. 199) with each item of the stew. Unconventional, maybe, but cooking is an ever-changing art and that's what makes it so exciting.   *Serves 8, with leftovers.*

30 ml (2 tbsp) olive oil
225 g (8 oz) streaky bacon rashers,
    rinded and diced small
6 large cloves garlic, chopped
2 shallots, finely chopped
450 g (1 lb) leeks, trimmed and thinly
    sliced
3 celery sticks, chopped
450 g (1 lb) veal or beef knuckle bones
    with marrow, if possible, cut up
450 g (1 lb) ham knuckle, chopped into
    small pieces
450 g (1 lb) stewing beef, cut into 2.5 cm
    (1 inch) cubes
1 × 2.3–2.7 kg (5–6 lb) ovenready
    roasting chicken
5 ml (1 tsp) salt
5 ml (1 tsp) freshly ground black pepper

1 quantity Meat Ball (p. 132)
45–60 ml (3–4 tbsp) plain flour
8 small turnips, peeled
8 small new potatoes
1 small green cabbage, cored and
    quartered
225 g (8 oz) carrots, peeled and cut into
    1 cm ($\frac{1}{2}$ inch) diagonal slices
900 g (2 lb) assorted pork sausages,
    including blood sausage and any other
    flavourful ones
2 × 425 g (15 oz) cans chick-peas,
    drained
100 g (4 oz) large shell pasta
AS A GARNISH
Olive oil or Garlic Mayonnaise
    (p. 199)

Heat the oil in a very large flameproof casserole and fry the bacon over a low heat until golden – about 10 minutes. Add the garlic, shallots, leeks and celery; cook for 15 minutes. Add the bones and meats (except the meat ball and sausages), add salt and pepper, and water to cover. Bring to the boil, reduce the heat to low and simmer gently, covered, for 1$\frac{1}{2}$ hours. Skim off the scum and fat that rise to the surface from time to time.

Divide the meat ball mixture in half, and shape it into 2 cylinders about 7.5 cm (3 inches) in diameter. Sprinkle flour on a board and roll the cylinders in it, coating them all over.

After 1$\frac{1}{2}$ hours of simmering, add the turnips, potatoes, cabbage, carrots, sausages, meat ball cylinders and chick-peas. If necessary, add some more boiling water to cover. Simmer for a further 30 minutes.

Remove the meats and vegetables from the broth and arrange them on 2 heated platters; keep warm. Strain the broth through a fine sieve and reduce it to about 1.7 litres (3 pints). Cook the pasta in the broth, at a rapid boil, until tender. Taste for seasoning.

Serve the broth and pasta as a soup, followed by the vegetables and meats with olive oil or Garlic Mayonnaise (Allioli).

Pelota

Pelota – Spanish for ball – is a recipe of Arab origin, although originally it did not use pork but other meat, especially lamb. It is part of many classic dishes such as Meat and Vegetable Stew with a Pasta Soup (Cocido Catalán) (p. 130), where it is made into two big cylinders; or Classic Paella with Shellfish, Chicken and Pork (Paella Valenciana de la Ribera) (p. 162), where it is shaped into small balls. These are also delicious simply as an appetizer, sautéed until golden; or cooked in Chicken Stock (Caldo de Pollo) (p. 191) with rice as a soup.   *Makes about 700 g (1½ lb).*

450 g (1 lb) minced pork	*3 large cloves garlic, finely chopped*
50 g (2 oz) soft white breadcrumbs	*25 g (1 oz) pine nuts*
(pp. 31–2)	*2.5 ml (½ tsp) salt*
2 eggs	*2.5 ml (½ tsp) freshly ground black pepper*
45 ml (3 tbsp) chopped parsley	*pinch of ground cinnamon*

Mix all the ingredients in a bowl and shape as described on p. 131.

Manzanas Rellenas al Horno

This is one of my favourite dishes at Agut d'Avignon, one of Barcelona's great restaurants. The person who deserves most of the credit for making Agut a culinary star is the late Ramón Cabau, the flamboyant genius of Catalan cooking. Ramón sold the restaurant in 1983, and died in 1987 – but Agut's standards have remained just as high. It features many Catalan dishes, such as these stuffed apples, which are typical of Gerona, north of Barcelona.   *Serves 6.*

6 large Bramley apples, about 225 g	*5 ml (1 tsp) salt*
(8 oz) each	*2.5 ml (½ tsp) freshly ground black pepper*
30 ml (2 tbsp) olive oil	*2 eggs*
25 g (1 oz) pine nuts	*225 ml (8 fl oz) dry white wine*
1 medium onion, finely chopped	*225 ml (8 fl oz) Brown Veal Stock*
3 large cloves garlic, finely chopped	*(p. 192), or more as needed*
350 g (12 oz) cooked lean ham, minced	*30 ml (2 tbsp) sugar*
350 g (12 oz) minced pork	
25 g (1 oz) soft white breadcrumbs	
(pp. 31–2)	

With the stem side down, cut the top quarter off each apple. With a vegetable corer or melon-baller, hollow out a pocket in the bottom three quarters of the apple. Remove the seeds and core without going all the way through to the bottom of the apple. With a vegetable corer or knife, enlarge the opening, shaping it like a funnel; reserve the apple pieces. Discard the seeds and core; chop the apple pieces and set aside.

Preheat the oven to 180°c (350°F) mark 4.

Heat the oil in a large frying pan and sauté the pine nuts until they turn golden. Add the onion and garlic and fry over a low heat until soft and golden – 10–15 minutes. Add the chopped apple pieces; stir and cook until tender – about 10 minutes. Off the heat, add the ham, pork, breadcrumbs, salt and pepper; stir and set aside. Beat the eggs lightly in a bowl; add the meat mixture and combine well. (It is better to do this with your hands so you can feel that the egg is distributed throughout the meat.)

Mound the stuffing into the apples, packing it inside the pockets; they should look like giant mushrooms. The stuffing will shrink during baking, so don't worry if they look too big; use up all the stuffing. Place the apples in an ungreased flameproof baking dish or tin and pour the wine around them. Bake in the oven for $1\frac{1}{4}$–$1\frac{1}{2}$ hours, until tender. While baking, there should always be a little liquid left in the pan; check periodically and add stock if needed, to make sure the juices don't burn (especially if you have an electric oven).

Remove the apples to a heated serving platter. Add the stock to the baking dish or tin. Cook over a high heat until reduced to the desired consistency; it should be a rather light sauce. Meanwhile, caramelize the sugar (see p. 33) by cooking it with 10 ml (2 tsp) water in a heavy saucepan over a medium-high heat, until it turns amber; stir into the sauce until caramel dissolves. Serve the apples surrounded with the sauce.

Melocotones Rellenos

· CATALAN – PRÉSSECS FARCITS ·

· PEACHES STUFFED WITH PORK AND ALMONDS ·

Here is an excellent Catalan combination of fruits and meat – this one comes from my mother's recipe file. It was one of my favourite dishes at home in the summertime, during the height of the peach season. It is interesting and unusual; the flavours mingle with extraordinary harmony.   *Serves 6.*

6 large, firm fresh peaches, total weight
    about 1.4 kg (3 lb)
FOR THE FILLING
75 g (3 oz) whole almonds
100 g (4 oz) minced pork
15 g ($\frac{1}{2}$ oz) soft white breadcrumbs (pp. 31–2)

1 egg
2.5 ml ($\frac{1}{2}$ tsp) salt
1.25 ml ($\frac{1}{4}$ tsp) freshly ground black
    pepper
pinch of ground cinnamon

FOR THE PEACHES
30 ml (2 tbsp) olive oil
25 g (1 oz) butter
15–30 ml (1–2 tbsp) plain flour
50 ml (2 fl oz) full-bodied Spanish
    brandy

50 ml (2 fl oz) sweet muscat wine, such
    as Torres Malvasía de Oro
5 cloves
450 ml (¾ pint) Brown Veal Stock
    (p. 192)
salt to taste, if necessary

Preheat the oven to 180°c (350°F) mark 4.

With the help of a knife and melon-baller, remove the stones from the peaches, leaving them whole; don't peel or cut them in half. Reserve the stones.

To prepare the filling   Toast almonds in the oven for 15 minutes, then grind them finely. Mix them in a bowl with all the filling ingredients, and stuff the peaches with the mixture.

To prepare the peaches   Heat the oil and butter in a large frying pan. Put the flour on a dish and dip the stuffed side of each peach into the flour; sauté them over a medium heat, stuffing side down, until golden.

Transfer the peaches to a flameproof casserole, stuffed side up. Skim the fat from the contents of the pan; deglaze with the brandy and pour into the casserole. Add the muscat wine, cloves and veal stock. Bring the liquid to the boil, reduce the heat to low, add the reserved peach stones and simmer the peaches, partially covered, for 45 minutes.

Arrange the peaches on a platter, stuffing side up, and keep warm. Discard the stones. Reduce the liquid to 175–225 ml (6–8 fl oz). Taste for seasoning. Pour the sauce over the peaches and serve.

Carne con Peras

· CATALAN – CARN AMB PERES ·

· VEAL WITH PEARS ·

This is yet another Catalan dish of meat cooked with fruit, here in a veal stew. It is a recipe from my family's cook, Rosalía, which I remember relishing as a child. *Serves 6.*

6 small firm cooking pears, peeled and
    cored, stems left intact, whole or
    halved
90 ml (6 tbsp) Poire Williams liqueur or
    full-bodied Spanish brandy
1.6 kg (3 lb) boneless stewing veal, cut
    into 3.5–5 cm (1½–2 inch) cubes
3.75 ml (¾ tsp) salt
3.75 ml (¾ tsp) freshly ground black
    pepper

about 90 ml (6 tbsp) olive oil
3 medium onions, finely chopped
6 large cloves garlic, finely chopped
50 g (2 oz) pine nuts
125 ml (4 fl oz) dry white wine
2 bay leaves
90 ml (6 tbsp) sugar

Place the pears in a large bowl and pour the liqueur or brandy over them, tossing gently. Cover and marinate at room temperature for at least 30 minutes.

Season the veal with 1.25 ml ($\frac{1}{4}$ tsp) each salt and pepper. In a large frying pan, heat 50 ml (2 fl oz) of the olive oil and, over a medium to high heat, sauté the veal briefly, in small batches, to seal. Set the veal aside. Add more oil to the pan if necessary, and sauté two-thirds of the onions and garlic until soft – about 10 minutes. Add the veal and its juices, cover and cook over a very low heat for 30 minutes. Season with the remaining salt and pepper.

Meanwhile, in a flameproof casserole large enough to hold the pears, sauté the pine nuts in 30 ml (2 tbsp) of the oil until golden. Remove with a slotted spoon and drain on kitchen paper. Add the remaining onion and garlic and dry over a low heat until soft – about 10 minutes. Add the pears, stem side up, with their marinade, the wine, bay leaves and pine nuts; stir gently, bring the liquid to the boil and turn heat to very low. Cover and simmer for 20 minutes. Push the pears to the sides of the casserole and pour in the veal with its sauce. Cover and simmer for a further 30 minutes.

Remove the veal and pears to a heated serving platter, mounding the meat in the centre with the pears surrounding it. Discard the bay leaves. Cover and keep warm. Over a high heat, reduce the sauce until thickened to desired consistency. Taste for seasoning. Pour over the veal.

In a small pan, caramelize the sugar (see p. 33) by dissolving it with 30 ml (2 tbsp) water and cooking over a medium-high heat until it turns an amber colour. Pour over the pears. Serve immediately.

Filete de Ternera con Salsa de Anchoas

· CATALAN – *FILET DE VEDELLA AMB SALSA D'ANXOVES* ·

· *VEAL FILLET WITH ANCHOVY SAUCE* ·

Tiró Mimet, a tiny family-style bistro in the old part of Barcelona, specializes in traditional dishes from Catalonia, where chef/owner Xavier Grifoll has lived – and cooked – all his life. Xavier serves this elegant dish with Aubergine Tartlets (Tartitas de Berenjena) (p. 154). *Serves 6.*

FOR THE SAUCE
25 g (1 oz) butter
1 large onion, finely chopped
4 large cloves garlic, finely chopped
1 × 50 g (2 oz) can flat anchovy fillets, drained and finely chopped
15 ml (1 tbsp) Dijon mustard
125 ml (4 fl oz) full-bodied Spanish brandy
50 ml (2 fl oz) amontillado or other flavourful dry Spanish sherry

350 ml (12 fl oz) Enriched Veal Stock (p. 193) or 750 ml (1¼ pints) Brown Veal Stock (p. 192)
125 ml (4 fl oz) double cream
FOR THE VEAL
1.6 kg (3 lb) boneless loin of veal
2.5 ml (½ tsp) salt
1.25 ml (¼ tsp) freshly ground black pepper
15 g (½ oz) butter
15 ml (1 tbsp) olive oil

To prepare the sauce   Melt the butter in a non-metallic pan; add the onion and garlic and fry for 10 minutes over a low heat. Stir in the anchovies and mustard. Add the brandy and, when hot, flambé (pp. 32–3). Pour in the sherry and stock; cook until reduced to 350 ml (12 fl oz). Transfer to a food processor or blender and purée. With the motor running, add the cream. Strain through a fine sieve. Taste for seasoning. Reserve.

To prepare the veal   Tie the loin at 2.5 cm (1 inch) intervals, and cut between strings, to make 12 medallions or little rounds. Season them with salt and pepper. Heat the butter and oil in a large frying pan and, over a medium to high heat, quickly cook the veal for 2–3 minutes on each side or until barely done. Pour the sauce over, heat through and serve immediately.

Medallones de Ternera a la Naranja

· VEAL MEDALLIONS IN AN ORANGE SAUCE ·

Bilbao is a very conservative city, and Guría is a traditional restaurant with an old reputation where Genaro Pildaín, using top-quality ingredients, serves classic Basque dishes like nobody else. His wife, Nati, runs the elegant dining room with the style of a grand Basque lady. This outstanding recipe was inspired by one of Genaro's preparations.   *Serves 6.*

15 ml (1 tbsp) sugar
125 ml (4 fl oz) Gran Torres liqueur or
   Grand Marnier
350 ml (12 fl oz) Enriched Veal Stock
   (p. 193) or 750 ml (1¼ pints) Brown
   Veal Stock (p. 192)
125 ml (4 fl oz) orange juice
1 large orange

900 g (2 lb) veal tenderloin, trimmed and
   cut into 2.5 cm (1 inch) thick rounds
2.5 ml (½ tsp) salt
2.5 ml (½ tsp) freshly ground black pepper
25 g (1 oz) butter
15 ml (1 tbsp) olive oil
125 ml (4 fl oz) full-bodied Spanish
   brandy

In a saucepan, dissolve the sugar in 5 ml (1 tsp) water and cook over a medium to high heat until the sugar melts and caramelizes, turning a dark golden colour (see p. 33). Add the orange liqueur, stock and orange juice; cook over a high heat until reduced to about 450 ml (¾ pint). Set aside.

With a vegetable peeler, peel the orange very carefully to get thin strips with no pith left on them. Cut the peel into thin match-like strips. In a small saucepan, bring about 450 ml (¾ pint) water to the boil; add the orange peel and boil for 1 minute. Drain the peel and add it to the sauce; cook for 3 minutes. Set the sauce aside. Cut the orange into segments, discarding the pith and membrane; reserve.

Pat the veal dry and season with 1.25 ml (¼ tsp) each salt and pepper. Heat the butter and oil in a frying pan large enough to hold all the veal medallions. Add the veal and sauté quickly, over a medium to high heat, for 2 minutes on each side.

Pour in the brandy and, when hot, flambé (pp. 32–3). When the flames subside, add the sauce with the orange peel and cook for 5 minutes, coating the veal with the sauce. Transfer the veal pieces to a heated serving platter and keep warm. Increase the heat to medium-high, and reduce the sauce to desired consistency. Season, then pour the sauce over the veal and garnish with the orange segments.

Lomo de Cerdo a la Naranja

· PORK LOIN IN AN ORANGE SAUCE ·

Madrid is full of traditional bistro-style restaurants where you can eat wonderfully; Horno de Santa Teresa has been one of them for over twenty-five years. Under owners Pepe and Ángeles Iglesias' approving eye, Chef Angel López produces a variety of excellent dishes representative of most Spanish regions. This recipe was inspired by one of his creations.   *Serves 6.*

1.4–1.6 kg (3–3½ lb) boned loin of pork,
  bones reserved, see Note below
7.5 ml (1½ tsp) salt
3 large cloves garlic, finely chopped
450 ml (¾ pint) fresh orange juice
450 ml (¾ pint) dry white wine
225 ml (8 fl oz) Brown Veal Stock
  (p. 192)

450 g (1 lb) tart dessert apples, such as
  Granny Smith, peeled, cored and cut
  up
50 g (2 oz) sugar
1.25 ml (¼ tsp) freshly ground black
  pepper
AS A GARNISH
6 unpeeled orange slices

(Note: Ask the butcher to bone the loin, (it should be about 2.3 kg (5 lb) before boning), and to cut the bones into 16 pieces.)

Cut a groove about 2 cm (¾ inch) deep along the length of the loin, on the non-fat side. Season with 5 ml (1 tsp) of the salt, rubbing it along the whole loin. Sprinkle the garlic along the groove. Tie the loin with string at 2.5 cm (1 inch) intervals.

Place the loin, fat side down, in a flameproof casserole and brown it over a medium heat without added fat, turning it until golden on all sides. Remove the loin and add the pork bones, browning them in the fat. Set the bones aside and drain the fat from casserole. Return the loin to the casserole and add the bones, orange juice, wine, veal stock and apples. Bring to the boil, immediately reduce the heat to low and cook, uncovered, for 1 hour, turning it from time to time.

Remove the loin to a chopping board. Discard the bones. Purée the sauce in a food processor or blender and return to the pan. In a small saucepan, caramelize the sugar dissolved in 15 ml (1 tbsp) water (see p. 33), until it turns dark golden. Add to the sauce and stir until dissolved. Increase the heat to high and cook the sauce until reduced by half, or to desired consistency. Add the remaining salt and the pepper, and taste for seasoning.

Slice the pork thinly and arrange on a heated serving platter. Serve garnished with orange slices, and hand the sauce separately in a sauce-boat.

Lomo de Cerdo Relleno

· PORK LOIN STUFFED WITH ALMONDS, MUSHROOMS AND SAGE ·

This delicious pork dish comes from my mother's recipe file. There is one change I made: she used fresh truffles (her special source was much cheaper than in this country) in the stuffing, which indeed add an extraordinary flavour. But I found that the combination of a fresh herb such as sage with the other ingredients produced an excellent result. You won't miss those expensive, rare fungi!   *Serves 8.*

FOR THE STUFFING
100 g (4 oz) whole almonds
100 g (4 oz) minced pork
100 g (4 lb) cooked ham, finely chopped
100 g (4 oz) mushrooms, chopped
2 hard-boiled eggs, chopped
30 ml (2 tbsp) finely chopped sage
5 ml (1 tsp) salt, or to taste
2.5 ml (½ tsp) freshly ground black
  pepper, or to taste

1 egg
FOR THE PORK
1.6 kg (3½ lb) boned loin of pork,
  2.3–2.7 kg (5–6 lb) before boning,
  bones reserved, see Note below
45 ml (3 tbsp) olive oil
125 ml (4 fl oz) full-bodied Spanish
  brandy
450 ml (¾ pint) Brown Veal Stock
  (p. 192)

(Note: Ask the butcher to bone the loin, leaving some fat around it, and tie it at 1 cm (½ inch) intervals. Then slice the loin between each string, three-quarters of the way through, so it opens like a book. Cut the bones into about 16 pieces and reserve.)

To stuff the pork   Preheat the oven to 180°C (350°F) mark 4. Toast the almonds in the oven for 15 minutes, then grind them finely. Combine them in a bowl with the pork, ham, mushrooms, hard-boiled eggs, sage, salt and pepper. Mix well with the egg. Stuff the loin between the strings with this mixture. Tie the loin lengthways, twice around.

To cook the pork   Heat the oil in a flameproof casserole and sauté the loin over a medium heat, turning it around, until golden on all sides. Remove the loin and add the pork bones, browning them in the fat. Set the bones aside. Remove the fat from the casserole and deglaze with brandy. Add the stock and bones, bring to the boil and add the loin. Reduce the heat to low, cover and cook for 1 hour over a medium to low heat or until cooked through.

Transfer the loin to a chopping board. Discard the bones. Reduce the sauce by about one-third. Taste for seasoning. Remove the strings, slice the loin and serve warm, with the sauce handed separately in a sauce-boat.

Solomillo de Cerdo con Uvas

· PORK TENDERLOIN WITH GRAPES ·

La Merced is the finest restaurant in Logroño, capital of La Rioja region, and probably in that whole wine district. Owner Lorenzo Cañas transformed an old palace into this elegant establishment, which he decorated with grand style and impeccable taste. And if that were not enough, the cellar may be the best in La Rioja, with 52,000 bottles from the region alone!

I thought a dish with grapes would be a good one to represent this excellent restaurant.   *Serves 6.*

FOR THE SAUCE
45 ml (3 tbsp) olive oil
3 large cloves garlic, finely chopped
1 small onion, finely chopped
1 small leek, trimmed and chopped
1 medium carrot, finely chopped
225 g (8 oz) seedless red grapes
1 bay leaf, middle vein removed,
   crumbled
125 ml (4 fl oz) fresh orange juice
FOR THE PORK
1.4 kg (2½ lb) pork tenderloin, cut into 18
   pieces about 2.5 cm (1 inch) thick

2.5 ml (½ tsp) salt
2.5 ml (½ tsp) freshly ground black
   pepper
30 ml (2 tbsp) olive oil
125 ml (4 fl oz) full-bodied Spanish
   brandy
FOR THE CARAMELIZED GRAPES
25 g (1 oz) butter
50 g (2 oz) sugar
225 g (8 oz) small seedless red grapes
50 ml (2 fl oz) dry red wine

To prepare the sauce   Heat the oil in a frying pan; fry the garlic, onion, leek, carrot, grapes and bay leaf over a medium to low heat until very golden, almost brown – about 20 minutes. Transfer to a food processor or blender and purée with the orange juice. Strain through a fine sieve. Reserve.

To cook the pork   Gently pound the pork pieces to flatten them slightly. Season with salt and pepper. Heat the oil in a heavy frying pan wide enough to hold the pork. (It will shrink as it cooks, so you can crowd it in the skillet.) When oil is very hot, sauté the pork over a high heat – 2 minutes on each side. Add the brandy and, when hot, flambé (pp. 32–3) for 1 minute. Douse the flames with the reserved sauce. Remove the pork to a plate and reserve the sauce in the skillet.

To caramelize the grapes   In a small saucepan, heat butter and sugar. Cook over a medium to high heat, shaking the pan, until the sugar starts to turn golden. Immediately add the grapes and cook quickly, shaking the pan until the caramel is brown – about 1 minute. Add the wine, stir and remove the grapes with a slotted spoon. Cook for 1 further minute over a high heat, until the mixture starts to thicken. Stir into the reserved sauce. Taste for seasoning. Add the pork and cook until done – about 5 minutes. Serve immediately, garnished with the grapes.

Chuleta de Cerdo a la Catalana

· CATALAN – COSTELLA DE PORC A LA CATALANA ·

· PORK CHOPS STUFFED WITH PRUNES AND PINE NUTS, CATALAN STYLE ·

As mentioned several times in this book, any Catalan-style preparation is bound to have pine nuts and prunes or raisins. Naturally, over the course of my life in Catalonia, I have eaten many a dish with these ingredients – from my mother's Christmas turkey to pigs' trotters at Jaume de Provença in Barcelona – but interestingly enough, never pork. Yet I have found that the combination works beautifully with pork. *Serves 6.*

FOR THE STUFFING
350 g (12 oz) stoned prunes
175 ml (6 fl oz) port wine
15 ml (1 tbsp) olive oil
45 ml (3 tbsp) pine nuts
1.25 ml (¼ tsp) salt
pinch of freshly ground black
* pepper*

FOR THE PORK
6 pork chops, 225 g (8 oz) each, cut with
* a pocket for stuffing*
5 ml (1 tsp) salt
2.5 ml (½ tsp) freshly ground black pepper
125 ml (4 fl oz) port wine
225 ml (8 fl oz) Brown Veal Stock
* (p. 192)*

To prepare the stuffing Place the prunes in a saucepan and cover with cold water. Bring to the boil, reduce the heat and simmer, uncovered, for 20 minutes. Add 125 ml (4 fl oz) of the port. Bring to the boil, immediately reduce the heat to low, cover and simmer for 15 minutes. Drain prunes and reserve with liquid.

Heat the oil in a medium frying pan and sauté the pine nuts until golden. Add the prunes, pour in the remaining port and cook over a medium heat until reduced to a glaze. Season with salt and pepper.

To prepare the pork Stuff the pork chops with the filling; if there is any excess, reserve it – you can use it later in the sauce. Heat a wide frying pan and, over a high seat, seal the chops by frying for 1 minute on each side. Sprinkle with salt and pepper as they cook. Add the wine, stock, reserved prune liquid and any leftover filling; cover and cook over a low heat for 30 minutes or until done. Transfer the chops to a heated serving platter, together with any filling that may have oozed out. Increase the heat to half and reduce the sauce to desired consistency. Pour the sauce over chops and serve warm.

CUTTING THE MEAT FROM A LEG OF LAMB

To get the best results in the following lamb dishes, it is a good idea to trim the fat and gristle off the leg of lamb and cut it up yourself; just ask the butcher to bone the leg for you. It is easy to cut up a leg of lamb, and if you do it according to the following instructions, it will cook much better.

Remove the outer skin and some fat from the meat; don't trim all the fat, or the meat will dry while cooking. Separate the meat along the individual muscles; this will give you more solid cubes of meat. You will notice that the meat will divide along its natural seams: some muscle groups are flatter, some thicker. Cut the meat along the line of the muscles, and then across to make pieces about 5 cm (2 inches) square. By not cutting across 2 or 3 muscle groups – as most butchers would do – you will get solid pieces of meat; this is much more important than getting precisely even cubes. Cutting the meat along the muscles also ensures that all the meat in each muscle will cook evenly. (This is also important when boning a larger piece of meat into chops or steaks.)

One small leg of lamb, 2.3–2.7 kg (5–6 lb) should give you 1.4–1.6 kg (3–3½ lb) of lean meat. This will provide about 6 servings, as indicated in the following recipes.

Pierna de Cordero Rellena de Riñones a la Almendra

· CATALAN – CUIXA DE XAI FARCIDA DE RONYONS A L'AMETLLA ·

· LEG OF LAMB STUFFED WITH KIDNEYS AND ALMONDS ·

For the last few years, La Odisea has been a star in Barcelona. Young owner/chef Antonio Ferrer is as adventurous in his cuisine as his establishment's name suggests. I was fascinated to hear his saga; his love of cooking started in school at the age of 8 – he made the sausages there! Now that he's in his early thirties, his passion for experimenting and learning continues, and his talent is reflected in the refined dishes he turns out. His wife, Teresa, is the perfect partner in the dining room.

Among many preparations difficult to reproduce here, he serves a top-quality leg of lamb stuffed with fresh lamb's kidneys, which inspired me to develop this recipe. I was very pleased with the result – especially as it has converted more than one reluctant friend to kidneys! I only hope Antonio would approve of my adaptation of his idea. *Serves 6–8.*

FOR THE STUFFING
50 g (2 oz) flaked almonds
30 ml (2 tbsp) olive oil
10 large cloves garlic, finely chopped
1 large onion, finely chopped
450 g (1 lb) tomatoes, skinned and chopped
30 ml (2 tbsp) chopped parsley
15 ml (1 tbsp) finely chopped thyme
2.5 ml (½ tsp) salt
2.5 ml (½ tsp) freshly ground black pepper
125 ml (4 fl oz) full-bodied Spanish brandy

450 g (1 lb) calf's or lamb's kidneys, fat removed, thinly sliced
FOR THE LAMB
2.3 kg (5 lb) leg of lamb, boned and opened out
2.5 ml (½ tsp) salt
2.5 ml (½ tsp) freshly ground black pepper
15 ml (1 tbsp) olive oil
50 ml (2 fl oz) full-bodied Spanish brandy
450 ml (¾ pint) Brown Veal Stock (p. 192)

To prepare the stuffing   Preheat the oven to 180°c (350°F) mark 4. Toast almonds in the oven for 5 minutes. In a large frying pan, heat the oil and fry the garlic and onion over a low heat until soft – about 10 minutes. Add the tomatoes, parsley and thyme; cook over a medium heat until all the liquid has evaporated. Season with salt and pepper. Reserve 225 ml (8 fl oz) of this sauce.

Add the brandy to the remaining sauce in the pan and, when hot, flambé (pp. 32–3). Cook over a high heat until the liquid has evaporated; turn off the heat. Stir in the almonds and kidneys. (You may prepare this stuffing ahead of time; if so, let cool before adding the almonds and kidneys.)

To prepare the lamb   Lay the lamb flat, skin side down; season with salt and pepper, rubbing it over the meat. Cover with the filling. Bring up the 4 sides of the meat and secure with a metal skewer from top to bottom. With the sides secured, sew up the edges to enclose the filling. Don't worry if the shape of the leg isn't perfect, or if some of the filling comes out; it will just add flavour to the sauce.

In a large flameproof casserole, heat the oil and brown the lamb on all sides. Remove the lamb and deglaze the casserole with the brandy. Add 225 ml (8 fl oz) of the stock and the reserved tomato sauce. Return the lamb to the casserole and cook in the oven, uncovered, for 45 minutes or until cooked through. While cooking, check to see that the sauce in the casserole doesn't burn.

Remove the lamb to a chopping board. Pour the contents of the casserole into a food processor or blender, add the remaining stock and purée. Strain through a fine sieve. Taste for seasoning.

Serve the lamb sliced with some hot sauce poured over it, and hand the remaining sauce in a sauce-boat.

Cordero a la Miel

· LAMB WITH HONEY AND GREEN PEPPERS ·

Start preparation 10 hours ahead or the day before, by marinating lamb

Pepe García-Marín, owner of El Caballo Rojo in Córdoba, has done a terrific job of researching the origins of old *mozárabe* cooking in Spain, and of adapting the recipes to suit today's palate while keeping their authenticity. *Mozárabes* were the Christians who lived under Arab rule, in conflict; by the tenth century they were being persecuted and had to flee to Christian areas in the north.

This recipe is one of Pepe's finest achievements, and a classic example of *mozárabe* cooking. The blend of flavours with the combination of sweet and sour works out extremely well. I like to serve it with Rosemary-Raisin Wreath Bread (Pan de Romero) (p. 184) or Home-Style White Rice (Arroz Blanco Hervido) (p. 160) as an accompaniment. *Serves 6.*

FOR THE MARINADE
about 450 ml (¾ pint) dry flavourful
   Spanish sherry, such as amontillado
15 ml (1 tbsp) paprika
10 ml (2 tsp) salt
1.4–1.6 kg (3–3½ lb) boneless lamb, cut
   into 5 cm (2 inch) pieces
FOR THE LAMB
45–60 ml (3–4 tbsp) olive oil

2 medium onions, finely chopped
1 large green sweet pepper, cored, seeded
   and chopped
2.5 ml (½ tsp) saffron threads
125 ml (4 fl oz) sherry wine vinegar
175 g (6 oz) eucalyptus honey or other
   full-flavoured honey

To prepare the marinade   In a non-metallic bowl, combine 350 ml (12 fl oz) of the sherry with the paprika and salt. Marinate the lamb in it overnight or for at least 8 hours, covered and refrigerated, turning the meat occasionally.

Lift the lamb from the marinade. Measure the liquid and add more sherry to a total of 350 ml (12 fl oz). Reserve.

To prepare the lamb   In a large flameproof casserole, heat 30 ml (2 tsp) of the oil and over a medium to high heat sauté the lamb quickly, until lightly browned. Set the lamb aside. Add another 15–30 ml (1–2 tbsp) oil if necessary, and fry the onions and pepper gently for 10 minutes. Return the lamb to the casserole, add the sherry marinade and stir in the saffron. Bring to the boil, reduce the heat to low, cover and simmer for 1 hour.

Stir in the vinegar and honey. Cook, uncovered, over a low heat, for 30 minutes. Remove the lamb to a heated serving platter and keep warm. Rapidly cook the sauce in the pan to reduce to about 750 ml (1¼ pints). Taste for seasoning. Pour the sauce over the lamb. Serve warm.

Cordero Chilindrón

· LAMB IN A MILD DRIED PEPPER SAUCE ·

Start preparation at least 8 hours ahead, by marinating lamb

Chilindrón is a preparation for meats – lamb, kid or rabbit – indigenous to the regions of Aragón and southern Navarra, where the palate calls for heartier dishes; the sauce can sometimes be quite hot. It should always include dried red peppers, the *pimientos choriceros* or *del pico*, grown along the banks of the Ebro River. They are used dried because in the spring, when young lamb and goat are in season, there are no fresh peppers in the Ebro gardens; only the dried peppers from the former season are available, preserved the way they were in the old days.

Pimientos choriceros or *del pico* are not available in America or Britain, but I have found that *ancho* or *pasilla* chillis (also called dried *poblanos* or *pisados*) work very well. If you cannot find these, any other kind of sweet-mild, flavourful dried chilli peppers will do. Some *chilindrón* recipes include tomatoes, potatoes, peas, ham, even fresh or canned sweet peppers; but traditionally, dried ones should be used.

This recipe was inspired by the memorable *cordero chilindrón* I had at Pamplona's Josetxo restaurant, my favourite in that city. Chef Juan Oscáriz is 'supervised' by his mother-in-law, great cook and matriarch Felisa García – over 70 and still at the stove every day – who adds the traditional touch to Juan's more inventive, innovative recipes.

I like to serve this dish with fresh crusty Peasant Bread (Pan de Payés) (p. 179) or Saffron Rice (Arroz con Azafrán) (p. 161).   *Serves 6.*

*1.4–1.6 kg (3–3½ lb) boneless lamb, cut
   into 5 cm (2 inch) pieces*
FOR THE MARINADE
*225 ml (8 fl oz) dry white wine
4 large cloves garlic, peeled and crushed*
FOR THE LAMB
3 sweet-mild dried red chilli peppers

*60 ml (4 tbsp) olive oil
350 ml (12 fl oz) dry red wine
2 large cloves garlic, finely chopped
2 large onions, chopped
450 ml (¾ pint) Brown Veal Stock
   (p. 192)
about 2.5 ml (½ tsp) salt*

To marinate the lamb   Place the lamb pieces in a non-metallic bowl with the white wine and garlic cloves. Cover and refrigerate for at least 6 hours or overnight.

To prepare the lamb   Place the chilli peppers in a saucepan and cover with water. Bring to the boil and cook over a medium heat for 10 minutes. Remove from the heat, cover and steep for 45 minutes. Drain the peppers; gently stem and seed them. Set the peppers aside and discard the liquid.

Remove the lamb from the marinade and reserve the liquid. In a heavy frying pan, heat 30 ml (2 tbsp) of the oil and over a medium heat sauté the lamb quickly, turning it until it starts to brown on all sides. Transfer the lamb to a flameproof casserole. Deglaze the pan with 175 ml (6 fl oz) of the wine and reduce to a glaze; pour over the meat. Wipe the pan clean and heat a further 30 ml (2 tbsp) oil. Add the garlic and onions; fry until soft – 10–15 minutes. Add to the casserole. Pour the remaining wine into the pan and deglaze until reduced to a syrup. Add to the casserole, together with reserved peppers. Pour the reserved marinade with the garlic over the lamb. Add the stock and bring to the boil; immediately reduce heat to very low and cook, covered, for 1½ hours or until the lamb is very tender.

Remove the lamb from the casserole. With a slotted spoon, strain the vegetables and purée very finely in a food processor or blender. Increase the heat to high and reduce the sauce to 175–225 ml (6–8 fl oz). Return puréed vegetables to the casserole, stir and taste for seasoning; add 2.5 ml (½ tsp) salt, or to taste. Add the lamb and heat through, stirring. Serve immediately.

Cordero a la Pastoril

· *LAMB STEW, SHEPHERD STYLE* ·

Start preparation 1 to 3 days ahead, by marinating lamb

Sevilla restaurant is located in Granada, in one of the most colourful parts of this extraordinarily beautiful city: the Alcaicería quarter, in the heart of town, wonderful to explore. Founded in 1930, Sevilla is one of the most typical and traditional restaurants in the city. Owner Juan Mari Álvarez is cheerful and friendly, a true Andalusian at heart. This recipe was inspired by a dish I had there.   *Serves 6.*

1.4–1.6 kg (3–3½ lb) boneless lamb, cut
   into 5 cm (2 inch) pieces
FOR THE MARINADE
6 large cloves garlic, peeled and crushed
15 ml (1 tbsp) paprika
15 ml (1 tbsp) dried oregano
2 bay leaves, middle vein removed,
   crumbled
5 ml (1 tsp) crushed hot red pepper flakes
125 ml (4 fl oz) sherry wine vinegar or
   red wine vinegar

50 ml (2 fl oz) dry white wine
5 ml (1 tsp) salt
FOR THE LAMB
45 ml (3 tbsp) olive oil
225 ml (8 fl oz) dry white wine
about 900 ml (1½ pints) Brown Veal
   Stock (p. 192)
freshly ground black pepper to taste, if
   necessary

To prepare the marinade   Place the lamb pieces in a non-metallic casserole or bowl. Purée all the ingredients for the marinade in a food processor or blender. Toss with the lamb and cover. Refrigerate for at least 24 hours or as long as 3 days, turning the lamb pieces in the marinade once in a while. Remove the lamb from the refrigerator 2 hours before cooking.

To prepare the lamb   Heat the oil in a large, heavy frying pan. Over a medium to high heat, quickly brown lamb pieces lightly, in small batches; do not wipe the marinade from the meat. Reserve the marinade left in the bowl.

Transfer the lamb to a flameproof casserole. Pour the wine into the pan and deglaze; cook rapidly to reduce by half. Transfer to the casserole. Add the stock and reserved marinade and bring to the boil. Immediately reduce the heat to very low and simmer, covered, for 1½ hours or until the lamb is very tender. Check periodically to make sure the stew doesn't boil, just simmers.

Transfer the lamb to a heated serving platter and keep warm. Cook the sauce over a high heat until reduced by half or to desired consistency. Taste for seasoning. Pour the sauce over the lamb and serve.

Cordero al Ajillo

· LAMB STEW IN A GARLIC AND SWEET PEPPER SAUCE ·

Start preparation 8 hours ahead or the day before, by marinating lamb

This is another lamb stew recipe inspired by a restaurant in Granada, Los Manueles. Established in 1917, under current owner Ángel de la Plata it has gained a well-deserved reputation for quality and friendliness. It is customary for *granadinos* to sit below its arches watching the world go by while nibbling on some of its irresistible *tapas.   Serves 6.*

FOR THE MARINADE
2 large heads garlic (about 40 cloves),
  peeled and crushed
15 ml (1 tbsp) chopped oregano, or
  3.75 ml (¾ tsp) dried
15 ml (1 tbsp) chopped thyme, or 3.75 ml
  (¾ tsp) dried
225 ml (8 fl oz) dry white wine
1.4–1.6 kg (3–3½ lb) boneless lamb, cut
  into 5 cm (2 inch) pieces
FOR THE LAMB
3 large red sweet peppers

about 45 ml (3 tbsp) olive oil
225 ml (8 fl oz) dry white wine
350 ml (12 fl oz) Brown Veal Stock
  (p. 192)
2.5 ml (½ tsp) salt, or to taste
2.5 ml (½ tsp) freshly ground black
  pepper, or to taste
AS A GARNISH
1 head garlic, very thinly sliced, sautéed
  in olive oil until crisp and golden,
  drained on kitchen paper

To prepare the marinade   In a non-metallic casserole or bowl, combine all the ingredients for the marinade and add the lamb pieces. Marinate for at least 6 hours, turning the lamb in the marinade from time to time.

To prepare the lamb   Roast and peel the peppers (see p. 32). Remove the cores and seeds, and coarsely chop the flesh. Heat the oil in a large heavy frying pan. Quickly brown the lamb lightly over a medium to high heat, in small batches: reserve the marinade. Transfer the lamb to a flameproof casserole. Add the wine to the pan and deglaze; reduce by half. Add to the casserole, together with the marinade left in the bowl, the peppers and stock. Bring to the boil, immediately reduce the heat to low and simmer, partially covered, for 1½ hours or until the lamb is tender.

Remove the lamb to a heated serving platter and keep warm. Transfer the sauce in casserole with the garlic and peppers to a food processor or blender; purée and return to the casserole. Increase the heat to high and reduce the sauce until thickened to desired consistency. Add salt and pepper, and taste for seasoning. Pour the sauce over the lamb. Garnish with sliced sautéed garlic on top.

Tronzón de Tudanco al Tresviso

· BEEF STEAK WITH MUSHROOMS IN A BLUE CHEESE SAUCE ·

This dish was among many interesting ones I had at Risco, the delightful restaurant in Laredo, Cantabria, run by Zacarías and Inés Puente, and it inspired me to develop this recipe.

The region is well known for its excellent blue cheese, Tresviso-Picón, as well as for its beef, *tudanco*. Tresviso is a mixture of cow's, goat's and sheep's cheese, similar to the Cabrales-Picón of Asturias and French Roquefort. *Tudanco* is a breed of ox that lives in the mountains; it has a lot of flavour. The word *tronzón* means large cut, and it is similar to our sirloin.   *Serves 6–8.*

FOR THE SAUCE

100 g (4 oz) sharp blue cheese, such as
  Danish Blue
125 ml (4 fl oz) dry white wine
40 g (1½ oz) butter
125 ml (4 fl oz) double cream
2 large cloves garlic, finely chopped
450 g (1 lb) mushrooms, thinly
  sliced

FOR THE STEAK

1.4 kg (3 lb) piece of steak, sirloin or
  rump
3.75 ml (¾ tsp) coarsely ground black
  pepper
5 ml (1 tsp) salt
175 ml (6 fl oz) Enriched Veal Stock
  (p. 193) or 350 ml (12 fl oz) Brown
  Veal Stock (p. 192)

To prepare the sauce   In a bowl, cream the cheese and wine with a fork. Melt
15 ml (1 tbsp) of the butter in a saucepan; add the cheese/wine mixture and cream.
Bring to the boil and reduce by one third, stirring. Set aside.

Heat the remaining butter in a frying pan and, over a low heat, fry the garlic
until soft and golden; add the mushrooms and cook until they start to soften – 6–8
minutes. Transfer to the pan with the cheese sauce. (This sauce can be prepared
ahead of time, and reheated at the last minute.)

To cook the meat   Shortly before serving time, season both sides of the steak
with pepper. Heat a heavy frying pan, large enough to hold the steak, until very
hot. Sprinkle the salt in the pan and add the steak. Cook the meat quickly, over a
high heat – it shouldn't burn, but should get dark brown – about 5 minutes on
each side, depending on the thickness. The steak should be rare, as it will continue
to cook for a few minutes after it is removed from the heat. Transfer the meat to a
chopping board and let it rest for about 5 minutes.

Meanwhile, pour the stock into the frying pan and, over a high heat, stir and
scrape the bottom and sides of the pan with a spatula to loosen all the sediment.
Cook until reduced to about 125 ml (4 fl oz). Pour into the pan with the
mushroom sauce. Stir and taste for seasoning.

Cut the meat into thin slices. Pour any juices from the meat into the sauce.
Serve the steak slices with the sauce poured on top.

Solomillo con Frutas Secas

· CATALAN – FILET DE BOU AMB FRUITS SECS ·

· FILLET OF BEEF WITH DRIED FRUITS ·

This recipe from the great restaurant El Racó d'en Binu, near Barcelona, is irresistible.
The combination of meat and fruits, here again, is classic Catalan; but it takes Francesc
Fortí's stroke of genius to put it together. It is a rich, elegant dish, worth every calorie
and sure of winning the admiration of your guests.

I prefer to serve it without any accompaniment, just by itself with the fruits; or at
the most, with Home-Style White Rice (Arroz Blanco Hervido) (p. 160).   Serves 6.

8 dried figs
18 dried apricots
12 prunes
6 × 175 g (6 oz) fillet steaks, trimmed
22.5 ml (1½ tbsp) crushed green
   peppercorns
7.5 ml (1½ tsp) salt

25 g (1 oz) butter
125 ml (4 fl oz) full-bodied Spanish
   brandy
125 ml (4 fl oz) double cream
125 ml (4 fl oz) Enriched Veal Stock
   (p. 193) or 225 ml (8 fl oz) Brown
   Veal Stock (p. 192)

Place the figs, apricots and prunes in a saucepan and cover with boiling water. Leave to soak for about 2 hours.

Tie each steak around with string, to give it a round shape. Cover both sides of the steaks with the peppercorns, and sprinkle them with 5 ml (1 tsp) of the salt. Leave at room temperature for 1 hour.

Remove the fruits from the soaking water and cut them into 6 mm (¼ inch) slices. Over a medium to high heat, reduce the liquid in a saucepan to 75 ml (3 fl oz).

In a heavy frying pan large enough to hold all of the steaks, melt the butter and, over a medium to high heat, sauté them for 1 minute on each side. Add the brandy and flambé (pp. 32–3). Set the steaks aside. Add the fruits, reduced liquid in the saucepan, cream and stock to the pan. Increase the heat and reduce the sauce by one third, or to desired consistency. Add the remaining salt or to taste. Return the steaks to the pan and coat them with the sauce. Serve immediately.

VEGETABLES

Calabacines en Escabeche

· COURGETTES MARINATED IN VINEGAR AND MINT ·

This is a very simple *escabeche* preparation, the way of marinating foods in lemon or vinegar brought to Spain by the Arabs. Served cold, it makes a very refreshing first course; it can also be served as an accompaniment to cold meats. It is ideal in a summer buffet.   *Serves 6–8.*

1.4 kg (3 lb) small courgettes, topped and tailed
about 15 ml (1 tbsp) salt
about 125 ml (4 fl oz) olive oil

12 large cloves garlic, cut into slivers
15 ml (1 tbsp) finely chopped mint
125 ml (4 fl oz) finest-quality red wine vinegar, preferably balsamic vinegar

Cut the courgettes into thin slices lengthways. Layer them on a cloth over a baking sheet; sprinkle salt between each layer. Let them dry in the sun, if possible, for 2–3 hours; otherwise, if you have a gas oven, place them in it, unheated, with just the pilot light on, for 2 hours; if you have an electric oven, heat it to 110°c (225°F) mark 4, for 10 minutes, then turn it off and leave the courgettes there for 2 hours. And if you are short of time, just let the courgettes stand for 30 minutes and pat them dry.

Heat the olive oil in a frying pan and fry the garlic over a medium to low heat until golden. Remove with a spatula and set aside on kitchen paper. Pat the courgettes dry and, in the same oil, sauté them over a medium heat in small batches, until golden on both sides. Drain on kitchen paper and layer them in a deep serving platter or wide casserole. Sprinkle each layer with garlic and mint; reserve about 15 ml (1 tbsp) of the garlic slices. Pour the vinegar over, cover and marinate for at least 3–4 hours. Just before serving, sprinkle the reserved garlic slices on top.

'Escalivada'

· ASSORTED GRILLED VEGETABLES, CATALAN STYLE ·

Escalivar is the Catalan word for cooking over hot embers; escalivada is the equivalent of charcoal-grilled vegetables, rubbed with oil and cooked whole. I usually bake them in the oven this way, unless I am already charcoal-grilling.

Escalivada is a very common first course all over Catalonia in the summertime – the peak season for red peppers, tomatoes and flavourful narrow aubergines. You can make escalivada with any or all of the vegetables in the following recipe; very often in Spain you would just be served aubergine and red peppers, perhaps with onions. On a platter, they are colourful and attractive, like a mosaic. It also makes a very nice accompaniment for grilled meat or fish, roasts or barbecued chicken. If you are cooking these on a charcoal grill, add the escalivada; it will have especially good flavour.

Carles Camós, at his Big Rock restaurant in Palamós (Costa Brava), in northern Catalonia, serves as an appetizer tosta d'escalivada amb anxoves (Catalan for toast with escalivada and anchovies) – a simple but terrific idea. He toasts thin slices of Peasant Bread (Pan de Payés) (p. 179) – you can also use a good French bread – puts a little escalivada of red pepper, aubergine and onion over it, and an anchovy fillet on top. According to Carles, the secret is just to use fresh, ripe, high-quality vegetables. Serves 4.

2 tomatoes, halved crossways	2.5 ml (½ tsp) salt, or to taste
450 g (1 lb) small aubergines	1.25 ml (¼ tsp) freshly ground black
2 large red sweet peppers	pepper, or to taste
2 onions	AS A GARNISH
2 baking potatoes, halved lengthways	30 ml (2 tbsp) chopped parsley
about 60 ml (4 tbsp) olive oil	

Preheat the oven to 180°c (350°F) mark 4.

Rub all the vegetables with about 30 ml (2 tbsp) oil. Place them on a baking sheet (tomatoes cut side up). Bake for about 15 minutes for tomatoes, 45–60 minutes for aubergines and peppers (depending on size), 1 hour for onions and potatoes.

Peel the aubergines and peppers. With your fingers, tear them into very thin strips. Arrange all the vegetables on a large platter. Season with salt and pepper, drizzle about 30 ml (2 tbsp) oil over, and sprinkle with parsley. Serve warm or at room temperature.

'Ceballots'

· BAKED YOUNG ONIONS OR LEEKS ·

Springtime in Catalonia brings on the *calçotada* – a special fiesta held in the town of Valls that celebrates the arrival of *calçots* or *ceballots*, tender young onions about the size of small leeks. *Calçotadas* are outdoor gatherings where these seasonal delicacies are grilled on open wood fires – traditionally we use vine prunings which have been cut in the winter – until they are completely charred on the outside. You peel away the burned skins, douse them with the *romesco*-style sauce *salbitxada* and feast away. Meanwhile, there is plenty of music, wine and lots of merriment. Sometimes we dance the traditional Catalonian folk dance known as the *sardana*.

Since *ceballots* are not available in America or Britain, I have found that the recipe works very well with leeks. They are best cooked on an outdoor charcoal grill, which provides great flavours; but they are also delicious cooked on an indoor grill, or even baked in the oven.

Ceballots or leeks combine perfectly with any *romesco* sauce; but I think the recipe for Romesco-Style Sauce for Grilled Vegetables (Salbitxada) (p. 196), from Pere Valls of El Celler del Penedès restaurant, goes particularly well.   *Serves 6.*

1.4 kg (3 lb) young leeks, trimmed of all
    but 5–7.5 cm (2–3 inches) of the green
    part

about 125 ml (4 fl oz) olive oil
½ quantity Romesco-Style Sauce for
    Grilled Vegetables (p. 196)

Cut the leeks in half lengthways down to within 2.5 cm (1 inch) from the bottom or root end. Rub the leeks quite generously with olive oil, and cook them (over a charcoal grill, on an indoor grill or in a preheated 220°c (425°F) mark 7 oven) until they are very tender and golden. Depending on their size and cooking method, they may take from 30–60 minutes. Turn them over occasionally while cooking.

Serve the leeks warm, with the sauce on the side.

Cebollitas a la Crema y al Perfume de Tomillo

· CATALAN – CEBETES A LA CREMA I AL PERFUM DE FARIGOLA ·

· BUTTON ONIONS IN A CREAM AND THYME SAUCE ·

I had these delicious onions at Can Boix, the Pyrenean restaurant in Martinet where Josep Boix handles with perfection the local produce of the bountiful Catalan district La Cerdanya: in this case, the baby onions and the fresh mountain thyme, which abounds there. In fact, it imparted an extraordinary fragrance to an after-lunch hike!
Serves 4–6.

700 g (1½ lb) button onions
25 g (1 oz) butter
125 ml (4 fl oz) full-bodied Spanish
  brandy
5 ml (1 tsp) chopped thyme

350 ml (12 fl oz) Brown Veal Stock
  (p. 192) or Chicken Stock (p. 191)
125 ml (4 fl oz) double cream
1.25 ml (¼ tsp) salt, or to taste

Peel the onions by dipping them in a pan of boiling water for 5–10 seconds. Immediately drain and, when cool, cut out the bottom with a sharp knife. Squeeze the onion out of its outer layer; it will pop out peeled.

Melt the butter in a medium frying pan and, over a medium to high heat, sauté the onions quickly for 4–5 minutes, shaking the pan, until they start to colour. Add the brandy and when hot, flambé (pp. 32–3). Add the thyme and stock, and bring to the boil; reduce the heat to low and cook, uncovered, for 15 minutes or until the onions are just done but still crisp.

With a slotted spoon, transfer the onions to a heated platter and reserve. Increase the heat to high and reduce the stock in the pan to just about 30 ml (2 tbsp). Add the cream, stir and cook over a medium heat to thicken a little. Add the onions and salt; cook over a medium to low heat until tender – about 5 further minutes. Taste for seasoning. Serve immediately.

Confit de Cebollas

· CATALAN – CONFIT DE CEBES ·

· ONION RELISH ·

Roig Rubí is Catalan for ruby red – and also the name of a small restaurant in Barcelona run by chef/owner Mercedes Navarro, her daughter Imma and son Juan. They opened in 1982, named it after the colour of fine red wine and set out to serve authentic Catalan home-style cooking. The restaurant's setting, with its charming umbrella-covered patio, provides the pleasant feeling of being in someone's private residence.

Mercedes's food shows her innovative approach to simple ideas. This relish makes a delightful, tangy condiment which may be served hot to accompany roast meats or poultry – it is excellent with Veal Medallions in an Orange Sauce (Medallones de Ternera a la Naranja) (p. 136) or Poussins in a Sweet and Sour Sauce (Capones al Agridulce) (p. 110) – as well as cold with pâtés, cold meats or sausages.   Serves 4.

50 g (2 oz) butter
900 g (2 lb) onions, thinly sliced
350 ml (12 fl oz) medium-bodied dry red
  wine

125 ml (4 fl oz) sherry wine vinegar or
  red wine vinegar
1.25 ml (¼ tsp) salt, or to taste
30 ml (2 tbsp) clear honey

Heat the butter in a deep frying pan. Add the onions and cook over a low heat, very slowly, until soft and golden; it should take about 45 minutes. Add the wine, vinegar and salt; cook over a medium heat until the liquid is absorbed by the onions. Add the honey and cook slowly until the honey begins to caramelize. Taste for seasoning. Serve warm or at room temperature.

Espinacas a la Catalana

· CATALAN – ESPINACS A LA CATALANA ·

· SPINACH WITH PINE NUTS AND RAISINS, CATALAN STYLE ·

You will find this classic Catalan vegetable dish – again with pine nuts and raisins – in the menus of many regional restaurants. A favourite of mine is Quo Vadis's preparation, because they get such good fresh spinach from nearby La Bouquería market, the best in town, in Barcelona's old Ramblas promenade. That's about all there is to the dish; the idea is quite simple, yet ingenious and very tasty. It is the perfect accompaniment for pork or game.   *Serves 4.*

1.4 kg (3 lb) spinach, stemmed
30 ml (2 tbsp) olive oil
50 g (2 oz) pine nuts
25 g (1 oz) raisins

1.25 ml ($\frac{1}{4}$ tsp) salt, or to taste
1.25 ml ($\frac{1}{4}$ tsp) freshly ground black
  pepper, or to taste

Rinse the spinach well and place in a large saucepan. Cook over a medium heat, covered, with only the water that clings to the leaves, just until softened – about 10 minutes, tossing with 2 spoons from time to time. Drain the spinach and squeeze dry. Chop coarsely.

Heat the olive oil in a large frying pan. Add the pine nuts and raisins; sauté over a medium to high heat until the pine nuts are golden and the raisins plump – 3–4 minutes. Add the spinach, salt and pepper, and gently toss until well mixed. Taste for seasoning. Serve warm.

Pastelitos de Espinaca

· SPINACH CUSTARDS ·

These spinach/potato moulds make a very nice accompaniment for any meat dish. *Serves 6.*

225 g (8 oz) potatoes
25 g (1 oz) butter
50 g (2 oz) chopped onion
450 g (1 lb) spinach, stemmed and
  chopped
50 g (2 oz) Gruyère or Emmenthal
  cheese, grated

2 eggs, beaten
50 ml (2 fl oz) milk
2.5 ml ($\frac{1}{2}$ tsp) salt
1.25 ml ($\frac{1}{4}$ tsp) freshly ground black
  pepper, or to taste
about 50 g (2 oz) finely grated Parmesan
  cheese

Boil, peel and mash the potatoes finely, with a potato ricer, masher or fork (don't use a food processor or blender). While still warm, mix in half the butter with a fork.

In a medium frying pan, fry the onion in the remaining butter until soft. Add the spinach and cover; cook until softened – about 3 minutes. Transfer to a bowl and combine with the mashed potatoes, grated Gruyère or Emmenthal cheese, eggs and milk. Mix well with a fork. Add salt and pepper; taste for seasoning.

Preheat the oven to 180°c (350°F) mark 4.

Oil 6 × 125 ml (4 fl oz) ramekins. Flour and shake out the excess; sprinkle with Parmesan cheese, just to coat. Fill with the spinach mixture.

Place the ramekins in a roasting pan and pour in boiling water to come halfway up the sides of the ramekins. Bake in the oven until well risen – about 30 minutes. Preheat the grill.

When the ramekins have cooled, run a knife around the edges and unmould on to a serving platter. Sprinkle the remaining Parmesan over the tops. Place under the grill for a few moments, until golden. Serve immediately.

Tartitas de Berenjena

· CATALAN – PASTISSETS D'ALBERGÍNIA ·

· AUBERGINE TARTLETS ·

These attractive little tartlets are an idea from the Tiró Mimet restaurant, where chef Xavier Grifoll serves them as an accompaniment to his Veal Fillet with Anchovy Sauce (Filete de Ternera con Salsa de Anchoas) (p. 135). The sharp taste of the aubergine provides an interesting contrast to any meat dish with a sauce.   *Serves 8.*

FOR THE TARTLETS
1 *quantity Press-in Pastry (p. 177)*
FOR THE FILLING
45 ml (3 tbsp) olive oil
450 g (1 lb) aubergine, peeled and cut
  into 6 mm (¼ inch) cubes
30 ml (2 tbsp) finely chopped onion
15 ml (1 tbsp) finely chopped garlic
1 small red or green sweet pepper

(preferably red), cored, seeded and
  finely chopped
450 g (1 lb) tomatoes, skinned, seeded
  and chopped
2.5 ml (½ tsp) salt, or to taste
1.25 ml (¼ tsp) freshly ground black
  pepper, or to taste
1 egg, beaten
125 ml (4 fl oz) double cream

To prepare the tartlets   Preheat the oven to 220°c (425°F) mark 7.

Divide the pastry dough into 8 equal pieces and use to line 8 ungreased 125 ml (4 fl oz) ramekins; press the dough into the ramekins and up on the sides, distributing it evenly. Refrigerate for at least 15 minutes. Immediately bake in the oven for 10–15 minutes, or until golden. When slightly cooled, gently remove the pastry from the ramekins and set aside. Reduce the oven temperature to 190°c (375°F) mark 5.

To prepare the filling In a large frying pan, heat 30 ml (2 tbsp) of the oil and fry the aubergine over a medium heat, stirring, for 10 minutes. Set aside. Add the remaining oil to the pan and fry the onion and garlic over a low heat for 5 minutes. Add the peppers and cook for 10 minutes. Add the tomatoes and cook until all the liquid has evaporated. Return the aubergine to the pan, stir and cook, covered, for another 10 minutes. Season with salt and pepper, and taste for seasoning. Allow to cool slightly. In a bowl, mix the egg and cream with the vegetables.

To assemble the tartlets Fill the prepared pastry cases with the mixture. Bake on a baking sheet in the oven for 15 minutes. Serve immediately.

Tortilla de Berenjenas

· AUBERGINE OMELETTE ·

The idea for this aubergine omelette comes from my good friend Mercedes Molina, who is from Murcia, one of the main vegetable-growing regions in Spain. I've enjoyed *tortilla de berenjenas* at her home, as a first course or even as a light supper; I often serve this and Spanish Potato Omelette (Tortilla Española) (p. 170) for lunch, together with Bread with Tomato, Catalan Style (Pan con Tomate) (p. 185).   *Serves 6.*

90 ml (6 tbsp) olive oil
1 large onion, chopped
900 g (2 lb) aubergine, peeled and diced small

6 eggs
5 ml (1 tsp) salt
2.5 ml (½ tsp) freshly ground black pepper

Heat 60 ml (4 tbsp) of the olive oil in a wide frying pan and fry the onion slowly for 10 minutes. Add the aubergine and cook over a medium to low heat until very tender, stirring often with a spatula – about 15 or 20 minutes. In a bowl, beat the eggs with the salt and pepper; stir in the aubergine.

Heat the remaining oil in a 20–22.5 cm (8–10 inch) non-stick frying pan. When quite hot, pour in the aubergine mixture, reduce heat to low and cook, shaking the pan occasionally, until the bottom of the omelette is set – 15–20 minutes. Cover the pan with an inverted plate slightly larger than the pan, and turn out the omelette on to it; slide the omelette back into the pan. Cook until firm and set all the way through – about 5 minutes. Slide the omelette onto a serving platter. Serve warm or at room temperature.

Flanes de Verduras

· CATALAN – ASSORTIMENT DE FLAMS DE LLEGUMS ·

· GREEN PEA AND RED PEPPER FLANS ·

El Racó d'en Binu, the very special restaurant in Argentona, near Barcelona, serves these colourful flans made with whatever vegetables are in season. I have found that green peas and red peppers work best here, and they make a very lovely combination – both colour- and tastewise. Served together or individually, they are a perfect accompaniment to poultry dishes, such as Chicken Flavoured with Sherry, in a Sherry Sauce (Pollito de Grano al Vino de Jerez) (p. 108).   *Serves 6.*

FOR THE GREEN PEA FLANS
300 g (10 oz) shelled peas, fresh or
  frozen
125 ml (4 fl oz) single cream
3 eggs
2.5 ml (½ tsp) salt
2.5 ml (½ tsp) freshly ground white pepper

FOR THE RED PEPPER FLANS
700 g (1½ lb) red sweet peppers
125 ml (4 fl oz) single cream
3 eggs
3.75 ml (¾ tsp) salt
1.25 ml (¼ tsp) freshly ground white
  pepper

Preheat the oven to 180°c (350°F) mark 4.

To prepare the green pea flans   Cook the peas in a small amount of boiling water until tender – 5 minutes for frozen, 15 for fresh. Drain them and purée in a food processor or blender; add all the remaining ingredients and blend well.

Generously butter 6 × 125 ml (4 fl oz) ramekins, especially the bases, and fill them three-quarters full with the pea mixture. Cover with foil and place them in a roasting pan; pour in boiling water to come halfway up the sides of the ramekins. Bake in the oven for 35 minutes; when done, they should feel slightly firm to the touch.

Let them cool, so that they firm up a little more, before unmoulding. Then run a knife around the rim of each ramekin and invert on to a serving plate, giving it a tap to unmould. Serve warm; if made in advance, cover with foil and reheat in the oven.

To prepare the red pepper flans   Place the peppers on an ungreased baking sheet in the oven and roast them for 45 – 60 minutes, turning them around until the skin is blackened and blistered. When cool enough to handle, peel and seed them, squeezing them dry with your hands; reserve the juices. Purée the peppers and add the remaining ingredients, proceeding as for the pea mould recipe.

Place the pepper juices in a saucepan and cook over a high heat until reduced to just about 15 ml (1 tbsp). Pour around the flans on the platter. (After the custards are unmoulded, some liquid will ooze out from the peppers; this will blend with the reduced juices, making a nice sauce.)

Flanes de Setas

· CATALAN – FLAMS DE ROVELLONS ·

· MUSHROOM FLANS ·

This is an elegant, subtle but flavourful first course, worthy of your finest dinner parties. The recipe was inspired by a dish from El Racó d'en Binu, the excellent restaurant in Argentona, near Barcelona.

In his classic style, chef Francesc Fortí has taken the idea from a traditional Catalan dish – the delicious mushrooms called *rovellons*, which usually are simply grilled and sprinkled with fresh garlic and parsley. We don't have those special mushrooms here, but I have found that some flavourful dried ones result in a dish pretty close to his rendition.   *Serves 8.*

FOR THE FLANS
25 g (1 oz) flavourful dried mushrooms,
   such as chanterelles or porcini
25 g (1 oz) butter
3 large cloves garlic, finely chopped
350 g (12 oz) fresh mushrooms, thinly
   sliced
15 ml (1 tbsp) finely chopped parsley
2.5 ml (½ tsp) salt
1.25 ml (¼ tsp) freshly ground white
   pepper
150 ml (¼ pint) full-bodied Spanish
   brandy
4 egg yolks
3 whole eggs

225 ml (8 fl oz) single cream
FOR THE SAUCE
25 g (1 oz) butter
6 shallots, peeled and finely chopped
225 g (8 oz) fresh mushrooms, thinly
   sliced
50 ml (2 fl oz) amontillado or other
   flavourful Spanish sherry
225 ml (8 fl oz) Brown Veal Stock
   (p. 192)
125 ml (4 fl oz) double cream
2.5 ml (½ tsp) salt, or to taste
2.5 ml (½ tsp) freshly ground white
   pepper, or to taste

To prepare the flans   Soak the dried mushrooms in 350 ml (12 fl oz) lukewarm water for 30 minutes. Drain them, and reserve liquid.

Preheat the oven to 180°c (350°f) mark 4.

Melt the butter in a frying pan and add the garlic, fresh and dried mushrooms, and parsley. Sauté over a low heat until the mushrooms are soft – 10–15 minutes. Season with salt and pepper. Add the brandy and, when hot, flambé (pp. 32–3). Continue sautéeing for a further 2–3 minutes, until all the liquid has evaporated. Pour the mushroom mixture into a food processor or blender, and purée. Beat in the egg yolks and eggs. Stir in the cream and blend well. Strain through a medium sieve.

Butter the sides and bases of 8 × 125 ml (4 fl oz) ramekins, and pour in the mixture. Place the ramekins in a roasting pan and pour in boiling water to come one third of the way up the sides of the ramekins. Cover with foil and bake in the oven for about 40 minutes, or until a fine skewer inserted into the centre of the flans comes out clean.

To prepare the sauce   Melt the butter in a frying pan, add the shallot and fry over a medium to low heat until soft – about 5 minutes. Add the mushrooms and continue cooking until the mushrooms are soft – about 10 minutes. Strain the reserved liquid from soaking dried mushrooms and add it; increase the heat and cook rapidly until liquid is reduced by half – about 5 minutes. Transfer to a food processor or blender and purée very finely with the sherry, stock and cream. Strain through a fine sieve into a saucepan, and heat through. Add salt and pepper, and taste for seasoning.

To assemble the dish   Serve each flan on an individual dish and pour the hot sauce over and around.

Alcachofas con Piñones

· ARTICHOKE STEW WITH PINE NUTS ·

Since it was founded in 1925 by Pepe Sánchez-Gómez, Rincón de Pepe has undoubtedly become the best restaurant in Murcia, the southeastern region which is home of the Huerta Murciana, Spain's main vegetable garden. Current owner Raimundo González-Frutos has done a fantastic job of researching and developing a great variety of delicious regional recipes. Many use the Huerta's fresh produce, such as these baby artichokes. Fresh artichoke hearts may also be used.

I usually serve this dish as a first course, in a bowl; but it is also a nice accompaniment to grilled chicken or meats.   *Serves 4–6.*

125 ml (4 fl oz) red or white wine vinegar
36 fresh baby artichokes or artichoke
* hearts*
30 ml (2 tbsp) olive oil
100 g (4 oz) streaky bacon, rinded and
* finely diced*
1 large onion, finely chopped
3 large cloves garlic, finely chopped

450 g (1 lb) ripe tomatoes, skinned,
* seeded and chopped*
750 ml (1¼ pints) Chicken Stock (p. 191)
5 ml (1 tsp) salt, or to taste
1.25 ml (¼ tsp) freshly ground black
* pepper, or to taste*
25 g (1 oz) pine nuts

In a non-metallic bowl, combine the vinegar with 1.2 litres (2 pints) water. Remove the outer leaves from each artichoke; trim top and bottom. Lay the artichoke on its side and, with a small knife, cut away from the bottom toward the top on a slant, to form points. This is a pretty way of cutting the artichokes – the edges look scalloped, the bottoms are round and the tops pointed. As you trim each artichoke, immediately plunge it into the acidulated water.

Heat the oil in a non-metallic pan. Add the bacon and cook over a medium to low heat for 10 minutes, until golden. Add the onion and garlic and fry for 5 minutes. Add the tomatoes and cook over a medium heat for 10–15 minutes, until all the liquid has evaporated. Add the stock, salt and pepper; bring to the boil. Drain the artichokes and add to the pan. Reduce the heat to a simmer and cook, covered, for 30 minutes.

Transfer the artichokes to an earthenware casserole and keep warm. Bring the liquid to the boil and reduce to about 225 ml (8 fl oz). Taste for seasoning.

Meanwhile, toast the pine nuts in a heavy frying pan over a low heat, stirring, until golden. Pour the sauce over the artichokes and sprinkle with the pine nuts.

Pastel de Col

· CABBAGE TORTE ·

This is an excellent recipe from my mother's files, traditionally Catalan in style. *Serves 6.*

1 large green cabbage
45 ml (3 tbsp) olive oil
100 g (4 oz) streaky bacon, rinded and
   finely diced
2 medium onions, finely chopped
3 eggs, beaten
25 g (1 oz) soft white breadcrumbs
   (pp. 31–2)

50 ml (2 fl oz) milk
100 g (4 oz) grated Parmesan cheese
5 ml (1 tsp) salt, or to taste
5 ml (1 tsp) freshly ground black pepper,
   or to taste
900 g (2 lb) tomatoes, skinned, seeded
   and chopped
15 ml (1 tbsp) tomato purée

Cut the cabbage in half and cook in boiling salted water for 20 minutes, covered; drain and set aside.

Heat 15 ml (1 tbsp) of the oil in a frying pan and, over a medium to low heat, fry the bacon until golden – about 10 minutes. Add the pork and cook, stirring, for 3 minutes or until cooked. Remove the pork and bacon and reserve. Add the onions to the pan and fry over a medium to low heat for 15 minutes or until very soft.

Preheat the oven to 180°c (350°F) mark 4.

In a bowl, soak the bread in the milk. Stir in the eggs, pancetta, pork, onions, cheese, 2.5 ml (½ tsp) salt and 3.75 ml (¾ tsp) pepper, or to taste.

Butter a 20 cm (8 inch) springform cake tin. Separate the cabbage leaves and arrange a third of them to cover the base and sides of the tin, overlapping the edges. Spread half the pork mixture on top. Cover with another third of the cabbage leaves, and spread the remaining filling on top. Cover with the remaining cabbage, bringing the overhanging leaves up over the top. Bake in the oven for 40 minutes.

To prepare the tomato sauce Heat the remaining oil in a frying pan and cook the tomatoes over a medium heat until reduced to a sauce consistency – 15–20 minutes. Add the tomato purée and the remaining salt and pepper. Taste for seasoning.

Unmould the cabbage cake on to a serving platter. Spread the tomato sauce on top. Serve hot.

RICE, POTATOES AND PASTA

Arroz Blanco Hervido

The rice we use in Spain is the short-grain type, the equivalent of Italian arborio, which is thicker and tastier than long-grain. It is essential to prepare any of my rice recipes, and much better than long-grain to accompany sauce dishes.

This is the way Rosalía, our family cook, always prepared rice at home. You will find it retains its fluffiness and does not stick together, so it is not necessary to add any butter. A nice way to present it as an accompaniment to any main course (especially those with sauce) is in individual moulds, as directed below.   *Serves 6.*

5 ml (1 tsp) salt   2 lemon slices
350 g (12 oz) short-grain rice, see above

In a heavy saucepan, bring 3.4 litres (6 pints) water to the boil; add the salt. Add the rice and lemon slices. Stir the rice with a wooden spatula at the beginning, so it doesn't stick to the bottom. Boil the rice, uncovered, over a medium heat for 10 minutes or until the grains are just tender.

Remove the lemon slices; strain the rice through a colander and rinse under running cold water, to stop the cooking.

To serve   Rinse a 125 ml (4 fl oz) ramekin in cold water and pack the rice firmly in it, up to 6 mm ($\frac{1}{4}$ inch) from the top. Invert the ramekin on to a serving platter and tap against the surface; it will come out in a neat mound. Repeat until you use up all the rice, rinsing the mould each time; arrange the rice moulds attractively on the platter. Before serving, cover with foil and warm through in the oven.

Arroz con Azafrán

· SAFFRON RICE ·

This flavourful rice will be a fine accompaniment to many of the meat, poultry or fish dishes in this book.   *Serves 8.*

50 g (2 oz) butter
1 large onion, finely chopped
3 large cloves garlic, finely chopped
750 ml (1¼ pints) Chicken Stock (p. 191)
2.5 ml (½ tsp) saffron threads or 1.25 ml
   (¼ tsp) powdered saffron

5 ml (1 tsp) salt
1.25 ml (¼ tsp) freshly ground black
   pepper
350 g (12 oz) short-grain rice

Heat the butter in a wide saucepan with high sides. Fry the onion and garlic over a low heat until soft – 10–15 minutes. Meanwhile, bring the stock to the boil in a small saucepan; stir in the saffron, salt and pepper. Add the rice to the onion mixture and cook for 1 minute, stirring. Add the boiling stock; return to the boil, reduce the heat to low and simmer, covered, for 18 minutes. Remove from the heat and let stand for 5–10 minutes before serving.

Arroz con Pasas y Piñones a la Catalana

· CATALAN – ARRÒS AMB PANSES I PINYONS A LA CATALANA ·

· RICE WITH RAISINS AND PINE NUTS, CATALAN STYLE ·

Here is a traditional Catalan-style rice – with pine nuts and raisins – the way I have had it as an accompaniment at El Racó d'en Binu, the great restaurant in Argentona, near Barcelona. It makes a perfect complement for any meat or poultry dish, especially those with a sweet touch such as Poussins in a Sweet and Sour Sauce (Capones al Agridulce) (p. 110) or any dish cooked with fruits.   *Serves 6.*

25 g (1 oz) butter
25 g (1 oz) pine nuts
90 ml (6 tbsp) raisins

10 ml (2 tsp) salt
350 g (12 oz) short-grain rice

In a large, heavy saucepan, melt the butter and add the pine nuts and raisins; sauté over a medium to low heat, stirring, until the raisins plump up and the pine nuts turn golden. Meanwhile, bring 750 ml (1¼ pints) water to the boil with the salt. Add the rice to the pine nuts and raisins; stir and scrape the bottom, to loosen the brown bits attached to the pan.

Add the boiling water to the rice; reduce the heat to low and cook, uncovered, for 15 minutes. Taste for seasoning. Turn off heat and cover the pan with a cloth. Leave to stand for 5 minutes. Serve immediately.

Paella Valenciana de la Ribera

· CATALAN – PAELLA VALENCIANA DE LA RIBERA ·

· CLASSIC PAELLA WITH SHELLFISH, CHICKEN AND PORK ·

Paella is, indeed, regarded as the 'national dish' of Spain. There are as many recipes for paella as there are cooks in Valencia – or in Spain. This classic recipe comes from one of my favourite restaurants in the region: Galbis, located in L'Alcudia de Carlet, a little town 20 miles south of Valencia.

Chef Juan Carlos Galbis deserves credit for breaking paella-making records by cooking this dish for 2,500 people, in a huge paella pan 4 m (13 feet) in diameter. He explained to me that the first giant paella was made for 1,000 people in March 1979, and it originated from a bet made after many bottles of wine. . . . It required 500 kg (1,100 lb) of firewood and, among other ingredients, 110 kg (220 lb) rice.

The classic Paella Valenciana always has snails – the fresh flavourful ones from the local mountains. But unless you can find them fresh, I recommend you omit them. *Serves 8.*

1.4–1.8 kg (3–4 lb) ovenready chicken,
  cut into small serving pieces
450 g (1 lb) lean boneless pork, diced
12.5 ml (2½ tsp) salt
7.5 ml (1½ tsp) freshly ground black
  pepper
30 ml (2 tbsp) olive oil, or more as
  needed
½ quantity Meat Ball (p. 132)
8 large prawns in the shell
700 g (1½ lb) squid, cleaned and cut into
  rings, see Rice in a Casserole with
  Shellfish (p. 165)
1 large red sweet pepper, cored, seeded
  and cut into thin strips lengthways

4 large cloves garlic, crushed
1 large onion, finely chopped
1.4 kg (3 lb) tomatoes, skinned, seeded
  and chopped
8 live small clams, shells scrubbed
8 live mussels, shells scrubbed (if mussels
  are not available, use 16 clams)
550 g (1¼ lb) short-grain rice
350 g (12 oz) French beans, topped and
  tailed, cut into 2.5 cm (1 inch) pieces
5 ml (1 tsp) saffron threads or 2.5 ml
  (½ tsp) powdered saffron
2 dozen fresh snails in the shell (optional)
AS A GARNISH
1–2 lemons, each cut into 8 wedges

Pat dry the chicken and pork. Season them with 5 ml (1 tsp) salt and 2.5 ml (½ tsp) pepper. Heat the oil in a large heavy frying pan or paella pan; add the chicken and sauté over a medium to high heat until golden. Remove the chicken to a colander (pour the drippings back into the pan). Add the pork to the hot oil and sauté until just golden; set aside. Shape the meat ball mixture into small, walnut-size balls and sauté until golden; set aside. Pat dry the prawns and squid; season the squid with 1.25 ml (¼ tsp) each salt and pepper. Sauté the prawns until just coloured; set aside. Finally, add the squid and sauté for 2–3 minutes, stirring; set aside.

Reduce the heat to medium, add more oil if necessary and fry the pepper until golden; set aside. Add the garlic and onion and fry until soft. Add the tomatoes and cook quickly until all the liquid has evaporated.

In a large saucepan with about 225 ml (8 fl oz) water, steam the clams and mussels on a rack until they open – 4–5 minutes for mussels, 5–10 for clams. Discard any that do not open. Strain the cooking liquid through a fine sieve. Measure the liquid and add enough water to make a total of 1.4 litres (2½ pints).

About 45 minutes before serving, bring the liquid to the boil. Meanwhile, add the rice to the tomato sauce; stir and add the port, meat balls, squid, green beans, saffron, snails if used and the remaining salt and pepper. Sauté for 2–3 minutes, stirring. Add the chicken pieces; push them down and distribute them evenly.

Add the boiling liquid and cook over a medium to low heat for 20 minutes. (Cooking this dish evenly throughout the pan is essential. The rice should simmer with small bubbles, but not boil; stir a bit on the sides and turn the skillet around to prevent overcooking in the centre.) Five minutes before cooking time is up, add the shellfish and peppers on top, arranging them attractively.

Turn off the heat and place a cloth over the pan. Leave to stand for 10 minutes. Arrange lemon wedges around the pan and serve immediately. Never let more than 20 minutes pass before eating; as the Spanish saying goes, rice doesn't wait for you – *you* wait for it!

Arroz al Horno de Verano

· CATALAN – ARRÒS AL FORN D'ESTIU ·

· BAKED RICE WITH SUMMER VEGETABLES ·

Arròs al forn (baked rice) is probably the oldest of all Valencian rice dishes. It is also called *arròs passejat* or walked rice, from the days when households had no ovens, so the wife would take the casserole to the local baker and cook it in his oven.

This is another of the many outstanding rices I relished at Galbis restaurant near Valencia. Juan Carlos Galbis, whose father started the restaurant-inn in 1939, is a born cook; he has done more than anybody I know to research and develop traditional Valencian recipes. I especially liked this rice because it is easy to put together. Like all baked rices, it is traditionally cooked in a shallow earthenware casserole. For this recipe I use one 30 cm (12 inches) in diameter. *Serves 8.*

45 ml (3 tbsp) olive oil

100 g (4 oz) streaky bacon, rinded, finely
  diced

75 g (3 oz) chorizo or other flavourful
  spicy pork sausage with paprika,
  casing removed, cut into 2 cm (¾ inch)
  rounds

225 g (8 oz) pork blood sausage, such as
  Italian blood pudding or black
  pudding, casing removed, cut into
  2 cm (¾ inch) rounds

4 large cloves garlic, finely chopped

2 large red sweet peppers, cored, seeded
  and cut lengthways into thin strips

700 g (1½ lb) ripe tomatoes, skinned and
  chopped, unseeded

450 g (1 lb) French beans, topped, tailed
  and cut into 2.5 cm (1 inch) pieces

300 g (10 oz) frozen petits pois

425 g (15 oz) short-grain rice

5 ml (1 tsp) paprika

5 ml (1 tsp) turmeric

2.5 ml (½ tsp) saffron threads or 1.25 ml
  (¼ tsp) powdered saffron

5 ml (1 tsp) salt

5 ml (1 tsp) freshly ground black
  pepper

In a large pan, heat 15 ml (1 tbsp) of the oil and add the bacon, chorizo and blood
sausages. Cook over a low heat for 10 minutes.

Heat the remaining oil in a frying pan. Add the garlic and peppers; cook over a
medium heat for 8–10 minutes, or until the peppers start to turn golden. Add the
tomatoes and cook until all the liquid has evaporated. Transfer to the pan with the
sausages. Add the beans and 1 litre (1¾ pints) cold water. Bring to the boil, reduce
the heat to low and cook for 10 minutes, uncovered. Drain through a colander
into a large shallow ovenproof casserole (preferably earthenware). Measure the
liquid, and if it is less then 1 litre (1¾ pints), add water to make up this amount. Stir
the remaining ingredients into the casserole.

Preheat the oven to 200°c (400°F) mark 6.

(One of the good things about this rice dish is that it can be prepared ahead of
time up to this point, as Juan Carlos Galbis told me: 'in the morning, before you
go to the beach; and then when you come home, just add the water, put it in the
oven, let it cook by itself and it is ready to eat!')

Bring the liquid to the boil. Add to the casserole and place in the oven for 20–30
minutes, or until rice is cooked. (Timing will depend on the oven, especially
whether it is electric or not. If the rice gets dry before it's cooked, add a little more
water.)

Remove the rice from the oven, cover with a cloth and leave to stand for 10
minutes. Serve immediately.

Arroz Caldoso de Monte

· CATALAN – ARRÒS CALDÓS DE MUNTANYA ·

· RICE WITH RABBIT IN BROTH ·

This dish is literally named mountain rice, because it is made from the produce of the
Valencian mountains: rabbit, rosemary – and snails. Again, as in the paella recipe, I
have left these optional, for I feel that unless they are fresh they don't contribute

much. Rabbit is not essential either; you can substitute chicken.

This was my favourite of all the excellent rices I had at La Venta del Toboso, an old restaurant in the city of Valencia which Javier de Zárate acquired in 1983. He and chef Rafael Haba set out to serve some of the most traditional dishes of Valencian cuisine, of which this is indeed one. The dish has more liquid than paella; it should have the consistency of a stew.   *Serves 6–8.*

1 rabbit, cut into small serving pieces	*3 large cloves garlic, finely chopped*
10 ml (2 tsp) salt, or to taste	*5 ml (1 tsp) finely chopped fresh rosemary*
5 ml (1 tsp) freshly ground black pepper,	*5 ml (1 tsp) paprika*
or to taste	*2.5 ml (½ tsp) saffron threads or 1.25 ml*
50 ml (2 fl oz) olive oil	*(¼ tsp) powdered saffron*
450 g (1 lb) mushrooms, thinly sliced	*425 g (15 oz) short-grain rice*
450 g (1 lb) French beans, topped, tailed	*2 dozen fresh snails in the shell*
and cut into 2.5 cm (1 inch) pieces	*(optional)*
700 g (1½ lb) tomatoes, skinned, seeded	*1.8 litres (3¼ pints) Chicken Stock*
and chopped	*(p. 191)*

Pat the rabbit pieces dry and season with 2.5 ml (½ tsp) salt and 1.25 ml (¼ tsp) pepper. Heat the oil in a large flameproof casserole and sauté the rabbit over a medium heat until golden. Set the rabbit pieces aside. Add the mushrooms to the casserole and sauté for 5 minutes. Add the beans and cook for a further 5 minutes. Add the tomatoes and garlic, increase the heat and cook quickly until all the liquid has evaporated. Stir in the rosemary, paprika, saffron and remaining salt and pepper. Taste for seasoning.

Stir in the rice and snails, if used, and return the rabbit to the casserole. Bring the stock to the boil and pour it in. Return to the boil, reduce the heat to medium-low and cook for 18–20 minutes, or until the rice is just slightly underdone. Turn off the heat and leave the rice to stand for 5 minutes, or until cooked to the right consistency.

Since this dish is meant to be soupy, it should be served immediately or the rice will overcook.

Arroz a la Cazuela con Marisco

· CATALAN – ARRÒS A LA CASSOLA AMB MARISC ·

RICE IN A CASSEROLE WITH SHELLFISH ·

The recipe for this classic Catalan rice dish is inspired by the superb rendition I had at Els Perols de L'Empordà (The Pots of L'Empordà), a tiny home-style restaurant in Barcelona which specializes in the cuisine of the district of L'Empordà. Owners Reinaldo and Juli Serrat are from Palamós, a fishing town in the heart of that area, where they lived until opening the restaurant in 1982. She cooks and he runs the dining room; they are *the* staff. And her cooking faithfully features some of the best recipes of their home district, prepared with love and care and great enthusiasm.

The dish is traditionally cooked and served in a shallow earthenware casserole; I use one 30 cm (12 inches) in diameter. It is a fisherman's rice, always a little soupy, and typically served with Garlic Mayonnaise (Allioli) on the side – although I find it doesn't really need it.   *Serves 8.*

FOR THE SOFRITO
50 ml (2 fl oz) olive oil
450 g (1 lb) onions, finely chopped
1.1 kg (2½ lb) ripe tomatoes, skinned, seeded and chopped
FOR THE PICADA
2 large cloves garlic, finely chopped
30 ml (2 tbsp) chopped parsley
2.5 ml (½ tsp) saffron threads or 1.25 ml (¼ tsp) powdered saffron
3.75 ml (¾ tsp) salt, or to taste
3.75 ml (¾ tsp) freshly ground white pepper, or to taste

FOR THE RICE AND SHELLFISH
900 g (2 lb) squid
16 small live clams, shells scrubbed
16 small live mussels, shells scrubbed
30 ml (2 tbsp) olive oil
350 g (12 oz) short-grain rice
about 900 ml (1½ pints) Fish Fumet (p. 194)
16 large prawns in the shell
225 g (8 oz) large scallops
AS A GARNISH (OPTIONAL)
8 lemon wedges
½ quantity Garlic Mayonnaise (p. 199), make whole recipe and use half

To prepare the *sofrito*   Heat the oil in a large flameproof casserole. Add the onions and fry slowly over a low heat, stirring from time to time, until the onions are brown and almost caramelized; add small amounts of water if necessary, so they don't burn. It may take 45 minutes or more – the longer the better, as it will add more flavour to your dish. Add the tomatoes and increase the heat to medium; cook until all the liquid has evaporated.

To prepare the *picada*   In a food processor or with a mortar and pestle, finely mash the garlic, parsley, saffron, salt and pepper. Set aside.

To clean the squid   Pull out the heads and discard the quill and innards from the squid; rinse well under running water. Cut off the tentacles from the heads, remove the beaks by pressing the tentacle base so it pops out. Remove the purplish skin from the body sacs, and cut the bodies (with fins attached) into rings. Set aside the body rings and tentacles.

To steam the clams and mussels   In a large saucepan, bring about 125 ml (4 fl oz) water to the boil and steam the clams and mussels on a rack until they open – 4–5 minutes for mussels, 5–10 minutes for clams. Set them aside. Discard any that do not open. Strain the liquid through a fine sieve. Reserve.

To cook the rice and shellfish   In a frying pan, heat the oil; add the squid rings and tentacles. Sauté for 2–3 minutes, stirring. Add squid and its juices to the casserole with the *sofrito*. Stir in the rice and *picada*.

Measure the reserved liquid and add enough fish fumet to make a total of 1 litre (1¾ pints). Bring to the boil in a saucepan. Add to the casserole and cook gently over a medium heat for 10 minutes. Add the prawns and scallops, pushing them down into the casserole so they are covered with the liquid. Cook for a further 8 minutes (altogether the rice should cook 18 minutes; it will be underdone). Turn off the heat. Arrange the mussels and clams on top. Cover the casserole with a cloth and leave to stand for 5 minutes, or until rice is the right consistency.

Serve immediately, so the rice doesn't overcook (since it is meant to be a little soupy, if you wait the rice will continue to cook). If liked, garnish with lemon wedges, and hand the Garlic Mayonnaise (Allioli) separately in a sauce-boat.

Arroz Negro con Calamares Rellenos

· CATALAN – ARRÒS NEGRE AMB CALAMARS FARCITS ·

· BLACK RICE WITH STUFFED SQUID ·

'Black rice', in a sauce made from the squid's own ink, is a dish originally from the Catalan district of L'Empordà, but found all along the Mediterranean coast of Spain. I had an especially good *arroz negro con chipirones* (black rice with tiny squid) at El Plat, one of Valencia's finest restaurants specializing in rice dishes. The ink not only makes it totally black, but also contributes an unusual, wonderful flavour.

Spanish squid have a lot of ink, because they are caught with bait. So, to obtain more ink, it is a good idea to buy extra squid – double the amount – which you can use for other recipes such as Classic Paella with Shellfish, Chicken and Pork (p. 162), (Paella Valenciana de la Ribera) (p. 162) or Shellfish Stew, Barcelona Style (Zarzuela de Mariscos) (p. 100); squid freezes well. Cleaning and obtaining the ink from the squid is rather time-consuming, but well worth it.   *Serves 6–8.*

FOR THE SQUID
700 g (1½ lb) small squid, uncleaned,
   with their ink sacs (see above – best
   buy 1.4 kg (3 lb))
225 ml (8 fl oz) Fish Fumet (p. 194)
FOR THE FILLING
30 ml (2 tbsp) olive oil
2 large onions, finely chopped
6 large cloves garlic, finely chopped
30 ml (2 tbsp) chopped parsley
5 ml (1 tsp) chopped oregano or 2.5 ml
   (½ tsp) dried
25 g (1 oz) pine nuts
15 g (½ oz) soft white breadcrumbs
   (pp. 31–2)
1 hard-boiled egg, coarsely chopped
1 egg

FOR THE SOFRITO
450 g (1 lb) unpeeled ripe tomatoes,
   chopped
2 large red sweet peppers, cored, seeded
   and chopped
pinch of crushed hot red pepper flakes
1 bay leaf
FOR THE RICE
750 ml (1¼ pints) Fish Fumet
   (p. 194)
425 g (15 oz) short-grain rice
2.5 ml (½ tsp) salt, or to taste
2.5 ml (½ tsp) freshly ground black
   pepper, or to taste
AS AN ACCOMPANIMENT (OPTIONAL)
½ quantity Garlic Mayonnaise (p. 199),
   make whole recipe and use half

To obtain ink from squid   Pull the heads of the squid from their bodies and carefully lift the long, silvery ink sacs from the inner section of the tail. Don't worry if you get some of the inner section along with them, for they will be sieved anyway. Place the ink sacs in a small fine sieve over a bowl. Pour the fumet over the ink sacs; the sieve should rest in the fumet, so the ink sacs soak at least a couple of hours. From time to time, press and stir the ink sacs with a spoon against the sieve to extract as much ink as possible. At first the liquid will be just greyish, but it will become black after a while.

To clean the squid   Discard the quill and innards from each squid body; rinse well under running water. Cut off the tentacles from the head; remove the beak by pressing the tentacle base so it pops out. Remove the purplish skin from the body sacs, and pull the fins off; you will be left with a small white pouch. Finely chop the fins. Set the fins, pouches and tentacles aside separately.

To prepare the filling   In a medium frying pan, heat the oil and, over a low heat, fry the onions and garlic until soft. Set aside half. Add the chopped fins, parsley and oregano; stir and cook for 5 minutes. Transfer to a bowl. Toast the pine nuts in a small dry frying pan over a medium heat, shaking it, until golden. Stir them into the bowl, together with the breadcrumbs and eggs.

To stuff the squid   Fit a piping bag with a wide plain nozzle and put in the filling. Stuff squid bodies only half full, otherwise they will burst, since squid shrinks as it cooks. Close the tops with a wooden cocktail stick. Prick the squid bodies once or twice with a cocktail stick.

To prepare the *sofrito*   Arrange the stuffed squid in a large shallow flameproof casserole, or in a large, heavy, deep frying pan. Stir in the reserved garlic/onion, tomatoes, red peppers, pepper flakes and bay leaf; cook over a medium heat until all the liquid has evaporated – 20–30 minutes.

To cook the rice   Bring the fumet to the boil with the ink fumet. Stir the reserved squid tentacles, rice, salt and pepper into the casserole. Add the boiling liquid and cook over a medium heat for 20 minutes; gently move the rice around so it cooks evenly throughout the casserole. Turn off the heat, cover the casserole with a cloth and leave to stand for 10 minutes.

Remove the bay leaf and cocktail sticks, and serve immediately. If desired, hand the Garlic Mayonnaise (Allioli) separately in a sauce-boat.

Patatas Aliñadas con Gambas

· POTATO SALAD WITH PRAWNS ·

Potatoes are served very often as a *tapa* in Spain, and that's how I had these at Don Peppone, a homely restaurant in the charming village of Puerto de Santa María, near Jerez. Its pleasant garden and patio provide an ideal summer luncheon or informal dinner spot after a day at the nearby beach. And José Luis Gómez-Heredia is always there, welcoming his patrons like a perfect host in his own home.

I find the combination of potatoes with prawns, peppers and tomatoes in this recipe irresistible, whether as a first course on a hot day, as a light luncheon main course accompanied by a salad, or as an anytime potato salad.   *Serves 6–8.*

FOR THE PRAWNS
125 ml (4 fl oz) dry white wine
2–3 sprigs parsley
1 bay leaf
6 black peppercorns
1.25 ml (¼ tsp) crushed hot red pepper
    flakes
10 coriander seeds
450 g (1 lb) medium raw prawns in the
    shell
FOR THE DRESSING
175 ml (6 fl oz) olive oil

45 ml (3 tbsp) sherry wine vinegar, or
    more to taste
5 ml (1 tsp) salt, or to taste
5 ml (1 tsp) freshly ground black pepper,
    or to taste
FOR THE SALAD
900 g (2 lb) new potatoes
1 small red sweet pepper, cored, seeded
    and finely chopped
90 ml (6 tbsp) chopped parsley
2 medium unpeeled tomatoes, seeded and
    diced
50 g (2 oz) chopped onion

To cook the prawns   In a large saucepan, bring to the boil 225 ml (8 fl oz) water with all the ingredients for the prawns, except the prawns themselves. Add the prawns, reduce the heat to low and cook for about 4 minutes or until the prawns are pink. Drain and discard the liquid. Peel the prawns.

To prepare the dressing   In a large salad bowl, combine all the dressing ingredients, beating with a fork.

To prepare the salad   Boil the potatoes in salted water until tender. Drain.

While the potatoes are still warm, cut them into 2.5 cm (1 inch) pieces (or into quarters if they are small) and immediately toss them with the dressing in the bowl. Leave to stand for about 30 minutes.

Add the prawns and remaining ingredients to the potatoes in the bowl; toss to combine well. Taste for seasoning. Allow the flavours to mingle for at least 2 or 3 hours. Serve at room temperature.

Pastel de Patata con Romero

· POTATO, ONION AND ROSEMARY CAKE ·

The flavour of rosemary in this cake mingles very well with any Catalan meat dish cooked with fruit, such as Stuffed Peaches with Pork and Almonds (Melocotones Rellenos) (p. 133). It can also be served as a light luncheon dish with a seafood salad. *Serves 8–10.*

75 g (3 oz) butter
700 g (1½ lb) onions, thinly sliced
900 g (2 lb) new potatoes
5 ml (1 tsp) salt

2.5 ml (½ tsp) freshly ground black pepper
45 ml (3 tbsp) coarsely chopped rosemary
225 ml (8 fl oz) single cream

In a frying pan, melt the butter and fry the onions over low heat for about 30 minutes, stirring occasionally. They should become very soft and lightly golden, but not brown.

Preheat the oven to 180°c (350°F) mark 4.

Butter a 22.5–30 cm (9–10 inch) round baking dish or pie plate. Peel the potatoes and slice them very thinly by hand. Arrange a layer of potatoes in the dish, sprinkle with some salt and pepper, arrange a thin layer of onions on top, and sprinkle some rosemary over. Continue with alternate layers, ending with rosemary. Pour the cream over and around.

Cover with a piece of kitchen foil and bake in the oven for 1 hour. Remove the foil and cook for a further 20–30 minutes, or until the top turns golden and the potatoes are tender. Serve immediately.

Tortilla Española

· SPANISH POTATO OMELETTE ·

This is the most classic omelette in Spain. Mexican *tortillas* are practically unknown in Spain; *tortilla* always means omelette, and unless you order a *tortilla francesa* (French omelette) you are bound to get an unfolded one cooked like an Italian *frittata*, as in this recipe.

It is particularly interesting to note that the person credited with inventing the French omelette was a Spaniard, Francisco Martínez Montiño; he picked up the idea from a Spanish convent and took it to the court of King Philip III, for whom he was the chef, in the early seventeenth century. Our 'Spanish omelette' is of more recent origin, well into the nineteenth century.

Practically every bar in Spain serves *tortilla española* as a *tapa*, cut into small squares or wedges. At home we had it often for supper accompanied by Bread with Tomato, Catalan Style (Pan con Tomate) (p. 185) – a great combination. It also makes a perfect picnic or lunch dish, served at room temperature. Although it can be made ahead, I prefer to eat it shortly after making it, while it is still warm.

Travelling around Spain, you will find omelettes made with anything and everything, from seasonal vegetables to fish, meat and sausages. Worth mentioning is the *tortilla sacromonte*, typical of Granada, made with calf's brains and testicles. I wouldn't dare give you the recipe – although it can be quite delicious.   *Serves 6.*

900 g (2 lb) potatoes, peeled and sliced
   into thin 2 cm (¾ inch) rounds (this can
   be done in a food processor)
3.7 ml (¾ tsp) salt

2.5 ml (½ tsp) freshly ground black pepper
125 ml (4 fl oz) olive oil
2 large onions, thinly sliced
6 eggs

Season the potatoes with 2.5 ml (½ tsp) salt and 1.25 ml (¼ tsp) pepper. Heat half the oil in a non-stick frying pan, add the potatoes and cook over a medium heat until golden brown and crispy. Toss the potatoes around with a spatula so they don't clump together; but if they stick a bit, don't worry. Meanwhile, heat 30 ml (2 tbsp) of the remaining oil in another pan and fry the onions until soft and golden – about 20–30 minutes.

In a bowl, beat the eggs; stir in the remaining salt and pepper, and the onions. Set the potatoes aside, wipe the pan clean and heat the remaining oil. Stir the potatoes into the egg mixture and pour into the pan. Reduce the heat to low and cook until lightly golden on the bottom – about 8–10 minutes.

Place on top of the pan an inverted plate slightly larger than the pan, and turn out the omelette on to it; slide the omelette back into the pan. Cook until the eggs are set – 3–4 further minutes. Serve warm, preferably.

Pasta Casera

· BASIC HOMEMADE PASTA ·

Making pasta at home is very easy and great fun, especially if you have a food processor – and even more so if you have a pasta machine. It certainly is worth it; freshly made pasta is a treat in itself.   *Makes about 450 g (1 lb)*.

300 g (10 oz) plain flour
3 eggs

5 ml (1 tsp) salt
15 ml (1 tbsp) olive oil

Put all the ingredients into a food processor. Process until the dough forms a ball or pulls away from the sides of the bowl. Remove the dough, shape into a ball and place on a floured board. Cover with a clean tea-towel and leave to rest for 15 minutes.

Divide the dough into quarters and roll out 1 quarter at a time, keeping the remaining dough covered. I prefer to roll the dough out with a straight rolling pin without handles, as it allows more control. If you have a pasta machine, process the dough according to the manufacturer's instructions.

If you do it by hand, roll the dough as thin as possible. Always roll away from you, flipping the dough over from time to time. Add flour to the board if the dough becomes sticky. Cut the dough as directed in the recipe you are using. Let the pasta dry before cooking it.

To dry the pasta, I always hang it on the back of a chair. Allow it to dry to a non-sticky state but not until it becomes brittle, or it will crack when you cut it. The timing will depend on the humidity and temperature – about 30 minutes.

If the dish you are preparing does not require the full amount of this recipe, it is best to make the whole recipe anyway and save the rest for another time; or the trimmings can be cut into noodles, allowed to dry and stored airtight for use anytime in the future.

Canelones de Espinacas

· CATALAN – CANALONS D'ESPINACS ·

· SPINACH CANNELLONI ·

I always enjoyed this dish at home; my parents' cook, Rosalía, often made it as a first course on Sundays. I was thrilled to find a very special rendition at an equally special restaurant in Barcelona, Jaume de Provença, and I have adapted Rosalía's recipe accordingly.   *Serves 8.*

FOR THE PASTA
1 quantity Basic Homemade Pasta
  (p. 171)
15 ml (1 tbsp) salt
15 ml (1 tbsp) oil
FOR THE FILLING
1.8 kg (4 lb) spinach, stems removed
15 ml (1 tbsp) olive oil
2 large cloves garlic, finely chopped
1 medium onion, finely chopped
225 g (8 oz) prosciutto, chopped

2 hard-boiled eggs, coarsely chopped
2.5 ml (½ tsp) freshly ground black
  pepper, or to taste
2.5 ml (½ tsp) freshly grated
FOR THE CHEESE SAUCE
40 g (1½ oz) butter
40 g (1½ oz) plain flour
750 ml (1¼ pints) milk
225 g (8 oz) Gruyère or Emmenthal
  cheese, grated

To prepare the pasta   Roll the dough into thin strips 10 cm (4 inches) wide, either by hand or by using a pasta machine. Cut the strips into 10 cm (4 inch) squares. Allow them to dry for about 30 minutes.

Bring a large saucepan of water to the boil, with the salt and oil. Drop the pasta squares into the water, one at a time; after the water has returned to the boil, cook for 3 minutes. Drain and immediately plunge them into a bowl of cold water. Lay the pasta flat on clean tea-towels to drain.

To prepare the filling   Place the spinach in a large saucepan, with just the water that clings to the leaves after washing it. Cook over a low heat, covered, until softened. Drain and squeeze it dry; chop and set aside.

In a frying pan, heat the oil and add the garlic, onion and prosciutto. Cook over a low heat for 15 minutes or until golden. Add the chopped spinach, eggs, pepper and nutmeg. Taste for seasoning.

To prepare the sauce   Melt the butter over a low heat; add the flour and stir until well mixed. Add the milk all at once, stirring constantly with a whisk or wooden spoon, until the mixture comes to the boil and thickens slightly – about 5 minutes. (This should be a light white sauce.) Turn off the heat and stir in half the grated cheese.

Preheat the oven to 200°c (400°F) mark 6.

To assemble the dish   Stir 175 ml (6 fl oz) of the sauce into the spinach mixture. Distribute the filling evenly on the cannelloni squares; roll each up like a cigar and place on an ovenproof platter. Pour the remaining sauce over the cannelloni, and sprinkle the remaining cheese on top. Bake in the oven for 30 minutes. Just before serving, place under the grill for a few minutes, until the cheese turns golden and bubbly.

Lasagna de Salmón a la Salsa de Vino Blanco

· CATALAN – LASAGNA DE SALMÓ A LA SALSA DE VI BLANC ·

· SALMON LASAGNE IN A WHITE WINE SAUCE ·

The idea of combining a salmon mousse with freshly made pasta comes from one of my favourite restaurants in Barcelona, Azulete. I found the dish extremely delicate, the blend of flavours enhanced by a light, very complementary sauce.

For this recipe you will need a 1.1 litre (2 pint) rectangular terrine. I use a 7.5 × 25 cm (3 × 10 inch) lidded terrine; you can also use a 22.5 × 12.5 cm loaf tin. *Serves 8.*

FOR THE PASTA
½ *quantity Basic Homemade Pasta*
  (p. 171)
15 ml (1 tbsp) salt
15 ml (1 tbsp) oil
FOR THE SALMON MOUSSE
450 g (1 lb) skinned and boned fresh
  salmon, cut into chunks (about 700 g
  (1½ lb) with skin and bones)
2 egg whites
5 ml (1 tsp) salt
2.5 ml (½ tsp) freshly ground white pepper
225 ml (8 fl oz) double cream
50 g (2 oz) lumpfish roe

FOR THE SAUCE
25 g (1 oz) butter
2 medium carrots, finely chopped
3 medium celery sticks, finely chopped
1 medium onion, finely chopped
1 large red sweet pepper, cored, seeded
  and finely chopped
225 ml (8 fl oz) dry white wine
2.5 ml (½ tsp) salt
1.25 ml (¼ tsp) freshly ground white
  pepper
125 ml (4 fl oz) double cream
125 ml (4 fl oz) Fish Fumet (p. 194)

To prepare the pasta Roll out the pasta dough, cutting the sheets to approximately fit the size of the terrine. (The pasta will stretch as you cook it, so you can cut the sheets smaller. They will have to be trimmed to size later anyway.) You will need at least 5 pieces of pasta, and up to 8 or 9 if you wish. Let the pasta dry for about 30 minutes.

Bring a large saucepan of water to the boil, with the salt and oil. Drop the pasta pieces into the water, one at a time; after the water has returned to the boil, cook for 3 minutes. Drain and immediately plunge them into cold water. Remove from the water and place on clean tea-towels to drain. Using as a pattern a piece of greaseproof paper to fit the bottom of the terrine, cut the sheets to size.

To prepare the salmon mousse In a food processor, purée the salmon with the egg whites, salt and pepper until smooth. With the motor running, pour in the cream. Stop the motor and scrape down the sides of the bowl. Process again. Remove to a bowl and fold in the lumpfish roe.

To prepare the terrine   Preheat the oven to 180°c (350°F) mark 4. Butter the terrine. Place a piece of pasta on the bottom. Spread one quarter of the salmon mousse on top (if you are using more than 5 pasta sheets, use less mousse per layer). Continue alternating layers of pasta and mousse, ending with a piece of pasta on top.

Cover the terrine with a lid or foil. Place in a roasting pan and pour in boiling water to come halfway up the sides of the terrine. Bake in the oven for 30 minutes. To unmould, run a knife around the lasagne and turn out on to a board. Cover to keep warm.

To make the sauce   Melt the butter in a frying pan and add the carrots, celery, onion and red pepper; cook slowly for 20 minutes. Pour in the wine; cook for 10 minutes. Add the salt and pepper. Transfer to a food processor or blender; purée with the cream and the fumet. Strain through a fine sieve into a saucepan. Taste for seasoning and heat through.

To assemble the dish   Cut the lasagne into 8 serving wedges. Pour some sauce over, and hand the rest separately in a sauce-boat.

'Fideuà'

· *THIN PASTA NOODLES COOKED IN A FISH FUMET* ·

Fideuà is a Valencian dish made with noodles, which in Catalan are called *fideus*. Its origin is picturesque: a group of friends went on a picnic with the intention of making a paella, but they forgot the rice. Fortunately, they had some noodles on hand, so they used them instead, and to their delight, the dish turned out to be great!

Eugenia and Josep Pedrell – he represents the third generation of a fishing family – own Eugenia restaurant in the little coastal town of Cambrils, near Tarragona, where I ate the best *fideuà* in my memory. Cooking noodles this way was an old tradition with the fishermen along the Valencian and Catalan coast.

The trick here is to sauté the dry noodles in olive oil before cooking them in the stock, until they acquire a *rossejat* (Catalan for golden) colour. It is important to use a good fish fumet; a substitute such as commercial broth or clam juice won't be as good. This was the sound advice that Eugenia's chef, Blas Moreno, gave me as I watched him in the kitchen while he sautéed the noodles, stirring all the time until they turned golden brown. Then he beamed – 'See, now it is *rossejat*' – and went on adding ladles of his wonderful fish stock, little by little, until it was totally absorbed by the noodles. *Serves 4–6.*

45 ml (3 tbsp) olive oil
4 large cloves garlic, chopped
700 g (1½ lb) unpeeled tomatoes, chopped
1.4 litres (2½ pints) Fish Fumet (p. 194)
2.5 ml (½ tsp) saffron threads

225 g (8 oz) coiled vermicelli, or fine
   spaghetti
2.5 ml (½ tsp) salt, or to taste
AS A GARNISH
1 lemon, cut into 4 or 6 wedges

In a 2.3 litre (4 pint) saucepan, heat 15 ml (1 tbsp) of the oil and add the garlic. Cook until soft and add the tomatoes; cook for 3 minutes, stirring. Add the fumet, bring to the boil and reduce to 900 ml (1½ pints). Add the saffron threads; cover and set aside.

Heat the remaining oil in a wide flameproof casserole. Add the pasta, breaking it up with your hands in about 7.5 cm (3 inch) pieces as you add it. Over a medium heat, stir the pasta with a wooden spatula for a few minutes, until it is golden brown (the more colour the pasta acquires, the more flavour it will give to this dish; but be careful not to burn it).

Bring the fumet to the boil and pour into the pan with the noodles. Add the salt and continue cooking rapidly, stirring all the time, until the liquid is absorbed by the pasta. Cooking time will vary according to the size and material of the pan – probably 10–15 minutes. Taste for seasoning. Surround the *fideuà* with the lemon wedges and serve directly from the casserole.

BREADS AND PASTRY
DOUGHS

I recommend the use of unbleached flour when making breads and doughs. Chemicals are used to bleach flour, and as a health-conscious person I feel it is important to avoid any unnecessary chemicals in our diets. These chemicals were originally introduced because bleached flour produces a better machine-made dough for mass production.

On a trip to San Sebastián, I visited the bakery of Luis Galparsoro, who is justifiably proud of his excellent, healthy breads and rolls. He uses Manitoba flour in making his products, a Canadian flour made from hard grains which produces a high-gluten flour, giving a light, well-aerated dough. High-gluten flours are available in many health food stores. Gluten makes dough elastic, which is wonderful for breads but not good for puff pastry or for any pastries, really – gluten tends to make the pastry tough.

I never sift flour. To measure it, carefully scoop it up in a measuring cup and gently slide a knife over the top of the cup to remove excess flour; do not shake the cup to level the top of the flour. Even with careful measurement, sometimes you must add more flour or liquid to a recipe to make it turn out correctly. The moisture content of flour varies greatly, which makes it difficult always to follow a recipe exactly. You must get a feel for the dough you are working with.

For the following recipes I always use a food processor; it is especially invaluable in making bread doughs – it saves time and energy.

Pasta Prensada

· PRESS-IN PASTRY ·

This is a quick and easy pastry dough, great to use for tarts and tartlets, as it avoids having to roll out the pastry – you just press it into the tin. *Makes about 350 g (12 oz) dough.*

215 g (7½ oz) plain flour   1 egg
100 g (4 oz) chilled unsalted butter, cut
    into 2.5 cm (1 inch) cubes

In a food processor, mix together the flour and butter; process until the flour acquires the consistency of semolina. Add the egg and process until a ball forms. Press the pastry into the tins. Keep the pastry at room temperature for ease in pressing.

Always refrigerate this pastry for at least 15 minutes before baking. This will keep it from shrinking during baking.

Pasta Brisa

· PIE PASTRY ·

This recipe is excellent for baking savoury as well as sweet pastry dishes – quiches, sweet tarts, etc. It is a basic pastry dough, not flaky rich but thin and crispy. *Makes 450 g (1 lb) dough.*

215 g (7½ oz) plain flour   1 egg yolk
100 g (4 oz) frozen unsalted butter, cut   2.5 ml (½ tsp) salt
    into 1 cm (½ inch) cubes   75 ml (5 tbsp) ice-cold water

In a food processor, mix together the flour and butter. Process to combine until it reaches the consistency of semolina.

In a bowl, mix together the egg yolk, salt and water; add to the flour and butter mixture. Process until a ball forms. (If a ball doesn't quite form, remove the dough and knead with your hands for a short while – about 30 seconds.)

Shape into a ball, place in a plastic bag and refrigerate for about 30 minutes.

Pasta de Hojaldre

· PUFF PASTRY ·

This recipe dispels the idea that making puff pastry is only for professionals. It is not difficult to make, and a real treat for those special recipes.

You can buy puff pastry ready-made, but it will never taste as good as home-made – especially if you use good, fresh butter.   *Makes 450 g (1 lb) dough.*

150 g (5 oz) minus 15 ml (1 tbsp) plain flour
15 ml (1 tbsp) cornflour
3.75 ml ($\frac{3}{4}$ tsp) salt

225 g (8 oz) chilled unsalted butter, cut into 1 cm ($\frac{1}{2}$ inch) pieces
50–125 ml (2–4 fl oz) ice-cold water
flour for sprinkling

In a bowl, combine the flour, cornflour and salt. With your hands, work the butter and flour together; the butter pieces should flatten a bit but not be completely incorporated into the flour. Work quickly; the butter must not get warm. (If you are working in warm weather, refrigerate the dough for 10 minutes at this point.) Pour in enough iced water to draw the flour and butter together. The dough should stick together, but not in a neat ball – in fact, it will be a mess. Gather it into a mound in the bowl.

Flour a pastry board or marble, as well as your hands and rolling pin. Put the dough on the board, and roll it out to about 45 × 15 cm (18 × 6 inches). It will not be a neat rectangle at this point; there will probably be holes, which you can patch. It will help to use a dough scraper, as the dough will stick to the board. It is very important to roll only back and forth, not sideways or diagonally. Work quickly; overworking the dough raises the gluten in the flour and makes it too elastic to work with. Keep your board and rolling pin well floured.

Fold the top of the dough one third of the way down towards you, and then fold over again – as if folding a letter. Turn the open flap to your left, and roll the dough straight up the board into another 45 × 15 cm (18 × 6 inch) piece; it will be a neater rectangle this time. Each roll and fold of the dough is called a turn. Fold the dough again the same way as before – that is, do one more turn. Place the flat piece of dough in a plastic bag and refrigerate for 30 minutes.

Remove from the refrigerator and do 2 more turns. Refrigerate for a further 30 minutes.

Do 2 more turns. Now roll it out in any direction you want, to cut as directed in your recipe. Always cut puff pastry with a sharp knife, making a clean cut, the less you touch it with your fingers, the better it will rise.

Puff pastry, covered, will keep in the refrigerator for a week, and for 1 month in the freezer.

Pasta Akelaŕe

· CRISP PASTRY CRUST ·

I named this crusty, nutty dough after the Akelaŕe restaurant in San Sebastían, where I had it in a delicious wild strawberry tart. Wild strawberries are hard to come by here, but this crust will make any fresh fruit tart special. I use it in my Aunt Oriola's Lemon Tart (Tarta de Limón Oriola) (p. 207), and also filled with some ice creams such as Date-Nut Honey Ice Cream (Helado de Miel con Nueces y Dátiles) (p. 232) with Chocolate Sauce (Salsa de Chocolate) (p. 200) on top – why not! Rich, sinful and plain yummy.   *Makes a 22.5 cm (9 inch) pie crust.*

40 g (1½ oz) blanched almonds
50 g (2 oz) unsalted butter, at room
*   temperature*

150 g (5 oz) plain flour
30 ml (2 tbsp) sugar

Preheat the oven to 180°c (350°f) mark 4.
   In a food processor, grind the almonds finely. Add the remaining ingredients and process until there are no lumps of butter.
   Press the dough into an ungreased 22.5 cm (9 inch) loose-based flan tin; make a thin, even layer. Place in the oven and bake for 20 minutes, or until golden brown.

Pan de Payés

· CATALAN – PA DE PAGÈS ·

· PEASANT BREAD ·

This is the bread you find most often in Catalonia. It is simple to make with a food processor, and home-made bread is a great addition to any dinner.   *Makes 2 small loaves.*

15 g (½ oz) dry active yeast
15 ml (1 tbsp) sugar
450 ml (¾ pint) lukewarm water (40–46°c)

15 ml (1 tbsp) salt
800 g (1¾ lb) strong plain flour

In a food processor bowl, dissolve the yeast and sugar in the water; don't stir, just leave to stand for 5–10 minutes, to activate the yeast (when the yeast starts popping to the top, that means it is ready to work). Immediately add the salt and 65 g (2½ oz) flour; process to combine well. Add all the remaining flour; process for 2 minutes. Oil a bowl and place the dough in it, turning to coat it on all sides with oil. Cover with a cloth and put the bowl in a warm place for about 1 hour, or until the dough has doubled in size.

Punch down the dough to release the air, and let it rest for 3–4 minutes. Oil a large baking sheet. Shape the dough into 2 round mounds and place them on the baking sheet. Using a razor blade or a very sharp knife, make 3 parallel slashes on the tops. Cover again with a cloth and leave to rise in a warm place for 20–30 minutes, or until they again double in size.

Preheat the oven to 200°c (400°F) mark 6.

Place a pan of hot water on the bottom of the oven, or on the bottom rack if it is electric. Just before baking, spray the dough with water to obtain a harder crust. Bake for 30–35 minutes, or until the loaves are golden and sound hollow when thumped on the top. Remove to a rack and allow to cool.

Pan de Molde

· LOAF BREAD ·

This is the bread Koldo Lasa uses to make his Prawn Toast (Tosta de Gambas) (p. 82). It not only is perfect for that dish, but also makes great toast. It's fun and easy to make, especially with a food processor.   *Makes 2 standard-size loaves, about 8.5 × 20 cm (3½ × 8 inches).*

15 g (½ oz) dry active yeast
15 ml (1 tbsp) sugar
425 ml (14 fl oz) lukewarm water (40–46°c)
225 ml (8 fl oz) milk

25 g (1 oz) butter
5 ml (1 tsp) salt
800 g (1¾ lb) strong plain flour
1 egg

In a food processor bowl, dissolve the yeast and sugar in the water; don't stir, just leave to stand for 5–10 minutes, to activate the yeast (when the yeast starts popping to the top, that means it is ready to work). Meanwhile, heat milk to lukewarm, add the butter and salt and set aside. As soon as the yeast is activated, add 150 g (5 oz) of the flour and process for 1 minute. Add the milk mixture and egg, and process to combine. Add the remaining flour and process until the dough draws away from the sides of the bowl.

Oil two 8.5 × 20 cm (3½ × 8 inch) loaf tins. Divide the dough in half and put into the tins, pressing gently along the sides and corners to even out the surface somewhat. Cover with a cloth and leave to rise for 1 hour, or until doubled in size.

Preheat the oven to 220°c (425°F) mark 7.

Place the loaf tins in the oven and bake for about 30 minutes, or until they are golden on top and the bread shrinks away from the sides of the pans. Immediately remove the loaves from the tins and place on a rack to cool.

Bollos de Pan con Café

· WHOLEMEAL BREAD ROLLS WITH GROUND COFFEE ·

These bread rolls were the perfect accompaniment to a memorable lunch at the Arzak restaurant in San Sebastián; I just had to go to the bakery that afternoon to get the recipe. Owner Luis Galparsoro was delighted not only to share it with me but to proudly show me around his bakery – indeed an impressive, modern establishment which also happens to make great bread.

You will not notice any coffee flavour in these rolls; the ground coffee just provides an interesting texture, which I couldn't figure out until Luis told me what it was. The rolls are not strongly flavoured, so they will complement any dish. *Makes 12 medium rolls.*

25 g (1 oz) dry active yeast
45 ml (3 tbsp) clear honey
350 ml (12 fl oz) lukewarm water
   (40–46°c)
15 ml (1 tbsp) salt

15 ml (1 tbsp) ground coffee
45 ml (3 tbsp) vegetable oil
300 g (10 oz) strong plain flour
300 g (10 oz) strong wholemeal flour
about 45 ml (3 tbsp) cracked wheat

In a food processor bowl, dissolve the yeast and honey in the water; don't stir, just leave to stand for 5–10 minutes, to activate the yeast (when the yeast starts popping to the top, that means that it is ready to work). Immediately add the salt, ground coffee, oil and half the white flour; process to combine well. Add the wholemeal flour and remaining white flour; process for 2 minutes or until the dough draws away from the sides of the bowl.

Oil a bowl and place the dough in it, turning to coat it on all sides with oil. Cover with a damp cloth, put in a warm place and leave to rise until doubled in size – about 1 hour.

Punch down the dough. Divide it into quarters, and each quarter into 3 equal pieces. Form each piece into a ball, folding it over to make it smooth. Put the cracked wheat in a dish. Oil a large baking sheet (or two). Holding each ball at the bottom with your fingers, dip it into the cracked wheat and place well apart on the oiled sheet(s). Cover the rolls with a cloth and leave in a warm place to rise again for 30 minutes.

Preheat the oven to 220°c (425°F) mark 7.

Bake the rolls in the oven for 20 minutes or more, until they are dark brown and crusty. Remove to a rack and leave to cool.

Rollos de Pan

· BREAD RINGS ·

The idea for these attractive ring-shaped rolls came from the Sevilla restaurant in Granada, where I had some that were similar to accompany their tasty Lamb Stew, Shepherd Style (Cordero a la Pastoril) (p. 144). The rings are fun to make, and complement all the lamb dishes in this book as well as any meat or fish stew.   *Makes 12 medium bread rings.*

15 g (½ oz) dry active yeast
15 ml (1 tbsp) sugar
225 ml (8 fl oz) lukewarm water (40–46°c)
30 ml (2 tbsp) olive oil
5 ml (1 tsp) salt

365 g (12¾ oz) strong plain flour
FOR FINISHING
45 ml (3 tbsp) olive oil
5–10 ml (1–2 tsp) coarse salt (optional;
see Note at the end of recipe)

In a food processor bowl, dissolve the yeast and sugar in the water; don't stir, just leave to stand for 5–10 minutes, to activate the yeast (when the yeast starts popping to the top, that means it is ready to work). Immediately add the oil, salt and 150 g (5 oz) of the flour; process for 1 minute. Add the remaining flour and process until a ball forms or the dough draws away from the sides of the bowl. Continue to process for 1 minute.

Oil a bowl and place the dough in it, turning to coat it on all sides with oil. Cover with a cloth and leave to rise in a warm place until doubled in size – about 1 hour.

Punch the dough down to release the air. Divide it into quarters and then divide each quarter into 3 equal pieces. Work with 1 piece at a time and keep the remaining dough covered. With your hands, roll each piece of dough, making it into a 30–35 cm (12–14 inch) long roll. Press the edges together to form a ring. Place the rings on 2 oiled baking sheets, setting them 5 cm (2 inches) apart. Cover them with a cloth and leave to rise for a further 30 minutes.

Preheat the oven to 160°c (375°F) mark 5.

Place the rings in the oven and bake for 5 minutes. Brush with the olive oil. Bake for a further 10 minutes. Brush again with oil; if desired, sprinkle with salt. Bake for a further 5–10 minutes, or until the rings are golden brown. Remove to a rack and leave to cool.

(Note: If the dish to be accompanied by these bread rings will not blend well with their salty flavour, don't add the coarse salt. A dish such as Lamb in a Mild Dried Pepper Sauce (Cordero Chilindrón) (p. 143), for example, will go very nicely with these bread rings without the salt.)

Pan de Mollete

· *CHIGNON BREAD* ·

These delicious rolls, shaped to resemble the back of a woman's head with a bun or chignon at the nape of the neck, are so unusual-looking your guests will love them. I took the idea from the great Galician restaurant Chocolate, where Josefa Cores serves them with all her wonderful food. She told me they are typical of Galicia because so many women wear their hair in a low bun – a style that, in this region, is called *mollete*.

This recipe will yield 16 medium rolls, so you may want to halve the quantities. But if you have a large food processor or heavy-duty mixer, why not make them all? You will certainly have requests for seconds, and they are just as good warmed up the next day.   *Makes 16 medium rolls.*

50 g (2 oz) butter, at room temperature   *10 ml (2 tsp) salt*
450 ml (¾ pint) milk   *2 eggs*
25 g (1 oz) dry active yeast   *900 g (2 lb) strong plain flour*
30 ml (2 tbsp) sugar

In a saucepan, melt the butter in the milk over a low heat until lukewarm 40–46°c (105–115°f).

In a food processor or mixer bowl, dissolve the yeast and sugar in about 125 ml (4 fl oz) of the lukewarm milk/butter mixture; don't stir, just leave to stand for 5–10 minutes, to activate the yeast (when the yeast starts popping to the top, that means it is ready to work). Immediately add the salt, eggs, remaining milk/butter and 150 g (5 oz) of the flour; process to combine well. Gradually add the remaining flour; the dough will be sticky, but it doesn't matter – the less flour you use, the lighter the bread will be.

Oil a bowl and place the dough in it, turning to coat it on all sides with oil. Cover with a cloth and leave to rise in a warm place until doubled in size – about 1 hour.

Punch the dough down to release the air. Divide it into quarters, and each quarter into 4 equal pieces. Work the dough with your fingers into 16 smooth round balls. Place them on 1 or 2 oiled baking sheets. Cover with a cloth and leave to rise again for about 40 minutes.

Preheat the oven to 190°c (375°f) mark 5.

Form the rolls to resemble the back of a woman's head with a bun at the nape of the neck. Pinch up a small ball from each roll, working just off centre from the top of the roll (as if the woman's head were face down), to make it look like a chignon. The rolls will deflate a little, but don't worry; they will puff up in the oven.

Bake in the oven for 25–30 minutes, until golden and crusty. Remove to a rack and leave to cool.

Pan de Romero

· ROSEMARY-RAISIN WREATH BREAD ·

This bread is especially wonderful with lamb or meat dishes cooked with fruits – as in the Catalan recipes in this book. The aromatic pungency of the rosemary blends very well with any sauce that has a touch of sweetness. The bread will also look very nice on a buffet dinner table, decorated with rosemary sprigs.   *Makes 1 large wreath.*

15 g (½ oz) dry active yeast
5 ml (1 tsp) clear honey
225 ml (8 fl oz) lukewarm water
   (40–46° c)
225 ml (8 fl oz) milk
30 ml (2 tbsp) coarsely chopped rosemary

65 g (2½ oz) dark raisins
800 g (1¾ lb) strong plain flour
30 ml (2 tbsp) fruity olive oil
7.5 ml (1½ tsp) salt
AS A GARNISH (OPTIONAL):
a bouquet of fresh rosemary sprigs

In a food processor bowl, dissolve the yeast and honey in the warm water; don't stir, just leave to stand for 5–10 minutes, to activate the yeast (when the yeast starts popping to the top, that means it is ready to work). Meanwhile, heat the milk in a small saucepan until warm; set aside. In a small bowl, toss the chopped rosemary and raisins with 65 g (2½ oz) of the flour and set aside.

As soon as the yeast is activated, mix in the warm milk (it should be at 40–46°c (105–115°F)), olive oil, salt and 150 g (5 oz) of the flour; process for 1 minute. Add the remaining flour and process until the dough draws away from the sides. Turn the dough out on to a floured board and knead in the raisins and rosemary with their flour. Continue to knead until these are evenly distributed throughout the dough, and the surface is shiny and elastic.

Oil a bowl and place the dough in it, turning to coat on all sides with oil. Cover with a cloth and leave to rise in a warm place until doubled in size – about 1 hour.

Oil a pizza pan. Punch the dough down to release the air. Lift it and, holding it in both hands, punch your thumbs through the middle of the dough and pull it apart to make a large doughnut-shaped bread, about 30 cm (12 inches) in diameter. Be sure to make the hole in the centre quite large; it will close up as the bread bakes. Place on the oiled pizza pan, and slash it around the edges with a sharp knife or razor blade, to make it resemble a braided wreath. Brush the top with olive oil, and leave to rest for 5 minutes.

Place the loaf in a cold oven, turn the oven to 200°c (400°F) mark 6 and bake for 35 minutes, or until the crust is browned and the bread sounds hollow when tapped on the top.

Remove to a rack and leave to cool. Serve it on a wooden board, garnished, if desired, with the rosemary sprigs.

Pan con Tomate

· CATALAN – PA AMB TOMÀQUET ·

· BREAD WITH TOMATO, CATALAN STYLE ·

The idea for this bread couldn't be more simple – and yet I have found it only in Catalonia, usually served at country-style restaurants instead of plain bread. Sometimes it is accompanied by some Catalan anchovies (those from La Scala, on the Costa Brava, are *the* best), cold local sausages or cured ham.

That's how I serve it at home – as an appetizer with anchovies, prosciutto, salami or other cold sausages; I slice the bread very thin, and cut it in small pieces. I also find it a winner for a light lunch with Spanish Potato Omelette (Tortilla Española) (p. 170) and/ or Aubergine Omelette (Tortilla de Berenjenas) (p. 155). At home we often had it like that for supper on Sundays, when the cook had been off in the afternoon and had to whip up something quick! In fact, you can serve this bread *anytime*.   Serves 4.

8 large, thin slices of Peasant Bread
  (p. 179) or French bread
2 large cloves garlic, peeled and cut in
  half lengthways (optional)
2 large, very ripe tomatoes, cut in half
  crossways

30 ml (2 tbsp) olive oil
salt and freshly ground black pepper to
  taste

Toast the bread on both sides. If desired, rub the garlic, cut side down, on the bread. Cupping ½ tomato in your palm, rub 2 pieces of bread with each tomato half; squeeze the tomato so that not only the juice and seeds ooze on to the bread but also some of the pulp.

Drizzle the oil over, and sprinkle with salt and pepper to taste. This bread is best served while still warm.

Coca de Tomate y Pimiento

· CATALAN – COCA DE TOMÀQUET I PEBROT ·

· FLAT BREAD WITH TOMATO AND PEPPER TOPPING ·

The name *coca* is given to a number of different breads or pastries in Catalonia. There are two basic kinds: savoury and sweet. The first have a bread base; they are particularly traditional in the northeastern regions of Catalonia, such as L'Empordà and Maresme. These bread *cocas* are usually long and oval; they are often toasted, rubbed with half a fresh tomato – or with garlic – and sprinkled with olive oil and salt, in the style of the preceding recipe.

At L'Olivé restaurant in Barcelona, which specializes in traditional Catalan cuisine, *coca del Maresme torrada amb tomàquet* (Catalan for toasted *coca* from Maresme with tomato) is served with your meal instead of bread, much like Bread with Tomato, Catalan Style (Pan con Tomate) (p. 185). In the old days, this plain bread *coca* or *coca de forner* (baker's *coca*) was also called in Catalan *pa de torn* or return bread, because it was given 'in return' as change for a purchase at the bakery.

Sweet *cocas* are used in a very different way – for breakfast, midday snack or dessert; they are usually covered with candied fruit, pine nuts and sugar. Most of them have a religious connotation; perhaps the best known is *coca de San Juan*, eaten on St John's Day, 24 June. To me, they are a little too sweet, especially when they have sugar and candied fruit on top. Some are covered with only pine nuts and sugar, which I love; then they are more like my Pine Nut Tart (Tarta de Piñones) (p. 211).

The savoury *cocas* sometimes have on top different local produce such as herring or anchovies, peppers, stoned olives, cooked eggs or cold cuts. The following version makes a great party dish or, cut in squares, a convenient appetizer. It is best served warm (reheated at the last minute). For greater effect, serve it on a large wooden board and cut it at the table.   *Makes one 25 × 32.5 cm (10 × 15 inch) flat bread.*

FOR THE CRUST
15 g (½ oz) dry active yeast
5 ml (1 tsp) sugar
125 ml (4 fl oz) lukewarm water
(40–46°c)
125 ml (4 fl oz) olive oil
50 g (2 oz) finely chopped onion
125 ml (4 fl oz) dry white wine, at room
temperature
10 ml (2 tsp) salt
450 g (1 lb) strong plain flour

FOR THE TOPPING
45 ml (3 tbsp) olive oil
10 large cloves garlic, sliced or coarsely
chopped
450 g (1 lb) green peppers, cored, seeded
and cut into 1 cm (½ inch) dice
1.8 kg (4 lb) tomatoes, skinned, seeded
and chopped
5 ml (1 tsp) salt, or to taste
3.75 ml (¾ tsp) freshly ground black
pepper, or to taste
25 g (1 oz) pine nuts

To prepare the crust   In a food processor bowl, dissolve the yeast and sugar in the water; don't stir, just leave to stand for 5–10 minutes, to activate the yeast (when the yeast starts popping to the top, that means it is ready to work). Meanwhile, in a frying pan heat the oil and, over a low heat, soften the onion.

As soon as the yeast is activated, add the wine, salt and 150 g (5 oz) of the flour and process to combine thoroughly. Add the onion with its oil and a further 150 g (5 oz) of the flour; mix well. Add all the remaining flour; process for 2 minutes. Oil a bowl. Remove the dough from the food processor and place in the bowl, turning to coat it on all sides with oil. Cover with a cloth and leave to rise in a warm place until doubled in size – about 1 hour.

To prepare the topping   In a frying pan, heat the oil and add the garlic; fry over a medium heat until the garlic is golden and crunchy. Add the peppers and cook for a couple of minutes, stirring to prevent the garlic from burning. Add the tomatoes and season with salt and pepper. Cook briskly for 10–15 minutes, or until the tomatoes are reduced to a thick sauce. Taste for seasoning.

Preheat the oven to 200°c (400°F) mark 6.

Punch down the dough to release the air. Grease a 25 × 32.5 cm (10 × 15 inch) Swiss roll tin. Press the dough into the tin, shaping the edges up to make a border.

Pour the topping over the dough and spread to cover. In a small dry frying pan, toast the pine nuts over a low heat, stirring, until they colour. Sprinkle the pine nuts over the top of the *coca*.

Bake in the oven for 25–30 minutes, or until the dough edges are golden brown. Remove to a rack and leave to cool.

Roscón de Reyes

· *CATALAN – TORTELL DE REIS* ·

· *THREE KINGS' SWEET BREAD WITH ALMOND FILLING* ·

Start preparation at least 6 hours in advance, or the day before

Tortells are a most popular dessert in Catalonia; they are always round, shaped like a doughnut, and filled with anything rich and sinful – whipped cream, chocolate, pastry cream. At home we had them on Sundays; we would go to the pastry shop, which was invariably crowded, after mass. In Spain nobody makes *tortells* at home; they always come from a pastry shop.

Just like *cocas* (see preceding recipe), some *tortells* have religious ties. A memorable one is the *tortell de Sant Antoni*, eaten on his feast day, 17 January. He is the patron saint of animals – and affectionately nicknamed St Anthony of the Donkeys because of his reputed ability to cure the maladies of people *and* animals. Even today, in the memory of this St Anthony, on 17 January a parade is organized in Barcelona and other towns all over Catalonia, where the farmers take their animals to the church to be blessed. Inside the church, *tortells* are sold and also given to the animals after they are blessed.

Tortell de Reis is probably the one *tortell* eaten not only in Catalonia but elsewhere in Spain (where it is known as *Roscón de Reyes*) on 6 January, Epiphany or Three Kings' Day. The tradition of eating this *tortell* has very ancient roots, dating back to the fifteenth century, in France as well as in Spain. The celebration was also called Fiesta de la Haba or festivity of the fava bean, because a dried fava bean was hidden in the filling. In the old days, the fava bean was a symbol of bad luck; but later it lost its negative connotation, and whoever found it in his or her piece was the king or queen of the festival!

Even today, it is traditional to hide inside the filling a fava bean and/or a little prize, usually a tiny white ceramic piece – something silly like a duck or a shoe. I remember, as a child, buying *tortells* hoping to find the prized fava bean *and* prize. And I still keep in Spain my enviable collection of prizes gathered over the years.

This recipe is adapted from one of my favourite delicatessen/pastry shops in Barcelona, Mantequerías Tívoli. Sadurní Val proudly features a selection of sweet and savoury pastries, party dishes, cheeses and wines.

This *tortell* can be served as a dessert or as a teatime cake, and it is also superb for breakfast with a little sweet butter. For this to be a true *tortell de reis*, you *must* have a little ceramic or plastic toy – how about a tiny Spanish bull, like those on our Tres Torres bottle – to insert in the filling. The finder gets a kiss! *Makes one 30 cm (12 inch) ring.*

FOR THE DOUGH
15 g (½ oz) dry active yeast
90 g (3½ oz) sugar
125 ml (4 fl oz) lukewarm water
   (40–46°c)
75 g (3 oz) unsalted butter, at room
   temperature
3 eggs
2.5 ml (½ tsp) salt
5 ml (1 tsp) vanilla extract

30 ml (2 tbsp) orange zest (p. 31)
350 g (12 oz) strong plain flour
FOR THE FILLING
225 g (8 oz) ground blanched almonds
150 g (5 oz) sugar
90 ml (6 tbsp) fresh orange juice
1.25 ml (¼ tsp) almond extract
FOR THE FINISHING
1 egg
50 g (2 oz) flaked almonds

To prepare the dough   In a small bowl, dissolve the yeast and half the sugar in the water; don't stir, just leave to stand for 5–10 minutes, to activate the yeast (when the yeast starts popping to the top, that means it is ready to work). Meanwhile, in a food processor or mixer, beat the remaining sugar with the butter, eggs, salt, vanilla and orange zest. Add the yeast as soon as it is ready, and mix well. Add 150 g (5 oz) of the flour and beat vigorously. Add the remaining flour and continue to process until well mixed.

Transfer to a bowl (if you used a food processor), cover with a cloth and allow the dough to rise in a warm place until doubled in size. It may take as long as 2 hours.

Stir down the dough with a spoon or your fingers (this is a sticky dough) to release the air. Refrigerate for at least 2 hours and up to 3 days (it will also rise in the refrigerator).

To prepare the filling   In a food processor, process the almonds and sugar until the mixture starts to move up the sides of the bowl. Gradually add the orange juice, and flavour with the almond extract. (If you make this ahead of time, keep it covered in the refrigerator.)

To assemble the sweet bread   Stir down the dough again. Flour your hands and a board, and roll the dough into a 75 cm (30 inch) long log. Pat the log flat to about 12.5 cm (5 inches) wide. Spread the filling all the way down the centre of the log, to within 2.5 cm (1 inch) of the side edges. At this point, remember to insert a little 'prize' inside the filling!

Pinch the sides of the dough up and over the filling. Pinch the log ends together to form a circle. Place the bread, seam side down, on a buttered pizza pan or a large baking sheet.

To finish the *tortell*   Beat the egg in a small bowl and brush the top of the bread with it. Press the almonds all over. Allow the bread to rise, uncovered, for 20 minutes.

Preheat the oven to 200°c (400°f) mark 6.

Bake the bread in the oven for 25 minutes. Serve warm.

Empanada de Anchoas

· ANCHOVY AND ONION PIE ·

Empanadas are classic seafood or meat pies from Galicia. I had one of the best at my favourite Galician restaurant in Madrid, Combarro. Manuel Domínguez, a Galician, has faithfully taken to Spain's capital the classic fish and shellfish dishes of his region, with great success.

In this recipe I've used an anchovy filling – an idea of Manuel's – which works perfectly with the other ingredients. The dough using cornmeal is inspired by a unique corn *empanada* I had at Chocolate, the terrific Galician restaurant near Pontevedra. *Serves 8.*

FOR THE DOUGH
50 g (2 oz) yellow or white cornmeal
5 ml (1 tsp) salt
15 ml (1 tbsp) olive oil
15 g ($\frac{1}{2}$ oz) dry active yeast
10 ml (2 tsp) sugar
215 g (7$\frac{1}{2}$ oz) strong plain flour
FOR THE FILLING
45 ml (3 tbsp) olive oil
2 large onions, thinly sliced
3 cloves garlic, finely chopped
15 ml (1 tbsp) paprika

1$\frac{1}{2}$ × 50 g (2 oz) cans flat anchovy fillets,
or 13–14 large fillets, drained and
chopped
2.5 ml ($\frac{1}{2}$ tsp) freshly ground black
pepper, or to taste
450 g (1 lb) unpeeled tomatoes, puréed
2 hard-boiled eggs, chopped
25 g (1 oz) dark raisins
FOR THE CRUST
15 ml (1 tbsp) milk
15 ml (1 tbsp) cornmeal

To prepare the dough Bring 125 ml (4 fl oz) water to the boil and pour over the cornmeal. Stir in the salt and oil. Allow to cool.

In a food processor bowl, dissolve the yeast and sugar in 50 ml (2 fl oz) lukewarm water 40–46°c (105–115°F). Don't stir, just leave to stand for 5–10 minutes, to activate the yeast (when the yeast starts popping to the top, that means it is ready to work). As soon as the yeast is ready and the cornmeal has cooled to at least 46°c (115°F), add the cornmeal and flour to the yeast. Process to combine well, until the dough draws away from the sides of the bowl or forms a ball. Oil a bowl and put the dough in it, turning to coat it on all sides with oil. Cover and put in a warm place until doubled in size – about 1 hour.

To prepare the filling Meanwhile, heat the oil in a large frying pan; fry the onions and garlic slowly for 20 minutes over a low heat. Add the paprika, anchovies and pepper; cook, stirring, for 5 minutes. Add the tomatoes and cook for 2 minutes, stirring. Off the heat, stir in the hard-boiled eggs and raisins. Taste.

Punch down the dough and divide it in half. On a floured board, roll out half the dough into a circle about 30 cm (12 inches) in diameter. Place this circle of dough on an oiled baking sheet and spread the filling over, to within 2.5 cm (1 inch) of the sides. Roll out the remaining half of the dough into another 30 cm

(12 inch) circle and cover the filling. Roll up the edges, pinching the dough and turning the pie around to seal it, so that the edge resembles a coiled rope. Brush the top of the pie with the milk and sprinkle with the cornmeal. Allow the pie to rest in a warm place, uncovered, for 20 minutes.

Preheat the oven to 230°c (450°F) mark 8.

Place the pie in the oven and bake for 20–25 minutes, until golden. Serve warm, cut into wedges.

STOCKS AND SAUCES

Stocks will keep for 3–4 days in the refrigerator, or for 6 months frozen. It is better to freeze them in small batches – 300–600 ml ($\frac{1}{2}$–1 pint) for easier use.

It is a good idea to keep a bag of chicken and veal bones in your freezer, adding to it whenever you have any left over. When you have accumulated several pounds, make a stock.

It is best not to season basic stocks, but rather to do so in the final recipe. The following stock recipes can also be used as they are for soup – in that case with seasonings added.

After the fat has been removed, the stock may be reduced by half over a medium to high heat to produce a very rich stock, which will add great flavour to sauces. Then you may freeze it in ice cube trays, remove it from the trays and keep in a plastic bag.

Caldo de Pollo

· CHICKEN STOCK ·

This stock recipe is a basic one to keep on hand in your freezer. It will add richness to your dishes, without extra calories! *Makes about 3.4 litres (6 pints).*

2.3–2.7 kg (5–6 lb) chicken backs, necks
   and/or wing tips
450 g (1 lb) onions, sliced or coarsely
   chopped
450 g (1 lb) carrots, topped but
   unpeeled, sliced or coarsely
   chopped

2–3 leeks, sliced or coarsely chopped,
   with ⅔ of the green part
225 ml (8 fl oz) dry white wine
1 large bay leaf
3 sprigs parsley
8 black peppercorns
1 sprig fresh thyme (optional)

Preheat the oven to 230°c (450°f) mark 8.

Put the chicken carcasses, onions, carrots and leeks in a large roasting pan. Place in the oven for 1 hour, turning occasionally.

Transfer the contents of the pan to a large saucepan. Add the wine, and let it boil for 3–4 minutes to evaporate the alcohol. Transfer this liquid to the saucepan; add the remaining ingredients, and cover with about 3.4 litres (6 pints) water. Bring to the boil and immediately reduce the heat to low.

Remove the scum that forms on top. Simmer the stock, partially covered, for about 3 hours. During this time, it is a good idea to remove the scum occasionally as it rises to the top; but don't worry about the fat on the surface, you will be able to remove that easily after the stock is chilled.

Strain the stock through a colander, then through a fine sieve. Allow to cool at room temperature, then refrigerate overnight. It will then be easy to remove the fat from the surface, after it has hardened; lift it off carefully, as it may not be too hard. The stock is now ready to use as is, seasoned as necessary, or to be reduced in order to make a richer stock. (Never boil a stock that has not had the fat removed from it, or the fat becomes a part of the stock and is impossible to remove.)

Caldo de Ternera

· BROWN VEAL STOCK ·

This is a dark stock which will provide a lot of flavour for your meat dishes and sauces.   *Makes about 1.4 litres (2½ pints)*

1.8–2.3 kg (4–5 lb) veal bones
350 g (12 oz) carrots, topped but
   unpeeled, sliced or coarsely
   chopped
1 large onion, sliced or coarsely chopped
2 leeks, sliced or coarsely chopped, with ⅔
   of the green part

1 × 10–15 cm (4–6 inch) celery stick
   with the leaves
2 shallots, chopped
225 ml (8 fl oz) dry white wine
1 bay leaf
4 sprigs parsley
5 ml (1 tsp) whole black peppercorns

Preheat the oven to 230°c (450°f) mark 8.

Put the veal bones, carrots, onion, leeks, celery and shallots into a large roasting pan. Place in the oven for 1¼ hours, or until the bones and vegetables are browned. Turn them from time to time, especially toward the end of the cooking, so as not to burn the vegetables in the corners.

Transfer the contents of the pan to a large saucepan. Add the wine to the pan; over a medium heat, stir and scrape the bottom and sides to loosen all the sediment left in the pan. As you scrape, allow the wine to boil for 4–5 minutes to evaporate the alcohol.

Add this liquid to the saucepan. Add the remaining ingredients and 1.1 litres (2 pints) water, or to cover. Bring to the boil and immediately reduce the heat to low. Continue as directed in Chicken Stock (Caldo de Pollo) (p. 191) recipe.

Mi Salsa Española

· ENRICHED VEAL STOCK ·

Salsa española, or *sauce espagnole* in French, is an enriched brown stock thickened with flour. But I don't care for floury sauces, because flour doesn't add any flavour – only thickness and calories. It is worth the effort to use a more flavourful stock instead, enriched by making a double veal stock (that is, using a veal stock to make it, instead of water) and fresh vegetables. This, then, is my version of *salsa española*; you will see the difference when you use it as directed in several recipes in this book.   *Makes about 900 ml (1½ pints).*

450 g (1 lb) veal bones, cracked into
  small pieces
1 ham knuckle, cracked into 4 or 5 pieces
2 medium leeks, sliced or coarsely
  chopped, with ⅔ of the green part
1 celery stick, sliced or coarsely chopped
2 medium onions, sliced or coarsely
  chopped
225 g (8 oz) carrots, topped but
  unpeeled, sliced or coarsely chopped

450 ml (¾ pint) dry Spanish sherry
900 ml (1½ pints) Brown Veal Stock
  (p. 192)
1 bay leaf
450 g (1 lb) unpeeled tomatoes, chopped
1 sprig fresh rosemary
1 sprig fresh thyme or 2.5 ml (½ tsp)
  dried
6 black peppercorns
1 × 5 cm (2 inch) stick cinnamon

Preheat the oven to 230°c (450°F) mark 8.

Place the veal bones, ham knuckle, leeks, celery, onions and carrots in a large roasting pan. Place in the preheated oven for 1¼ hours, or until the bones and vegetables are browned. Turn them from time to time. Transfer to a large saucepan. Deglaze the roasting pan with the sherry, stirring and scraping, until reduced by half; pour into the saucepan. Add the veal stock and the remaining ingredients. Bring to the boil, and immediately reduce the heat to low. Simmer, covered, for about 2–3 hours. Continue as directed in Chicken Stock (Caldo de Pollo) recipe (p. 191).

Caldo de Pescado

· FISH FUMET ·

A good fish stock, or fumet, is essential for many fine seafood dishes. Bottled clam juice is not a good substitute; it is salty and will never add the flavour of a fumet.

This recipe is quick and easy to make. All you need are fish heads and bones, which you can obtain from your fishmonger. To make a good fumet, it is important to use only white fish – sole, plaice, cod, whiting, etc. Do not use oily fish such as mackerel. When preparing the fish trimmings, remove skins and fins, for they are oily.   *Makes about 2.3 litres (4 pints).*

1.4 kg (3 lb) fish heads and/or bones
125 ml (4 fl oz) olive oil
2 large or 3 small leeks, sliced or coarsely
  chopped, with ⅔ of the green part
1 large onion, sliced or coarsely
  chopped

1 medium carrot, topped but unpeeled,
  sliced or coarsely chopped
450 ml (¾ pint) dry white wine
1–2 sprigs parsley, with plenty of stems
1–2 bay leaves
2–3 sprigs fresh thyme, or 1 tsp if dried

Rinse the fish heads and bones thoroughly; unless they are absolutely fresh, soak them in cold water for 10–15 minutes. Drain.

Heat the oil in a large saucepan. Add the leeks, onion and carrot; sauté for about 5 minutes, stirring, until they start to colour. Add the wine and boil for 5 minutes to evaporate the alcohol. Add the fish heads and bones, herbs and 1.4 litres (2½ pints) cold water; bring to the boil, immediately reduce the heat to very low and remove the scum on the surface. Simmer slowly, partially covered, for 30 minutes. During this time, skim off 2–3 times any scum that rises to the surface.

Strain the fish stock through a colander, gently pressing down the bones and vegetables with a spoon, and then through a fine strainer into the container where you will store it. Let cool before refrigerating or freezing.

ROMESCO

Romesco is truly indigenous to Catalonia, specifically to the city of Tarragona and its surroundings. An annual festival associated with its preparation is held there on the arrival of summer, the prime season for the vegetables which are essential to the sauce. A competition is then organized, based on cooking the best *romesco*; the winner is awarded the title of Mestre Major Romescaire, or Grand Master *Romesco* Maker.

The origin of *romesco*, in fact, is not as a sauce but as a dish: Fish Stew, Tarragona Style (Romesco de Pescados) (p. 101). It was a simple way to cook fish for fishermen all along the coast from Vilanova – a fishing village 20 miles south of Barcelona – to Valencia. They made it when out at sea, using their lesser-quality catch (naturally saving the best to sell), with a strong sauce, which became known as *romesco*. Later on, the sauce came to be made separately, and today is served mainly to accompany grilled, poached or deep-fried fresh fish. Purists maintain, though, that *romesco* is not a sauce but a dish.

Romesco is based on primary Catalan ingredients: hazelnuts or almonds, red peppers, garlic, onions, tomatoes, herbs or spices and – most important – a very good, fruity olive oil.

In many restaurants in Catalonia you will be served with a little bowl of *romesco* as well as Garlic Mayonnaise (Allioli) (p. 199), especially with grilled or fried fish, even without asking for it. Often, both sauces are blended together.

I have selected here a few of my favorite *romesco* sauces from different chefs in Catalonia. They can be combined with recipes in this book as well as with almost anything – salads, grilled meats or vegetables, pasta, rice, and so on.

The ingredients in a *romesco* sauce should be finely ground, which in the old days was done with a mortar and pestle; today it can be done much more efficiently in a food processor. All *romescos* should rest at room temperature for at least 3–4 hours before serving, for the flavours to mingle.

Salsa Roja

· CATALAN – SALSA VERMELLA ·

· ROMESCO-STYLE SAUCE FOR GRILLED FISH ·

Salsa vermella, as Eugenia Pedrell – owner of the Eugenia restaurant in Cambrils, near Tarragona – calls this sauce in Catalan, translates as 'red sauce'. It is a light, fresh and zesty *romesco*-style sauce. It goes particularly well with grilled fish. *Makes about 450 ml (¾ pint)*.

1 large slice of white bread, cut 1 cm (½ inch) thick	225 g (8 oz) unpeeled ripe tomatoes, chopped
50 ml (2 fl oz) red wine vinegar	10 ml (2 tsp) paprika
65 g (2½ oz) whole almonds	2.5 ml (½ tsp) salt
	125 ml (4 fl oz) fruity olive oil

Preheat the oven to 180°c (350°F) mark 4.

Soak the bread in the vinegar to soften. Toast the almonds in the oven for 15 minutes. Grind them finely in a food processor. Add all the remaining ingredients except the oil, and purée. With the motor running, add the oil slowly. Taste for seasoning.

'Xató'

· ROMESCO-STYLE SAUCE FOR 'XATONADA' ·

Xató is a sharp and nutty *romesco*-style sauce, with a buttery smoothness. It is traditionally served with Catalan Tuna Salad ('Xatonada') (p. 72), as Pere Valls does at his El Celler del Penedès restaurant – but I find it wonderful with just about anything.   *Makes about 750 ml (1¼ pints).*

150 g (5 oz) whole almonds
1 medium red sweet pepper
3 large cloves garlic, coarsely chopped
15 ml (1 tbsp) fresh parsley
2.5 ml (½ tsp) salt

1.25 ml (¼ tsp) freshly ground black
   pepper
125 ml (4 fl oz) red wine vinegar
175 ml (6 fl oz) fruity olive oil

Preheat the oven to 180°c (350°F) mark 4. Toast the almonds in the oven for 15 minutes; grind them finely in a food processor. Roast the red pepper over a flame or in the oven (see p. 32) until the skin starts to blacken; peel, seed and cut it up.

Add the red pepper, garlic and parsley to the food processor; purée. Add the salt, pepper and vinegar, and process until they form a smooth paste. With the motor running, gradually add the oil in a thin stream. Taste for seasoning. The sauce should have a thick consistency and very sharp flavour. Depending on the strength of the vinegar used, you may need more or less oil.

'Salbitxada'

· ROMESCO-STYLE SAUCE FOR GRILLED VEGETABLES ·

This version of *romesco* is typically served with Baked Young Onions or Leeks ('Ceballots') (p. 151) or other grilled vegetables. The colour is a beautiful light terracotta, and the flavours a harmonious, rich blend of all its ingredients. Pere Valls serves an excellent *salbitxada* at El Celler del Penedès restaurant, from which I adapted this recipe.   *Makes about 450 ml (¾ pint).*

15 ml (1 tbsp) olive oil, for frying
1 large slice of white bread, cut 1 cm
   (½ inch) thick
65 g (2½ oz) whole almonds
1.25 ml (¼ tsp) crushed hot red pepper
   flakes
3 large cloves garlic
225 g (8 oz) unpeeled ripe tomatoes

1 × 100 g (4 oz) can pimientos, drained
1.25 ml (¼ tsp) paprika
1.25 ml (¼ tsp) salt, or to taste
2.5 ml (½ tsp) freshly ground black
   pepper, or to taste
50 ml (2 fl oz) red wine vinegar
125 ml (4 fl oz) fruity olive oil

Preheat the oven to 180°c (350°F) mark 4.

Heat the oil in a small frying pan and, over a medium heat, fry the bread until golden on both sides.

Toast the almonds in the oven for 15 minutes. Grind them finely in a food processor, together with the fried bread, pepper flakes and garlic. Add the tomatoes, pimientos, paprika, salt and pepper; purée until they form a smooth paste. Add the vinegar and process again. With the motor running, add the oil slowly, in a thin stream. Taste for seasoning.

Romesco de L'Olivé

· ROMESCO SAUCE WITH ANCHO CHILLIS, ONION AND PAPRIKA ·

The following are two of my favourite *romesco* sauces, both from restaurants in Barcelona which specialize in classic Catalan cuisine: L'Olivé, tiny and innovative; and Cal Isidre, traditional and home-style. I have simply given their recipes the name of the restaurant. They both use *nyoras* – the unique Catalan dried red peppers – and hazelnuts as well as almonds, which provide earthy full flavours. Josep Olivé uses onion and paprika, which contribute a rounder, milder taste; and Isidre Gironés bakes the vegetables for a sweeter, tangier flavour.

Both sauces are excellent with lamb barbecued pork or chicken, or any grilled meat. *Makes about 750 ml (1¼ pints).*

2 medium dried red chilli peppers
65 g (2½ oz) whole almonds
65 g (2½ oz) hazelnuts
15 ml (1 tbsp) olive oil, for frying
1 large slice of white bread, cut 1 cm (½ inch) thick
3 large cloves garlic
50 g (2 oz) chopped onion

225 g (8 oz) unpeeled ripe tomatoes, cut up
10 ml (2 tsp) paprika
3.75 ml (¾ tsp) salt
1.25 ml (¼ tsp) freshly ground black pepper
about 30 ml (2 tbsp) red wine vinegar
125 ml (4 fl oz) fruity olive oil

Preheat the oven to 180°c (350°F) mark 4.

Cover the chillis with water in a saucepan. Bring to the boil and cook for 10 minutes over a medium to low heat. Turn off the heat, cover and steep for 30 minutes. Remove the cores and seeds, and discard the water.

While the chillis soak, toast the nuts separately in the oven for about 15 minutes. Rub the hazelnuts in a damp tea-towel to remove most of the skins.

Heat the oil in a small frying pan and, over a medium heat, fry the bread until golden on both sides.

In a food processor, grind the nuts finely with the garlic and fried bread. Add the chillis, onion, tomatoes, paprika, salt and pepper. Purée until they form a smooth paste. Add the vinegar and process again. With the motor running, pour in the oil slowly, in a thin stream. Taste for seasoning.

Romesco de Cal Isidre

· ROMESCO SAUCE WITH CHILLIS AND BAKED GARLIC/TOMATO ·

Makes about 450 ml (¾ pint).

2 medium dried red chilli
  peppers
25 g (1 oz) whole almonds
25 g (1 oz) hazelnuts
1 large head garlic
1 large unpeeled ripe tomato
15 ml (1 tbsp) olive oil, for frying

1 large slice of white bread, cut 1 cm
  (½ inch) thick
1.25 ml (¼ tsp) crushed hot red pepper
  flakes
50 ml (2 fl oz) wine vinegar
2.5 ml (½ tsp) salt
125 ml (4 fl oz) fruity olive oil

Preheat the oven to 180°c (350°F) mark 4.

Cover the chillis with water in a saucepan. Bring to the boil and cook for 10 minutes over a medium to low heat. Turn off the heat, cover and steep for 30 minutes. Remove the cores and seeds, and reserve 30 ml (2 tbsp) of the water.

Toast the almonds and hazelnuts separately in the oven for about 15 minutes. Rub the hazelnuts in a damp tea-towel to remove most of the skins.

Put the whole head of garlic and the tomato on an ungreased baking sheet. In the oven, bake the garlic for 45 minutes and the tomato for 20 minutes. Cut off about a quarter of the garlic head top, and squeeze the pulp out. Peel the tomato.

Heat the oil in a small frying pan and, over a medium heat, fry the bread until golden on both sides. Grind it finely in a food processor, together with the nuts and pepper flakes. Add the tomato, garlic pulp and chillis; process until they form a smooth paste. Add the vinegar, salt and reserved water from cooking the chillis; process to combine. With the motor running, add the oil slowly, in a thin stream. Taste for seasoning.

Salsa Mayonesa

· MAYONNAISE ·

Makes 350 ml (12 fl oz).

1 egg, at room temperature
1 egg yolk, at room temperature
6.25 ml (1¼ tsp) Dijon mustard
225 ml (8 fl oz) safflower oil or another
  vegetable oil

125 ml (4 fl oz) extra virgin olive oil
25 ml (1 fl oz) lemon juice
1.25 ml (¼ tsp) salt, or to taste
pinch of cayenne

In a blender or food processor fitted with a metal blade, combine the egg, egg yolk and mustard. Mix the oils and lemon juice together in a jug and add slowly, with the motor running, in a thin stream; the mixture will thicken and become a mayonnaise. Season with the salt and cayenne.

If the mixture separates or does not thicken, you can correct it as follows: pour all but 15 ml (1 tbsp) of the separated mayonnaise into another container. Add 15 ml (1 tbsp) water to the mayonnaise left in the blender or food processor. With the motor running, add the separated mayonnaise slowly; the mixture should attain the right consistency – if not, try again. It will work! Keep refrigerated.

Allioli

· GARLIC MAYONNAISE ·

Best to prepare this sauce a day ahead

Makes about 350 ml (12 fl oz).

22.5 ml (1½ tbsp) finely chopped garlic
1 egg, at room temperature
125 ml (4 fl oz) extra virgin olive oil

225 ml (8 fl oz) safflower oil or another
   vegetable oil
15 ml (1 tbsp) lemon juice

In a blender or food processor fitted with a metal blade, purée the garlic with the egg. Mix the oils with the lemon juice in a jug. With the motor running, add slowly in a thin stream. Process for a further additional 10 seconds. Transfer to a bowl, cover and refrigerate. You may use the *allioli* immediately, but I prefer it the next day, after the flavours mingle and mellow.

Allioli de Miel

· CATALAN – ALLIOLI DE MEL ·

· HONEY GARLIC MAYONNAISE ·

This and the next *allioli* recipe are a creation of Montse Guillén and typical of her inventiveness: adding a new note to an old traditional Catalan recipe such as *allioli*. Both sauces are featured at her Barcelona restaurant. Montse likes to serve them to accompany grilled meats, such as lamb chops. *Makes about 350 ml (12 fl oz).*

1 egg
30 ml (2 tbsp) finely chopped garlic
225 ml (8 fl oz) olive oil

45 ml (3 tbsp) clear honey
2.5 ml (½ tsp) salt

In a blender or food processor fitted with a metal blade, purée the egg with the garlic. With the motor running, gradually add the oil in a thin stream until it thickens like a mayonnaise. Add the honey and salt, process to blend and taste for seasoning. Keep refrigerated until serving time.

Allioli de Manzana

· CATALAN – ALLIOLI DE POMA ·

· APPLE GARLIC MAYONNAISE ·

In addition to the serving suggestions mentioned in the former recipe, I find this apple *allioli* goes very well with Rabbit and Prune Terrine (Terrina de Conejo con Ciruelas) (p. 51) and with the pork loin recipes in this book.   *Makes about 600 ml (1 pint).*

450 g (1 lb) tart dessert apples, such as
    Granny Smith, peeled, cored and cut
    into 2.5 cm (1 inch) pieces
5 ml (1 tsp) finely chopped garlic

150 ml (¼ pint) olive oil
1.25 ml (¼ tsp) salt, or to taste
1.25 ml (¼ tsp) freshly ground white
    pepper, or to taste

Place the apples in a saucepan and cover with water. Bring to the boil, reduce the heat to low, cover and simmer until tender – about 30–45 minutes. Drain the apples and place them in a food processor or blender. Add the garlic and purée finely. With the motor running, gradually add the oil in a thin stream. Add the salt and pepper, and taste for seasoning. Keep refrigerated until ready to serve.

Salsa de Chocolate

· CHOCOLATE SAUCE ·

If you like chocolate, this is the ultimate sauce. It is especially delicious over ice cream, as in Caramelized Nut Ice Cream with Hot Chocolate Sauce (Helado de Frutos Secos al Caramelo con Salsa de Chocolate) (p. 236) or with fresh fruit. I also love to marinate strawberries in an orange brandy liqueur (such as Gran Torres or Grand Marnier) and dip them in this chocolate sauce.   *Makes about 350 ml (12 fl oz).*

225 ml (8 fl oz) double cream
50 g (2 oz) unsweetened cooking
    chocolate
75 g (3 oz) chocolate chips

22.5 ml (1½ tbsp) finest-quality Spanish
    brandy
5 ml (1 tsp) vanilla extract

Heat the cream in the top of a double boiler over boiling water, or in a heavy-bottomed small saucepan. Melt the chocolate and chocolate chips in the cream, stirring over a very low heat, until combined into a smooth sauce. Off the heat, add the brandy and vanilla. Serve hot.

If you make this sauce ahead, reheat it in a double boiler, stirring, so it does not separate.

DESSERTS

Tocinillos de Cielo

The name of these rich, mellow tarts of silky texture literally translates as 'little pigs from heaven'. They are found all over Spain, in restaurants as well as in bakeries. They may be small tarts or made in only one mould, in which case it is called *tocino de cielo*.

Actually, this dessert originated in the south of Spain; history has it dating back to 1611, in Jerez. The winemakers in that area used a lot of egg whites for filtering their wines, and they had no use for the yolks. King Philip III decided to give them to the Clarisas order of nuns, which he had founded. They first used them in a dessert still made all over Spain, *natillas*, a light custard consisting of egg yolks, milk and sugar. According to records, this went on for quite a while – until one day the head cook became ill, and another nun had to take over. She mistakenly omitted the milk, so the *natillas* came out firm like flans. When she served them, one nun started using her knife and fork to eat them, joking that she 'had to cut this dessert like a pig' – to which another nun retorted, 'but a pig from heaven, because it is *so* delicious!'

Even today, popular belief has it that in order to ensure fine weather for a special party, one should send 2 or 3 dozen eggs to the Clarisas nuns because their prayers have an influence over the elements.

For this recipe you need 6 × 125 ml (4 fl oz) ramekins. Don't fill them to the top; they will be easier to unmould. This is such a rich dessert that you will probably want to serve just 1 *tocinillo* per person. *Serves 6.*

FOR THE CARAMEL
90 ml (6 tbsp) sugar
FOR THE TARTS
200 g (7 oz) sugar
1 × 5–7.5 cm (2–3 inch) stick cinnamon

thinly pared zest of 1 lemon
6 egg yolks
2 whole eggs
AS AN ACCOMPANIMENT
150 ml (¼ pint) whipped cream

To caramelize the moulds   In a small, heavy saucepan, dissolve the sugar with 15–30 ml (1–2 tbsp) water and cook over a medium heat until the sugar melts and turns golden. To facilitate caramelizing, have the ramekins warm by the time the caramel is ready. Pour the caramel into the ramekins; it must coat the bottom and most of the sides. This may be a little tricky, as caramel gets very hot. Work quickly, 1 or 2 ramekins at a time, using potholders if you have them and turning the ramekins around to coat the sides; a teaspoon may also help. (If the caramel should harden in the ramekins before you have a chance to coat the sides, you may soften it by placing them in a pan of boiling water.)

To prepare the tarts   Dissolve the sugar with 50 ml (2 fl oz) water in a heavy saucepan, preferably one with a pouring lip. Add the cinnamon stick and lemon zest. Cook over a medium heat to 112°c (230°F) on a sugar thermometer, or thread consistency. Remove from the heat and set aside for 1 minute. Discard the cinnamon stick and lemon zest.

While the sugar syrup is cooking, beat the egg yolks and whole eggs lightly with a fork in a medium bowl; do not beat to a froth. Add the sugar syrup to the eggs in a very thin stream, stirring with a fork, so the egg yolks won't curdle. Strain through a fine sieve into a jug, and pour into the caramelized ramekins.

To cook the *tocinillos*   This is the most delicate part, for the tarts must be steamed, not baked. If you have a steamer, it is easier to do it on top of the stove because this will give you better control. Place the ramekins on the steamer rack, making sure the water is below the rack level. The water should boil, otherwise it won't produce enough steam to cook them. Place a double-layered cloth on top of the steamer, and cover tightly with a lid.

(You can also cook them in the oven, inside a large roasting pan containing about 2.5 cm (1 inch) boiling water. The ramekins must not touch the water, however; place them on a rack and, if necessary, put the rack on top of a folded cloth. Form a tent of foil and cover the entire pan to hold in the steam. Place in a preheated 180°c (350°F) mark 4 oven.)

Cook for about 15 minutes, or until a skewer inserted into the centre of the ramekins comes out clean and the surface is firm and puffed up. Be very careful when opening the lid of the steamer (or the foil tent over the pan) – steam will scald you very easily!

To assemble the dish   As soon as the ramekins are cool enough to handle, unmould them on to a serving platter or individual plates. To unmould, run a knife around the edges and tap the ramekins against the plate; they will come out easily. With a spoon, scoop out as much as possible of the liquid caramel in the ramekin, and spoon it over the *tocinillos*. Serve decorated with whipped cream.

Flan de Coco al Caramelo

· CARAMELIZED COCONUT FLAN ·

Flans are classic Spanish desserts, and the following two are favourite recipes from my mother's file. The first is light and subtly flavoured with the coconut; the second combines the full taste of apples with a light, interesting texture – and of course, coming from my family, they both are enhanced by a dash or so of fine brandy!

Coconut is often eaten raw in Spain, and the summer stands on the boulevards of the seaside resorts usually sell it cut into wedges, side by side with other children's delights such as sugar-coated almonds and candyfloss. As a child, I remember relishing this crunchy refreshment on balmy Mediterranean afternoons. *Serves 8.*

FOR THE CARAMEL
100 g (4 oz) sugar
FOR THE FLAN
900 ml (1½ pints) milk
1 vanilla pod, split in half lengthways
peel of 1 lemon
5 egg yolks

5 whole eggs
150 g (5 oz) sugar
45 ml (3 tbsp) Miguel Torres or another
    fine-quality Spanish brandy
generous 50 g (2 oz) shredded coconut
FOR THE DECORATION
25 g (1 oz) shredded coconut

To prepare the caramel   In a small, heavy saucepan, dissolve the sugar in 30 ml (2 tbsp) water. Cook over a medium to high heat until the sugar melts and turns medium brown. Don't stir, just shake the pan around. Immediately pour the caramel into a 1.1 litre (2 pint) ring mould. With oven gloves on both hands, rotate the mould gently, swirling the caramel to cover the bottom and part of the sides, keep moving the mould around until the caramel is almost set.

To prepare the flan   Preheat the oven to 180°c (350°F) mark 4.

Combine the milk, vanilla pod and lemon zest in a saucepan and cook over a very low heat for 10 minutes. Cover and set aside for 15 minutes. In a food processor or blender, beat the egg yolks, eggs and sugar until light and foamy. Discard the vanilla pod and lemon zest. Pour the hot milk into the egg mixture in a slow, steady stream, beating constantly. Stir in the brandy and coconut. Immediately pour the mixture into the mould, and place it in a roasting pan. Pour in boiling water to come halfway up the sides of the mould. Bake in the oven for 50 minutes, or until a skewer inserted into the centre comes out clean.

Let the flan cool at room temperature, then chill. Meanwhile, in a dry frying pan toast the coconut for the decoration, stirring, until golden.

To assemble the dish   Unmould the flan on to a dessert platter with a rim. Spoon the caramel left in the mould on top of the flan. Garnish with toasted coconut around the top of the flan. Serve at room temperature or chilled.

Flan de Manzana al Caramelo

· CARAMELIZED APPLE FLAN ·

Serves 6–8.

FOR THE CARAMEL
65 g (2½ oz) sugar
FOR THE FLAN
40 g (1½ oz) butter
900 g (2 lb) tart dessert apples such as
  Granny Smith, peeled, cored and
  coarsely chopped
125 ml (4 fl oz) Miguel Torres or another
  fine-quality Spanish brandy

6 eggs
100 g (4 oz) sugar
5 ml (1 tsp) ground cinnamon
FOR THE DECORATION
225 ml (8 fl oz) double cream
30 ml (2 tbsp) icing sugar
2.5 ml (½ tsp) vanilla extract
1.25 ml (¼ tsp) ground cinnamon

To prepare the caramel   Caramelize a 1.1 litre (2 pint) ring mould with the sugar and 15–30 ml (1–2 tbsp) water, proceeding as directed in Caramelized Coconut Flan (Flan de Coco al Caramelo) (p. 203).

To prepare the flan   Preheat the oven to 180°c (350°f) mark 4.

In a heavy saucepan, melt the butter and cook the apples over medium to low heat, covered, for 15 minutes. Add the brandy; when hot, flambé (pp. 32–3). Cook for 2–3 minutes, shaking the pan. In a bowl, beat the eggs with the sugar and cinnamon. Stir in the apples.

Pour the apple mixture into the caramelized mould, and place in a roasting pan. Pour in boiling water to come halfway up the sides of the mould. Bake in the oven, uncovered, for 45 minutes or until a skewer inserted into the centre comes out clean.

To prepare the decoration and assemble the dish   Whip the cream with the icing sugar and vanilla. As soon as the flan is cool enough to handle, unmould it on to a serving platter. Spoon the caramel over the flan. Spoon the cream into the centre of the flan, sprinkling the top with cinnamon. Serve warm or at room temperature.

Flan de Moras con Salsa de Moras

· CATALAN – FLAM DE MÓRES AMB SALSA DE MÓRES ·

· BLACKBERRY FLAN WITH A BLACKBERRY SAUCE ·

If you like blackberries and can get them fresh during their short season, don't miss making this dessert, a creation of the Neichel restaurant in Barcelona. Jean-Louis Neichel, an Alsatian, is one of my favourite chefs in the city; his way of handling the finest ingredients is impeccable, always enhancing their freshness with unusual, new-style personal ideas.   *Serves 6–8.*

FOR THE FLAN
225 ml (8 fl oz) milk
5 ml (1 tsp) vanilla extract
100 g (4 oz) sugar
4 egg yolks
1 sachet powdered gelatine
125 ml (4 fl oz) blackberry liqueur

450 g (1 lb) fresh blackberries
225 ml (8 fl oz) double cream
FOR THE SAUCE
225 g (8 oz) fresh blackberries
65 g (2½ oz) sugar
30 ml (2 tbsp) blackberry liqueur

To prepare the flan   In a heavy saucepan, combine the milk, vanilla, sugar and egg yolks. Heat gently and cook over a low heat, stirring constantly, until the custard thickens and coats the back of a spoon; it will take about 15 minutes.

In a small saucepan, dissolve the gelatine in the liqueur, stirring over a low heat until the gelatine is dissolved. Add to the custard. Refrigerate the custard until it begins to set – about 45 minutes.

Meanwhile, with a fork or potato masher, crush 100 g (4 oz) of the blackberries and mix with the remaining whole berries. Whip the cream until it forms stiff peaks. Remove the custard from the refrigerator; fold in the blackberries and the cream. Pour the mixture into a 1.7 litre (3 pint) ring mould. Refrigerate for at least 3–4 hours, or until set.

To prepare the sauce   In a food processor or blender, purée the blackberries with the sugar and liqueur. Strain through a fine sieve.

To assemble the dish   Unmould the flan by dipping it into a pan or sink filled with hot water for 5 or 6 seconds. Invert the mould on to a serving platter, and pour some sauce around it. Hand the remaining sauce separately in a sauce-boat. Serve chilled.

Flan de Fresas con Su Salsa de Fresas Frescas

· CATALAN – FLAM DE MADUIXES AMB SALSA DE MADUIXES FRESQUES ·

· STRAWBERRY FLAN IN A FRESH STRAWBERRY SAUCE ·

I enjoyed this strawberry flan, among other good things, at Hostal del Priorato, a quaint Catalan country restaurant in Banyeres, south of Barcelona. Chef/owner Miguel Puig prepares excellent traditional dishes, some of them with a new approach, such as this one.

When I tried it at home, it was delicious – but after boiling the strawberries to get a concentrated syrup, the colour was greyish and unappealing. As I looked through my kitchen window, mulling over the problem, the hummingbirds picking at my fuchsias gave me an idea: they wouldn't mind if I took one drop of the red food colour I use to tint the syrup for their feeding, would they? (Naturally, I didn't need to tell my guests either.) Well, the flan came out great, and also looking pretty.   *Serves 4–6.*

FOR THE FLAN
200 g (7 oz) sugar
125 ml (4 fl oz) sweet muscat wine
15 ml (1 tbsp) lemon juice
700 g (1½ lb) fresh strawberries, hulled
8 eggs

1 drop red food colouring (optional)
FOR THE SAUCE
450 g (1 lb) fresh strawberries, hulled
65 g (2½ oz) sugar
30–45 ml (2–3 tbsp) framboise liqueur,
    or to taste

Preheat the oven to 180°c (350°F) mark 4.

To prepare the flan   In a large saucepan, combine the sugar, wine, lemon juice and strawberries. Bring to the boil and boil vigorously for 5 minutes. Pass through a medium sieve or food mill into a bowl. Beat the eggs well and strain them through a fine sieve into the bowl with the strawberry mixture. If desired, add drop of red food colouring. Pour the mixture into a 1.2 litre (2 pint) mould, cover with foil and place in a roasting pan. Pour in boiling water to come halfway up the sides of the mould. Bake in the oven for 40 minutes. Allow to cool at room temperature, then chill.

To prepare the sauce   In a food processor or blender, purée the strawberries with the sugar and liqueur. Strain through a fine sieve.

To assemble the dish   Turn out the flan on to a serving platter. Spoon some of the sauce over it, and hand the remaining sauce separately in a sauce-boat.

Corona de Naranja

· CATALAN – CORONA DE TARONJA ·

· ORANGE FLAN IN A CROWN ·

Nicolás is a tiny restaurant in the colourful quarter of Chamberi in Madrid – near Malasaña, one of the most animated districts in the city at night. José Antonio Méndez opened this family-run place in 1984. He features home-style, well-made dishes; among them a simple but delightful orange flan which inspired me to develop this recipe.

I find this flan makes a perfect combination with Orange Ice Cream (Helado de Naranja) (p. 232); I make it in a ring mould and put the ice cream balls in the centre, surrounding the mould with whipped cream. Or it can be served with the cream alone – it's delicious either way.   *Serves 4–6.*

FOR THE CARAMEL
100 g (4 oz) sugar
FOR THE FLAN
225 ml (8 fl oz) fresh orange juice
200 g (7 oz) sugar
6 eggs

FOR FINISHING
225 ml (8 fl oz) double cream
30 ml (2 tbsp) orange liqueur, such as
    Gran Torres or Grand Marnier
15 ml (1 tbsp) sugar

To prepare the caramel   Caramelize a 1.2 litre (2 pint) ring mould with the sugar, proceeding as directed in Caramelized Coconut Custard (Flan de Coco al Caramelo) (p. 203).

Preheat the oven to 180°c (350°f) mark 4.

To prepare the flan In a bowl, beat together the orange juice, sugar and eggs, to blend thoroughly. Pour the mixture into the caramelized mould. Cover with foil and place in a roasting pan. Pour in boiling water to come halfway up the sides of the mould.

Bake in the oven for about 40 minutes, or until a skewer inserted into the centre of the mould comes out clean. (The surface should be slightly firm.)

To prepare the garnish and assemble the dish When cold, turn out the flan on to a round serving dish. Whip the cream until it forms soft peaks. Add the liqueur and sugar and whip a little more, until stiff. Using a piping bag, pipe the cream decoratively around the sides of the flan.

Tarta de Limón Oriola ˙

· AUNT ORIOLA'S LEMON TART ·

This is an old recipe from my Aunt Oriola, a dessert I often asked her to make for me when she offered to bring something to my parties. It is not new-style cuisine or low in calories – rather, it's sinfully rich and worth every bite.

I have made one change: she used a *pâte sucrée* as a crust; I use instead Crisp Pastry Crust (Pasta Akelaŕe) (p. 179), which I actually find much tastier – and certainly more Spanish! *Serves 10–12*.

FOR THE PASTRY
1 quantity *Crisp Pastry Crust*
  (p. 179)
FOR THE CUSTARD
4 eggs, separated, at room temperature

1 × 400 g *(14 oz) can sweetened*
  condensed milk
50 ml *(2 fl oz) fresh lemon juice*
22.5 ml *(1½ tbsp) lemon zest (p. 31)*
125 ml *(4 fl oz) milk*

Preheat the oven to 180°c (350°f) mark 4.

To prepare the pastry Prepare the crust as directed in the recipe, using a 20–22.5 cm (8–9 inch) loose-based flan tin. Press the dough up the sides of the tin to about 6 cm (1½ inches); try to make it very thin on the bottom, and thicker on the sides. Bake in the oven for 30 minutes, or until golden.

To prepare the custard In a large bowl, beat the egg yolks with the condensed milk, lemon juice and lemon zest. Stir in the milk. Beat the egg whites until stiff but not dry. Fold them carefully into the mixture.

To prepare the tart Pour the lemon custard into the pastry case and bake in the oven for 35–40 minutes, or until the top starts to get golden and a skewer inserted into the centre comes out clean. (During the baking process the filling will rise, but after it comes out of the oven it will fall to the crust level.) Serve at room temperature.

Tarta Templada de Limón

· *WARM LEMON TART* ·

The idea for this zesty tart came from chef Toya Roqué of the Azulete restaurant in Barcelona. It has a delightful balance of sweet and sharp, rich and tangy.   *Serves 6–8.*

FOR THE PASTRY
1 quantity Pie Pastry (p. 177)
FOR THE FILLING
75 g (3 oz) unsalted butter, at room
    temperature

200 g (7 oz) sugar
15 ml (1 tbsp) lemon zest (p. 31)
5 eggs, separated, at room temperature
125 ml (4 fl oz) lemon juice

To prepare the pastry crust   Preheat the oven to 220°c (425°F) mark 7.

Roll out the pastry thinly to fit a 25–27.5 cm (10–11 inch) loose based flan tin with low sides. Place a piece of foil over the pastry, and fill it with rice or beans. Bake blind in the oven for 15 minutes.

Remove the foil and beans from the pastry and bake for a further 5–10 minutes, until lightly golden. Reduce the oven temperature to 190°c (375°F) mark 5.

To prepare the filling   While the pastry is baking, cream the butter and sugar with the lemon zest in a food processor until the sugar is dissolved. Add the egg yolks and blend, then add the lemon juice and blend again.

Whip the egg whites until stiff but not dry. Fold them into the lemon mixture and pour into the baked pastry case. Bake in the oven for 35–40 minutes, or until golden on top. Serve warm. (If you make it ahead of time, warm it up for 10 minutes in a preheated 180°c (350°F) mark 4 oven just before serving.)

Tarta de Espinacas

· *SWEET SPINACH TART* ·

This was my favourite among an array of irresistible desserts at Jolastoky, a superb restaurant in the Basque city of Bilbao owned by Sabino and Begoña Arana. Your most discriminating guests will be delighted with the combination of flavours in this tart. And although it looks very special, it really is not difficult to make.   *Serves 6–8.*

FOR THE PASTRY
1 quantity Puff Pastry, chilled
    (p. 178)
FOR THE CUSTARD
450 ml (¾ pint) milk
pared zest of 1 lemon

200 g (7 oz) sugar
6 egg yolks
300 g (10 oz) frozen chopped spinach,
    defrosted and drained
15 ml (1 tbsp) lemon juice, or to taste
2.5 ml (½ tsp) freshly grated nutmeg

FOR THE MERINGUE
4 *egg whites, at room temperature*

pinch of salt
65 g (2½ oz) sugar

Preheat the oven to 220°c (425°F) mark 7.

To prepare the pastry case   Roll out the pastry and cut it into 2 × 25 cm (10 inch) circles (use a plate as a pattern). Cut the circles cleanly with a knife; do not tear the pastry, or it will not rise properly. Using a sharp knife, draw a circle on 1 of the rounds 5 cm (2 inches) from the edge (don't cut all the way through the dough, however, for better rising). Dip your finger in water and moisten a 5 cm (2 inch) area around the edge of the other round. Place the round with the circle on top of the one with the moistened edge; lay it down carefully, but don't press down the dough or adjust the edges with your fingers, or the pastry won't puff up properly.

Immediately bake in the oven for 10 minutes. (If you don't bake it immediately, keep it refrigerated.) Reduce the oven temperature to 190°c (375°F) mark 5 and bake for a further 20 minutes, or until the pastry is golden and the base starts to brown.

Remove the pastry from oven and immediately cut, with a sharp knife, through the inner circle you made earlier, carefully lifting out the lid. If there is any soft puff pastry inside the shell, scoop it out so you will be left with a neat round box. Discard the lid (if you can resist having it as a snack).

This pastry case can be made up to 3 days ahead, and warmed up just before serving in a preheated 150°c (300°F) mark 2 oven for 5 minutes.

To prepare the custard   Heat the milk with the lemon zest in a saucepan. Cover and set aside for 10 minutes. In a bowl, beat together the sugar and egg yolks. Discard the lemon zest and add the egg and sugar mixture to the hot milk. Cook over a low heat, stirring constantly, until the mixture thickens enough to coat the back of a spoon. Squeeze the spinach dry; stir it into the custard. Add the lemon juice and nutmeg; taste for seasoning. Set aside.

To prepare the meringue   Beat the egg whites with the salt until stiff. Gradually beat in the sugar, until stiff and glossy.

To assemble the dish   Increase the oven temperature to 220°c (425°F) mark 7.

Just before serving, heat the spinach custard gently and cook for about 5 minutes, stirring. Pour the custard into the pastry case and spoon the meringue over the top, spreading it to the edges of the filling. Fluff the surface with the bottom of a fork to make little peaks. Bake in the oven for about 5 minutes, or until the meringue is set and slightly golden. Serve immediately.

Tarta de Música

· MUSICIAN'S TART ·

Postre de músic, or musician's dessert, is one of Catalonia's simplest desserts – nothing more than a mixture of dried fruits and nuts. The name comes from the old days when musicians, usually young and poor, travelled around the countryside. They were not paid much but always got some food, and if their music was really good, a dessert treat: raisins, hazelnuts, almonds, pine nuts – whatever the farmer had to hand.

Tarta de músico is a sophisticated version of that humble dessert made into a delicious tart.   *Serves 8.*

FOR THE PASTRY
1 quantity Pie Pastry, chilled
   (p. 177)
FOR THE FILLING
225 g (8 oz) moist dried figs, stemmed
100 g (4 oz) stoned dates
75 g (3 oz) raisins
75 g (3 oz) sultanas
25 g (1 oz) unsalted butter
15 ml (1 tbsp) plain flour
225 ml (8 fl oz) cold milk
150 g (5 oz) sugar
3 egg yolks

125 ml (4 fl oz) Miguel Torres or another
   fine-quality Spanish brandy
50 ml (2 tbsp) lemon juice
FOR THE TOPPING
40 g (1½ oz) hazelnuts
40 g (1½ oz) blanched almonds
40 g (1½ oz) whole walnuts
40 g (1½ oz) pine nuts
FOR SERVING
225 ml (8 fl oz) double cream
30 ml (2 tbsp) finest-quality Spanish
   brandy, or to taste
15 ml (1 tbsp) sugar, or to taste

To prepare the pastry case   Preheat the oven to 220°c (425°F) mark 7.
   Roll out the chilled pastry to fit a 25 cm (10 inch) loose based flan tin. Line the pastry with foil and beans. Bake blind for 15 minutes. Remove the foil and beans.
To prepare the filling   In a saucepan, combine the dried fruits with 350 ml (12 fl oz) water. Bring to the boil, reduce the heat to low, cover and cook for 10 minutes. Uncover, increase the heat to medium-high and cook, stirring, until all the liquid has evaporated. Purée the fruit in a blender or food processor.
   Reduce the oven temperature to 180°c (350°F) mark 4.
   In a medium saucepan, melt the butter; add flour and stir. Add the milk and sugar, stir and cook over a medium heat until the sugar has melted. Meanwhile, in a bowl beat the egg yolks with the brandy; add to the hot milk and cook over a low heat, stirring constantly, until the custard thickens – about 15 minutes. Add the puréed fruits and lemon juice; taste and add more lemon juice and brandy if necessary. Pour the mixture into the prepared pastry case.
To prepare the topping   Toast the hazelnuts in the oven for 12 minutes. Rub them in a damp tea-towel, so most of the skins come off. Toast the almonds for 10 minutes, or until they start to colour. Increase the oven temperature to 190°c (375°F) mark 5. Sprinkle the hazelnuts, almonds, walnuts and pine nuts over the

tart, and pat them down with your hand. Bake in the oven for 45 minutes, or until the nuts and pastry are golden.

To prepare the accompaniment In a bowl, beat the cream until it forms soft peaks. Mix in the brandy and sugar.

Serve the tart at room temperature or slightly warm, accompanied by the cream.

Tarta de Piñones

· CATALAN – PASTÍS DE PINYONS ·

· PINE NUT TART ·

Start preparation 5–6 hours ahead

Here is another classic Catalan idea: a tart of pine nuts over *cabell d'angel* or angel's hair, a filling used very often for sweets in Catalonia.

You can usually buy little pine nut tartlets at pastry shops all over Catalonia, but I have had this exquisite tart, home-made, only at one of Barcelona's most elegant restaurants, Vía Veneto. José Monje, an enthusiastic and enterprising restaurateur, acquired it in 1980 and took on a noted young cook, Josep Bullich; together they set out to bring their cuisine to the top rank. I must add, it is my father's favourite restaurant when he wants to entertain someone lavishly – that's where he took my mother recently for their 50th wedding anniversary! *Serves 6–8.*

1.4 kg (3 lb) spaghetti squash or
  pumpkin
½ quantity Puff Pastry, chilled (p. 178),
  make the whole recipe and freeze half

200 g (7 oz) sugar
150 g (5 oz) pine nuts

Steam the squash or pumpkin over boiling water until tender when pierced with a fork – about 30–40 minutes.

To prepare the pastry Roll out the pastry to a 30 × 17.5 cm (12 × 7 inch) rectangle (or longer, if you have a long enough plate to serve it on). Cut out the rectangle with a sharp knife, making a clean cut; handle the pastry as little as possible. Place the pastry rectangle on a baking sheet, prick the bottom all over with a fork and refrigerate for at least 30 minutes.

Preheat the oven to 180°c (350°f) mark 4.

To prepare the filling Cut the squash or pumpkin in half and discard the seeds (try to remove only the seeds and not the stringy part to which the seeds are attached). With a fork, scrape the sides of the interior and scoop out the flesh.

In a roasting pan, combine the squash or pumpkin with the sugar and bake in the oven, stirring occasionally, until the mixture is very tender and beginning to brown from caramelizing; it should lose all its crunch and become a dark golden colour. This may take 3–4 hours. Toward the end, you may want to cook it on the stove so you can watch it better.

Increase the oven temperature to 200°c (400°F) mark 6.

While the squash or pumpkin mixture cools, bake the pastry for 12 minutes. During this time, prick it with a fork once or twice.

To assemble the dish   Spread the filling over the pastry, leaving a border all around. Place the pine nuts on top, pressing them into the filling. Bake in the oven for about 30 minutes, or until the nuts are golden. Serve barely warm or at room temperature.

Tarta de Santiago

· SANTIAGO ALMOND TORTE ·

Can be made 1 or 2 days ahead

I enjoyed this torte at several restaurants in Madrid, and was puzzled to see that it was exactly the same every time – until I found out the story behind it from Félix Colomo, who serves it at his colourful Posada de la Villa. A little old lady, Purita, used to make them at a restaurant she owned, which did not prosper; so she now prepares them at home and supplies them to other restaurants.

Tarta de Santiago is named after the Galician city of Santiago de Compostela. And sure enough, later on I found it all over Galicia, one of the best at the excellent Vilas restaurant in Santiago.

As this torte is not too sweet, it goes very well with a glass of fine sherry or red wine, or even as an accompaniment to a sharp cheese and fruit as dessert.   *Serves 10–12.*

100 g (4 oz) unsalted butter, at room
    temperature
200 g (7 oz) sugar
15 ml (1 tbsp) lemon zest (p. 31)
4 eggs, at room temperature
30 ml (2 tbsp) Miguel Torres or another
    fine-quality Spanish brandy

100 g (4 oz) plain flour
200 g (7 oz) whole almonds, finely
    ground
FOR FINISHING
about 45 ml (3 tbsp) icing sugar

Preheat the oven to 180°c (350°F) mark 4.

Cream the butter and sugar together until light and fluffy. Add the lemon zest and eggs; beat until smooth. Stir in 125 ml (4 fl oz) water and the brandy; add the flour and mix well. (If the mixture curdles, don't worry about it.) Fold in the almonds.

Butter a 22.5 cm (9 inch) springform tin and pour the almond mixture into it. Bake in the oven for about 40 minutes, or until the centre springs back when pressed lightly with your finger and the cake shrinks away from the side of the tin. Leave to stand for 10 minutes; then remove the cake from the tin and cool on a rack. When completely cooled, sprinkle the top of the cake with finely sifted icing sugar.

This torte can be prepared ahead of time, and will last for at least a week, if kept in a tin. If you make it ahead of time, sprinkle the sugar on top just before serving.

Bizcocho de Chocolate con Crema Inglesa

· CHOCOLATE TORTE WITH A LIGHT CREAM CUSTARD ·

These days there is as much of a passion for chocolate in Spain as there is in the United States and Britain, and most restaurants feature some kind of chocolate torte. I had one that left particularly fond memories at El Amparo, the outstanding restaurant in Madrid, and it inspired this recipe: it is chocolate-chocolate at its best. The light custard and candied orange peel make this a most distinctive dessert, but the torte stands very well on its own.   *Serves 12.*

FOR THE TORTE
50 g (2 oz) unsalted butter, at room
  temperature
150 g (5 oz) sugar
1.25 ml (¼ tsp) salt
2.5 ml (½ tsp) vanilla extract
3 eggs
100 g (4 oz) minus 15 ml (1 tbsp) plain
  flour
15 ml (1 tbsp) cornflour
15 g (½ oz) soft white breadcrumbs
  (pp. 31–2)
40 g (1½ oz) unsweetened cooking
  chocolate
100 g (4 oz) plain chocolate chips
30 ml (2 tbsp) orange liqueur, such as
  Gran Torres or Grand Marnier

FOR THE GLAZE
50 g (2 oz) unsalted butter
50 g (2 oz) unsweetened cooking
  chocolate
15 g (½ oz) semi-sweet chocolate chips
15 ml (1 tbsp) orange liqueur
FOR THE CUSTARD
400 ml (14 fl oz) single cream
4 egg yolks
150 g (5 oz) sugar
30 ml (2 tbsp) orange liqueur
FOR THE CANDIED ORANGE PEEL
200 g (7 oz) sugar
12 strips thinly pared orange peel, about
  1 mm (1/16 inch) wide and 6–7 cm
  (2¼–2¾ inches) long, as directed below

Preheat the oven to 180°c (350°F) mark 4.

To prepare the torte   In a mixer or food processor, cream the butter and sugar together with the salt and vanilla. With the motor running, beat in the eggs. Combine the flour, cornflour and breadcrumbs; beat into the mixture.

In a small heavy saucepan, melt the chocolates together with the liqueur, stirring over a very low heat. As soon as they melt, remove from the heat and blend into the torte mixture.

Butter a 20–22.5 cm (8–9 inch) springform cake tin. Line the base with buttered greaseproof paper.

Pour in the chocolate mixture and bake in the oven until the surface feels firm to the touch – about 25 minutes for a 20 cm (8 inch) tin and 20 minutes for a 22.5 cm (9 inch) tin. The centre of the cake should seem a little underdone. Remove the cake from the oven and leave in the tin for 30 minutes. Invert on to a rack to cool. Remove the lining paper.

To prepare the glaze   While the cake cools, melt the butter in a small heavy saucepan. Add the chocolates and the liqueur; slowly melt them together over a very low heat, stirring. As soon as they are melted, remove from the heat.

Place the cake on a rack over a plate, and pour the glaze over. Smooth quickly with a spatula, spreading the glaze over the top and around the sides of the cake.

To prepare the custard   Scald the single cream in a non-metallic pan. In a heavy saucepan, beat the egg yolks with the sugar; cook over a low heat, stirring, until slightly warm. Whisk in the single cream; stirring constantly, cook until the custard thickens enough to coat a spoon – about 15 minutes. Add the liqueur and whisk briskly to cool.

Pour the custard through a fine sieve into a bowl. Place this inside a larger bowl filled with ice cubes. Stir the custard with a whisk until it is cool (it should be cooled immediately, so it will end up thick and smooth). Cover and refrigerate until serving time.

To prepare the candied orange peel   Combine the sugar and 225 ml (8 fl oz) water in a saucepan, and bring to the boil. Add the orange peel strips and cook them at a simmer, but not a boil, for 30 minutes. Remove the peel to an oiled plate and allow to cool. The peel should be pliable, not brittle.

To assemble the torte   Cut the cake into 12 equal pieces. Pour the custard on to a large round serving platter. Place pieces of cake over, in a circle, like flower petals. Arrange a piece of candied orange peel on top of each piece of torte, lengthways.

(This torte can be prepared a day ahead, but it should be assembled with the custard sauce at the last minute so the bottom of the torte does not get soggy.)

Filloas con Piña y Salsa de Naranja

· THIN PANCAKES WITH PINEAPPLE IN AN ORANGE SAUCE ·

Filloas are a typical Galician dessert: thin pancakes filled with pastry cream and sautéed in oil. I had never cared for them until I tasted this version at Madrid's delightful Sacha restaurant. Owner Pitila Mosquera, who is from Galicia, adds a touch of originality to all her traditional recipes, and this is a fine example of her cooking talent. *Serves 4–6. (Makes 12–14 pancakes.)*

FOR THE PANCAKES
3 eggs
100 g (4 oz) plain flour
175 ml (6 fl oz) milk
7.5 ml (1½ tsp) sugar
5 ml (1 tsp) vanilla extract
about 25 g (1 oz) butter for frying
FOR THE FILLING
2 egg yolks
40 g (1½ oz) sugar
22.5 ml (1½ tbsp) plain flour

175 ml (6 fl oz) milk
100 g (4 oz) canned crushed pineapple
   in its own juice, no sugar added,
   drained
FOR THE SAUCE
40 g (1½ oz) sugar
60 ml (4 tbsp) Miguel Torres or another
   fine-quality Spanish brandy
60 ml (4 tbsp) orange liqueur, such as
   Gran Torres or Grand Marnier
150 ml (¼ pint) orange juice

To prepare the pancakes   In a food processor or blender, combine all pancake ingredients except the butter, and blend until very smooth. Leave the batter to stand for about 30 minutes before cooking.

Prepare the pancakes as directed in Thin Pancakes Stuffed with Crab (Crêpes de Txangurro) (p. 86). You should have 12–14 pancakes.

To prepare the filling   In a bowl, beat together the egg yolks, sugar and flour until well mixed. Heat the milk in a small saucepan. Add the hot milk to the egg mixture in a thin stream, stirring. Pour back into the saucepan and cook over a low heat, stirring, until the custard thickens and coats the back of a spoon. Fold in the pineapple.

To assemble the pancakes   Spread 1 heaped tablespoon of the filling over each pancake, on the side that didn't get golden. Roll it like a cigar. Arrange the *filloas* on a platter and reserve. (The *filloas* may be prepared up to this point and refrigerated until needed.)

To make the sauce   In a saucepan large enough to hold all the *filloas*, dissolve the sugar in 15 ml (1 tbsp) water. Cook over a medium to high heat until it caramelizes and turns golden brown. Watch so it doesn't burn – but don't stir the pan, just shake it gently. Add the brandy and orange liqueur; it will hiss, but don't worry. Ignite and flambé (pp. 32–3) – be careful not to burn yourself! Pour the orange juice into the pan to dowse the flames. Cook quickly over a medium heat, stirring with a wooden spatula, until thickened and reduced a little – about 1–2 minutes (the sauce will continue to thicken when the *filloas* are added, so don't reduce too much now). Reduce the heat to low and add the *filloas*, basting them with the sauce until heated through.

Serve 2–3 *filloas* to each guest, with some of the sauce on top.

Terrina de Frutas con Muselina de Almendras

· *FRUIT TERRINE WITH ALMOND-BUTTERCREAM FILLING* ·

Prepare 1 day in advance, or at least 10 hours ahead

This terrine, with the colourful fruits – strawberries, kiwi and pawpaw or mango – encased in a fluffy filling surrounded by liqueur-soaked sponge cake, is one of the most visually attractive desserts in my repertoire. On my trips around Spain I've had similar versions several times in Madrid, Barcelona and the Basque Country; but Peñas Arriba, the exceptional new-style restaurant in Madrid run by 'Chiqui' Seco and chef Javier Otaduy, gave me the best recipe.

To make this cake you will need a 22.5 × 12.5 cm (9 × 5 inch) bread loaf tin and a 25 × 37.5 cm (10 × 15 inch) baking sheet – and a little skill to place the fruits so they come out in a colourful triangle when the slices are cut. The sponge cake, while easy to make, can be replaced by sponge fingers; you will need 175 g (6 oz).   *Serves 8–10*.

FOR THE SPONGE CAKE
4 eggs, 2 whole and 2 separated
3.75 ml (¾ tsp) baking powder
1.25 ml (¼ tsp) salt
150 g (5 oz) sugar
5 ml (1 tsp) vanilla extract
100 g (4 oz) plain flour
125 ml (4 fl oz) orange liqueur, such as
    Gran Torres or Grand Marnier
FOR THE FILLING
215 g (7½ oz) icing sugar

150 g (5 oz) unsalted butter, at room
    temperature
150 g (5 oz) blanched almonds, very
    finely ground
300 ml (½ pint) cream, stiffly whipped
about 8 large strawberries, hulled
1 large kiwi fruit, 100–150 g (4–5 oz),
    peeled and quartered lengthways
½ large ripe pawpaw or mango, peeled,
    seeded and cut into 4 pieces
    lengthways

To prepare the sponge cake   Preheat the oven to 200°c (400°F) mark 6. In a food processor or blender, beat the whole eggs and the egg yolks, baking powder, salt, sugar and vanilla until thick – about 2 minutes. Add the flour; process for a few seconds, just enough to blend – don't overmix. Transfer to a bowl. Whisk the egg whites until stiff; fold them lightly into the mixture, without overfolding.

Butter a 25 × 37.5 cm (10 × 15 inch) Swiss roll tin, and line it with greased greaseproof paper or non-stick baking parchment. Pour in the mixture, evening it out with a spatula. Bake in the oven for 8–10 minutes, just until it starts to colour and feels firm to the touch; don't let it get golden. Turn the cake on to a clean tea-towel and carefully remove the paper while still warm. Trim the edges with a sharp knife.

Cut the cake into 2 rectangles: one as wide as the length of your loaf tin, and long enough to cover the long sides and bottom of it (22.5 × 22.5 cm/9 × 9 inches). Cut out another rectangle to cover the top of the loaf tin (22.5 × 12.5 cm/ 9 × 5 inches). Sprinkle both rectangles with the liqueur. Line the sides and bottom of the loaf tin with the first rectangle and reserve the second.

To prepare the filling   Cream the sugar and butter together. Add the almonds and blend until thoroughly mixed. Transfer to a bowl. Fold in the whipped cream.

To assemble the terrine   Put a layer of filling over the bottom of the tin lined with the sponge cake. Cut off the tips and tops of strawberries and arrange them in a continuous line along the centre of the pan; press the fruit down with your fingers into the filling, lining it up evenly. Cover with another layer of filling. Cut off the tips and tops of the kiwi and pawpaw or mango pieces. Arrange the kiwi and pawpaw in 2 continuous lines next to each other, both cut side down, on top of the filling along the edges of the pan. Pile the remaining filling on top, evening it out with a spatula. Cover with the reserved rectangle of sponge cake, pressing down gently.

Cover the tin with foil and place a weight on top. Refrigerate overnight or for at least 9 hours before serving (in fact, it can be made up to 4 days ahead).

Serve on individual plates, cut into 2 cm (¾ inch) slices, so that each colourful slice shows the pattern of the fruit.

Pudín de Frutas Secas al Licor de Naranja

· DRIED FRUIT PUDDING WITH ORANGE LIQUEUR ·

The next three recipes are all from my Aunt Oriola. They are great home-style fruit desserts (this one with dried, the others with fresh fruits); each has a distinctive touch that seems very Spanish to me. And naturally, they all use some of my family's products – whether wine, brandy or orange liqueur. *Serves 6–8.*

FOR THE CARAMEL
100 g (4 oz) sugar
FOR THE PUDDING
450 ml (¾ pint) milk
25 g (1 oz) unsalted butter
100 g (4 oz) soft white breadcrumbs
(pp. 31–2)
225 ml (8 fl oz) orange liqueur, such as
Gran Torres or Grand Marnier

225 g (8 oz) mixed dried fruits, (raisins,
sultanas, apricots, dates, figs),
chopped
3 eggs, beaten
FOR THE DECORATION
225 ml (8 fl oz) double cream, whipped
with 30 ml (2 tbsp) sugar and 15 ml
(1 tbsp) orange liqueur

Preheat the oven to 180°c (350°F) mark 4.

To prepare the caramel Caramelize a 1.2 litre (2 pint) ring mould with the sugar, proceeding as directed in the recipe for Caramelized Coconut Flan (Flan de Coco al Caramelo) (p. 203).

To prepare the pudding Bring the milk to the boil and add the butter, stirring until it melts. Combine with the breadcrumbs in a food processor and process to make a thin paste. Transfer to a bowl and mix in the liqueur, fruits and beaten eggs. Pour into the prepared mould.

Place the mould inside a roasting pan and pour in boiling water to come halfway up the sides of the mould. Bake in the oven for 40 minutes, or until a skewer inserted into the centre comes out clean.

To assemble the dish Allow to cool for 10–15 minutes before unmoulding on to a round serving plate. Garnish with whipped cream, mounding it in the centre.

Pinchitos de Fruta al Licor de Naranja

· BAKED FRUIT ON SKEWERS SPRINKLED WITH ORANGE LIQUEUR ·

This dessert is a perfect, light end to a fine meal. You will need 12 × 25 cm (10 inch) long wooden kebab skewers. Soak them in water for 30 minutes before using them, so they won't burn during grilling. *Serves 6.*

½ *large pineapple, peeled, cored and cut*
 into 4 × 1 cm (½ inch) slices, each cut
 into 2.5 cm (1 inch) wedges
4 *medium bananas, cut into 1 cm (½ inch)*
 slices
4 *large seedless oranges, peeled and*
 segmented, with the membrane

5 *ml (1 tsp) ground cinnamon*
50 *g (2 oz) sugar*
50 *ml (2 fl oz) orange liqueur, such as*
 Gran Torres or Grand Marnier

Preheat the grill.

Skewer the fruit, beginning and ending each skewer with pineapple, until all the fruit is used up.

Line a baking tin with aluminum foil and arrange the fruit skewers in it. Mix the cinnamon with the sugar in a bowl, and sprinkle over the fruit.

Grill the fruit as close to the heat as possible, turning once, until browned – about 3–5 minutes. Remove from the oven and sprinkle 5 ml (1 tsp) liqueur over each skewer. Serve immediately.

Peras al Vino Tinto

· *PEARS IN RED WINE WITH STRAWBERRY SAUCE* ·

You can't go wrong with pears cooked in red wine – but these are the best ever. The natural tartness of the wine is perfectly balanced with the sweetness of the strawberry sauce.   *Serves 6.*

FOR THE PEARS
6 *large ripe, firm dessert pears*
1 × 750 *ml (1¼ pint) bottle full-bodied dry*
 red wine
100 *g (4 oz) sugar*
2 × 6 *cm (2½ inch) sticks cinnamon*
FOR THE FILLING
75 *g (3 oz) cream cheese, at room*
 temperature

50 *g (2 oz) sugar*
50 *ml (2 fl oz) whipped cream*
dash of finest-quality Spanish brandy
FOR THE SAUCE
350 *g (12 oz) fresh strawberries*
50 *g (2 oz) sugar*

To prepare the pears   Peel the pears and core them whole, from bottom to top, making a cylindrical hole. In a saucepan, bring the wine to the boil with the sugar and cinnamon. Reduce the heat to low and simmer the pears in the wine for about 30 minutes, or until they are very tender but not mushy. Keep basting the pears with the wine while simmering, so that they will take on the colour of the wine. Remove the pears from the pan and discard the cinnamon sticks. Bring the liquid to the boil and reduce it to 175–225 ml (6–8 fl oz). Set aside.

To prepare the filling   Mix the cream cheese with the sugar in a food processor or blender. Transfer to a bowl and fold in the whipped cream. Stir in a dash of brandy, to taste.

Using a piping bag, pipe the filling into the pears. Place them in a bowl. Pour the reduced wine over. Chill.

To prepare the sauce   Purée the strawberries with the sugar in a food processor or blender until the sugar dissolves completely. Chill.

To assemble the dish   At the last minute, cover the pears with the strawberry purée, or hand it separately in a sauce-boat.

Manzana Gratinada

· CATALAN – POMA GRATINADA ·

· APPLE GRATIN ·

I fell in love with this surprisingly simple, flavourful dessert at the Azulete restaurant in Barcelona. The kind of apples chef/owner Toya Roqué uses in Spain are similar to Golden Delicious, but I find that Cox's Orange Pippins and Granny Smiths work even better. Don't use Bramley or other cooking apples, as they do not hold their shape well.   *Serves 6.*

FOR THE APPLES
900 g–1.1 kg (2–2½ lb) Cox's Orange
   Pippin or Granny Smith apples
15 ml (1 tbsp) lemon juice
200 g (7 oz) sugar

FOR THE TOPPING
150 g (5 oz) blanched almonds
100 g (4 oz) sugar
50 g (2 oz) butter
2 eggs

To prepare the apples   Peel, core and thinly slice the apples. Put them into a bowl with water to cover and add the lemon juice to prevent them from discolouring.

In a saucepan large enough to hold all the apple slices, combine the 200 g (7 oz) sugar with 350 ml (12 fl oz) water; bring to the boil. Drain the apple slices and add them to the pan. Cook over a brisk heat for 5 minutes.

Butter a gratin dish or a small pie plate. Remove the apple slices from the syrup with a slotted spoon, and pile them into the baking dish.

Preheat the oven to 220°c (425°F) mark 7.

To prepare the topping   Finely grind the almonds and sugar in a food processor. Cut the butter into small pieces and add to the mixture; process until smooth. Add the eggs and process to blend. Pour this mixture over the apples.

Bake in the oven for 15 minutes or until the top is puffed and golden. Serve warm.

Nueces Caramelizadas con Nata

· CARAMELIZED WALNUTS WITH WHIPPED CREAM ·

Baeza is a little village in Andalucía, 30 miles northeast of Jaén, just off the road from Madrid to the south. I had been told it was worth the detour to go for lunch at Juanito, a roadside restaurant owned by Juanito and Luisa Salcedo and their son, Damián. Luisa's good old peasant country cooking has become famous, and the restaurant has received numerous awards.

So I decided to get up early one day and go there for lunch, on a trip from Madrid to Córdoba. It was packed – I learned later that it always is – and fortunately, it *was* worth it. Luisa has rescued traditional recipes from that part of Andalucía, which she executes with down-to-earth perfection. This dessert, in its simplicity, is a winner. *Serves 6.*

225 ml (8 fl oz) double cream
15 ml (1 tbsp) sugar

45 ml (3 tbsp) clear honey
150 g (5 oz) walnut halves

Whip the cream until it forms soft peaks; add the sugar and whip to stiff peaks.

In a frying pan, cook the honey over a medium heat until it starts to foam. Add the walnuts and cook, stirring, until the walnuts turn a dark golden colour from the caramelized honey.

Place a mound of whipped cream in the middle of each individual serving plate or bowl. Arrange the walnuts, straight from the pan, on top. Serve immediately, while the walnuts are still hot. The whipped cream will just start to melt, with a very nice visual effect and a great texture contrast.

Pan de Higos y Chocolate

· FIG AND CHOCOLATE LOAF ·

Excellent figs are produced in the area around Alicante, south of Valencia. One of the desserts I had at Els Capellans, in Elche, was *pan de higos*, which literally translates as fig bread; but rather than figs in a dough, this merely consisted of some wonderful local dried figs, pressed into the shape of a loaf of bread, with the addition of some powdered sugar. That gave me the idea for this easy yet terrific recipe. It is very rich indeed, so this 'loaf' will go a long way; a thin slice per serving may be more than enough. The good news is, it will keep for 2–3 weeks or even a month, in an airtight tin. It would also make a delightful little Christmas gift!   *Serves about 12.*

150 g (5 oz) whole almonds
175 g (6 oz) semi-sweet chocolate chips

450 g (1 lb) dried figs, stemmed and cut up
about 25 g (1 oz) icing sugar

Preheat the oven to 180°c (350°f) mark 4. Toast the almonds in the oven for 15 minutes. Immediately grind them finely in a food processor; add the chocolate and process to mix. The chocolate will melt from the heat of the almonds and all will stick together. Add the figs and process to combine thoroughly.

Butter a springform tin and sift in about half the icing sugar. Coat the tin with the sugar and shake out the excess. (If you don't have a springform tin, line a loaf tin with a piece of foil, so it will be easier to unmould.)

Press the fig mixture firmly into the tin. Unmould on to a serving plate and sift more icing sugar over the top of the loaf. Serve at room temperature.

Higos Pasos Rellenos

· FIGS STUFFED WITH CHOCOLATE AND NUTS ·

At the end of a memorable meal and several desserts at La Muralla, the gastronomic haven in Huelva, in western Andalucía, I was served these figs as an after-lunch treat – and found myself going back for more. You can't go wrong with figs, nuts and chocolate; but the combination here is truly irresistible.   *Makes 24 stuffed figs.*

FOR THE FIGS
50 g (2 oz) sugar
125 ml (4 fl oz) orange liqueur,
  such as Gran Torres or Grand
  Marnier
24 dried figs

FOR THE STUFFING
90 g (3½ oz) plain chocolate
25 g (1 oz) shelled pistachio nuts
25 g (1 oz) shelled walnuts
FOR THE DECORATION
24 walnut halves

To prepare the figs   In a saucepan, combine the sugar with the liqueur and 450 ml (¾ pint) water. Bring to the boil and boil for 1 minute. Add the figs, reduce the heat to low and cook at a simmer for 10–15 minutes, or until the figs have softened slightly. Turn off the heat and leave the figs to steep in the syrup for 30 minutes–1 hour. Remove the figs and reserve. Cook the syrup over a medium to high heat until just before it reaches thread consistency (110°c (225°F) on a sugar thermometer.

To prepare the stuffing   In a food processor, finely grind together the chocolate, pistachios and walnuts. Stir 15 ml (1 tbsp) of the fig syrup into the chocolate mixture. Discard the remaining liquid.

Preheat the oven to 180°c (350°F) mark 4.

To assemble the dish   Cut off the stem ends from the figs. With your finger, poke a hole in the stem end of each fig to make a pouch. Fill with some of the stuffing. Close up the fig opening by pinching it together firmly (don't worry if the figs don't close all the way).

Place the figs, stem side up, on an ungreased baking sheet. Push them down slightly to make them stand upright. Press a half walnut into the opening of each fig. Bake for 12 minutes and serve immediately, while still warm, or at room temperature.

Tejas Gigantes

· GIANT TUILE BISCUITS ·

Tuiles are fun to make, but these are particularly distinctive because of their size. I first had them at one of Madrid's smartest restaurants, Zalacaín, where they bring you one giant tuile on a silver platter as a treat with coffee, and the waiter breaks it into pieces with a spoon. Tuile biscuits are quite popular in Spain – especially in the Basque Country, for they originated in the town of Tolosa, near San Sebastián. Maybe that's why they are so special at Zalacaín, whose owner Jesús María Oyarbide is a Basque.

You will need three things to make these giant tuiles successfully: (1) a dry day, (2) 2 × 30 cm (12 inch) pizza pans and (3) 1 empty 1.5 litre (magnum) Bordeaux-shaped wine bottle. Of course, I don't have much of a problem there because my family makes 3 wines – Viña Sol, Tres Torres and Coronas – in this size. So the worst that can happen is that you have to go to the off licence, buy a magnum and then drink it before you can make these wonderful biscuits – it will be worthwhile!

The reason you need a dry day is because in damp weather these *tejas* will get soggy very quickly. I have made them, however, on a rainy day in Sausalito pretty close to dinnertime and they were still crisp when I served them. They won't last much longer; but that's not a big problem anyway, as it is unlikely there will be any left over. *Makes 3 × 25 cm (10 inch) tuiles.*

65 g (2½ oz) flaked almonds
65 g (2½ oz) nibbed almonds
150 g (5 oz) sugar
90 ml (6 tbsp) plain flour
15 ml (1 tbsp) cornflour

pinch of salt
5 ml (1 tsp) vanilla extract
2 egg whites
100 g (4 oz) unsalted butter

Preheat the oven to 180°c (350°F) mark 4.

In a bowl, mix together the almonds, sugar, flour, cornflour, salt, vanilla and egg whites. Melt the butter in a small saucepan; don't let it get too hot. Stir the butter into the bowl and combine thoroughly.

Butter a 30 cm (12 inch) pizza pan. Pour one third of the mixture in the middle of the pan. Using a fork, spread the mixture so it covers a circle to within 5 cm (2 inches) from the sides of the pan. Spread as thinly as possible; if there are some holes don't worry, they will fill in during the baking.

Bake in the oven for 8–10 minutes. After 7 or 8 minutes, watch carefully; the biscuit should be golden in the middle and brown on the sides, but don't let it burn.

To form the tuiles, have a 1.5 litre (magnum) wine bottle ready by the time the tuile is baked. Use a long metal spatula to loosen it from the pan. Put the second pizza pan on top and flip it over. Holding the pan with one hand and the bottle with the other, flip the tuile gently over the bottle (the reason for flipping from one pan to the other is so that the better-looking side of the biscuit will be on top).

The biscuit will cool quickly and take the shape of the bottle – a giant tuile. Leave it over the bottle for just a couple of minutes (if left too long, it tends to stick to the glass) and then remove the bottle, letting the tuile stand on its own.

Make the second and third tuiles in the same manner. Make sure the pizza pan is very clean before buttering it again, and wipe off the bottle each time.

Even on a dry day, these *tejas* should be baked not more than a few hours before serving time, as they are fragile and will absorb moisture. However, if they do lose their crunchiness, just reheat them in the oven and form them again. If you don't succeed in making a perfect tuile the first time and it breaks, just put it on the buttered pizza pan again, reheat in the oven and re-form it.

'Panellets'

· CATALAN AUTUMN BISCUITS ·

Hallowe'en is a festivity unknown in Spain; however, we do celebrate 1 November as All Saints' Day. This is a national holiday – and a particularly important date for those whose name is not in the registry of saints, as they celebrate their saint's day on 1 November. You see, birthdays pass almost unobserved in Spain – in fact, it is considered impolite to congratulate a lady on her birthday – but saints' days are important festivities. So for instance, if your name is Theresa, you would have your saint's day on St Theresa's day, 15 October. But if your name is, say, Eve, since Eve was not a saint your saint's day will be 1 November.

You may wonder what all this has to do with food. Well, Spaniards have a tendency to associate any religious holiday with something to eat, and *panellets* (little breads, in Catalan) are a traditional treat on All Saints' Day. They are made only at this time of the year, when yams are in season. I have fond memories of spending many a cosy 1 November afternoon around a fireplace with a group of friends, eating more *panellets* than I should have, with yams and chestnuts roasted over a wood fire.

The most typical *panellets*, *panellets de piñones*, are made with the basic dough and just covered with pine nuts; similar confections can be found in the rest of Spain under the name *empiñonados*, literally translated as 'covered with pine nuts'. But there are many different kinds, and we traditionally serve a selection of them. I have chosen here a few favourites and given different quantities, which you may adapt according to your taste. I suggest you make the full *panellet* dough recipe and then 2 or 4 different flavours – the way we would do it in Spain.

PANELLET DOUGH

Makes about 700 g (1½ lb)

100 g (4 oz) yam or sweet potato	1 egg yolk
200 g (7 oz) sugar	2.5 ml (½ tsp) vanilla extract
215 g (7½ oz) blanched almonds, finely ground	5 ml (1 tsp) lemon zest (p. 31)

Boil the yam until tender – about 30 minutes, depending on size. Peel and mash it. In a food processor, mix the yam together with the rest of ingredients, until you have a soft dough. Leave to stand for at least 30 minutes before using in any of the following recipes.

PANELLETS DE PIÑONES (PINE NUT PANELLETS)

Makes 18–20 biscuits

½ *quantity* Panellet *Dough (p. 223)*   *15–30 ml (1–2 tbsp) milk*
150 g (5 oz) pine nuts

Preheat the oven to 180°c (350°F) mark 4.

Make small walnut-size balls of dough and coat them with pine nuts. Brush them lightly with milk. Place on an oiled baking sheet, 2.5 cm (1 inch) apart. Bake in the oven for 15 minutes.

PANELLETS DE CHOCOLATE (CHOCOLATE PANELLETS)

Makes 15–18 biscuits

25 g (1 oz) cocoa powder   *25 g (1 oz) ground almonds*
½ *quantity* Panellet *Dough (p. 223)*

Preheat the oven to 180°c (350°F) mark 4.

Mix the cocoa with the dough. Shape the dough into walnut-size balls and roll them in the ground almonds. Place on an oiled baking sheet, 2.5 cm (1 inch) apart. Bake in the oven for 10–15 minutes, just until they start to colour.

PANELLETS DE CASTAÑAS (CHESTNUT PANELLETS)

Makes about 20 biscuits

175 g (6 oz) chestnuts, peeled   *pinch of freshly grated nutmeg*
225 ml (8 fl oz) milk   *about 25 g (1 oz) ground almonds*
½ *quantity* Panellet *Dough (p. 223)*

Preheat the oven to 180°c (350°F) mark 4.

Simmer the chestnuts in the milk for 35 minutes, covered. Grind the chestnuts with the milk in the food processor; add the dough and nutmeg. Shape the dough into walnut-size balls and coat with ground almonds. Bake as directed in Chocolate *Panellets* recipe.

PANELLETS DE CAFÉ (COFFEE PANELLETS)

Makes 8–10 biscuits

¼ *quantity* Panellet *Dough (p. 223)*   *15 ml (1 tbsp) sugar*
5 ml (1 tsp) instant coffee   *8–10 whole coffee beans*

Preheat the oven to 180°c (350°F) mark 4.

   Mix the dough with the instant coffee, shape into walnut-size balls and roll them in sugar. Put 1 coffee bean on top of each biscuit, pressing it in slightly. Bake as directed in Chocolate *Panellets* recipe.

PANELLETS DE AVELLANAS (HAZELNUT PANELLETS)

Makes 10–12 biscuits

¼ *quantity* Panellet *Dough (p. 223)*   *15 ml (1 tbsp) sugar*
65 g (2½ oz) roasted hazelnuts, filberts,   *8–10 whole hazelnuts, roasted and*
  skinned and finely ground   *skinned*

Preheat the oven to 180°c (350°F) mark 4.

   Mix the dough with the ground hazelnuts, shape into walnut-sized balls and roll them in sugar. Place a whole hazelnut in the centre of each biscuit. Bake as directed in Chocolate *Panellets* recipe.

PANELLETS DE CLAVO (CLOVE PANELLETS)

Makes 8–10 biscuits

¼ *quantity* Panellet *Dough (p. 223)*   *15 ml (1 tbsp) sugar*
1.25 ml (¼ tsp) ground cloves

Preheat the oven to 180°c (350°F) mark 4.

   Mix the dough with the cloves. Shape into walnut-size balls and roll them in sugar. Bake as directed in Chocolate *Panellets* recipe.

PANELLETS DE COCO (COCONUT PANELLETS)

Makes 10–12 biscuits

¼ *quantity* Panellet *Dough (p. 223)*   *15 ml (1 tbsp) sugar*
40 g (1½ oz) sweetened shredded coconut

Preheat the oven to 180°c (350°F) mark 4.

   Mix the dough with the coconut. Shape into walnut-size balls and roll them in sugar. Bake as directed in Chocolate *Panellets* recipe.

Pelotitas del Profesor

· HAZELNUT MERINGUE BISCUITS ·

The name of these biscuits actually translates as 'professor's little balls' – and naturally, there is a story behind it. When I had them at Madrid's Asturian restaurant La Máquina, former director Eduardo Méndez Riestra explained to me that the recipe comes from a bakery in a little Asturian town named Salas, whose owner was affectionately called 'the professor'. The biscuits had no name, but one day a tourist who went to buy them asked the 'professor' for his *pelotitas* – a word she probably associated with the shape of the biscuits. He naturally found that quite amusing, and from then on the biscuits had a name. The 'professor' died long ago, and today the biscuits are still made at the same bakery by his niece.

If you make these on a damp day, don't leave them uncovered or they might get soggy. Keep them in a tightly closed tin and they will last for quite a while.   *Makes about 15 small biscuits.*

150 g (5 oz) hazelnuts
50 g (2 oz) sugar

2.5 ml (½ tsp) vanilla extract
2 egg whites

Preheat the oven to 180°c (350°F) mark 4. Toast the hazelnuts in the oven for 15 minutes. Rub them in a damp tea-towel, to remove most of the skins.

Grind the nuts very finely in a food processor, together with the sugar, vanilla and 1 of the egg whites. Beat the remaining egg white until very stiff (you should be able to turn the bowl over without the egg white falling out). Fold the egg white into the nut mixture until well mixed. Increase the oven temperature to 200°c (400°F) mark 6.

Line a baking sheet with non-stick baking parchment. Using two teaspoons, drop small heaps of the mixture on to the baking sheet, spacing them 2.5–5 cm (1–2 inches) apart. Bake in the oven for 10–15 minutes, or until they start to brown. Remove from the oven, leave for a few minutes, then carefully remove from the lining paper with a spatula and transfer to a wire rack to cool completely.

'Carquinyolis'

· HARD ALMOND BISCUITS ·

Carquinyolis are typical Catalan biscuits, found in different versions in most pastry shops of the region. They have one thing in common: they are always hard – sometimes too much so for my taste. These are just delightfully crunchy.   *Makes about 50–60 biscuits.*

225 g (8 oz) blanched almonds
450 g (1 lb) plain flour
200 g (7 oz) sugar
15 ml (1 tbsp) baking powder
2.5 ml (½ tsp) salt
30 ml (2 tbsp) lemon zest (p. 31)

100 g (4 oz) chilled unsalted butter, cut
  into small pieces
3 eggs
5 ml (1 tsp) vanilla extract
5 ml (1 tsp) almond extract

Preheat the oven to 180°c (350°f) mark 4. Toast the almonds in the oven for 10 minutes (they will bake later with the biscuits, so don't let them turn golden). Set aside.

In a food processor, combine the flour, sugar, baking powder, salt and lemon zest. Add the butter and process briefly just to cut into the dry ingredients. Add the eggs, vanilla and almond extract. Process again very briefly; don't overmix, the dough should not be too smooth. Transfer to a bowl and fold the almonds into the dough quickly with your hands, until evenly distributed.

Butter a baking sheet. Shape the dough into 3 logs lengthways on the baking sheet; they should be about 5–6 cm (2–2½ inches) wide and 2–2.5 cm (¾–1 inch) high. The dough will spread during baking, so leave 2.5 cm (1 inch) between each log.

Bake in the preheated oven for about 25–30 minutes, or until the dough starts to turn golden. Remove from the oven and immediately, while still hot, cut the logs into 2 cm (¾ inch) thick slices. Place the slices, cut side down, on the baking sheet and return to the oven. Bake for further 15–20 minutes, or until golden.

These delicious biscuits will keep for quite a while, stored in a tightly closed tin – but I've never been able to make them last more than a week!

ICE CREAMS AND SORBETS

There are few better treats for an ice cream lover than home-made ice cream and sorbet. And indeed, with one of the excellent ice cream makers available today, the difference will be worthwhile. In the following ice cream and sorbet recipes, I have assumed that you have such a machine; but here are the directions if you don't have one.

To prepare ice cream and sorbet without a machine Refrigerate the mixture in a bowl until completely chilled. Freeze until firm about 2.5 cm (1 inch) from the edge of the bowl. Beat with an electric mixer to blend thoroughly. Cover and freeze until partially firm. Repeat the process twice more. Freeze until set.

Sorbete de Vino Tinto a la Hierbabuena

· CATALAN – XARRUP DE VI NEGRE A LA MENTA ·

· RED WINE SORBET WITH MINT ·

This is an idea from Cal Joan, the quaint country restaurant in Vilafranca del Penedès – home of my family's winery. Naturally, Joan and now his son, Quico, have always used one of our wines, Coronas, to make this sorbet, and that's what I use myself. In any case, the secret to this recipe is to use a fine medium-bodied dry red wine; a harsh red will give you a harsh, unpalatable sorbet. *Makes about 1.2 litres (2 pints).*

200 g (7 oz) sugar
5 fresh mint leaves
1 × 750 ml (1¼ pint) Torres Coronas or

another bottle fine medium-bodied dry
red wine
125 ml (4 fl oz) fresh orange juice
45 ml (3 tbsp) lemon juice

In a small saucepan, combine the sugar and mint leaves with 125 ml (4 fl oz) water. Bring to the boil and boil for 1 minute. Allow to cool, then remove the mint leaves.

Pour the wine into a non-metallic bowl. Add the sugar syrup, orange and lemon juice, and stir. Chill and make into sorbet according to the instructions for your ice cream machine.

Sorbete de Apio

· CELERY SORBET ·

This is an understated, refreshing sorbet, perfect as a palate cleanser between courses. The idea came from Madrid's Cabo Mayor restaurant; owner Víctor Merino created it because he likes celery so much. Its success was a surprise even to him!   *Makes 600 ml (1 pint).*

700 g (1½ lb) celery, with leaves, cut into
1 cm (½ inch) pieces

50 ml (2 fl oz) lemon juice
150 g (5 oz) sugar

In a large non-metallic saucepan, bring to the boil 1.4 litres (2½ pints) water with all the ingredients. Reduce the heat to low and cook, covered, for 25 minutes.

Strain through a fine sieve, pushing the celery down with a spoon; return the strained liquid to the pan and cook over a high heat until reduced to 750 ml (1¼ pints). Chill and make into sorbet according to the instructions for your ice cream machine.

If you have kept the sorbet in the freezer, leave it out for 15–20 minutes before serving it, so it will not be frozen hard. Serve in large wine glasses, for greater effect.

Sorbete de Gazpacho con Gambitas

· GAZPACHO SORBET WITH PRAWNS ·

Gazpacho is such a refreshing, healthy vegetable combination, it is a natural to make a sorbet out of it. The idea comes from José Carlos Capel, the Madrid writer who has taught me a lot about Andalusian gastronomy. He has written about gazpachos, too, and while commenting on that subject over dinner one evening, he told me how delicious his gazpacho sorbet with tiny prawns was. And he was right!

This will make a perfect palate freshener between courses, whetting your appetite for the main dish, or before dessert, instead of a salad.   *Makes 800 ml (1¼ pints).*

FOR THE GAZPACHO
450 g (1 lb) unpeeled ripe tomatoes,
   cut up
100 g (4 oz) chopped onion
5 ml (1 tsp) chopped garlic
¼ cucumber, peeled and cut up
1 small red sweet pepper, cored, seeded
   and coarsely chopped
350 ml (12 fl oz) tomato juice
30 ml (2 tbsp) sherry wine vinegar or red
   wine vinegar

15 ml (1 tbsp) finest-quality olive oil,
   extra virgin if possible
3.75 ml (¾ tsp) salt
15–30 ml (1–2 tbsp) hot chilli sauce
AS A GARNISH
225 g (8 oz) small peeled cooked prawns
5 ml (1 tsp) olive oil
7.5 ml (1½ tsp) sherry wine vinegar or red
   wine vinegar
hot chilli sauce (optional)

To prepare the gazpacho   In a food processor or blender, purée the tomatoes, onion, garlic, cucumber and red pepper. Add the tomato juice, vinegar, oil, salt and chilli sauce to taste. Process to combine well. Taste for seasoning.

Strain the gazpacho through a medium sieve. Measure and add water to equal 750 ml (1¼ pints). Chill and make into sorbet according to the instructions for your ice cream machine.

To prepare the garnish   If the prawns are salty, rinse them under running water and pat them dry. Toss them in a bowl with the oil and vinegar. Taste for seasoning and add chilli sauce to taste, if liked. Leave to marinate in the refrigerator for 1–5 hours. Drain the prawns on paper towels, then garnish each sorbet.

Sorbete de Manzana con Pasas

· APPLE SORBET WITH RAISINS ·

Start preparation at least 6 hours in advance

Luis Irizar is considered by many the father of 'New Basque Cuisine'. After living and cooking in San Sebastián for many years, he moved to Madrid and in October 1982 opened the Irizar restaurant. His classic Basque recipes have a personal, interesting approach to cooking; an example is his apple sorbet, which inspired me to develop this recipe.   *Makes about 1.4 litres (2½ pints).*

50 g (2 oz) raisins
125 ml (4 fl oz) dark rum
900 g (2 lb) tart dessert apples, such as
   Granny Smith

150 g (5 oz) sugar
900 ml (1½ pints) cider

Soak the raisins in the rum for at least 4–5 hours. Peel, core and quarter the apples; place them in a saucepan with the sugar and cider. Cook over a medium heat, uncovered, until very tender – about 30 minutes. Pass the apples through a medium sieve or a food mill. Stir in the raisins and rum.

Chill and make into sorbet according to the instructions for your ice cream machine. (Because of the consistency of the apples, it may take this sorbet a little longer to freeze.)

Sorbete de Moras

· BLACKBERRY SORBET ·

Blackberries make wonderful iced desserts. I had a memorable *sorbete de moras* at Josetxo – my favourite restaurant in Pamplona, capital of Navarra – which inspired this recipe. It made a perfect, light dessert after an excellent summer lunch. *Makes about 1.5 litres (2¾ pints)*.

450 g (1 lb) fresh blackberries
300 g (10 oz) sugar

15 ml (1 tbsp) lemon juice
225 ml (8 fl oz) double cream

Purée the blackberries in a food processor or blender. Combine the sugar with 1.5 litres (2¾ pints) water in a large saucepan and add the blackberry purée. Bring to the boil and cook over a high heat until reduced by half. Strain to remove the seeds. Allow to cool. Add the lemon juice and cream. Chill and make into sorbet according to the directions for your ice cream machine.

Leche Merengada

· MERINGUED MILK SORBET ·

This is my version of *leche merengada*. The one you find all over Spain in bars and ice cream and coffee houses during the summertime has no alcohol in it, but I find it much better this way! It would make a lovely dessert on a hot summer evening, perhaps accompanied by Hard Almond Biscuits ('Carquinyolis') (p. 226).

The origin of *leche merengada* is traced to Valencia, from where it went to Catalonia. It appeared for the first time in 1747, and was very popular throughout the nineteenth century, along with other iced drinks and ice creams. My favourite place to have it is at Chocolatería de Santa Catalina (St Catherine's Chocolate House) in Valencia. Don't miss it if you are there in the summertime. *Makes about 1.7 litres (3 pints)*.

90 g (3½ oz) sugar
thinly pared zest of 1 lemon
1 × 6 cm (2½ inch) stick cinnamon
90 ml (6 tbsp) orange liqueur, such as
   Gran Torres or Grand Marnier
1.2 litres (2 pints) single cream

2 egg whites, at room temperature
50 ml (2 fl oz) Miguel Torres or another
   fine-quality Spanish brandy, or to taste
FOR FINISHING
ground cinnamon

In a saucepan, combine the sugar, lemon zest, cinnamon stick, orange liqueur and cream. Cook over a low heat without boiling for 10 minutes. Cover and leave to infuse for 15 minutes. Transfer to a bowl. Discard the lemon zest and cinnamon stick.

Beat the egg whites until stiff. Fold them into the mixture. Add brandy to taste. Chill. Make into sorbet according to the instructions for your ice cream machine.

Sprinkle the top lightly with cinnamon and serve.

Helado de Miel con Nueces y Dátiles

· DATE–NUT HONEY ICE CREAM ·

Jockey, the great Madrid restaurant, serves a honey ice cream which inspired this recipe. I thought some dates and walnuts would go well here; and they certainly do. *Makes about 1.2 litres (2 pints).*

900 ml (1½ pints) milk	175 g (6 oz) stoned, chopped dates
4 whole eggs	50 g (2 oz) chopped walnuts
175 g (6 oz) honey	

In a large, heavy saucepan, beat together the milk, eggs and honey. Heat the mixture and cook over a low heat, stirring constantly, until it thickens – about 15 minutes. (If it should curdle, don't worry; it won't be noticeable after processing the ice cream.) Chill.

Fold the dates and walnuts into the custard. Make into içe cream according to the instructions for your ice cream machine.

Helado de Naranja

· CATALAN – GELAT DE TARONJA ·

· ORANGE ICE CREAM ·

I've had orange ice cream at several restaurants in Barcelona, perhaps the most memorable at Florián, a small refined establishment where Rosa Grau presents a very personal, imaginative cuisine. She and her husband, Javier García-Ruano, opened Florián in 1980 and have since built up an excellent reputation for their quality and uniqueness.

Rosa's orange ice cream inspired me to develop this recipe, acclaimed by many guests as the most delicious ice cream they've ever had. Hers didn't have candied orange zest, but I find it contributes a particularly interesting texture which combines very well with the richness of the ice cream and the freshness of the orange juice. (It is important to use fresh orange juice.)

This ice cream goes particularly well with Orange Custard in a Crown (Corona de Naranja) (p. 206). A nice way to serve it is by scooping balls of ice cream into the centre of the ring.   *Makes about 1.2 litres (2 pints)*.

FOR THE CANDIED ZEST
200 g (7 oz) sugar
30 ml (2 tbsp) orange zest (p. 31)
225 ml (8 fl oz) freshly squeezed orange
    juice, strained

FOR THE ICE CREAM
2 egg yolks
125 ml (4 fl oz) single cream
pinch of salt
225 ml (8 fl oz) double cream

To prepare the candied zest   Combine the sugar and orange zest in a heavy saucepan with 125 ml (4 fl oz) water. Bring to the boil and boil until the syrup darkens or reaches 130°c (250°F) on a sugar thermometer (firm-ball consistency). Remove from the heat and immediately add orange juice to the syrup. Stir well; the caramelized zest will stick together in a candied lump. Pour through a fine sieve into a container, reserving the orange syrup. Spread the candied zest on a small buttered dish and leave to dry.

To prepare the ice cream   Beat the egg yolks, single cream and salt together in a small heavy saucepan. Cook over a low heat, stirring all the time, until the mixture thickens enough to coat the back of a spoon – about 15 minutes. Add the reserved orange syrup to the egg mixture. Pour through a fine sieve into a bowl, and chill.

Beat the double cream until it forms stiff peaks; fold it into the custard mixture. Don't worry about the lumps of cream you will probably get; they will disappear when the ice cream is processed. Chop the candied zest and add to the ice cream mixture.

Make into ice cream according to the instructions for your ice cream machine.

Helado de Crema Catalana con Salsa de Avellanas

· CATALAN – GELAT DE CREMA CATALANA AMB SALSA D'AVELLANES ·

· CATALAN CARAMEL CUSTARD ICE CREAM WITH HAZELNUT SAUCE ·

Crema Catalana is a delicious custard served very often as dessert in Catalonia. The nicest thing about it is the caramelized sugar on top, which is made by sprinkling sugar over the custard and burning it with a red-hot iron plate. In the old days it was done with the central iron circle in the wood stoves used in homes. These stoves had iron tops, built into concentric circles; you would take out with a handle as many circles as necessary to fit the size of your pan. The central circle would be about 7.5 cm (3 inches) in diameter, and this was used to burn the sugar top. You raised it with a handle and just touched the surface of the sugar so it would caramelize.

These days such iron plates are sold commercially in Spain, but are seldom found in the United Kingdom. Instead, you can use a flat metal spatula and heat it on a gas stove or another heating element with a flame. Or you can caramelize the sugar and make spun sugar to top each ice cream mould, as directed below.

The idea of making *crema catalana* into an ice cream comes from the always imaginative Jaume Bargues, chef/owner of Jaume de Provença restaurant in Barcelona. This is characteristic of his talent: taking a very old, classic Catalan recipe and adding his personal touch to make it into a creation of his own.   *Makes about 1.2 litres (2 pints).*

FOR THE ICE CREAM
750 ml (1¼ pints) single cream
225 ml (8 fl oz) double cream
1 vanilla pod, split in half lengthways
thinly pared zest of 1 lemon
8 egg yolks
150 g (5 oz) sugar
90 ml (6 tbsp) Miguel Torres or another
  fine-quality Spanish brandy, or to taste

FOR THE SAUCE
40 g (1½ oz) hazelnuts
450 ml (¾ pint) milk
4 egg yolks
50 g (2 oz) sugar
FOR THE CARAMEL TOPPING
60–70 ml (4–5 tbsp) sugar

To make the ice cream   In a non-metallic saucepan, heat the single and double creams gently with the vanilla pod and lemon zest to just below boiling point; cover and set aside for 10–15 minutes. Remove and reserve the lemon zest and vanilla pod.

In a heavy saucepan, beat the egg yolks and sugar together with a whisk. Slowly whisk the cream mixture into the eggs. Cook over a low heat, stirring constantly, until the mixture thickens and coats the back of a spoon – about 15 minutes. Remove from the heat and whisk briskly to cool. Stir in the brandy. Leave to cool at room temperature. Chill and make into ice cream according to the instructions for your ice cream machine.

Fill 16 × 50 ml (2 fl oz) moulds with the ice cream, cover and place in the freezer for at least 30 minutes. Run a knife around the edges of each mould. Dip the moulds for just a few seconds in hot water and unmould on to a baking sheet. Return them to the freezer until just before serving; they must be served frozen very hard.

To prepare the sauce   Preheat the oven to 180°C (350°F) mark 4. Toast the hazelnuts in the oven for 12 minutes. Rub them in a damp tea-towel to remove most of the skins. Grind them very finely in a food processor.

Heat the milk with the reserved lemon zest and vanilla pod to just below boiling point; cover and set aside. In a saucepan, beat the egg yolks with the sugar; make the custard as described above. Discard the lemon zest and vanilla pod. Stir in the ground hazelnuts (if they form lumps, blend in the food processor until smooth). Refrigerate until ready to serve.

To assemble the dish   Just before serving, pour about 30 ml (2 tbsp) of the sauce on each plate. Place a metal spatula over a flame until red hot (unless you are making spun sugar as directed below). Sprinkle about 5 ml (1 tsp) sugar on top of each ice cream mould, and immediately burn the sugar with the red-hot metal spatula. Place 2 ice cream moulds on each plate, and serve immediately.

Alternatively, to make spun sugar topping   Caramelize 60 ml (4 tbsp) sugar with 15 ml (1 tbsp) water, proceeding as directed in the Caramelized Coconut Flan (Flan de Coco al Caramelo) recipe (p. 203). Do not let the caramel get dark; remove from the heat as soon as it turns light golden, since the caramel will continue to cook and darken.

Stir the caramel with a fork to cool. After 1–2 minutes, lift the fork from the caramel; when you see that threads begin to form, string the threads over each ice cream mould, working quickly with the fork. The caramel topping should not be thick – just a thin latticework of sugar threads over each one.

Helado de Pasas al Pedro Ximénez

· RAISIN ICE CREAM WITH CREAM SHERRY ·

The idea of combining a raisin ice cream with sherry would have to come from Jerez – of course! Outside the sherry district I've had it with Chocolate Sauce (Salsa de Chocolate) (p. 200), which is a nice dessert too; but only in the south have I tasted it with a dash of cream sherry. The first time was at El Faro, one of Cádiz's most colourful restaurants. Gonzalo Córdoba started the restaurant as a small eating spot in the old part of the city where he served fresh fish from the bay, plainly cooked. Today his menu is quite extensive, still featuring some of the best seafood from the nearby waters, based on traditional recipes from the area.

Another restaurant worth mentioning which features this ice cream is the charming, casual Bigote (Moustache, the nickname of the founder) in Sanlúcar de Barrameda. This is a taverna-style eatery where Bigote's sons, Paco and Fernando Hermoso, serve their top-quality local fish cooked in the simplest fisherman's style. After a feast of seafood, nothing could have been better than their raisin ice cream.   *Makes about 1.5 litres (2¾ pints).*

150 g (5 oz) raisins
125 ml (4 fl oz) Miguel Torres or another
   fine-quality Spanish brandy
1.2 litres (2 pints) milk
200 g (7 oz) sugar

8 egg yolks
About 30 ml (2 tbsp) per serving fine
   Spanish cream sherry, or a Pedro
   Ximénez

Soak the raisins in the brandy for at least 2–3 hours.

Scald the milk in a saucepan. In a bowl, beat the sugar with the egg yolks. Beat the mixture into the hot milk, stirring. Cook over a low heat, stirring all the time, until it thickens and coats the back of a spoon – about 15 minutes. Set aside.

Drain the raisins, reserving the brandy. Chop the raisins very finely in a food processor or blender; add them with the brandy to the custard. Allow to cool to room temperature, then chill. Make into ice cream according to the instructions for your ice cream machine.

Serve in individual bowls, pouring sherry on top.

Helado de Frutos Secos al Caramelo con Salsa de Chocolate

· CARAMELIZED NUT ICE CREAM WITH HOT CHOCOLATE SAUCE ·

Wallis is a new, very 'in' restaurant in Madrid, with an elegant decor and most interesting cuisine. Chef/owner Iñaki Izaguirre blends very innovative ideas with some old classics from his home region, the Basque Country where he was born, and Navarra, where he lived and cooked for a long time. After I had tasted an impressive array of his specialities, he recommended his *copa Don Ignacio* for dessert, which I loved, and it gave me the idea to develop this recipe.   *Makes 1.3 litres (2¼ pints).*

65 g (2½ oz) blanched almonds	8 egg yolks
65 g (2½ oz) hazelnuts	125 ml (4 fl oz) Miguel Torres or another
200 g (7 oz) sugar	fine-quality Spanish brandy
65 g (2½ oz) walnut pieces	75 g (3 oz) honey
900 ml (1½ pints) milk	1 quantity Chocolate Sauce (p. 200)
1 × 5 cm (2 inch) stick cinnamon	

Preheat the oven to 180°c (350°f) mark 4. Toast the almonds and hazelnuts in the oven for about 12 minutes, or until the almonds start to colour. Rub the hazelnuts in a damp tea-towel to remove most of the skins.

In a heavy frying pan, caramelize half the sugar (see Caramelizing, p. 33) by dissolving it with 15–30 ml (1–2 tbsp) water. Cook over a medium heat, until it starts to turn golden. Add the almonds, hazelnuts and walnuts; stir with a wooden spoon until the nuts are coated with caramel and acquire a dark, golden colour. Transfer the caramelized nuts to a large buttered plate, spreading them out. When they have cooled and hardened, grind them very finely in a food processor. Set aside.

In a saucepan, scald the milk with the cinnamon stick. Meanwhile, in a bowl, beat the egg yolks with the remaining sugar. Whisk the egg mixture into the hot milk and cook over a low heat, stirring constantly, until the custard thickens and coats the back of a spoon – about 15 minutes. Turn off the heat; stir in the brandy, honey and ground nuts. Allow to cool at room temperature, then chill. Make into ice cream according to the instructions for your ice cream machine.

Serve in individual bowls, pouring hot chocolate sauce on top.

BEVERAGES

Sangría

· RED WINE AND FRUIT PUNCH ·

This is my personal recipe for sangría, the refreshing, popular Spanish punch. It is a very colourful drink for a party, great for the summertime. I serve it in a large glass bowl, and peel the lemons and oranges leaving the skins in one piece, so they look like festive spirals hanging from the sides of the bowl.

The quantities of brandy, orange liqueur and gin can be adjusted at your discretion; I always pour rough amounts, depending on my mood – and my guests. If you find you went overboard, just add more wine, fruits, soda, etc., and make more of it. I never have any left over!

I must add that it is much against the will of my brother Miguel, our perfectionist winemaker, that I give out this recipe. It is his strong feeling that wine should never be mixed with soda and fruit – and he is right, in fact. But I remember our teenage summer parties when he would skilfully mix healthy amounts of our winery products into tasty punches, which kept everybody going merrily until hours later than our parents would have liked. Well, that's what sangría is about – a drink not to be taken seriously, but just for the fun of it. *Serves 8 or more.*

3 × 750 ml (1¼ pint) bottles Tres Torres
   or another full-bodied dry red wine
2 large lemons, peel thinly pared in one
   long spiral, flesh thinly sliced
2 large oranges, peel thinly pared in one
   long spiral, flesh thinly sliced
2 large peaches, when in season, sliced
45 ml (3 tbsp) sugar, or to taste
125 ml (4 fl oz) Miguel Torres or another
   fine-quality Spanish brandy, or to taste

125 ml (4 fl oz) orange liqueur, such as
   Gran Torres or Grand Marnier, or to
   taste
50 ml (2 fl oz) gin, or to taste
any other fresh fruits such as strawberries
   and grapes, except melon
600–700 ml (1–1½ pints) club soda water
ice cubes

Place all the ingredients, except soda and ice cubes, in a large glass bowl or jug. Stir well. Taste to adjust ingredients if necessary. Cover and refrigerate for at least 4 hours before serving. Just before serving, add the soda and ice cubes. (If you make it more than 6 hours before serving, add fruits like strawberries at the end, so they don't get mushy.)

Zurracapote

· SPICED RED WINE ·

Prepare at least 2 days in advance

I learned about this zesty wine drink from José Ramón Aguiriano at the historic restaurant Dos Hermanas (Two Sisters) in Vitoria, founded by his grandmother and great-aunt more than a century ago. Today José Ramón continues their fine cooking tradition.

Vitoria is the capital of the southern Basque province of Álava, home of the fine red wines of Rioja Alavesa. I have had *zurracapote* there cold and warm, mild and explosive – depending on the proportions of wine, fruits and their grape alcohol, *aguardiente* – but always a treat.   *Serves 4–6. Makes about 1.2 litres (2 pints).*

1 × 750 ml (1¼ pint) bottle Torres Corona
   or another medium-bodied dry
   red wine
40 g (1½ oz) sugar

3 × 6 cm (2¼ inch) sticks cinnamon
thinly pared zest of 1 lemon
75 ml (3 fl oz) Miguel Torres or another
   fine-quality Spanish brandy

Bring one third of the wine slowly to the boil with the sugar, cinnamon and lemon peel. Simmer for 15 minutes over a heat. Turn off the heat; add the remaining wine and the brandy, and stir.

Transfer to a plastic or glass container, cover and leave at room temperature for at least 48 hours to mature.

Serve at room temperature, strained into glasses.

'Cremat'

· CATALAN HOT COFFEE AND BRANDY ·

This is a very old, classic recipe from the Catalan fishermen of the Costa Brava, the coastal area north of Barcelona. They have traditionally prepared this comforting beverage to warm their bodies as well as their spirits while singing their sensual songs, *habaneras*.

Toward the end of the nineteenth century, many Catalans emigrated to Cuba to seek their fortunes; when they came back, full of good memories of the 'Caribbean Pearl', as they called it, and its beautiful women, they sang melancholy songs evoking days past, named *habaneras* after the city of Havana. They had discovered *cremat* there, the great combination of Antilles rum and Cuban coffee; and back home they continued to enjoy the beverage – often substituting the local brandy for the rum – together with their nostalgic songs. After the long day's work at sea, the *cremat*'s flames provided the perfect accompaniment for the evening.

Today there are performances of *habaneras* held during the summer in the Costa Brava; the fishermen sing them while *cremat* flows abundantly. *Habaneras* reflect the exuberant flavour of the tropical island: lyrical hymns to distant dreams, nostalgia and love. Perhaps one of the most popular is 'La Bella Lola' ('Beautiful Lola'), and the lyrics illustrate those feelings:

After a year without seeing land,/because the war prevented it,/I went to the port to find/the one that I adored./Ah! what a pleasure I felt/when at the beach she waved her handkerchief at me,/then she came to me and hugged me,/and in that embrace I thought I'd die./

In Catalonia, *cremat* is traditionally prepared in a wide, flameproof casserole – as I've had it at L'Avi Pau in Cunit, a restaurant famous for its theatrical presentation of *cremat*. This beverage is more fun to prepare in front of your guests; it can be heated over a chafing dish burner.   *Serves 6–8.*

350 ml (12 fl oz) Miguel Torres or
 another fine-quality Spanish brandy
40 g (1½ oz) sugar
1 × 5–7.5 cm (2–3 inch) stick cinnamon
3 long thinly pared strips each lemon and
 orange zest

1.2 litres (2 pints) freshly brewed, strong
 hot coffee
15 ml (1 tbsp) coffee beans

In a wide flameproof casserole, heat the brandy with the sugar, cinnamon, lemon and orange zest. When hot, ignite with a match and flambé (p. 31) for about 1 minute, stirring with a ladle. Dowse the flames with the coffee. Add the coffee beans and serve immediately, ladling into coffee cups.

'Euskal Akaita'

· BASQUE COFFEE WITH BRANDY AND PRUNES ·

The recipe for this traditional Basque coffee was given to me by Juan José Lapitz, the gastronomic writer who has been my main guide and mentor throughout my visits to the Basque Country. He prepared it for me at the Basque Gastronomic Society in San Sebastián – where only men are members and cooks – after a dinner cooked by him and the society's president. It was indeed the finishing touch to a superb meal! *Serves 8.*

350 ml (12 fl oz) plum brandy, such as
    slivovitz, or a fine-quality Spanish
    brandy, such as Miguel Torres
65 g (2½ oz) soft dark brown sugar
900 ml (1½ pints) freshly brewed strong
    hot coffee

8 dried prunes, stoned
225 ml (8 fl oz) double cream, lightly
    whipped, just to give it some body
5 ml (1 tsp) powdered instant coffee

In a jug, mix the brandy and sugar; stir. Add the hot coffee. Place a prune in each glass and pour in the coffee mixture. Float the cream on top and sprinkle the instant coffee over the cream.

Queimada

· WITCH'S BREW ·

Catalonia has *cremat*, Basque Country has *euskal akaita* – and Galicia has *queimada*. And in the good Galician tradition, this drink has a background of superstition. It is the brew around which goblins and *meigas* (Galician for witches) are conjured up while the cauldron flames in the dark and bewitching songs are chanted in low, monotonous tones.

   That's the story, as was told to me by a cheerful group of Galicians around a midnight *queimada* at Galloufa, a cosy restaurant in the little village of Villagarcía de Arosa. Just about every Galician has a recipe for *queimada*, and one thing you cannot reproduce is Galloufa's excellent grappa-style spirit.

   After all I've said, obviously this is a great drink to prepare in front of your guests, so I have adapted the recipe accordingly. And if possible, serve it from a wide, shallow flameproof casserole – the effect will be even more spectacular.   *Serves 8.*

90 ml (6 tbsp) sugar
350 ml (12 fl oz) grappa or a fine-quality
    Spanish brandy, such as Miguel
    Torres
450 ml (¾ pint) Torres Corona or another
    medium-bodied dry red wine

thinly pared zest of 1 large lemon
1 large Cox's Orange Pippin or Golden
    Delicious apple, peeled, cored and cut
    into wedges
15 ml (1 tbsp) coffee beans

In a heavy saucepan dissolve the sugar with 15–30 ml (1–2 tbsp) water; cook over a medium to high heat until the sugar caramelizes and turns dark gold. Add the grappa or brandy (it will hiss, but don't worry) and scrape with a spatula to dissolve the caramel. Meanwhile, heat the wine in a separate pan. Transfer the caramel/brandy mixture to a round casserole or whatever container you are serving from. Add the lemon zest, apple and coffee beans.

Right away, so the brandy stays hot, take the casserole to the room where your guests are. Ignite with a match and flambé (pp. 32–3). Now you can turn off the lights and invoke the witches! Stir the *queimada* with a long spoon for a few minutes, while flames beautifully light the room in the dark. . . .

When you have had enough of a show, dowse flames with hot red wine. Serve very warm in small glasses or cups.

A Tour of
SPAIN'S
FINEST
WINE
REGIONS

To understand Spanish wine, it is important to realize that *everybody* in Spain drinks it. Wine for Spaniards is a staple, it is not a luxury. Spain's per capita annual consumption is 15 gallons – compared to 2.4 gallons in the United Kingdom.

The Phoenicians and the Greeks, in the fifth and fourth centuries B.C., were the real initiators of wine growing in Spain. Later on, 2,000 years ago, the Romans established and extended the cultivation of the vines. At that time, more than 100 varieties of *Vitis vinifera* wine grapes were grown in the Iberian Peninsula.

Spain has 4.2 million acres of land planted in vineyards – more than any other country in the world. Yet the average annual wine production in the last decade has been about 800 million gallons, so it is only the number four producer after France, Italy and the Soviet Union.

There are 30 wine-growing areas in Spain covered by an Appellation of Origin (Denóminación de Origen), or specific regions controlled by legislation which regulates their viticulture and winemaking practices – equivalent to the French Appellation Contrôlée or the Italian Denominazione d'Origine Controlata. This chapter will be a tour only of the main regions, those I feel produce today the most interesting wines.

Very broadly, Spain can be divided into three main wine-producing areas: (1) The south, with the highest temperatures and most sun, is the home of the great aperitif and dessert wines in areas such as Sherry, Montilla-Moriles and Málaga. (2) The drier, arid central zone makes a wide range of sound but less delicate wines for everyday drinking. (3) The northern belt of Spain – Galicia, Upper Duero, Rioja and Catalonia – for reasons of soil as well as climate produces the great Spanish table wines.

RIOJA

The Denominación de Origen Rioja is part of the upper valley of the Ebro River; it gets its name from one of its tributaries, the Oja River (Río Oja). North and south of the Ebro the land is rugged, with few but fertile plains, making it one of the best agricultural areas of Spain. The rivers play an important role in Rioja; besides the Oja, there are several Ebro tributaries. The gentle slopes rising above the rivers are the home of many of the region's vineyards.

The Tirón, the Oja and the Najerilla rivers form the Rioja Alta (High Rioja). Further east, from the cities of Logroño to Alfaro, four more Ebro tributaries – the Iregua, the Leza, the Cidacos and the Alhama – form the Rioja Baja (Low Rioja). From the mouth of the Tirón River to that of the Alhama, the Ebro descends 725 feet, so there is a big change in climate and vegetation between these two areas. The western region, or High Rioja, is influenced by the Atlantic Ocean; whereas the eastern, Low Rioja, has a Mediterranean climate.

A third region is named Rioja Alavesa after the province of Álava, north of Rioja Alta. According to Professor Antonio Larrea, enologist and Rioja historian, Rioja Alta produces better wines for aging, because of the climate, whereas the wines of Rioja Alavesa are softer and with less acidity, better for earlier drinking.

The Grapes

There may have been vineyards in Rioja 5,000 years before Jesus Christ, but the heyday of Rioja came after the phylloxera plague started in France in the 1860s. As the great vineyards of Bordeaux became infested with the insect, some French winemakers went to Spain and established themselves in Rioja, which is only 300 miles south. They introduced their vinification and aging methods, most significantly the use of oak. Eventually phylloxera also hit Rioja and the rest of Spain, until at the turn of the century, the method of grafting on to American phylloxera-resistant rootstock was developed and the vineyards were replanted.

These same grapes continue to be grown today. The reds are mostly Tempranillo and Garnacha (the French Grenache), which make up 30 and 40 per cent of Rioja's vineyards respectively, with tiny quantities of Graciano and Mazuelo. For the whites, it is mainly Viura (the Macabeo of Catalonia) with 13 per cent of the total. The noble European grapes, such as Cabernet and Merlot, have been planted only experimentally and are not authorized for wines bearing the Denominación de Origen Rioja.

The total vineyard acreage in Rioja is 100,000 acres. Most of the wineries don't own vast vineyards; the largest is probably owned by CUNE, with over 1,000 acres, and Domecq with 700–800 acres planted. There are 60 *bodegas* which make wine and label it, and about 40 of them export some of the wine they produce. In a normal year, the total Rioja production is 29 million gallons. Harvest rarely starts there before mid-October, whereas in Catalonia or Jerez, for example, it usually starts in early September.

The Expansion of the Seventies

The late sixties saw the beginning of the arrival of outside capital in Rioja. Some of the large *bodegas* of Jerez came into the area, acquiring old established wineries such as Paternina and Franco Españolas. But the great expansion came between 1970–1973; several new wineries were built, among them Domecq, Olarra, Marqués de Cáceres, Berberana, Lan, Montecillo, Lagunilla and Alavesas.

A Winery Tour of Rioja

We will start our tour in the town of Haro, capital of Rioja Alta, and then move east to Rioja Alavesa, ending in Logroño, following the course of the Ebro River all the way.

The most striking impression when you visit the wineries in Rioja is how different one can be from another. Cold fermentation is used by almost all the large *bodegas* today, and many employ the latest technology – yet 15–25 per cent of the wine is still crushed by stomping! There is contrast in the ageing, too: some wineries will age their red wines no longer than two years in oak, whereas others – such as López de Heredia – keep them up to seven years. The cooperage used is mostly American white oak, except for a few French barrels.

LÓPEZ DE HEREDIA   Haro (Rioja Alta) (941) 310127 and 310244   Founded in 1877 by Rafael López de Heredia and today run by his grandson, Pedro, López de Heredia is one of the most conservative wineries in Rioja. A relatively small, family-owned business (under 50 employees), it prides itself on the traditional style and craftsmanship of its wines. The winery has its own cooper's shop and, faithful to the past, still ferments its wines in oak and ages them in old barrels for a long time – the whites 4–5 years, and up to 7 for their red Reservas. The top wine is Viña Tondonia, named after a vineyard on its 420-acre estate. Most of the production is sold in Spain; only 25 per cent is exported, the United States being the main market.

LA RIOJA ALTA   Haro (Rioja Alta) (941) 310346 and 310467   Established in 1890, this is another medium-sized winery making excellent wines in the traditional Rioja style. Its finest wine, in memory of that date, is called Reserva 890 – a wine of limited production, just about 1,000 cases, of which very little is exported. The second label is Reserva 904, available at select wine stores. The '70 vintage is a classic Rioja with an elegant oaky character.

COMPAÑÍA VINÍCOLA DEL NORTE DE ESPAÑA (C.V.N.E.)   Haro (Rioja Alta) (941) 310650   One of the first exporters of Rioja to the United States, CUNE (its pronounceable acronym) is well known for its white Monopole as well as for its reds, Viña Real Plata and Viña Real Oro, the latter considered in Spain one of the best Rioja Reservas. The founding family still retains control of the winery, which was established in 1879. It was greatly expanded in 1940, when it was the first in Rioja to use cement vats for wine storage; it was further enlarged in 1970 and 1980.

Though the winery owns over 1,000 acres of vineyards, it also buys grapes from local farmers. Its wines have been awarded numerous prizes in international competitions, dating back to 1885.

BODEGAS BILBAÍNAS   Haro (Rioja Alta) (941) 310147   Founded in 1901 by Santiago Ugarte, a Basque from Bilbao, Bilbaínas is today one of the wineries with longest-standing tradition in Rioja. The Ugarte family still retains control, and third-generation Santiago Ugarte is one of the directors.

A medium-sized company, its emphasis is on consistent quality. It owns 625 acres of vineyards, mostly in Rioja Alta around Haro, which provide it with about 25 per cent of its needs. The vinification plant is modern and efficient – a sign that the current generation is working toward establishing a prestigious, high-quality image for the winery.

The United States is one of its main export markets, where it was among the first to establish its brand as a quality Spanish wine. The semi-sweet Brillante white and rosé, dry whites Viña Paceta and Cepa de Oro, reds Viña Zaco and Viña Pomal, and especially the red Reservas, Vendimia Especial and Gran Reserva (aged in oak for 4 years), are excellent representatives of its style. It also produces a very pleasant sparkling wine, Royal Carlton.

BODEGAS MUGA   Haro (Rioja Alta) (941) 310498 and 311825   Isaac Muga's winery, founded by his father in 1932, is not large: he makes 40,000–45,000 cases a year of premium wines, in the fine old style. The wines, neither pasteurized nor cold-treated, are aged 2–4 years mostly in American oak and some French

Limousin; they are clarified with egg whites and filtered to a minimum if at all; the bottles are packed horizontally in wooden cases as well as in cartons. Respect for tradition and craftsmanship works for him to produce elegant red wines, with great personality. Muga exports some of his production.

GRANJA REMÉLLURI   Labastida (Rioja Alavesa) (941) 331274   In the mid 1960s Jaime Rodríguez-Salís, a Basque industrialist from Irún, acquired the Remélluri farm (*granja*) in Labastida. With its eighteenth-century farmhouse and 170 acres of land, the farm had once belonged to the convent of Monte Toloño Monastery. From the back garden you can see the Toloño mountain, and off the front balcony the most marvellous view of the entire Rioja, its vineyards sprawling endlessly in the distance.

An enthusiast of Rioja wines, Jaime embarked on the task of building a château-style winery. From 10,000 bottles in the first vintage, 1971, Granja Remélluri is now producing over 200,000. The wines are aged 3 years in American and French Limousin oak, and at least 1 year in the bottle before release.

BODEGAS DOMECQ   Elciego (Rioja Alavesa) (941) 106001   The great Jerez family set out in 1973 to enter the Rioja wine business by acquiring 750 acres of vineyard land and building a most impressive winery with the latest technology.

Their production is now about 400,000 cases, mostly from their own grapes. All the vineyards planted since '73 are trellised, something fairly unusual in Rioja. Their reds are aged in American oak, from $1\frac{1}{2}$ years for the regular wines to $2\frac{1}{2}$ for the Reservas; they look for fruit and varietal character, rather than for oak. Their white, made from Viura, has no oak at all but fresh, clean fruit. Their reds are well made, round and consistent in quality.

Domecq is very export-minded, and 30 per cent of its sales go abroad. In the United States it sells under the Privilegio label – a wine with a story behind it. In 1773 there was a dispute between two Rioja towns over the right to plant vineyards: the grape growers of Laguardia were opposed to new plantings in Elciego. The Elciegans took the case to the Supreme Court of Castile, which ruled in their favour, based on a 'privilege' (*privilegio*) awarded to the town by King Sancho of Navarre in the year 1165; hence the full name of the wine is Privilegio del Rey Sancho.

MARQUÉS DE RISCAL   Elciego (Rioja Alavesa) (941) 106000   Founded in 1860 by the Marquis of Riscal, Camilo Hurtado de Amézaga, this is the oldest winery in Rioja. Its underground cellar – built in 1860 – keeps an outstanding library of old vintages, dating back to the founding years. Winemaker Javier Salamero attributes their longevity partly to the fact that in those days they had Cabernet Sauvignon in them.

The fine quality of Riscal wines probably goes back to 1868, when the Marquis hired the services of a respected French enologist, Jean Pinau, to make his wines. As early as 1895, the wines of Riscal were awarded the first medal ever won by a Spanish wine – which has been shown on their label since – and at a Bordeaux exposition no less, in competition with the local French wines.

Everything surrounding Riscal has great history – including the town where it is located, Elciego (the Blind Man), named after a roadside inn owned by a blind man where travellers stopped to rest on their way to Basque Country. At some point, 50 or 60 years ago, the entire village was dependent on Riscal. The winery may be considered the last remnant of a good feudalism, where a nobleman created an enterprise and was able to instil in the families and workers around him the same devotion and enthusiasm he had. Today the workers are shareholders, and their attachment to the winery is still strong.

BODEGAS RIOJANAS Cenicero (Rioja Alta) (941) 454050 Founded in 1890, Bodegas Riojanas has been controlled for several generations by the Artacho family. It exports 50 per cent of its production. Here it sells the Monte Real and Viña Albina labels, both white and red Reservas. Viña Albina is made in a lighter style than Monte Real, and on the label it shows several prizes the wine has won over the years.

MARQUÉS DE CÁCERES Cenicero (Rioja Alta) (941) 454000 Enrique Forner, a native of Valencia who owns Château Camensac and Larose Trintaudon in Bordeaux, came down to Rioja in 1968 and decided to create his third 'château' there.

His first vintage, 1970 – the year the winery was completed – was released in 1975. Forner's philosophy of winemaking is indeed quality-oriented, and it shows in the classic style of the wines. His basic red as well as the Reserva are good exponents of a new ideology in Rioja winemaking, happily blending tradition with the latest technology. Cáceres white is fresh and with fine floral aromas, yet intense and complex. The reds are aged for a maximum 18 months in oak, American and French Limousin, which contributes an elegant trace of spiciness in perfect balance with the fruit from the Tempranillo grape.

BODEGAS MONTECILLO Fuenmayor (Rioja Alta) (941) 440125 Established in 1874 by brothers Alejandro and Celestino Navajas, the winery was family-owned until sold in 1973 to the Jerez family firm of Osborne. The existing structure was expanded, and new vinification and ageing plants were built. Under the keen direction of winemaker Gonzalo Causapé and with an enthusiastic, highly professional team, the winery has evolved from a small quality business to a prestigious 300,000–400,000-case-a-year operation.

The red wines – Viña Cumbrero, Viña Monty and Montecillo – all have great character and good balance between fruit and oak; the Gran Reservas are especially fine, the best being a '73 Montecillo black label. The white Viña Cumbrero is fresh and crisp, without any trace of oak.

FAUSTINO MARTÍNEZ Oyón (Rioja Alavesa) (941) 110701 The Martínez family had been making wine since the 1850s, but it was in 1930 that Faustino Martínez decided to bottle his products. His son, Julio Faustino Martínez, carries on the family tradition. Today the winery owns about 600 acres of vineyards, and it is the number one exporter of Reserva and Gran Reserva wines in Rioja.

The evolution of Faustino Martínez is astonishing. Here is a family of grape growers who one day decided to make wine – and not only did they succeed, but they have become one of the top wineries in Rioja.

MARQUÉS DE MURRIETA   Castillo de Ygay, Logroño (Rioja Alta) (941) 258100   This is an old prestigious name representative of quality wines from Rioja in the United States as far as 20 or 30 years ago. It was in 1872 that the Marquis Luciano Murrieta acquired the Ygay estate near Logroño, and began making fine wines in the style of Bordeaux. Today the beautiful château-style winery owns 350 acres of vineyards, and the wines are all estate-bottled.

Murrieta was one of the first wineries in Rioja to export its wines, despite the small production: 90,000 cases/year, of which about 50 per cent are sold abroad. The white is made from Viura and the reds from Tempranillo, the latter aged 2 or 3 years in American oak. Its red Reserva, Castillo Ygay, is a particularly good exponent of the quality of Murrieta wines, and the old vintages occasionally found in specialist shops are proof of their long life.

BODEGAS OLARRA   Logroño (Rioja Alta) (941) 235299 and 235388   This is probably the most California-style winery in Rioja. It was built in 1972 by a Basque industrialist, Luis Olarra; he recently sold the winery, but winemaker Ezequiel García has stayed on. Olarra is a wonder of technology and efficiency, different from anything else in Rioja. Yet it has maintained the best of Rioja's tradition, blending it with the most modern enological advances.

Olarra has looked for a style of its own. The whites and reds, especially the Reserva Cerro Añón, have been a hit ever since the first vintage, 1970. Its marketing team is highly professional and consumer-oriented, and the sales – 300,000 cases in '83 – are one-third export, including the United Kingdom. Despite the winery's youth, the wines have won numerous awards because of their elegance and personality.

GALICIA

Winemaking in Galicia goes back to the eleventh century. But it was in the fourteenth century that the British, always searching for areas which could produce fine wine, came to Galicia, and they made a good white port-style wine for a while. Unfortunately, in the sixteenth century they were forced to leave – the Catholic Church became fearful that the trade with 'heretics' would corrupt the locals' souls. So they went farther south, to Portugal; they established themselves in Oporto, and the history of port began.

About 65 per cent of the wines made in Galicia are red, yet the best are white. The reds are consumed locally; they are generally rough and quite acidic. The best whites, all consumed locally, can be elegant and delightful. Because the consumption is twice the amount produced, a lot of grapes, and even wine, are imported from other areas – and sold as native. Fraud is quite common, aided by the fact that Galicians distrust labels; they believe a bottle with a label is a clear indication that the wine was made 'chemically'. Thus good wine is hard to find; and when you do, it's very expensive.

While winemaking is rudimentary, the grapes are grown with immense care; nothing else is tended with such devotion in Galicia. To avoid cryptogamic diseases caused by the abundant rains, vines are planted on arbors. The best vineyards are located on the sunny slopes above the rivers; altitude hurts quality because of the scarce sun in the region, and the plains give large quantities of mediocre grapes.

After phylloxera struck Galicia, most of the vineyards were replanted with the white Palomino grape from Jerez – called Jerez in Galicia – because it is heartier than the indigenous varieties and produces a larger yield. And this is the only area in Spain where I've seen hybrid grapes. The variety, called Catalam, is originally from California and produces bountiful crops of ordinary white and red wines. Fortunately, an effort is being made to bring back the noble local varieties as the basis for the great wines of Galicia.

Alvarinho is the best Galician grape, and the price paid for it is the highest in Spain. Alvarinho is a Specific Appellation or Denominación Específica, applicable to any wine made from that grape regardless of the area, rather than a Denominatión de Origen such as the Galician regions Ribeiro or Valdeorras. Treixadura and Torrontés are the finest varieties in Ribeiro, and Godelho in Valdeorras.

The Alvarinho variety seems related to the Alsatian and German Riesling, brought back via the Camino de Santiago (the pilgrim route described in the section on Galicia in 'The Flavour of Spain', p. 21). Of course, some maintain that it was actually the other way around: Alvarinho was taken from Galicia to northern Europe and there it became Riesling. And indeed, at its best it has the fruit and elegance of a fine European Riesling.

A Winery Tour of Galicia

ASOCIACIÓN DE COSECHEROS DE ALVARINHO   Sisam, Cambados **(Pontevedra)** (986) 710052   The co-op system in Galicia works very differently from co-ops in other areas of Spain; here it plays a very important role in the quality improvement of the wines. President Daniel Casalderrei is enthusiastic about the new installations at this co-op as well as about further plans underway, and is proud of the results already obtained.

The winery is indeed a model of cleanliness and efficiency. With 17 members in the *Asociación*, the production is only about 300,000 bottles; so unlike the big co-ops, Casalderrei can control the growers who turn their grapes in for vinification. Faithful to tradition, he seldom labels the wines – the members want it that way! Regardless, he turns out some lovely bottles, with delicate and elegant aromas. And naturally, he proudly feels that Alvarinho makes the best wines in the world.

PAZO DE BAYÓN   **Villagarcía de Arosa (Pontevedra)** (986) 500789   *Pazo* is the Galician word for farmhouse – but this is more like a château. Situated near the delightful town of Villagarcía de Arosa, Pazo de Bayón is in a movie-style setting, with its castle rising over the estate, its vineyards and trees and little paths sprawling over the lush valley. Justo Álvarez de la Fuente, an industrialist from Ávila, is a most friendly host who takes pleasure in showing a wine lover around. And if all this were not enough, Pazo de Bayón makes a terrific Alvarinho; only 80,000 bottles a year, most sold locally, but well worth searching for.

SANTIAGO RUIZ   Sam Miguel de Tabagom (Pontevedra) (986) 610568 Nestled in the far southwest corner of Galicia, where the Minho River flows into the Atlantic Ocean, forming a natural boundary with Portugal, is the district of O Rosal, producer of some truly charming Alvarinhos. At the very southern tip of O Rosal is the village of Sam Miguel, where Santiago and Isabel Ruiz make the most renowned Alvarinhos in the area. Santiago's family has been making wine at that property since the 1700s. His production has not increased much from that time: in 1984 – an excellent year – he made 15,000 bottles!

Santiago Ruiz makes wine as his father and grandfather did: with great love and care, the old way, in a tiny cellar behind his home, next to a museum of memorabilia and old wine artifacts. Right there is his 'bottling machine' – the same one his grandfather had used since 1908. Yet he ferments in stainless steel and uses a modern pressing machine to crush the grapes. Heralded by connoisseurs and wine writers in Spain, his wine is not only very difficult to obtain but also quite expensive.

Watching the sunset from his verandah, with a marvellous view of the Minho River and Portugal in the distance, Santiago will sing for you the praises of Galician wines – definitely the best in the world. And while tasting his, you will agree!

COOPERATIVA DEL RIBEIRO   Ribadavia (Orense) (988) 470175   This cooperative is a far cry from the one in Alvarinho. It has about 1,000 members, produces 4–5 million bottles a year, and the members' input varies from 22 pounds to 88,000!

The varieties planted are the indigenous Treixadura and Torrontés, plus a lot of the lesser Palomino. One of the problems there is that the grapes have always been harvested in large plastic bags, in which they may sit in the sun for a day until the harvest truck comes by to pick them up. The growers were up in arms when the co-op stopped selling the bags to discourage such practice. Now the finest varieties are harvested in boxes, and the members are encouraged by financial incentives to plant more of the better varieties.

About 80 per cent of the co-op's wines are sold with a label. Its top brand is Bradomín, a 100 per cent Treixadura and Torrontés varietal of lovely golden colour, with fine aromas reminiscent of banana and tropical fruits. Viña Costeira is pale, fresh and crisp, with a touch of bubbliness, made mostly from the two indigenous varieties with some Palomino.

CASTILLA-LEÓN

This is a vast area with various wine-growing districts, but probably the finest wines are made in the only 2 regions covered by a Denominación de Origen:

Rueda and Ribera del Duero, the last a D.O. only since 1982. Both are located on the banks of the upper Duero River. The first is best known for its white wines, the second for its reds – notably the legendary Vega Sicilia.

Ribera del Duero is an area of extraordinary beauty. During the cold, rigorous winters, the snow-covered mountains in the background seem to want to protect the vineyards sprawling in the valleys. In an October visit there, the autumn colours were spectacular. The vineyards had taken on a fiery red hue due to the early frosts – one of the main problems for the vineyards in the area – and the landscape exuded a certain peaceful serenity.

The main grapes planted in the district are Tinto Fino (same as Rioja's Tempranillo), Garnacha and three French varieties: Cabernet Sauvignon, Merlot and Malbec. Ribera del Duero and Penedès, in Catalonia, are the only two D.O.s which authorize foreign grapes to be used in their wines.

Rueda's vineyards are mostly planted with Verdejo, a white grape indigenous to the region. Viura and Palomino are also grown; they make harder, less elegant wines. At its best, Verdejo produces wines of pale golden colour, dry, almost austere, with character and individuality, finishing off with a slightly grassy, refreshing aftertaste.

A Wine Tour of the Upper Duero

VEGA SICILIA   Valbuena de Duero (Valladolid) (983) 300393 and 220318
For decades, any lover of Spanish wines has known about the great wine of Vega Sicilia – probably since Sir Winston Churchill proclaimed it his favourite. Today the wines continue to have an enviable level of quality and a well-deserved prestige throughout Spain as well as abroad.

The winery is located on the right bank of the Duero River, 25 miles east of Valladolid. The estate dates from 1864, when Eloy Lecanda brought the French vines Cabernet Sauvignon, Merlot and Malbec down from Bordeaux and planted them alongside various Spanish varieties.

All Vega Sicilia wines are estate-bottled; the production is quite limited, although in 15 years it has gone from 30,000 bottles to 200,000 in 1984. The property has about 300 acres of prime soil planted with vineyards along the gentle slopes rising from the Duero: 70 per cent Tinto Fino, 20 per cent Cabernet Sauvignon and 10 per cent Malbec/Merlot. The winery exports some of its production, but only a few cases reach the United Kingdom – hardly enough to satisfy the curiosity and appreciation for the wine in this country!

The wines are made following the traditional methods handed down from Vega Sicilia's first winemaker, the notable 'Chomín'. They spend between 3 and 10 years in oak, mostly American, plus 1 or 2 in the bottle before release. Those with bigger potential are first kept 3–4 years in large wooden vats.

The premier label is the Vega Sicilia 'Único', an elegant, complex red, with exceptional character reminiscent of a great Bordeaux yet with its very own personality. The other red, Valbuena, is velvety and soft, with a deep bouquet and excellent balance between fruit and oak.

To me, Vega Sicilia has achieved a mythical reputation thanks to the unique character of its wines – something similar to what Château Latour has done in Bordeaux. You may like one vintage more than another; but they all have that unmistakable individuality which is the mark of a great wine. For that, and for showing the world how fine a Spanish wine can be, Vega Sicilia deserves the utmost respect.

ALEJANDRO FERNÁNDEZ   Pesquera de Duero (Valladolid) (983) 881023
Alejandro is a man in his fifties who has always loved wine. After amassing a sizeable fortune in his business, in 1970 he decided to build a winery in Ribera del Duero and to produce the best red wine in the world. Today he has 70 acres, planted mostly with the finest local grape, Tinto Fino.

The first vintage, 1974, was released in 1976. Alejandro makes about 100,000 bottles of two reds, Pesquera Tinto and Gran Reserva, which have recently won many prizes – and when I tasted the '80 Gran Reserva, I realized why. Three years in American oak had mellowed out its intense, robust body; the nose was rich with breed and character, and the lingering aftertaste had enough good tannin to augur a long life.

MARQUÉS DE GRIÑÓN   Rueda (Valladolid) (983) 868116   A recent newcomer to Rueda is Carlos Falcó, Marquis of Griñón. In 1974 he and his partner, Antonio Sanz, built a winery equipped with the latest winemaking technology.

Their white, sold under the label Marqués de Griñón, is made exclusively from the Verdejo grape. They produce 15,000 to 18,000 cases and are already exporting to the United States and other countries. It is a dry, aromatic wine, with abundant fruit and marked varietal character; with no wood ageing, it is a fine example of the elegant whites that can be produced in the area.

Also very exciting are the red wines they are making from a 35-acre Cabernet Sauvignon vineyard near Toledo. Their '82 and '83, tasted out of the cask, showed great promise and fine Cabernet fruit in the nose. They will be released after 2 years' ageing in American oak.

CASTILLA-LA MANCHA

This is the largest wine-producing region of Spain, accounting for 70–75 per cent of the country's wine production. There are four Denominaciones de Origen in the area, the main ones being La Mancha – which by itself makes up about 40 per cent of Spain's total – and Valdepeñas; the other two are Almansa and Méntrida.

Driving through the miles and miles of vineyards in La Mancha, you will admire the endless rows of tidy, well-kept vines tended lovingly like gardens. Here and there a windmill sprinkles the landscape with a dot of white, as in Don Quijote's time.

La Mancha is an immense plateau, with an average altitude of 2,000 feet and 1.2 million acres planted – the largest vineyard concentration in the world. There are in La Mancha about 2,000 wineries, making a total of 400 million gallons of wine per year. The climate is dry and extreme, with sparse rainfall and temperatures that reach minus 10 degrees F in the winter and 110 degrees F in the summer.

Valdepeñas is a much smaller district, planted with 86,000 acres of vineyards; it was part of La Mancha until 1968, when it became a separate Denominación de Origen. Valdepeñas wines are more stable – owing to their own natural constitution – and travel better than those from the rest of the region; therefore the district has been Madrid's traditional wine purveyor since the eighteenth century.

Valdepeñas is quite a wine town; with a population of 25,000 or 30,000, it has 400 wineries – and they all look alike! The village is full of caves, housing the traditional huge *tinajas*, 4,200-gallon earthenware jars with conical bottoms, shaped like the ancient Roman amphoras; wine has been made, stored and even transported in them since time immemorial. In fact, *tinajas* are the next best thing to temperature-controlled fermentation. They dispel the heat produced during the process as the air circulates around inside the container, producing a natural ventilation which cools the fermenting grape juice.

Although *tinajas* are typical of all La Mancha, their largest concentration has always been in the Valdepeñas district. Today, with modern enological techniques, they are falling into disuse – but most wineries still have some. Since 1982, the attractive boulevard leading into Valdepeñas, Avenida del Vino, has 126 *tinajas* lining the sides of the street – a clever idea of Mayor Esteban López, who rescued them as they were thrown away by wineries that had no more use for them.

The region of Castilla-La Mancha produces three types of wine: white from the Airén grape, reds mostly from Cencibel (yet another name for Rioja's Tempranillo) and *claretes* from a mixture of 85 per cent white and 15 per cent red. The reason for the existence of these *claretes* is that Cencibel is much more expensive than Airén, which has a higher yield and characteristically produces soft wines, low in acidity.

Traditionally, La Mancha has been the big producer of ordinary wines in Spain, much of it shipped in bulk abroad or to other Spanish wine districts for blending. But in the last 5–10 years, a handful of pioneering wineries have been applying new production methods and moving away from *claretes*. They are making some crisp, young whites with clean fruit from the Airén grape, and light, fruity reds from Cencibel; both are excellent value for the money. Fortunately, they are changing the idea – so deeply rooted in yesterday's Spain – that the higher the alcohol content and the older the vintage, the better the wine.

The cooperatives play an important role in the area. There are 86 of them in La Mancha, making about 60 per cent of all the district's wines. Their storage capacity is staggering: anywhere between 2 and 10 million gallons each. With these figures in mind it is easy to understand that La Mancha has enormous surpluses of wine – which the government subsidizes by buying vast amounts at minimum prices for distillation into alcohol. Lately, however, steps have been taken in the right direction. A 'Quality Plan' has been established, giving financial help to wineries to help them introduce temperature-controlled fermentation and other technological improvements.

A Winery Tour of Valdepeñas and La Mancha

LUIS MEGÍA   Valdepeñas (Ciudad Real) (926) 320600   Founded in 1947 by Luis Megía, the winery was recently sold to a leading Spanish bank, although Luis and his team have stayed on. The change has, in fact, been very positive for the quality of the wines, as large sums of capital have been invested in the company. This is encouraging, and speaks for the success of these new higher-quality wines.

Megía is the most technologically advanced producer in Valdepeñas. Fermentation is done under controlled temperature in stainless-steel tanks, with selected yeasts; yet *tinajas* are still used to clarify the wines. Production is 3 million gallons per year, of which some is exported to the United Kingdom.

COOPERATIVA LA INVENCIBLE   Valdepeñas (Ciudad Real) (926) 320458 This is the largest and oldest co-op in Valdepeñas, an incredible operation with over 1,000 members which produces 30 per cent of all the district's wine – about half bottled and half in bulk. The smallest member brings in 11 tons of grapes, and the biggest 550 to 750 tons. During harvest time, it is an amazing sight to watch the long row of tractors lining up at day's end to deposit their load of grapes at the winery; the line goes on and on through the streets of Valdepeñas.

The vinification is handled with great efficiency. The tractors go through a station at the entrance where a sample of the must is extracted and the sugar content measured; the computer prints a card which will be the receipt for the grape grower at profit-sharing time. As the grapes are unloaded into the presses, the whole transaction has taken just about five minutes!

FÉLIX SOLÍS   Valdepeñas (Ciudad Real) (926) 322400   Since Félix Solís established the small winery Bodega del Cura (priest's cellar) in 1925, it has become one of the largest and most modern wineries in Valdepeñas, as well as the number one exporter and bottled wine producer in the area. Mr Solís is still president of the family-owned company.

The winery produces fresh, young, cold-fermented whites and clean, pleasant reds. The red Reservas are aged in *tinajas* and in American oak for 1 year or longer, which contributes their creamy, vanilla-like character. All in all, their price/quality ratio is excellent; few regions in the world can match it.

VINÍCOLA DE CASTILLA   Manzanares (Ciudad Real) (926) 610450   In 1976, the former conglomerate Rumasa went all out to build the ultimate winery in La Mancha: a technologically advanced, quality-oriented operation which would take full advantage of the vast potential of La Mancha wines.

General Manager Alfonso Monsalve and winemaker Alberto Pérez have great confidence in the future of the district's wines. Very export-oriented, they started shipping to the United States in 1983, mostly with the labels Viña Bonita, Espada and Señorío de Guadianeja.

Of particular interest are their experimental plantings (50 acres) of Cabernet Sauvignon, for which Alberto believes there are great microclimates in La Mancha. And indeed, I was impressed with the fruit displayed by the young '84.

Their '79 Reserva, a blend of 90 per cent Cencibel and 10 per cent Cabernet aged in American oak, has good balance and a nice touch of vanilla in the finish. In general, their wines are clean, honest and well made, terrific value for the price.

COOPERATIVA NUESTRO PADRE JESÚS DEL PERDÓN Manzanares (Ciudad Real) (926) 610309   This modern co-op was the first in La Mancha to attempt, back in 1970, a change in the vinification of white wines toward more emphasis on the fruit. It has over 700 members and a capacity of 8.2 million gallons.

Pascual Herrera oversees the production, assisted by young cellar master Pepe Casalderrey. As we tasted the wines, I could see how they look for youth and freshness in the whites, and for clean fruit in the reds.

JEREZ

To me, the wines of Jerez have an aura of mystery about them. It still is something of an enigma why the *flor* (flower), or layer of yeast that grows spontaneously on the surface of the wine, appears in this privileged Denominación de Origen.

Few wines in the world can boast as illustrious a literature as *jerez*, or sherry. And such prestige is due to the excellence of their wines, achieved through centuries of fine winemaking. 'If I had a thousand sons,' said Shakespeare's Falstaff, 'the first humane principle I would teach them should be, to forswear thin potations, and to addict themselves to sack [sherry].'

Fino sherry is *the* aperitif wine in Spain, yet its consumption is limited. The *jerez* drinker is usually sophisticated, and also very loyal – somewhat like the classical music lover. In southern Spain *jerez* is part of the lifestyle, and in Madrid it is the most popular aperitif; but in the rest of Spain, the habit of serving it is not as deeply rooted.

During my last visit to Jerez, I tried to understand why sherry is not more popular in the United States. And it occurred to me that maybe the problem is the same as in northern Spain: people don't know when to serve it. Yet it should fit the American lifestyle so well! A fino, for example, is a refreshing aperitif which entices the palate for the meal to come. And after dinner, an old amontillado or a fragrant oloroso are certain to enhance any dessert.

One possible reason for confusion, I believe, is that the label usually reads 'sherry' rather than *jerez*. Many people don't realize that the *true* sherry, *jerez*, comes only from a relatively small region – 50,000 acres – in southwest Spain, in the triangle formed by the towns of Jerez de la Frontera, Sanlúcar de Barrameda and Puerto de Santa María. Furthermore, Spain is the only country that can use the word 'sherry' alone on the label. California, Australia, Chile, South Africa or Cyprus must have the name of the region or country preceding the word sherry – as in Californian or Australian sherry. Unfortunately, many consumers associate true Spanish sherry with the sweet, less expensive, poorer quality product from other countries.

Another problem is that a delicate fino or manzanilla does not have a long life in the bottle – at the most, 1 or 2 years – and since it has no vintage, it is difficult to be sure that the bottle you buy is at its peak.

The grapes and the soil   The main grape in Jerez is Palomino, planted in 92 per cent of the district's soil. Pedro Ximénez accounts for another 5 per cent, and Moscatel 2 per cent.

The soil in Jerez is the famous white, chalky *albariza*, found mainly on gentle slopes. With a high calcium carbonate content, it is very absorbent and, when it dries out, it reflects the heat and keeps the humidity in the plant's roots. Thus the vines can overcome the torrid Andalusian summer.

The flor   The key factor in *jerez* wines is the *flor*, or film of saccharomyces yeast which protects the wine from oxidation and transforms the alcohol into aldehyde, giving sherry much of its flavour, aroma and character. The *flor* has been transferred to other areas of the world, but it grows spontaneously only in the Spanish Sherry, Montilla and Upper Duero districts, and in the French Jura.

Several yeasts produce *flor*, but the quality one is formed by *Saccharomyces ellipsoideus*. This thrives on oxygen, glycerine and alcohol, and it develops perfectly at the autumn and spring temperatures in Jerez – in wines of an alcohol content around 15.5 per cent. The wine, right after fermentation, is transferred to *botas* or butts (the 130-gallon casks of American oak used in Jerez), which are not filled to the top, in order to encourage development of the *flor*. For some unexplained reason, the *flor* will not develop in every *bota*. Whether or not it does determines which classification of sherry will be produced.

The classification: finos, olorosos and amontillados   From December to January, the cellar master or *capataz* will watch the development of every butt, periodically tasting each one by dipping the *venencia* (a long, narrow cup at the end of a rod) with a clean, swift stroke, to extract a sample. Those butts marked with *una raya* (1 stripe) will be selected for finos. Those marked with *dos rayas* (2 stripes) will usually be destined for olorosos. The classification goes down to 4 stripes, for wines that can be used only for distillation into brandy. If the classification is undetermined, the *capataz* will mark the butt with *raya y punto* (stripe and dot).

After this, the young wines are fortified with alcohol accordingly, in order either to encourage or to eliminate further growth of the *flor*: the finos up to 15.5 per cent to encourage it, and the olorosos to 18 per cent to kill it off. Those butts marked as undetermined will be tasted again after 5 or 6 months; their definitive trend will then be established and they will be fortified accordingly.

In order for a wine to be a fino, it has to stay in the butt with the *flor* for at least a year. If a fino is allowed to age, it will evolve into an amontillado. In the finos, the film of *flor* is pale yellow; in the amontillados it is thinner and greyish, and it dies after 2–3 years, falling to the bottom of the butt. Finos are light, very dry wines of pale straw colour, with clean pungent aroma and a special, almost green-olive taste; they should be drunk cold. Amontillados have an elegant amber colour, more body and fullness, a marked dry palate and a nutty quality reminiscent of hazelnuts.

Most of the olorosos on the market are semi-sweet, but there also exist excellent dry ones. They are scarce, though, because a good one needs to be 8 years old. At its best, a dry oloroso will have an old-gold amber colour, acquired after the long ageing in wood. The bouquet will be intense and clean, and on the palate it will display a luscious first impression – due to the high glycerine content – evolving into a complex aftertaste, somewhat like walnuts.

The solera system   The wines of Jerez are aged by the traditional method of *soleras*, which is aimed at maintaining consistency in the quality. *Soleras* are the bottom-row butts (thus *soleras*, from *suelo* or floor); those on top, the *criaderas* (from *criar*, or nurture), contain the younger wine. As the sherry is drawn from the *soleras* for bottling or shipping – a maximum of one third from each butt per year – the *solera* is refilled with new wine from the butts right above, called *primera* (first) *criadera*; the new wine will then acquire the characteristics of the older wine. The *primera criadera* in turn will be refilled with wine from the *segunda* (second) *criadera*, or the butts on the third tier, and so on. (This process is known as 'refreshing' the *solera*.) Obviously, *jerez* is a blended wine; a specific brand is usually made of a special blend of *soleras*, which will determine the style of the wine characteristic of that particular winery.

Manzanilla   The town of Sanlúcar, right on the Atlantic Ocean, has a peculiarity: the wines made there as finos come out as manzanillas. If a fino *solera* is taken to Sanlúcar, in 2–3 months it will acquire the style of manzanilla. The name manzanilla means chamomile, and the wine is soft, very aromatic, with that slight appealing bitterness and pale straw colour of chamomile tea. The *flor* in Sanlúcar grows differently from the *flor* in Jerez – although the towns are only 15 miles apart – because of the proximity of the ocean, which imparts to the wine a subtle and complex bouquet reminiscent of the ocean breeze.

Manzanilla must be made in old oak butts – some are up to 300 years old – so it does not acquire the flavour of wood. In spring and autumn, as the *flor* grows more abundantly, it sinks down to the bottom of the butt and naturally clarifies the wine, turning it paler in colour; then some more *flor* forms on the surface.

Some Jerez wineries – such as Valdespino, Domecq and González Byass – also have *bodegas* in Sanlúcar and produce a manzanilla; but only those with the ideal conditions can grow it. A manzanilla can hold for 1 or 2 years if the temperature doesn't go above 80°F; if it leaves Sanlúcar, however, it turns into a fino soon afterward.

An aged manzanilla will evolve into a manzanilla *pasada*, just as a fino will develop into an amontillado, after the *flor* dies.

Pedro Ximénez and cream   The Pedro Ximénez grape takes its name from a Spanish translation of Peter Siemens, the German soldier in Charles V's army who allegedly brought it to Spain from the Rhine. It is harvested in a different way from Palomino. In order to obtain a high concentration of sugar, the bunches of grapes are left out in the sun for two weeks, until they reach a concentration of

26–28° Brix. (Actually, a more efficient method is used today by most wineries to increase the sugar content without exposing the grapes to rains and night moisture; but the theory is the same.) After the grapes are crushed, the grape juice or 'must' is fortified before the fermentation ever takes place.

A certain amount of Pedro Ximénez is added to oloroso to produce cream sherries, which have the body of an oloroso with the lusciousness of the PX grape. Wines made from 100 per cent PX are rare, but they exist; they have the colour of mahogany and are mellow and velvety, almost like a nectar, with the unmistakable 'burnt' character of the variety.

Palo cortado   Palo cortado is a rare variety of oloroso that grows no *flor* but is very delicate, with certain characteristics of an amontillado, especially a fresher aroma and a hazelnut-like scent. Its name means 'cut stripe', because the *capataz* will mark the butt with a stripe and a line through it. An authentic palo cortado is considered by experts to be the 'king' of *jerez*.

The new white wines of Jerez   An interesting phenomenon is occurring in Jerez: a few wineries – notably Barbadillo – have started to produce crisp, fresh wines from Palomino. Cold-fermented and released early to capture the fruit of the grape, they are finding a good market locally as well as in the rest of Spain.

A Winery Tour of Jerez

The wineries in Jerez are grand, and their owners friendly and hospitable. They are well prepared to receive visitors, who are welcomed with a style and flair unique to this area.

GONZÁLEZ BYASS   Jerez de la Frontera (Cádiz) (956) 340000   This is one of the largest wineries in Jerez, founded in 1835 by Manuel María González. His uncle, José Ángel de la Peña – affectionately called 'Tío Pepe' – owned a *bodega* in Sanlúcar and initiated Manuel into the fascinating world of *jerez* wine. Uncle Pepe requested that a few butts be set aside for his private use in his nephew's *bodega*; and that's what gave the name to the firm's most popular sherry, Tío Pepe, the largest selling fino in the United States. Today, the Gran Bodega Tío Pepe contains 75,000 butts of *soleras* for this fino alone, which accounts for about 80 per cent of the winery's sales.

Another great cellar there is Las Copas. Built in 1974, it has the most modern vinification plant in Jerez, crushing 2,000 tons per day. Altogether, González Byass's facilities occupy an area of 133 square miles, and the estate has 3,000 acres of vineyards – the largest vineyard property owned by a single *bodega* in Jerez.

Extremely well organized to receive visitors, the winery is certainly worth a tour. And don't miss the unusual attraction of the oloroso-loving mice, which have been drinking the wine for 40 years by climbing up a mouse-size ladder to a sherry glass!

PEDRO DOMECQ   Jerez de la Frontera (Cádiz) (956) 331800   The firm was established in 1816 by a French nobleman, Pierre Domecq-Lembeye, a true wine lover who came to Jerez from London and built the first Domecq winery. He appropriately changed his name to Pedro and started a dynasty which to this day is one of the most prestigious in Jerez. In 1823 King Ferdinand VII visited the winery and, impressed by what he saw, made Domecq a nobleman and allowed him to use the royal crown in the family and company crest.

Today Domecq is an empire, still 75 per cent controlled by the family. José Ignacio Domecq – affectionately called 'The Nose' because of the size and great gustatory qualities of his – is chairman of Domecq International. His son, José Ignacio Domecq, Jr ('The Nose, Jr'), who learned from his father the art of tasting, is in charge of production and quality control. There are 261 Domecq first cousins in the current seventh generation, but only 8 in the business – one of them the managing director, Ramón de la Mora Figueroa Domecq.

Domecq offers a wide range of wines. Fino La Ina is the top-selling brand – about 40 per cent of its sherry sales. It is a delightful aperitif, with a clear, pale topaz colour and a delicate aroma of mature flowers and fruits. The Primero Amontillado is excellent, complex and very dry, available in the United States in small quantities. So is Río Viejo Oloroso, mellow and luscious. Celebration Cream and the 100 per cent PX, Viña 25, are classics of the style. Domecq's Double Century sherries are its standard line – fino, amontillado, oloroso and cream – at very good prices. And on the expensive end, the Rare Sherries are extraordinary: Sibarita Amontillado, Palo Cortado, Imperial Oloroso and Venerable PX.

SANDEMAN   Jerez de la Frontera (Cádiz) (956) 331100   El Hombre de la Capa Negra ('The Man with the Black Cape') or 'The Don Figure' is a familiar sight in Spain and Portugal, but its history is less well known. It goes back to 1790, when George Sandeman founded the House of Sandeman in London and shipped the first true vintage port. The sherries have been shipped from Jerez since 1809. In 1980 the company was acquired by Seagram's, but the Sandeman family is still involved in the business, with David Patrick Sandeman as the chairman. 'The Don Figure', their trademark since 1928, is a figure dressed in a stylized Portuguese student's cape, sporting a wide-brimmed hat such as those still worn by the caballeros (noblemen) of Jerez.

Sandeman's best-selling sherry in the United States is Dry Don, a medium-dry amontillado which fills your mouth with a mellow, nutty flavour. Character is a medium-dry oloroso, versatile and complex, with a lingering pleasant aftertaste. Don Fino is dry and light, fresh in the nose and deliciously fragrant. Armada Cream, with the touch of lusciousness from Pedro Ximénez, is full-bodied and much more complex than most cream sherries on the market.

WILLIAMS & HUMBERT   Jerez de la Frontera (Cádiz) (956) 331300   Dry Sack – a blend of oloroso, amontillado and Pedro Ximénez – is one of the most popular home-bottled sherries selling abroad. And for good reason; it is not too dry despite the name, the 'sack' packaging is smart and attractive, and it is easy to drink chilled or on the rocks.

Exported to 140 countries, Dry Sack accounts for 95 per cent of the firm's sales;

but its Pando Fino and Canasta Cream are best-sellers too. Pando is a light, very pleasant fino, fresh and dry. Canasta Cream, named after the basket in which the bottle is cradled, is a smooth, mellow, classic cream. The rare Dos Cortados is a palo cortado of medium amber colour, deep and subtle bouquet, dry and elegant.

VALDESPINO   Jerez de la Frontera (Cádiz) (956) 331450   I owe this old winery many a nice time over a glass of its rare oloroso, amontillado and palo cortado. Its Hartley & Gibson line of sherries – manzanilla, fino, amontillado and cream – are terrific value, and I always have a bottle on hand at home. I was also delighted to find that Manuel de Argüeso, the Pedro Ximénez I had used with great results to enhance my Raisin Ice Cream with Cream Sherry (Helado de Pasas al Pedro Ximénez) (p. 235), was Valdespino's brand, too!

Brothers Rafael and Miguel Valdespino are the current generation of the oldest family of Spanish origin in Jerez. Their roots go back to 1264, when King Alfonso X, the Wise, knighted 24 families in Jerez and granted them land. The company was established in 1877, although the Valdespinos had been making wine at their *bodega* since 1430. They have one of the oldest cellars in Jerez, dating back to the 1600s, which has been kept almost the same. Everything at Valdespino, even today, breathes age and tradition!

OSBORNE   Puerto de Santa María (Cádiz) (956) 855211   Osborne is the major *jerez* winery in Puerto de Santa María. You can't miss the two big iron bulls at the entrance of the town by the gate of their Bodegas del Tiro. In fact, all over Spain you can't miss the brave-looking black bull, always strategically placed on top of a hill – the clever ad for Osborne's Veterano brandy. The bull logo comes from the association with the family's cattle-raising business. The bullring of Puerto de Santa María, one of the most beautiful and famous in the world, was built by Tomás Osborne, son of the founder.

The company was established in 1772 by Thomas Osborne, a British merchant. Today, fourth-generation Enrique Osborne is president of the board of directors. But the current heart of the winery is Manuel Robles, the enterprising general manager since 1978.

ANTONIO BARBADILLO   Sanlúcar de Barrameda (Cádiz) (956) 360352   A tour of Jerez would be incomplete without visiting the home of manzanilla: Sanlúcar, the charming port on the Costa de la Luz (Coast of Light) just northwest of Jerez. And in Sanlúcar, *the bodega* to visit is Barbadillo, quite large yet family-run. Antonio Pedro 'Toto' Barbadillo is at the helm of the company; he and cousin Juan Carlos represent the fifth generation of this old family to run the company since it was founded by Benigno Barbadillo in 1821.

If you find yourself near there, I highly recommend you try some of their manzanillas – or better yet, stop by and visit the winery. I can assure you that you will receive a warm, hospitable welcome!

CATALUNYA (CATALONIA)

In exploring the wines of Catalunya, or Catalonia – home of my family's winery – I enlisted the help of my friend Mauricio Wiesenthal, author of several books on Spain, its art, peoples and lifestyles, as well as about other Latin cultures. He is also an authority on wines and gastronomy, and contributing editor to a Spanish food and wine magazine.

Catalan wines today are a far cry from what they were just a few years ago. As in many other wine areas of Spain, quantity rather than quality had been the determining factor in the past. Towards the end of the nineteenth century, the most typical rural industry in Catalonia was the distillation of brandy and spirits, or *aguardientes*. But in recent years, the vineyard acreage has decreased while the quality of the wines has improved proportionally. The Catalan winemakers' determination has brought the most modern technology, and their creativity has prompted them to experiment in the adaptation of new grape varieties (Cabernet Sauvignon, Chardonnay, Pinot Noir, Riesling, Gewürztraminer, etc.) to their soil and climate.

As a result, the wines have reached such a level of quality that they now rank with the finest in the world at international competitions. Yet they have not lost their local character; there is a certain unity among Catalan wines, a style they have in common even if each district – and winemaker – has a distinct personality. There are seven different Denominaciones de Origen in Catalonia, and they all have something in common which sets them apart from the rest of Spanish wines. The whites are aromatic, fresh and elegant; the reds are well aged, round and full-bodied.

The commercial 'discovery' of these Catalan wines dates from the 1970s; but winemaking is an old art in Catalonia. Back in the first half of the fourteenth century, some lovely sparkling wines were made which the writers of the time called 'subtle' and 'tingling'. The full-bodied, soundly structured wines of Priorato were made by the monks in the medieval monasteries. And the pale wines of Alella, brilliant and delicate, were very popular in Barcelona at the turn of the century. Catalonia has always had a certain universal vocation which enabled it to adapt to the changes of the times with great flexibility. And today its wines have adapted themselves to the tastes of a period which enjoys youth and natural elegance over heaviness and excess oak.

The Denominaciones de Origen

One important factor in Catalonia is the diversity of its climate and soil. The Mediterranean provides the area with mild temperatures, yet the high mountains of the Catalan coastal system contribute the cold winters and cool summer nights which are ideal for growing white aromatic grapes and making fresh, fragrant white wines.

The seven Catalan Denominaciones de Origen are: Alella, Ampurdán-Costa Brava, Conca de Barberá, Priorato, Penedès, Tarragona and Terra-Alta. There are other small districts which produce wines of great quality, such as Raimat, near

Lérida; and most important, the *cavas* or sparkling wines produced by the *méthode champenoise*, which is a Denominación Específica or Specific Appellation, physically located 98 per cent on Penedès but not part of the Denominación de Origen.

A special mention must be made of Catalan brandies, which have created a style of their own. They are made from the distillation of the area's white wines in copper pot stills – some by the *charentais* process of double distillation used in Cognac – and aged in American or French Limousin oak.

Alella

Located just north of Barcelona, Alella is well known for its white wines of pale straw colour, aromatic and fruity. The main wineries are Cooperativa de Alella, producer of the Marfil brand of dry and semi-dry white, rosé and red; and Bodegas Alta Alella, which markets the white Marqués de Alella label. The latter uses very modern winemaking methods, fermenting the musts under controlled temperatures to make young, fresh and lively wines.

Ampurdán–Costa Brava

This district's vineyards, located north of Gerona, bordering France, are probably the most ancient in Catalonia. One of the oldest enology manuals in Europe was written in 1130 by the monk Ramón Pere de Novàs at the monastery of Sant Pere de Roda, its ruins rising today over the rugged Mediterranean coastline. Most of Ampurdán's wines are fresh, young rosés, made primarily from the Garnacha and Cariñena grapes.

The most important winery is Cavas del Ampurdán, established in 1930 and located in the historic fourteenth-century Perelada castle. It produces white, rosé and red wines, as well as *cavas* and a slightly carbonated, very pleasant and refreshing white, Blanc Pescador, made from Parellada and Macabeo grapes.

Another grower, Cellers Santamaría, has had a family winemaking tradition since the nineteenth century. In the village of Capmany it produces a high-quality rosé and red in small quantities.

Conca de Barberá

This is a district full of medieval legends, vineyards and almond orchards. Situated just north of Tarragona, it produces fine, aromatic and fruity rosés. The Knight Templars and the Cistercian monks began growing grapes here as early as the twelfth century. The historic heart of the area is the grandiose Monastery of Poblet, where the kings and queens of Catalonia and Aragón were buried. It is still possible to visit the Gothic cellar where Poblet wines were produced and aged. It is said that the monks had already discovered modern winemaking techniques; they fermented their wines at cool temperatures, sprinkling the tanks with water pumped from a well.

The area's white wines, made from Parellada and Macabeo grapes, are light and aromatic; they are sold mostly for the production of sparkling wine to firms in San Sadurní de Noia. My family feels the district's wines have a bright future, and in our Milmanda Castle estate near Poblet we have already planted some noble European grapes – Chardonnay, Pinot Noir and Cabernet – which we believe will soon produce high-quality wines.

Priorato

This is another historic area, once under the jurisdiction of the Carthusian Scala Dei order of monks. The impressive ruins of the monastery still rise among the vineyards, just west of Tarragona. Garnacha was the classic grape variety of the aromatic, full-bodied and slightly sweet Priorato red wines. Today, however, the vineyards are planted mainly with Cariñena, which gives a sturdy wine, suitable for ageing. Most of the district's wines are made from a blend of both grapes; they are rich in colour and alcohol. When they are well made, the softness and aroma of Garnacha is nicely coupled with the powerful structure of Cariñena. The best-known firms are Bodegas Müller and Scala Dei.

Tarragona

The land of the old Tarraco, of ancient Roman history, has a serene and classic beauty. Olive, almond and hazelnut trees stretch over the landscape among the vineyards. The area's wines were already famous at the Roman tables, and highly appreciated in the days of Emperor Augustus. Its production is so bountiful that the wines are exported throughout the world; such abundance has sometimes affected the quality required by their historic reputation. The main varieties planted are Macabeo, Xarel-lo and Parellada for whites, and Tempranillo and Cariñena for reds.

The best-known winery is Bodegas Müller, established in 1851; it produces mostly young, fresh white wines. It is also famous for its sweet wine for the Holy Mass, made according to the canons dictated by the Vatican.

Penedès

This is the wine-producing district par excellence in Catalonia. It not only makes the finest table wines, which constitute one of the great enological achievements in the second half of this century, but also is the home of the renowned Spanish *cavas* or sparkling wines. Grapes have been growing here since the fourth or fifth century BC. The Penedès Denominación de Origen covers an area of 385,000 acres, of which about 62,000 are planted with vineyards. The DO's capital is Vilafranca del Penedès, 30 miles southwest of Barcelona.

The Penedès climate and soil are very diverse. In less than 20 miles, the vineyards climb from sea level to an altitude well over 2,000 feet; this provides dramatic landscapes and a great variety of microclimates. The area is divided into 3 sub-zones: Low Penedès, with vineyards planted up to 400 feet; Middle or Central Penedès to 1,300 feet; and High Penedès, where vines grow at an elevation of 2,300 feet. Such variation allows the acclimation of very different grape varieties.

The traditional red grapes – Cariñena, Garnacha, Tempranillo and Monastrell – are grown mostly in the Low Penedès, along the Mediterranean. The Middle

Penedès produces the classic whites from Xarel-lo and Macabeo, which are the basis for the area's sparkling wines. It is also most suitable for the noble European red varieties Cabernet Sauvignon, Cabernet Franc, Pinot Noir and Merlot, and for the whites Chardonnay and Sauvignon Blanc. The High Penedès, with its rainy and cooler climate, is ideal for growing the fine, elegant local white Parellada and the French Sauvignon Blanc, as well as the aromatic Alsatian and German varieties Riesling, Gewürztraminer and Muscat d'Alsace.

In the Penedès, good winemakers grow their own grapes, select the vine stocks and varieties, oversee their pruning and study the adaptation of the prime grapes. A tour of the area provides a picturesque sight of well-kept trellised vineyards on neatly worked, clean soil. From the large cooperatives to the small family wineries in the traditional Catalan *masías* (farmhouses), a wide range of wines is made: whites full of youth and aroma or well-aged and buttery, occasionally reminiscent of honey; fresh, fruity rosés; reds complex and noble or full-bodied and sturdy; lively spritzy whites and elegant sparkling *cavas*; or aperitif and dessert wines, including the maderized *rancio* wines and the traditional sweet *malvasía* of Sitges, itself an institution among Spanish dessert wines.

Typical of the Catalan character is the will to create, change and improve, and many vineyards are continually in a state of change, trying new grapes, new methods and new blends.

The *bodegas* of Penedès fall into two categories: those that are introducing more and more noble grapes from Europe and producing wines of a more international character, rather than traditionally Spanish; and those *bodegas* that are content with the grapes and the wines they have always grown. In the middle are a number of wineries that are trying new varieties while relying on those they already have. Fortunately they can exist side by side, each making some very successful wines.

The Sparkling Cava Wines

The small town of San Sadurní de Noia, 7 miles from Vilafranca del Penedès and about an hour's drive from Barcelona, has been the headquarters for the sparkling wine industry in Spain since 1872, when José Raventós brought the *méthode champenoise* to his family *bodegas*, Codorníu, and to Spain.

The grapes used in *cava* wines are generally a mixture: Parellada for elegance and suppleness, Macabeo for aroma and finesse, and Xarel-lo for body and freshness. The red grapes Garnacha and Monastrell are used for the rosés.

Today there are over 100 *cava* wineries in Spain, 83 of them in Penedès. The Consejo Regulador del Cava (Regulatory Council of Cava), an organization under the Ministry of Agriculture, plays a very important role in controlling the quality of *cava* wines. Its regulations are strict; the name *cava* appears only on bottles produced by the *méthode champenoise* (the method used for Champagne), which means that the wine has become sparkling as a result of undergoing a secondary fermentation in the bottle. The cheaper Charmat process (known in France as *cuve close*, and in Spain as *granvas*) can never produce the same quality. The Council also sets controls for the minimum 9-month ageing of the base wine or *cuvée* (if vintage-dated, minimum ageing is 3 years) and for other areas, such as the compulsory bottling date on the cork.

Most Americans wonder why Spanish *cava* wines can be sold for such a low price, given their quality. First of all, the price of the wine before the second fermentation is not high. But it is mainly due to the technology, introduced by Codorníu in 1972, when José María Raventós was manager of the company. The Raventós family was committed to the *méthode champenoise*, and while others – in Spain and France – were trying to perfect the cheaper Charmat process, Codorníu set out to mechanize the *méthode champenoise* and bring down the cost.

It used to take skilled specialists 3–6 weeks to complete the task of 'riddling', or turning each bottle a little bit every day until the sediment produced by the second fermentation settles in the cork end, prior to expulsion. Now, at the larger wineries, this operation is accomplished manually by a *girasol* (sunflower) or mechanically by a *giropallet*, a huge crate with an octagonal base which holds 504 bottles and tilts them a bit every 8 hours.

Such automation, however, can be done only at the large wineries; the smaller ones cannot afford it. With 45 million bottles of *cava* produced in 1984, the Codorníu group is the world's largest *champenoise*-method producer of sparkling wines. Second in Spain comes Freixenet, with 34 million bottles, and third is Castellblanch (now part of the Freixenet group) with 6 million.

The story of the small *cava* producers is also a happy one: they are making excellent wines and easily selling them in the domestic market at pretty high prices. They are mostly vineyard owners who make their *cava* with little mechanization, family style. The largest of them is Monistrol, with 2 million bottles in '84, followed by Juvé i Camps with about 1 million; the rest make under 1 million – and are happy to stay that way.

A Winery Tour of Catalonia

JEAN LEON   Plà del Penedès (Barcelona) (93) 899–5033   Representative of those winemakers seeking to explore new and exciting techniques is Jean Leon. Born in Spain, he went to America in the 1950s and eventually opened La Scala restaurant in Beverly Hills. In 1962 he acquired a 375-acre vineyard in Plà del Penedès, 3 miles from Vilafranca, with a small farmhouse which he turned into a winery. He then obtained cuttings of Cabernet Sauvignon, Cabernet Franc, Chardonnay and Pinot Noir from France, and proceeded to adapt them to his estate. At present one third of his vineyard is in full production, planted with Cabernet Sauvignon and Chardonnay, and the quality of his grapes is among the best.

All of Jean Leon's wines are made from his own grapes and aged in a beautiful underground cellar. His production is about 200,000 bottles per year, mostly sold locally and in the United States.

HEREDAD MONTSARRA   Torrelles de Foix (Barcelona) (93) 892–2897 This winery is located in a historic sixteenth-century farmhouse built over the ruins of more ancient constructions, as evidenced by its Roman underground cellar. The estate belonged to the aristocratic family of the Marquis of Spain until it was acquired by the Balaguer family in 1748.

José María Balaguer began in 1974 to bottle and label varietal wines made from the indigenous white grapes of Penedès: Parellada, Macabeo and Xarel-lo. Today the estate has 250 acres of vineyards planted with these varieties, as well as some Chardonnay in the experimental stages. None of the wines are aged in wood, most are bottled young and each tastes of the grape from which it is made. The winery's Parellada is the most interesting varietal, a wine with lovely aroma, fine fruit and crisp finish.

MONT MARÇAL   Castellví de la Marca (Barcelona) (93) 891–8281   Established in 1975 by Manuel Sancho, Mont Marçal has acquired a well-deserved reputation among wine lovers in the few years of its existence.

Its 150 acres of vineyards are planted with the traditional Penedès varieties – Parellada, Xarel-lo and Macabeo – as well as with some noble European grapes such as Chardonnay and Cabernet Sauvignon; Sylvaner is also in the experimental stages. The wines are made with the most modern technology, in cold-fermented stainless-steel tanks, and the reds are oak-aged. Their production, sold in Spain and also exported to Europe and the United States, includes whites, reds and *cava*. Of particular interest are their fresh and aromatic white Vi Novell (Catalan for new wine), another white made with some Chardonnay, and their Reserva red, with great character and breed.

MASÍA BACH   San Esteve de Sesrovires (Barcelona) (93) 771–4052   Two enterprising brothers, Pere and Ramón Bach, after making their fortune in the textile industry in the twenties, decided to become winemakers. They acquired a beautiful 850-acre estate near San Sadurní, planted it with vineyards and olive trees, built a great mansion (a Catalan *masía*) and established Masía Bach in 1929. Unfortunately, after the Spanish Civil War the winery went into decline, until it was acquired by Codorníu in 1975. Under the auspices of winemaker Ángel Escudé, they set out to revive the old *bodega* – a task that has been accomplished well. The renovated mansion today enjoys its splendour once more, with the charming modernist, woodpanelled salons decorated with beautiful stained glass and tiles, and a superb Florentine-style staircase. Truly worth a visit!

The firm owns 85 acres of the original estate and buys most of the grapes for its wines, made from the traditional Penedès varieties. A special point of interest is their ½-mile-long, 80-foot-deep cellar, built in 1924, destined for oak ageing of their red wines.

The firm's legendary brand is the white Gran Reserva Extrisímo, a luscious, mellow, well-aged sweet white wine of silky texture. Extrisímo Seco is a fine dry white, characteristic of Penedès, with the fresh aroma of the Parellada variety.

MARQUÉS DE MONISTROL   Monistrol de Noia (Barcelona) (93) 891–0276 A great enologist and promoter of Spanish agriculture, José María Escrivá de Romaní, Marquis of Monistrol, established this winery in 1882 and around it grew the picturesque village of Monistrol de Noia, near San Sadurní.

Monistrol's whites, rosés, reds and *cava* wines are produced according to the most modern technology, vinified in stainless steel and aged in impressive underground cellars. Among their top brands are the white Blanc de Blancs, fresh and fruity, with a pleasant hint of carbonation; and Blanco Seco, dry and delicate, made with the traditional Penedès varieties.

HEREDAD SEGURA VIUDAS San Sadurní de Noia (Barcelona) (93)899–5111 This estate, which dates back to the eleventh century, is today part of the Freixenet group. Its 270 acres of vineyards sprawl along the banks of the Noia River, with the legendary Montserrat mountains in the background. Besides Segura Viudas, two other wines, Conde de Caralt and René Barbier – a historic label established in 1880 – are made at the winery.

The facilities are modern and efficient, with a beautiful bottling plant, large groups of horizontal presses and long underground, multilevelled ageing cellars. In addition, a wine library keeps a collection of the estate's best Reservas over the years.

The sparkling wines are sold under the brand name Segura Viudas; Conde de Caralt are white wines, and René Barbier whites and reds, the latter including some well-aged Reservas. All of them are made from the traditional Penedès grapes.

RAIMAT Raimat (Lérida) (973) 724008 Established in 1914 by the Raventós family, this impressive winery ranks high today among the first-quality wine producers of Catalonia. They have succeeded in reviving viticulture in an area of drier and warmer climate then Penedès, which traditionally had not been devoted to vineyards.

The estate includes close to 2,000 acres of vineyards, planted with the Catalan grapes Parellada, Macabeo, Garnacha, Cariñena and Tempranillo, as well as with some noble European varieties such as Cabernet Sauvignon, Chardonnay and Merlot.

The winery, designed in 1922 according to the classic modernist turn-of-the-century style, is worthy of a visit. The wines are made with the latest technology, using temperature-controlled stainless-steel tanks, and the reds are carefully aged in oak casks. Among the various brands, their varietal Cabernets and Chardonnays are especially notable: the reds complex and velvety, the whites fresh and aromatic, and both with great character.

CODORNÍU San Sadurní de Noia (Barcelona) (93) 891–0125 The main building of the Codorníu *bodega* is a nineteenth-century 'national monument' of fascinating architecture, set in beautiful gardens just outside San Sadurní. The winery dates from 1551 and has belonged to the Raventós family since 1659, when the Codorníu heiress, María Ana, married Miguel Raventós. Today its vast 5-tier underground cellar is the longest in the world; it winds around for 15 miles and holds more than 100 million bottles. The current managing director is Manuel Raventós, representing the fourth generation since José Raventós started to make sparkling wines in 1872.

If you are near Barcelona or Tarragona, a visit to Codorníu is a wine lover's must. Not only the wines but the cellars, the museum of old wine presses, the gardens, the entire tour is memorable – including the 500-year-old oak tree which welcomes you at the entrance.

Codorníu wines are smartly packaged and have an individual style. The best known are Blanc de Blancs, Brut Clásico and the top of the line, Gran Codorníu.

FREIXENET   San Sadurní de Noia (Barcelona) (93) 891–0125   Freixenet is the number-one-selling sparkling wine imported into the United States. Its characteristic black bottle (which everybody remembers even if they can't pronounce the name) and its aggressive marketing have made it the leader. Besides the Cordón Negro brand in the black bottle, also sold here are the less expensive Carta Nevada, the premium brand Brut Nature, and the top of the line Brut Barroco.

The estate of La Freixeneda (ash grove in Catalan) has belonged to the Ferrer family since the thirteenth century. In 1889, Pedro Ferrer, nicknamed 'Freixenet', started to make sparkling wine. His son José Ferrer is the current president.

After Freixenet's recent purchase of the sparkling wines Castellblanch, Segura Viudas, Conde de Caralt and René Barbier – once owned by the holding company Rumasa – it is now a close second to Codorníu in size. The winery has kept up almost constant expansion in an attempt to fill the phenomenal demand.

During the Rumasa days, a large investment was made to transform Segura Viudas into one of the most modern sparkling wine *bodegas*. The entire operation is mechanized, and their cellars house about 10 million bottles.

TORRES   Vilafranca del Penedès (Barcelona) (93) 890–0100 and 890–2504 It is appropriate to end this tour of Spanish wineries with a visit to my family's *bodega*, sharing our history and what I feel we have contributed to Spanish viticulture.

My family has owned vineyards and made wine since the seventeenth century, but our entry into the world market actually had its beginnings in 1858, when Jaime Torres set off for America to make his fortune. Eventually settling in Havana, Cuba, he worked and saved diligently for seven years and in 1865 invested his savings in a fledgling oil company. Shortly thereafter, a world-wide oil boom made him a wealthy man.

Jaime reinvested in oceangoing sailing ships and organized the first shipping line between Barcelona and Havana. Then he returned to Barcelona and began construction of the large wine cellar, inaugurated in 1870. Upon his death in 1906, his brother Miguel took over the winery operation. Miguel's eventual successor was Juan Torres, father of the present owner, Miguel Torres – my father.

Miguel was only twenty-three when his father died in March 1932; but assisted by his mother, Josefa, he took charge of the winery management. Those were difficult days in Spain, and all over Europe. The Spanish Civil War started in July 1936 and lasted three years. In January 1939, during an air raid in Vilafranca del Penedès, several bombs hit our winery. A huge 160,000-gallon vat, full of wine, was destroyed during the explosions. The streets became real rivers of wine; the damage was overwhelming. The efforts of three generations lay in ruins.

However, from the ashes and the debris arose, firm and powerful, the will to rebuild. There was no capital, so Miguel applied for credit. In spite of the difficulties of that time, the reconstruction began very soon and was finished in early 1940.

While former generations had always exported wine and brandy in bulk, it was Miguel who decided to embark on the estate-bottling venture and to create prestige for each Torres label.

To this day, my father remembers with nostalgia and pride his first selling activities in Barcelona. He would personally visit restaurants and retail stores; if the buyer was busy with customers, he would apologize and wait patiently. Then he would pull out of his briefcase some samples of wine or brandy and coerce the prospective buyer into tasting them, while explaining with enthusiasm the history of their production and ageing. By the late 1950s, Torres brandy had acquired a small but influential patronage. Compared with the sherry brandies, Miguel's was different: it had a softer bouquet and a French style.

In the mid 1960s, my brother Miguel, Jr – our winemaker – started to experiment with adapting the noble European grapes to our soil and climate. First he planted Cabernet Sauvignon and Pinot Noir, then Chardonnay, Sauvignon Blanc, Riesling, Gewürztraminer, Muscat d'Alsace and Cabernet Franc. All these varietals are today blended to produce our wines, and experimental plantings are still going on with other grapes such as Merlot and Petite Sirah, which we also expect to use for our wines in the future.

These noble grapes have changed the whole picture of Penedès wines. Today many fine winemakers in Spain – not only in Catalonia but in other Spanish wine regions as well – are following the path set by my brother since the 1960s.

In 1973, our winery pioneered in Spain the use of temperature-controlled fermentation for white wines; keeping the temperature low to ensure a slower fermentation produces more aromatic and fruity wines. At the same time, we also began using stainless-steel tanks to ferment our reds. Many wineries all over Spain are now using these methods to make their wines.

Perhaps the main contribution my family has made to Spanish viticulture has been to change the concept of wine appreciation in Spain. Today most Spaniards realize that wine does not necessarily need to be old in order to be good; that the varietal character and the nobility of the grape is extremely important; that Spanish wines do not have to be an imitation of French, they can have their own personality and the winemaker's individual style, which makes them different from all others.

Today, Torres is the largest individually owned producer of premium wines in Spain; they can be found, under only one label, in 85 countries all over the world. The secret of our success is brand image, personal approach and our own, personal style. The quality of a wine is determined by four factors: climate, soil, grape variety and – most important – the winemaker. In our case, I feel we have found the right combination of the four, led by a winemaker who is not only innovative and creative but has one attribute that is fundamental: he is never content with the results obtained in the last harvest and always looks forward to doing better next year.

APPENDIX:
THE
RESTAURANTS
OF SPAIN

Throughout my travels in Spain I visited hundreds of restaurants, the finest of which gave me the ideas to develop most of the recipes in this book. Below is a list of these restaurants, as well as the region and town where they are located and the recipes they inspired. They are all worth a visit, so I hope the list will be a helpful reference when planning your next trip to Spain.

CATALUNYA

VILAFRANCA DEL PENEDÈS

El Celler del Penedès   Caracoles Picantes (Snails in a Piquant Sauce); 'Xatonada' (Catalan Tuna Salad with a *Romesco*-Style Sauce); 'Xató' (*Romesco*-Style Sauce for 'Xatonada'); 'Salbitxada' (*Romesco*-Style Sauce for Grilled Vegetables).

Cal Joan   Habas a la Catalana (Broad Bean Stew, Catalan Style); Sorbete de Vino Tinto a la Hierbabuena (Red Wine Sorbet with Mint).

BARCELONA

Azulete   Tartaletas de Caracoles a las Hierbas Aromáticas (Snail Tarts with Mushrooms and Aromatic Herbs); Ensalada Templada de Lentejas y Conejo al Curry (Warm Curried Lentil and Rabbit Salad); Silla de Conejo Rellena can Verduras (Stuffed Rabbit Saddle with Vegetables); Mollejitas a la Salsa de Miel y Vinagre de Jerez (Sweetbreads in a Honey and Sherry Vinegar Sauce); Lasagna de Salmón a la Salsa de Vino Blanco (Salmon Lasagne in a Light Cream Sauce); Tarta Templada de Limón (Warm Lemon Tart); Manzana Gratinada (Apple Gratin).

Montse Guillén   Crema de Tomillo (Thyme Cream Soup); Allioli de Miel (Honey Garlic Mayonnaise); Allioli de Manzana (Apple Garlic Mayonnaise).

L'Olivé   Ensalada de Col Lombarda con Boquerones (Red Cabbage Salad with Anchovies); Coca de Tomate y Pimiento (Flat Bread with Tomato and Pepper Topping); Romesco de L'Olivé (*Romesco* Sauce with *Ancho* Chillis, Onion and Paprika).

Tritón   'Esqueixada' (Catalan Shredded Cod Salad).

Cal Isidre   Langostinos a la Crema de Perejil (Prawn in a Parsley Cream); Romesco de Cal Isidre (*Romesco* Sauce with *Ancho* Chillis and Baked Garlic/ Tomato).

Jaume de Provença   Bacalao a la Catalana con Pasas y Piñones (Catalan-Style Cod with Pine Nuts and Raisins); Bacalao a la Mousse de Allioli (Cod in an *Allioli* Mousse); Chuleta de Cerdo a la Catalana (Pork Chop Stuffed with Prunes and Pine Nuts, Catalan Style); Canelones de Espinacas (Spinach Canneloni); Helado de Crema Catalana con Salsa de Avellanas (Catalan Caramel Custard Ice Cream with Hazelnut Sauce).

Neichel   Salmón al Vapor con Salsa de Vino Tinto (Fresh Salmon in a Red Wine Sauce); Flan de Moras con Salsa de Moras (Blackberry Flan with a Blackberry Sauce).

Casa Costa   Zarzuela de Mariscos (Shellfish Stew, Barcelona Style).

Reno   Capones al Agridulce (Poussins in a Sweet and Sour Sauce).

Tiró Mimet   Pato con Aceitunas (Duck with Olives); Filete de Ternera con Salsa de Anchoas (Veal Fillet with Anchovy Sauce); Tartitas de Berenjena (Aubergine Tartlets).

Quo Vadis   Perdiz con 'Farcellets' de Col a la Ampurdanesa (Partridge with Cabbage Croquettes, L'Empordà Style); Espinacas a la Catalana (Spinach with Pine Nuts and Raisins, Catalan Style).

Agut d'Avignon   Pato con Higos (Duck with Figs); Manzanas Rellenas al Horno (Baked Stuffed Apples).

La Odisea   Pierna de Cordero Rellena de Riñones a la Almendra (Leg of Lamb Stuffed with Kidneys and Almonds).

Roig Rubí   Confit de Cebollas (Onion Relish).

Els Perols de L'Empordà   Arroz a la Cazuela con Marisco (Rice in a Casserole with Shellfish).

Mantequerías Tívoli   Roscón de Reyes (Three Kings' Sweet Bread with Almond Filling).

Vía Veneto   Tarta de Piñones (Pine Nut Tart).

Florián   Helado de Naranja (Orange Ice Cream).

ARGENTONA

El Racó d'en Binu   Sopa de Tomate y Hierbabuena con Almendras (Cold Tomato Mint Soup with Almonds); Solomillo con Frutas Secas (Beef Tenderloin with Dried Fruits); Flanes de Verduras (Green Pea and Red Pepper Flans); Flanes de Setas (Mushroom Flans); Arroz con Pasas y Piñones a la Catalana (Rice with Raisins and Pine Nuts, Catalan Style).

FIGUERAS

Ampurdán   'Garum' (Roman Dip); Terrina de Conejo con Ciruelas (Rabbit and Prune Terrine); Mousse de 'Escalivada' (Aubergine, Pepper and Tomato Dip); Ensalada de Habas a la Hierbabuena (Broad Bean Salad with Mint); Rodaballo Soufflé a la Albahaca (Turbot with Basil Soufflé).

PALAMÓS

Big Rock   Mousse de Endibias con Salsa de Cabrales (Chicory Mousse with Blue Cheese Sauce); 'Suquet' de Pescado (Fish Stew with Potatoes, Costa Brava Style); 'Escalivada' (Assorted Grilled Vegetables, Catalan Style).

MARTINET

Can Boix   Crema de Hinojo (Cream of Fennel Soup); Cebollitas a la Crema y al Perfume de Tomillo (Button Onions in a Cream and Thyme Sauce).

MERANGES
Can Borrell   Tarta de Puerros (Leek Tart); Crema de Tomillo (Thyme Cream Soup).

SITGES
Mare Nostrum   Sopa de Pescadores (Fishermen's Soup, Mediterranean Style).

PALS
Sa Punta   Ensalada de Endibias y Aguacates a la Salsa de Cabrales (Chicory and Avocado Salad with a Blue Cheese Sauce); Guisantes Estofados a la Menta Fresca con Almejas (Pea Stew with Fresh Mint and Clams).

SANT FELÍU DE GUIXOLS
Eldorado Petit   'Trinxat' de Rape (Catalan Shredded Monkfish Salad); Langosta con Pollo 'Mar y Montaña' (Lobster and Chicken with Nuts and Chocolate).

CUNIT
L'Avi Pau   Pescado 'A l'All Cremat' (Fish in a Burned Garlic Sauce); 'Cremat' (Catalan Hot Coffee and Brandy).

TORREDEMBARRA
Casa Morros   Romesco de Pescados (Fish Stew, Tarragona Style).

VILANOVA I LA GELTRÚ
Peixerot   Zarzuela de Mariscos (Shellfish Stew, Barcelona Style).

CAMBRILS
Eugenia   'Fideuà' (Thin Pasta Noodles Cooked in a Fish Fumet); Salsa Roja (*Romesco*-Style Sauce for Grilled Fish).

BANYERES
Hostal del Priorato   Flan de Fresas con su Salsa de Fresas Frescas (Strawberry Flan in a Fresh Strawberry Sauce).

VALENCIA

ELCHE
Els Capellans   Ensalada de Naranja y Aguacate (Orange and Avocado Salad); Pan de Higos y Chocolate (Fig and Chocolate Loaf).

VALENCIA
El Plat   Arroz Negro con Calamares Rellenos (Black Rice with Stuffed Squid).
La Venta del Toboso   Arroz Caldoso de Monte (Rice with Rabbit in Broth).
Chocolatería de Santa Catalina   Leche Merengada (Meringued Milk Sorbet).

L'ALCUDIA DE CARLET
Galbis   Paella Valenciana de la Ribera (Classic *Paella* with Shellfish, Chicken
and Pork); Arroz al Horno de Verano (Baked Rice with Summer Vegetables).

MURCIA/

MURCIA
Rincón de Pepe   Ensalada de Zanahoria al Jerez (Carrot Salad with Sherry);
Alcachofas con Piñones (Artichoke Stew with Pine Nuts).

ANDALUCÍA

SEVILLA
Las Golondrinas   Zanahorias Aliñadas (Carrots Seasoned with Herbs).

PUERTO DE SANTA MARÍA
El Fogón   Ajo Blanco de Málaga (Cold White Gazpacho from Málaga with
Garlic and Almonds); Crema de Remolacha (Beetroot Cream Soup).
Don Peppone   Patatas Aliñadas con Gambas (Potato Salad with Prawns).

CÓRDOBA
El Caballo Rojo   Salmorejo de Córdoba (Thick Gazpacho from Córdoba);
Cordero a la Miel (Lamb with Honey and Green Peppers).

DÚRCAL (GRANADA)
El Molino   Atún Mechado al Horno (Braised Tuna Studded with Anchovies).

GRANADA
Sevilla   Cordero a la Pastoril (Lamb Stew, Shepherd Style); Rollos de Pan
(Bread Rings).
Los Manueles   Cordero al Ajillo (Lamb Stew in a Garlic and Sweet Pepper
Sauce).

SAN ROQUE
Los Remos   Ensaladilla de Bonito (Bonito Salad with Peppers, Onions and
Tomatoes); Rape con Nueces (Monkfish in a Walnut Cream Sauce).

HUELVA
La Muralla   Hojaldre de Mollejas al Aroma de Alcaparras (Sweetbreads in Puff
Pastry with a Caper Sauce); Higos Pasos Rellenos (Figs Stuffed with Chocolate
and Nuts).

BAEZA
Juanito   Nueces Caramelizadas con Nata (Caramelized Walnuts with Whipped
Cream).

CÁDIZ
El Faro   Helado de Pasas al Pedro Ximénez (Raisin Ice Cream with Cream Sherry).

SANLÚCAR DE BARRAMEDA
Bigote   Helado de Pasas al Pedro Ximénez (Raisin Ice Cream with Cream Sherry).

MADRID

MADRID
Sacha   Pâté de Salmón Ahumado (Smoked Salmon Pâté); Filloas con Piña y Salsa de Naranja (Thin Pancakes with Pineapple in an Orange Sauce).

El Amparo   Mousse de Salmón y Aguacate (Salmon and Avocado Mousse); Pollito de Grano al Vino de Jerez (Chicken Flavoured with Sherry, in a Sherry Sauce); Bizcocho de Chocolate con Crema Inglesa (Chocolate Torte with a Light Custard).

La Máquina   Pâté de Cabrales a la Manzana (Blue Cheese Pâté with Apples); Pelotitas del Profesor (Hazelnut Meringue Biscuits).

El Cenador del Prado   Crema Fría de Melón a la Hierbabuena (Cold Melon Cream Soup with Mint).

Zalacaín   Zanahoria Rallada con Naranja y Piñones (Shredded Carrot Salad with Orange and Pine Nuts); Tejas Gigantes (Giant Tuile Biscuits).

La Gabarra   Ensalada de Aguacate con Tomate (Avocado and Tomato Salad).

Wallis   Ensalada de Aguacate y Pimientos Rojos (Avocado and Red Pepper Salad); Helado de Frutos Secos al Caramelo con Salsa de Chocolate (Caramelized Nut Ice Cream with Hot Chocolate Sauce).

Cabo Mayor   Ensalada de Aguacate y Pimientos Rojos (Avocado and Red Pepper Salad); Ensalada de Verduras con Dos Gustos de Salmón (Vegetable Salad with Fresh and Smoked Salmon); Sorbete de Apio (Celery Sorbet).

O'Pazo   Trucha Escabechada (Trout Marinated in Vinegar with Onions and Carrots).

Príncipe de Viana   Bacalao al Ajoarriero (Cod in a Tomato and Red Pepper Sauce).

Jockey   Pescado Braseado en Hojas de Col con Salsa al Cava (Braised Fish Wrapped in Cabbage Leaves with a Champagne Sauce); Helado de Miel con Nueces y Dátiles (Date-Nut Honey Ice Cream).

Peñas Arriba   Escalopas de Salmón con Vieiras y Pimientos Verdes (Salmon with Scallops in a Green Pepper Sauce); Terrina de Frutas con Muselina de Almendras (Fruit Terrine with Almond-Buttercream Filling).

Horno de Santa Teresa   Lomo de Cerdo a la Naranja (Pork Loin in an Orange Sauce).

Combarro   Empanada de Anchoas (Anchovy and Onion Pie).

Nicolás   Corona de Naranja (Orange Flan in a Crown).

Posada de la Villa   Tarta de Santiago (Santiago Almond Torte).

Irizar   Sorbete de Manzana con Pasas (Apple Sorbet with Raisins).

CASTILLA-LEÓN

ARANDA DE DUERO

Mesón de la Villa   Pollo Escabechado (Chicken Marinated in Vinegar and Wine, Spices and Herbs).

VALLADOLID

La Fragua   Lengua Empiñonada (Braised Tongue with Pine Nuts).

GALICIA

VILAXOÁN

Chocolate   Fideos con Almejas (Noodles with Clams); Pan de Mollete (Chignon Bread); Empanada de Anchoas (Anchovy and Onion Pie).

SANTIAGO DE COMPOSTELA

Vilas   Callos a la Gallega (Tripe with Chick-peas, Ham and Sausage, Galician Style); Tarta de Santiago (Santiago Almond Torte).

VILLAGARCÍA DE AROSA

Galloufa   Queimada (Witch's Brew).

ASTURIAS

OVIEDO

La Máquina   Fabada Asturiana (Bean Stew with Sausages, Asturian Style).

CANTABRIA

LAREDO

Risco   Pâté de Anchoa con Caviar (Anchovy Pâté with Caviare Mayonnaise); Tronzón de Tudanco al Tresviso (Beef Steak with Mushrooms in a Blue Cheese Sauce).

PAÍS VASCO

SAN SEBASTIÁN

Akelafe   Caracoles sin Trabajo con Salsa de Berros (Effortless Snails in a Watercress Sauce); Ensalada Templada de Bonito (Warm Bonito Salad with

Vegetables); Rape con Romero (Monkfish with Rosemary); Mollejas de Ternera al Oporto (Veal Sweetbreads in a Port Sauce); Pasta Akelaŕe (Crisp Pastry Crust).

Bar Oquendo   Tartaletas de Riñones (Kidney Tartlets).

Panier Fleuri   Tarta de Cebolla (Onion Tart).

Arzak   Pastel de Krabarroka (Basque Fish Mousse); Crêpes de Txangurro (Thin Pancakes Stuffed with Crab); Bollos de Pan con Café (Wholemeal Bread Rolls with Ground Coffee).

Rekondo   Pimientos Rellenos de Bacalao (Red Peppers Stuffed with Cod).

Kokotxa   Chicharro con Juliana de Verduras (Mackerel with a Julienne of Leeks and Carrots).

Casa Alcalde   Hígado Glaseado con Manzana y Naranja (Glazed Liver with Apple and Orange).

BERGARA
Hostal Lasa   Tosta de Gambas (Prawn Toast); Pan de Molde (Loaf Bread).

VITORIA
Dos Hermanas   Bacalao al Ajoarriero (Cod in a Tomato and Red Pepper Sauce); Zurracapote (Spiced Red Wine).

BEASAÍN
Castillo   Riñones al Jerez (Kidneys in a Sherry Sauce).

BILBAO
Guría   Medallones de Ternera a la Naranja (Veal Medallions in an Orange Sauce)

Jolastoky   Tarta de Espinacas (Sweet Spinach Tart).

NAVARRA

PAMPLONA
Josetxo   Bacalao al Ajoarriero (Cod in a Tomato and Red Pepper Sauce); Cordero Chilindrón (Lamb in a Mild Dried Pepper Sauce); Sorbete de Moras (Blackberry Sorbet).

LA RIOJA

LOGROÑO
La Merced   Solomillo de Cerdo con Uvas (Pork Tenderloin with Grapes).

INDEX